Racial Politics in American Cities

Racial Politics in American Cities

Second Edition

Edited by

Rufus P. Browning
San Francisco State University

Dale Rogers Marshall
Wheaton College

David H. Tabb
San Francisco State University

An imprint of Addison Wesley Longman, Inc.

New York • Reading, Massachusetts • Menlo Park, California • Harlow, England
Don Mills, Ontario • Sydney • Mexico City • Madrid • Amsterdam

Racial Politics in American Cities, Second Edition

Copyright © 1997, 1990 by Longman Publishers USA,
A Division of Addison Wesley Longman, Inc.
All rights reserved.
No part of this publication may be reproduced,
stored in a retrieval system, or transmitted
in any form or by any means, electronic, mechanical,
photocopying, recording, or otherwise,
without the prior written permission of the publisher.

Longman, 10 Bank Street, White Plains, N.Y. 10606

Executive editor: Pamela A. Gordon
Editorial assistant: Chia Ling
Production editors: Linda Moser, Barbara Gerr/Professional Book Center
Production supervisor: Edith Pullman
Cover design: Inez Sovjani
Compositor: Professional Book Center

Library of Congress Cataloging-in-Publication Data

Racial politics in American cities / edited by Rufus P. Browning, Dale
    Rogers Marshall, David H. Tabb.—2nd ed.
        p.   cm.
    Includes bibliographical references (p.   ) and index.
    ISBN 0-8013-1535-2
    1. Afro-Americans—Politics and government.   2. Hispanic
Americans—Politics and government.   3. United States—Race
relations.   4. Municipal government—United States—History—20th
century.   I. Browning, Rufus P.   II. Marshall, Dale Rogers.
III. Tabb, David H.
E185.615.R214   1997
323.1'73—dc20   96-30443
                                                          CIP

4 5 6 7 8 9 10-MA-0099989796

Contents

PART III BARRIERS TO COALITIONS 95

CHAPTER 4 NEW YORK: THE GREAT ANOMALY
John Mollenkopf   **97**

CHAPTER 5 AN EXAMINATION OF CHICAGO POLITICS FOR EVIDENCE OF POLITICAL INCORPORATION AND REPRESENTATION
Dianne M. Pinderhughes   **117**

Preface

The first edition of this book was the outgrowth of an invitation to organize a forum for the American Political Science Association's magazine, *PS*. The book was thus an illustration of the contribution that professional associations can make to scholarship.

After our earlier book on minority mobilization in California cities, *Protest Is Not Enough*, won two prizes from the American Political Science Association for the best book on American public policy and the best book on ethnic relations, Cathy Rudder, now the executive director of the association, asked us to do the forum. We asked distinguished scholars to apply the framework we developed in *Protest* to other major American cities. That forum, published in summer 1986, was the catalyst for the first edition of this book.

The first edition, published in 1990, was well received and widely used in colleges and universities. Since that time, so many political, economic, and social changes have occurred at the national, state, and local levels that we decided to do a second edition. This edition includes many of the same authors and cities but all those chapters have been substantially revised to take account of recent developments. There are two new cities and authors—a chapter on Baltimore by Marion Orr and a separate chapter on San Francisco by Richard DeLeon—and new authors—Dianne Pinderhughes on Chicago and Rodney Hero on Denver and Pueblo.

We wish to express our thanks to all the authors who shared their expertise, the University of California Press and the American Political Science Association for permission to draw heavily on earlier work, and to Pam Gordon, Chia Ling, Linda Moser, and Barbara Gerr at Longman who have worked with skill and commitment on the book.

We would also like to thank the anonymous reviewers who provided careful and helpful critiques of the manuscript.

We dedicate this book to our children. We hope that their generations will continue to give priority to the struggle for racial justice:

Marla, Ross, Charles, and Mark Browning

Jessica, Cynthia, and Clayton Marshall

Kevin, Lisa, and Jonah Tabb

Racial Politics in
American Cities

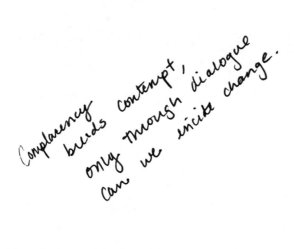

Complacency breeds contempt, only through dialogue can we incite change.

part **I**

Problems and Possibilities

introduction

Can People of Color Achieve Power in City Government? The Setting and the Issues

Rufus P. Browning, Dale Rogers Marshall, and David H. Tabb

The long and terrible history of racial domination in the United States has twice led to great, ultimately irresistible national movements; prolonged political conflict, sometimes violent; and death and destruction. The movement to abolish slavery finally achieved the Fourteenth Amendment but failed to secure for the former slaves the rights of citizens. Nearly a century later, the civil rights movement endeavored to span the chasm between the ideals of democracy and political equality and the American practice of extreme inequality, violent suppression, and exclusion from the most fundamental rights and liberties of people of African descent—the right to vote, the right to equal treatment before the law, the rights of free speech and assembly.

THE CIVIL RIGHTS MOVEMENT AND BLACK PROTEST

Waves of political mobilization, demand, and protest, sometimes peaceful, often violent, swept across the United States from the late 1950s to the mid-1970s. The assault on the institutionalized structures of racial exclusion and domination was felt in all cities with significant black populations. The mobilization of Latinos, who have a long history of engagement with civil rights issues, accelerated too. First came the civil rights movement, challenging the exclusion of African Americans from politics, government, and education, etching scenes that will forever be in the American consciousness—National Guardsmen escorting black children into school through mobs of enraged whites, lunch counter sit-ins, Governor Wallace—"segregation today, segregation tomorrow, segregation forever"—blocking the doorway of the University of Alabama to federal officials, Martin Luther King, Jr.'s, impassioned plea for equality from the steps of the Lincoln Memorial, marches in Selma and Birmingham in Alabama and the attacks on them, the murder of civil rights workers, burnings of black churches.

Mass violence erupted in the mid-sixties. Riots in Los Angeles, Detroit, Newark, and dozens of other cities both expressed and aroused fear, anger, and hatred. Leaders struggled to control events and prevent cities from burning. The riots were followed by recriminations, investigations, and heightened demands.

The federal government initiated programs aimed at poverty, racial inequality, and discrimination—and at defusing protest. President Lyndon Johnson pushed aggressively for the passage of the Civil Rights Act of 1964. the Voting Rights Act of 1965, and the "war on poverty" created by the Economic Opportunity Act of 1964. These were followed by Model Cities and a tidal wave of other programs in employment, housing, education, and health, many of which changed the activities and resources of city governments but also the prospects and resources of blacks, Latinos, the unemployed, low-income workers, and inner-city residents. During the first Nixon administration (1969–1973), the federal system of grants to cities was reorganized but continued to expand with the institution of general revenue sharing and block grants.

Since the 1970s, the great passion and commitment of the civil rights movement has been defused by its achievements, both real and symbolic. The support of whites for fundamental civil rights, evoked with the deeply moral and religious voice of Martin Luther King, Jr., could not be sustained and transformed into support for an economic agenda that beckoned after federal power had been applied to voting registration and to the integration of schools and universities. The movements for civil rights and black power were also suppressed by assassination of their strongest and most charismatic leaders—King and Malcolm X—and eclipsed by other issues, in particular the war in Vietnam; and they suffered the attrition of exhaustion, fear, and generational change.

With a series of Republican and moderate Democratic presidencies beginning in 1969, the organizations that carry the mantle of the black civil rights movement, such as the National Association for the Advancement of Colored People, the Southern Christian Leadership Conference, and the Urban League, lost visibility and access to the federal government and became less active. Electoral organization and officeholding at all levels, by African Americans especially but also by Latinos and Asians, have grown nationwide as the dramatic protests that so gripped public attention in the sixties virtually ceased.

In cities where African Americans and Latinos have risen to positions of authority as mayors, council members, and top managers and administrators, the politics of mobilization and mass action have been replaced by the politics of administration, implementation, planning, and economic development, and sometimes by crises of competence and corruption, as in governments generally. Open conflict within and between minority groups now represented in city governments has sometimes replaced the unity that was once attained when the city and its white, established power holders were the common enemy.

THE STRUGGLE FOR DEMOCRACY IN CITY POLITICS

A significant part of the denial of civil rights and of rights to nondiscrimination in employment, education, and housing and to equal treatment by government occurred at the local level where people lived, worked, and voted, and were subject to the imposition of police power and other local regulation. Accordingly, a significant part of the civil rights movement and of local mobilization by blacks, Latinos, and other groups aimed to force city governments to end their massive, blatant, common, and virtually complete discrimination and exclusion, and to engage the power of city governments on the side of reducing discrimination in private employment and housing. These historic efforts became not only tests of the ability of groups to sustain a high level of political activity and achieve their goals, but tests as well of the American polity itself, a running experiment on the proposition that groups who were excluded in a racially obsessed society could realize the democratic promise of the American political ideal.

The continuing efforts of African Americans and Latinos for access to government and for responsive policies in the cities, and the response to their efforts, are the subjects of this book. As we shall see, these struggles have achieved changes that are striking in their scope and significance. Standing in 1960 and looking forward from the near-total exclusion of African- and Latino-American people from government in the United States at that time, it would have seemed incredible that an African American could become a general in the U.S. Army or the powerful Speaker of the California Assembly or that blacks would be mayors of New York, Los Angeles, Chicago, Philadelphia, Washington, Seattle, and many other cities.

On the other hand, the value of the benefits gained is questioned by some; the momentum of the effort has greatly slowed, its successes have been uneven over time and from city to city, and its gains are subject to attack and reversal. Since the 1960s, a long tide of reaction to racial and other social change has steadily strengthened forces at all levels of government that would dismantle programs intended to counterbalance the discrimination that remains common; these forces would cut funding that many people of color and their organizations and leaders believe is necessary for continued progress and have come to regard as rightful compensation for the barriers presented by a racialized society. In the courts, decisions are entered against affirmative action in government contracting and in admissions and financial aid in higher education. In California, the cleverly misnamed California Civil Rights Initiative aims to undo a wide range of state affirmative action programs. And in the largest cities in the country—Los Angeles, New York, Chicago, Philadelphia—African-American mayors have been replaced in recent years by significantly more conservative whites. Perhaps the great expansion of officeholding by African Americans was merely temporary, to be followed by the reestablishment of white rule at the local level and by reversal of legislative gains at all levels.

Even with the expansion of officeholding by blacks and Latinos, it is still true that many cities with substantial black or Latino populations have no minority representation in city council and mayoral offices, or very little. Even where black or Latino officials hold office, how much power do they have? Can black and Latino officeholders really make city governments responsive to the interests of their groups?

We will concede that in some cities they can control local policies on some issues and at least some departments of city government—although control of police departments in particular seems especially difficult in many settings, as in Los Angeles. Even so, can minority-group officeholders make any headway against the most painful and intractable problem of people of color in a racialized society—unemployment and poverty, now higher than in the early 1970s—as help from the federal level is cut? As the pie of municipal resources shrinks between declining federal aid and state taxing and spending limits, can minority officeholders still carve out a larger piece of it for people of color? If they try to reallocate resources to their people, can they still attract the investors and financial institutions on which cities depend for investment and economic growth? These are questions that ask us to look beyond the achievement of local office to the problematic nature of power in a racialized society in which by far the greater power remains in the hands of the dominant group.

In short, even with the growing number of black and Latino officials, it may be that the limited powers of cities in a federal system and in a capitalist society render that gain more symbolic than real. Will the forces that now attempt to reverse the gains of the sixties and seventies succeed? The outcome remains in doubt.

African Americans and Latinos ("population of Hispanic origin," in the terminology of the Census) are the two largest minority groups in the United States, accounting for about 21 percent of the national population in 1990 and much larger proportions in many states and cities. The quality of their mobilization and their capacity to sustain political power in cities are crucial to their ability to gain continuing access at the national level of government as well as their ability to have a voice in the governance of the cities where most of them live. And because many contenders for state and national office learn from their first and formative experience in city politics, it is important to understand the diverse lessons those experiences teach.

Most important, this book offers a current report on the efforts of racially subordinated groups to gain power by election—continuing experiments in democracy carried out in frustration over persistent racially determined inequality and in a desperate race to stave off the explosion of rage.

THE CITIES

This book addresses these questions by bringing together 13 chapters on the political mobilization and political power of African Americans and Latinos in 21 cities, listed in order of size in 1990:

New York	Oakland, CA
Los Angeles	Sacramento, CA
Chicago	Miami, FL

Philadelphia   Birmingham, AL
San Jose   Stockton, CA
Baltimore   Hayward, CA
San Francisco   Vallejo, CA
New Orleans   Berkeley, CA
Denver   Pueblo, CO
Atlanta   Daly City, CA
                    Richmond, CA

These include the four largest cities in the country—Los Angeles, New York, Chicago, and Philadelphia—and other major cities in diverse regions. Of this group, Atlanta, San Francisco, and Oakland have black mayors; Miami and Denver, Latino mayors.

To locate these 21 cities in the universe of all U.S. cities, Figure I.1 places them and the other 534 U.S. cities with populations greater than 50,000 in a plot showing the size of each city's population and the proportion of that population that is white and non-Hispanic. The cities described in this book range in size from Richmond, California, with 87,000 people in 1990, to New York, with 7.3 million. As you can see in Figure I.1, most cities are clustered in the upper left quadrant: relatively small, mostly white. The cities of this book include the largest cities and other cities

FIGURE I.1   Size of city population and proportion of that population that is white, non-Hispanic for U.S. cities with populations greater than 50,000 in 1990

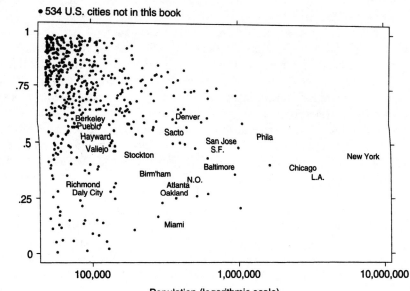

of various sizes, and their white, non-Hispanic populations are concentrated in the range of 25 percent to 63 percent, except for Miami at 12 percent. In this middle range, the size of the nonwhite and Hispanic population is large enough for real political strength if these groups are mobilized, but typically not so large that the role of whites is negligible. In short, this is a range in which the political opportunities for racial/ethnic minorities are good, but coalition will typically be necessary.

WHAT IS POLITICAL POWER IN CITIES?

All the chapters in this book use a framework we developed in our work on California cities that is discussed in chapter 1 (Browning, Marshall, and Tabb 1984). Here we identify the main outlines of the framework to alert you to common themes and points of difference in the accounts of particular cities.

Look at the question—What is political power?—from the perspective of people who have long been excluded from holding office or from any significant influence over city government. Suppose they decide to contest their exclusion in the arena of city politics, and power over city government is the target of their efforts. They know they have achieved power when they wrest concessions from an unwilling city hall; when they win office against determined opposition; when they succeed in forming a coalition that defeats an incumbent group; when their coalition is able to change the policies and personnel of city government; and when they are able over a period of years to institutionalize the changes they sought.

Examples of demands that African Americans and other groups have won in this way include representation in elective offices, access to employment in city government, appointments to head city agencies, application of the enforcement powers of city government to reduce or punish discrimination, and equitable allocation of funds for city services. This list makes it evident that we are focusing on concrete interests that lie clearly within the authority of city governments.

The goal of representation has been at the center of the struggle for political equality of blacks and Latinos. Viewed from the perspective of their virtual exclusion from city governments in the late 1950s, it is an astonishing achievement that many people of color now hold office as mayors, council members, and other officials. As important as representation is, however, it does not guarantee a group control over city government. The mere presence of people of color in office does not ensure that they will try to realize a particular vision of group interests or that they will be able to influence their governments. Even a large minority on a city council may have little or no influence over city government in the presence of a resistant and united majority.

To change the direction of city government in the face of opposition requires control of local legislation, programs, spending, governmental structure, and governmental personnel over an extended period of time. This means that blacks and Latinos, if they are to achieve their political goals in any city, have to secure majority control or support of a majority of the city council and of the mayor over a period of years. The key to control of city government to gain fairness and other values has to be a *governing coalition*. A group either has to constitute a majority on its own or it has to participate in a coalition that is able to dominate the city council on issues of greatest concern to it and able to secure reelection. Such a coalition does not have to consist entirely of blacks and Latinos, but it does have to have a strong commitment to their interests if they are to obtain the changes in city government policies that they want.

The key is coalition, not just representation. Even substantial minority-group representation—30 percent to 40 percent of a city council—might have little or no effect on policy if these members are opposed at every turn by an entrenched and intransigent governing coalition determined to resist. Where minority groups fall short of 50 percent of the voting-age population, as they usually do, coalition between the groups and with liberal whites is a possible and necessary way to replace a resistant governing coalition if they are to gain access to city government. In short, representation alone is not enough to control city government, and the formation of biracial and multiracial coalitions is a necessary step in the struggle for governmental power.

Political Incorporation

We use the term *political incorporation* to refer to the extent to which group interests are effectively represented in policy making. We *measure* the political incorporation of a group by the extent to which it is represented in a coalition that dominates city policy making on issues of greatest concern to the group. This measure involves a supposition—that coalition control of city government really does, at least typically, "effectively represent" a group in policy making. This is not an assumption but a hypothesis to be tested against the results of such control.

Political incorporation as a measure thus refers to a range of possibilities of group presence in city government. At the lowest level a group is not represented at all—there are no officials from the group, and the group does not participate in a coalition that controls city government on the issues of greatest concern to it. At the next level, there is some representation, but on a council dominated by a coalition resistant to minority interests. Finally—the strongest form of incorporation—a group has an equal or leading role in a dominant coalition that is strongly committed to minority interests. The highest levels of political incorporation may afford substantial influence over policy.

What Did Blacks and Latinos Want of City Governments?

First, they wanted to end their exclusion from government and the political process. They wanted respect from government, access to it, positions in it, and real influence over policies and programs of special interest to them. They wanted to be able to get the attention of city government, to have their concerns taken seriously. They wanted to hold office and to shape city policies and spending priorities.

Second, they wanted a share of the benefits of government and an end to discrimination. Starting from nearly zero in many cities, they wanted increased minority employment in city government. They wanted to see minority administrators in top city jobs. They wanted minority businesses to get some of the city's contracts and purchases. If economic development funds were considered, they wanted minority business districts to get a share. They wanted police to stop shooting and beating minority suspects. They wanted low-income housing, parks and recreation programs, police protection, libraries, and health and other services in minority neighborhoods.

They wanted, in short, government that included them, that was fair, and that was responsive to a broad range of deeply felt demands. But because racism was pervasive rather than rare, because whites controlled all the functions of city governments and discrimination was accepted practice, because people in power hold on to it and do not willingly give it up, a prolonged struggle would be necessary if minority demands were to be satisfied even partly.

What Form Would the Struggle Take?

Groups pursue political objectives in several ways. Aside from terrorism, groups may petition or pressure government from outside—the interest-group strategy—or they may achieve representation and a position of influence from inside—the electoral strategy. These are not mutually exclusive approaches, and large groups such as blacks and Latinos typically pursue both. Which strategy is dominant in a given setting, however, will shape the path of the political action that emerges.

We can portray a successful protest strategy for a newly mobilizing group as follows:

Group mobilization	Demand and protest activity	Appointments and minority representation	Governmental responsiveness on policy

The group mobilizes and applies pressure to city government with protest and demands. The governing coalition in city government may respond by appointing one or more minority representatives to vacancies as they occur on the city council; in any case, the coalition responds positively to some of the group's demands.

Where a group is sufficiently large or is able to find allies for a coalition, an electoral strategy might be feasible. We can diagram a successful electoral strategy as follows:

Group mobilization	Competition for elective office	Group representation and incorporation	Governmental responsiveness on policy

In this scenario, the focus is on electoral mobilization. If successful, it leads to representation and some level of group incorporation into city government; the extent of incorporation, in turn, determines the extent to which city government is responsive to group interests. Protest may be carried out, but its primary function is to arouse minority populations and their potential supporters, to raise the level of anger and create the possibility and the determination to act. The position in city government achieved by minority-group officeholders, rather than group pressure on city government, will, in this scenario, lead to responsiveness.

There is nothing inevitable to these scenarios: a coalition in power may be utterly unresponsive to minority demands or electoral effort may lead to no victories and no representation. Still, they constitute possible ways of influencing city governments.

URBAN POLITICS AND ECONOMIC POWER

The interest-group and electoral strategies are commonplace for all of us because they are the stuff of typical public discourse about politics and political power. The formation of coalitions, the importance of political leaders in framing issues and building coalitions, mobilization for protest and for elections, public disputes about policy and public funds—these elements of news and talk about politics are both familiar and real, but it is important to understand that the emphasis on them, the assumption that they are important, is a matter of perspective. In political science, this perspective is called the *pluralist* perspective. It is a view of politics as contention among many groups for control of political institutions, with the presumption that those institutions are significantly autonomous, that they possess real authority, and that they control important resources.[1]

A *class* or *structural* perspective, in contrast, sees politics from a different vantage point, looking not at the decisions of a given city government but rather at the relationship between government and the economic structure of society. Through the structural lens, we observe that government is not autonomous but is fundamentally constrained by the relationship between government and the structure of business interests: "Private property, market competition, wealth and income inequality, the corporate system, and the stage of capitalist development pervasively shape the terrain on which political competition occurs" (Mollenkopf 1992, 27).

In the structural view, city politics reveals deep and lasting inequalities that government can do little about, and the forces that produce and maintain inequality are likely to be more important than the limited autonomy of local government and the limited benefits that governmental action might secure. The structure and dynamic of capitalism, the institutional power of local corporations, and the cumulative inequalities embedded in capitalist institutions exert profound effects on urban politics and government.

Consider how the transformational dynamic of capitalism can undermine the prosperity of a group. African Americans migrate from the South to escape from the

---

[1] Here and in subsequent paragraphs we are drawing on Mollenkopf (1992, ch. 2) and on Alford and Friedland (1985).

oppression of sharecropping and to seek employment in the great industries of Detroit, Chicago, and Cleveland. Decades of struggle to overcome the racism of employers and of white workers eventually yield great gains of employment and income. Then these gains are steadily undermined beginning in the 1970s as global competition drains market share and employment from steel, automobiles, machinery, and other manufacturing industries. Unemployment and poverty among African Americans increase again, and a portion of the African-American population is mired without hope or opportunity in big-city ghettoes. The wealth those industries created is no longer available to finance local governments and local needs; it disappears or moves elsewhere, leaving behind the people who depended on it. Even if people of color have gained control of city governments in such a setting, they will be under constant pressure to compete with other cities for outside investment; that is, they will be under pressure to reduce taxes and to channel resources toward infrastructure attractive to investors, thus reducing resources for new programs.

In addition to the overarching structure and transformational dynamic of the global capitalist system, organized, powerful local economic elites may dominate city government. To express the possibility that strong economic institutions mold city government to their interests, we must refer to a broader governing coalition— a coalition of political and economic leaders that the latter seek to form and control, and which is in turn able to control city government. To differentiate this broader coalition from a governing coalition located entirely within the political/governmental sphere, it is called a *regime* (Stone 1989, 2).

Seen from the structural perspective, elections and voting are of limited interest because they cannot explain why city governments behave as they do; instead, the extent of structural inequality and the power of local economic elites in a city constitute the fundamental explanation: "the unequal distribution of economic, organizational, and cultural resources has a substantial bearing on the character of actual governing coalitions" in cities (Stone 1989, 9).

Though often presented as opposed, the pluralist and structural perspectives are, we believe, complementary. They are both necessary; they offer different truths and allow us to see different possibilities, but neither has a viable claim to be *the* truth. Their different central claims are both at least sometimes true, and we must employ both to understand urban politics fully.

Between them, the two theoretical perspectives identify five fundamental elements of urban political systems. This list does not exhaust the institutions with power over city governments—for example, it does not include state and federal governments—but it does identify the key actors in the immediate vicinity of local institutions:

1. Political "entrepreneurs," leaders who are typically coalition builders and who seek to lead city government
2. Public sector "producer interests" within government—administrators, employees, unions
3. Popular or constituency interests who may express their demands through elections and interest-group activity

4. Private market interests, especially corporations with discretion over local capital investment

5. A dominant political coalition—"a working alliance among different interests that can win elections for executive office and secure the cooperation it needs from other public and private power centers in order to govern" (Mollenkopf 1992, 38). This *governing coalition* is the product of the efforts of political entrepreneurs who build support from the other key actors.

This *governing-coalition approach* borrows from the pluralist view the proposition that a key interaction takes place between popular interests (3) and political entrepreneurs (1) as the latter seek to develop viable coalitions (5). From the structural approach, the governing-coalition perspective borrows the proposition that another key interaction occurs in the broader sphere between the political coalition that is able to dominate city government (5) and private market interests (4). It is also possible that public employees (2) play significant roles in the allocation of public money and privilege.

Although we accord private market interests a prominent place in any account of the capabilities and inclinations of city government, we also look for the possibility that political entrepreneurs and the alliances they may build are able to create significant autonomy for the political sphere.

Thus the achievement of political power by a hitherto excluded group in or over city government must overcome two potential obstacles—the presence of a dominant political coalition that will not give up power without a struggle, and the presence of market interests that may organize to dominate and shape any political coalition.

HOW THIS BOOK WORKS

The authors of the chapters of this book apply these frameworks to the cities they know best, testing the adequacy of the frameworks against new evidence and extending them as they encounter patterns of power and frustration not readily encompassed by them. By the end of the book, we should understand not only how the movement for political power unfolded in some of the largest and most important American cities but also the possibilities of the future: the adequacy of political incorporation of the previously excluded groups, the extent to which they pursue the broader goals of the movement, and what they might do in pursuit of those goals.

REFERENCES

Alford, Robert R., and Roger Friedland. 1985. *Powers of Theory: Capitalism, the State, and Democracy.* Cambridge: Cambridge University Press.

Browning, Rufus P., Dale Rogers Marshall, and David H. Tabb. 1984. *Protest Is Not Enough*. Berkeley: University of California Press.

Mollenkopf, John H. 1992. *A Phoenix in the Ashes: The Rise and Fall of the Koch Coalition in New York City Politics*. Princeton, N.J.: Princeton University Press.

Stone, Clarence N. 1989. *Regime Politics: Governing Atlanta 1946–1988*. Lawrence: University Press of Kansas.

chapter **1**

Mobilization, Incorporation, and Policy in Ten California Cities

Rufus P. Browning, Dale Rogers Marshall, and David H. Tabb

Why did blacks and Latinos mobilize strongly in some cities but not in others? Why did mobilization lead to significant minority incorporation in some city governments but not in others? Where incorporation was achieved, did it lead to power and responsive policies? Overall, was the movement successful?

Ten cities in northern California were studied in the 1960s and 1970s (Browning, Marshall, and Tabb 1984). The cities were revisited in 1993–1995 to reassess the political mobilization, incorporation, and policy influence of people of African and Latino origin, to reexamine the conditions for biracial and multiracial coalitions, and to review differences in racial politics among those cities and explanations for their differences.

In this chapter, we elaborate on the framework presented in the Introduction to understand why minority mobilization unfolded in diverse ways, and with notably different results, in various cities.[1] Study of these cities enables us to assess the successes and failures of minority mobilization in local settings and the conditions that led to success or failure; this assessment, valid for cities in northern California, is then a set of hypotheses about the achievements and evolution of the minority movement in other regions and in cities with very different characteristics and histories.[2] To understand the emergence and evolution of the national movement in the

---

[1] Portions of this chapter are drawn from the authors' *Protest Is Not Enough* (1984); *Racial Politics in American Cities* (1990); and "Mobilization, Incorporation, and Policy: Ten California Cities Revisited," a paper prepared for the 1995 Annual Meeting of the American Political Science Association.

[2] Without intending to diminish in any way the significance of political effort by other groups, we use the terms *minority* or *people of color* to refer, for ease of expression, primarily to blacks and Latinos, but also sometimes including Asian Americans. We do not mean to imply by our shorthand that blacks and Latinos are generally united or have identical goals and interests.

cities is to understand why it evolved in different ways, depending on social, economic, historical, and political factors that varied, and still vary, from city to city.

Understanding variation is essential for political action as well. Political action occurs in the context of each city's distinctive history and other shaping characteristics. Political activists and leaders and people generally must understand how their city differs from others in order to apply effectively the lessons learned elsewhere. Thus, to make our understanding relevant to action, we must understand variation—both what is different about particular cities and the patterns of difference across all cities.

Looking at many cities at once inevitably brings out different aspects of city politics than an examination of one city. Studies of one city, for example, take the population makeup of the city as given, and search in the ebb and flow of political competition, leadership, and policy for explanations and evaluations of change. But the population differences between cities are likely to be of great interest in comparative studies of many cities. So it is here. In the comparative view of ten cities presented in this chapter, we bring out the structure of population characteristics that shape the political dynamics and possibilities of cities. When you read the chapters on particular cities, keep this structure in mind to assess how it shapes the politics of each city.

TEN CITIES IN THE SIXTIES

We studied the largest cities in the region—San Francisco, San Jose, Oakland, and Sacramento—and a group of smaller cities with substantial black or Latino populations: Berkeley, Stockton, Richmond, Hayward, Daly City, and Vallejo. In 1990, their total populations ranged from 87,000 to 782,000; combined black and Latino populations ranged from 26 percent to 58 percent—large enough in all of these cities to have substantial influence in city politics, if they could unite or form an alliance with liberal whites and other groups. (See Table 1.1 for city-by-city data on population and other variables.) Constitutionally, all these cities are in the progressive reform tradition, with nonpartisan elections, city managers, and professional civil service systems. All had at-large elections for city council in the early 1960s, but the larger cities later changed to district elections, typically as part of efforts to secure the representation of minorities. The authority and prominence of the mayor's office is much greater in the larger cities.

As noted in the Introduction, groups pursue political objectives in two ways: they petition government from outside (the interest-group strategy) or they achieve representation and a position of influence inside (the electoral strategy). By the late 1950s, blacks in several of these California cities already had considerable experience both with electoral mobilization and with moderate forms of protest. Blacks in Berkeley in the 1930s focused on picketing and on increasing black voter turnout to demonstrate opposition to discrimination in public accommodation and employ-

TABLE 1.1 Minority population and representation in ten northern California cities

City	Population, 1990				Electoral system[1] (year of adoption)	City Council – 1994			
	Total (1000)	Percent				Size[2]	Black	Latino	Asian
		Black	Latino	Asian					
San Jose	782	4.7	26.6	19.5	D (1980)	11	1	2	1
Daly City	92	7.5	22.4	42.3	A–L	5	0	1	1
Stockton	211	9.6	25.0	22.8	D (1971)	7	1	1	1
Hayward	111	9.8	23.9	15.5	A–L	7	1	1	0
San Francisco	724	10.9	13.9	29.1	A–L[3]	11	1	1	1
Sacramento	369	15.3	16.2	15.0	D (1971)	9	1	1	1
Berkeley	103	18.7	14.7	8.3	D (1986)	9	2	0	0
Vallejo	109	21.2	10.8	23.0	A–L	7	0	0	1
Richmond	87	42.8	14.5	11.3	A–L	9	3	1	0
Oakland	372	43.9	13.9	14.8	D (1981)	8	3	1	1
Mean	296	18.4	18.2	20.2	Total	83	13	9	7
Standard deviation	264	14.1	5.7	9.9	Percent	100	16	11	8

[1] A–L=at-large, D=district elections.

[2] Councils include mayors except in San Francisco, where the mayor does not sit on the Board of Supervisors.

[3] Voters chose district elections in 1977 but reverted to at-large elections in 1980.

SOURCE: Department of Commerce, Bureau of the Census, *1990 Census of Population, Summary of Population and Housing Characteristics, California* (Washington, DC: Government Printing Office, 1992).

ment; black candidates ran organized campaigns for city council, not with the expectation of winning but as a way of registering protest (Nathan and Scott 1978, 10). With the rapid influx of blacks to work in defense plants during World War II and continuing migration afterward, their electoral prospects improved. Blacks became active in the state Democratic party and were instrumental in selecting black delegates to the 1948 Democratic convention. In that year as well, the Black Caucus was formed in Berkeley, and W. Byron Rumford became the first black elected to the California State Assembly, from a district of predominantly black neighborhoods in north Oakland and south Berkeley. The Caucus screened and selected black candidates so that multiple candidates would not split the black vote (Nathan and Scott 1978, 133). As the civil rights movement gathered force in the late 1950s and early 1960s, the electoral strategy in particular was already at least well practiced, if not well established, where leadership and conditions were optimal in parts of the San Francisco Bay Area.

As the civil rights movement spread in northern California in the early 1960s, it was testing with nonviolent protest the boundaries of the rights of assembly and petition in many cities and towns across the country. Those gatherings—large-scale marches and rallies, boycotts, and sit-ins—were peaceful, usually intensely un-wanted or forbidden by local authorities, and sometimes disruptive or costly to their targets. Nonviolent protest became civil disobedience, and organized nonviolent ac-tivity was increasingly overshadowed by spontaneous violent protest. Thus a range of strategies was being acted out by the late 1950s, extending to widespread vio-lence in the mid-1960s.

In northern California as elsewhere, African Americans and Latinos wanted the most basic civil rights—to hold public office, to be treated equally under the law, to end discrimination. They wanted access to education, to government, and to gov-ernment employment and business. They wanted to enjoy the same benefits of lo-cal government that white citizens took for granted. They certainly wanted police to stop shooting, beating, and harassing people of color.

What path would blacks and Latinos in northern California take as they pur-sued these goals? Would it be a peaceful path, focused on voter registration and turnout and the recruitment of minority candidates? Would it follow the direction of traditional interest-group effort, concentrating more on articulation of interests and demands than on elections? Would it take the more threatening stance of sometimes violent protest?

The answer was not one path but many paths in different cities as the move-ment unfolded. The dominant effort in a given city was shaped by characteristics of the minority community, of the white population and historical race relationships, and of the local political system and its response to minority mobilization.

The Structure of the Situation—Resources of Population and Political Commitment

For activists, a fundamental political resource was the size of minority populations. Black and Latino populations varied greatly in these cities: in 1970, from a mere 2 percent to 36 percent, and from tiny communities of fewer than 2,000 to groups of more than 100,000. We should expect the politics of mobilization and competition to play out very differently in cities where group populations are relatively large from where they are small.

Table 1.1 shows 1990 population figures, and the populations of all three groups shown there have increased in most cities; however, the pattern of group concentration is roughly the same as it was in the 1960s and 1970s. African Ameri-cans were and are more concentrated in a few cities; Asians and Latinos tend to be more widely dispersed across all these cities.

Both the magnitude of protest and the importance of group voting are contin-gent on the numbers of people who can be mobilized, but the incentive to pursue protest or voting in a given city depends on different aspects of group size. The ability to mount large-scale protest depends on the absolute number of people who can be mobilized for protest. In contrast, the ability to mount a powerful electoral challenge depends not on numbers but on the percentage that those numbers constitute of the electorate. In these cities, numbers and percentages of group populations are not closely related. For instance, San Francisco's large black population in 1970—about 96,000—constituted only 13 percent of the city's population and somewhat less of the city's voting-age population; but Richmond's 29,000 blacks were a potent 36 percent of its population. So groups in these cities varied not only with respect to their basic population resources but also in the extent to which those resources equipped them for protest or for electoral mobilization, for neither, or for both.

As populations of people of color increased after World War II, the partisan balance in these cities was shifting too. Democratic voter registration grew rapidly. By 1962, it ranged from 53 percent to 73 percent of registered voters, but Republicans still constituted majorities on half of these city councils. At the same time the civil rights movement was gaining momentum, Democrats in these cities were moving to capitalize on Democratic majorities among voters. For Democrats, the task was to mobilize Democratic voters to replace Republicans; blacks and Latinos were likely sources of such support. For blacks and Latinos, the task was to mobilize people of color and form alliances with liberal whites in order to replace all-white, conservative coalitions that had no intention of responding positively to minority demands; racially liberal whites were likely to come from the ranks of liberal Democrats.

The tasks of the civil rights movement and the replacement of Republican, conservative coalitions were related but not identical. They were not identical because many Democrats were not sufficiently liberal on the racial, social, and economic issues important to blacks and Latinos to support a minority-oriented coalition. Many whites of both parties did not want to concede anything to blacks and Latinos, and even those who were willing to grant some minority demands often preferred not to share leadership with minority leaders. The extent to which white Democrats were eager or willing to work closely and cooperatively with blacks and Latinos varied considerably from one city to the next.

As black mobilization intensified, local activists thus faced quite different structures of political opportunities and problems. Both the ideological commitments of liberal activists and the structure of the situations in which they sought control of city government powerfully shaped their incentives to actively seek minority support and to make significant concessions to get it.

PATTERNS OF MINORITY MOBILIZATION

We can summarize the evolution of the movement in these ten cities by describing minority initiatives and white responses and their consequences, ranging from continued exclusion of minorities from city government to some form of inclusion in a governing coalition, often in a subordinate role, occasionally in an equal or dominant role.

Demand-Protest

The pattern of group mobilization in a given city was very strongly shaped by group size. In every city where black or Latino populations were large in an absolute sense, intense, sustained demand and protest activity developed.

Mobilization was shaped also by the extent of political support from white liberals. Where white populations were more willing to support black and Latino candidates and their positions on issues, demand and protest tended to occur at higher levels and with greater frequency.

During the 1960s and 1970s, San Francisco and Oakland experienced substantial racially related rioting and other violence in addition to organized and persistent pressure on city government, including rallies, marches, sit-ins, picketing, and numerous dramatic and successful efforts to focus media attention on minority issues. In several smaller cities, local minority groups generated some demand activity, such as meetings with city officials to request their consideration of problems. Although the relationship between black population and level of black demand-protest is very close, this correlation does not mean that size of black population was the only factor involved in the production of intense demand-protest. Cities with large black populations were also large cities, and organizers gravitated to them with size of city and the availability of media attention in mind. A very large, vociferous rally in San Francisco, with clever arrangements to involve the mayor as the target of demands, would almost certainly be covered by the San Francisco media, would be distributed throughout the greater Bay Area, and would stand a chance of being picked up by the national media. Events in the larger cities were intrinsically more interesting to the media than what was happening in smaller population centers.

White hostility to black political interests typically diminished demand-protest; liberal support encouraged it, no doubt by raising expectations that demand-protest would be effective. More recently, although the level of demand-protest is certainly lower than in the 1960s, it is still evoked by events that gave rise to it then, such as the deaths of African-American suspects during police chases or in police custody. The largest cities—Oakland, San Francisco, and San Jose—remain the major sites of demand-protest activity.

Electoral Mobilization

The electoral mobilization of black populations was shaped by a different calculus of resources and opportunities. Numbers generate massive protest, but percentages win elections. And because black and Latino populations in all these cities fell well short of electoral majorities in 1960 and 1970, electoral victory depended on the support of liberal whites. The most successful electoral efforts therefore always involved the creation of cohesive electoral coalitions of blacks and whites, sometimes with Latinos as well. Such coalitions formed slates of candidates, carefully recruiting and controlling the number of minority and white candidates so as not to split the minority vote, developed common platforms, shared funds, and organized common publicity and canvassing; sometimes they established continuing citywide, partylike organizations.

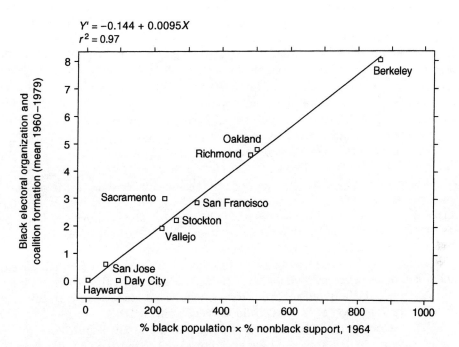

$$Y' = -0.144 + 0.0095X$$
$$r^2 = 0.97$$

FIGURE 1.1   Black electoral organization and coalition formation 1960–1979 as a function of black population and liberal support in 1964

SOURCE: Adapted from Browning, Marshall, and Tabb 1984, 119.

Key to electoral mobilization/coalition formation scale:
8: Black leaders conduct centralized recruitment of black candidates on bi/multiracial coalition states
6: Black and white organizations form coalitions; organizations negotiate presence of black candidates on coalition slates
4: Black organizations recruit and endorse black candidates; no bi/multiracial coalition
2: Black organizations endorse black candidates
0: Occasional black candidates run without significant endorsements

In the often tense atmosphere of minority protest in the 1960s and 1970s, conditions did not always permit formation of such coalitions. Nevertheless, the extent of coalition formation efforts by blacks was strongly shaped by the combination of black population and liberal support (by whites, Latinos, and other groups). Figure 1.1 shows the relationship. In cities where black populations and supportive nonblacks (mostly whites) were found together in adequate numbers, blacks mobilized for electoral politics and formed coalitions with their nonblack supporters.

Black population and liberal support are represented by their product on the horizontal axis of Figure 1.1 because their effects on coalition formation were interdependent.[3] An example makes this clear. Consider a black population that made up 25 percent of a city's electorate. With no liberal support for black candidates,

[3] Support for black candidates and interests among nonblacks was estimated from votes on a 1964 statewide proposition widely understood to be antiblack; see Browning, Marshall, and Tabb (1984, 282).

that 25 percent could not elect sufficient council members to control city government. In this situation, blacks had little incentive to expend a great deal of energy in a futile effort to contest elections. On the other hand, if liberals other than blacks also constituted 25 percent of the electorate, both groups stood an excellent chance of winning control of the city council, if they could unite around a common slate of candidates. In that situation, the incentive to organize a cohesive biracial slate and to establish partylike control over minority candidacies was very strong. That political incentive depended on the presence of both groups in sufficient numbers in a city's electorate. Thus, the impact of size of black population and of support from nonblack liberals on electoral mobilization was contingent on the level of the other factor. Neither group could go it alone; together, they could win.

The contingency of the two groups is expressed numerically by the product of their percentages. The product expresses the political reality that even a substantial black population—say, 35 percent—had little hope of taking control of city government without sizable support from liberal nonblacks. And roughly equal sizes of the two groups, as in Berkeley, was better than unequal sizes.

In cities where blacks and liberals together accounted for nearly half, or more than half, of the electorate—Berkeley, Oakland, and Richmond—blacks did indeed consistently take the long step from recruitment and endorsement of black candidates to the formation of biracial coalitions with white activists.

The pattern of the 1960s and 1970s persists in the 1990s. Figure 1.2 shows the same relationship that appears in Figure 1.1, updated to the 1990s. We lack an estimate of nonblack support in 1994 equivalent to the 1964 support figure, so in Figure 1.2 we simply take the product of the 1964 support and the 1990 black population as the variable on the horizontal axis. The relationship with black electoral organization in 1994 is still strong, though not quite as close as for the 1960s–1970s period. Figure 1.2 both supports the finding from the 1960s–1970s data and suggests that the racial liberalism of nonblack populations has been quite stable in these cities.

Latino and Asian Mobilization

Latinos also mobilized in many cities but typically less vigorously than blacks. For many reasons, Latino mobilization not only occurred later, for the most part, but was also usually not so unified, so well organized, or so intensely pursued. Latinos, more recent arrivals in these cities, are on average better off than blacks. In some cities, they are culturally and politically fragmented into several nationality groups (Central and South Americans as well as Mexican Americans). Significant numbers are not citizens. Some consider themselves culturally but not racially different from whites and are therefore less inclined to insist on an autonomous group political role. Their political experience may predispose them not to turn to government for solutions to problems. Finally, Latinos are more evenly distributed in these cities than blacks are, probably because housing discrimination is not so intense for Latinos as for blacks. In 1990, blacks constituted more than 40 percent of city populations in two of the cities shown in Table 1.1 whereas Latinos did not exceed

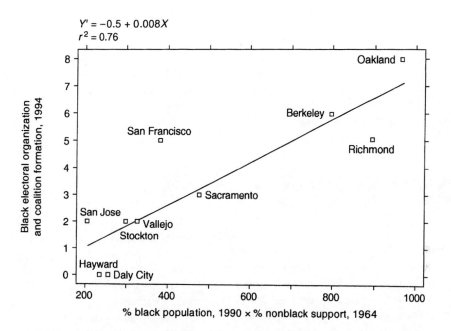

FIGURE 1.2 Black electoral organization and coalition formation in 1994 as a function of black population, 1990, and liberal support, 1964

Key to electoral/coalition formation scale:

8: Black leaders conduct centralized recruitment of black candidates on bi/multiracial coalition slates

6: Black and white organizations form coalitions; organizations negotiate presence of black candidates on coalition slates

4: Black organizations recruit and endorse black candidates; no bi/multiracial coalition

2: Black organizations endorse black candidates

0: Occasional black candidates run without significant endorsements

27 percent in any city, even though the mean percentages of the two groups were about equal. This observation suggests that Latinos may be significant forces in many cities but are less likely to achieve the sort of leading role African Americans have attained in cities where they are highly concentrated, such as Oakland and Richmond.

Latino mobilization, because it came later and because black mobilization was already under way, also depended on black mobilization to some extent. In a given city, black demand-protest tended to stimulate Latino demand-protest. And just as black coalition formation depended on the presence of liberals (including Latinos), the ability of Latinos to participate in electoral coalitions was contingent on the presence of sizable black populations.

However, Latinos in some cities have mobilized strongly at the community level. In the Fruitvale district of Oakland, for example, Latino organizations banded together to operate a community clinic and other services and persuaded city hall to build a new library as part of an effort to develop the community and generate employment.

Asian mobilization has centered dominantly on housing issues, particularly tenants' rights. In the 1960s, Asian groups in San Francisco's Chinatown organized to prevent the demolition of a hotel whose residents were primarily Chinese. Since that time, dense networks of community organizations have been built in both Oakland and San Francisco focusing on health, education, employment, and self-sufficiency issues in addition to housing. Like Latinos, Asian community organizations vary in their country of origin. During the 1990s, we observe many Asian groups working together to bring about change in their communities and in local government programs and budget allocations.

PATTERNS OF COALITION AND POLITICAL INCORPORATION

In the period 1960–1979, African Americans achieved high levels of political incorporation in two cities, Berkeley and Oakland; they were equal or dominant partners in liberal or progressive biracial coalitions that controlled city governments continuously for many years. In other important cities in the region—San Francisco, Sacramento, San Jose, and the smaller city of Richmond—African Americans became major political forces and major partners in coalitions led by whites that also took strongly liberal positions on racial issues and produced rapid gains in government employment, government contracting, and group representation on boards and commissions. Political incorporation resulted directly from electoral organization and biracial coalition formation (Figures 1.1 and 1.2) and was very closely related to it: the higher the level of electoral organization, the greater was the resulting political incorporation.

The results of the strongest forms of political incorporation were striking. African Americans in these cities went within a decade from virtually complete exclusion to positions of substantial equality in terms of the kinds of offices and authority they held and in terms of the assumptions about policy that guided those city governments.

In a group of smaller cities with more conservative white populations and/or smaller black populations—Hayward, Vallejo, Daly City, and Stockton—mobilization was weaker and African Americans achieved little in the way of political incorporation.

Latinos—mainly Mexican but also Central American in some cities—gained less incorporation in 1960–1979; where they did so was mainly where blacks and supportive whites were both present in significant numbers and needed Latino support to challenge conservative coalitions that controlled city governments. (Asians were not studied in our earlier work.)

The sequence of mobilization, formation of biracial (occasionally multiracial) coalitions, successful electoral challenge, office holding and exercise of governmental powers, and the implementation of responsiveness was a path tightly structured by the passionate determination of the civil rights and black power movements and the political realities of these diverse cities. The most vigorous mobilization and coalition formation occurred if and only if African Americans and racially liberal whites were present in sufficient numbers to constitute almost an electoral majority if they could be combined. The strongest forms of political incorporation appeared only where numbers, commitment, and timing could be brought together success- fully to replace conservative governing coalitions for years at a time. The most vig- orous policy response to the demands of African Americans was achieved where the strongest forms of incorporation were instituted.

Decades of political effort had produced a great breakthrough in political equality and in the reduction of governmental discrimination. The breakthrough was still unevenly achieved, however, and many problems were not effectively alle- viated by it. Widespread unemployment and poverty and terrible health problems associated or intensified with poverty remained. Inner-city populations continued to face inadequate education with constrained funding induced by the great tax-revolt victories of Proposition 13 (1978) and its successor tax- and spending-limitation in- itiatives as well as by cutbacks at the federal level. Even strong and determined bi- racial coalitions that controlled city governments felt compelled to compete for pri- vate investment with the usual tools available to cities, though they were also sometimes able to come to arrangements with developers that produced low- and moderate-income housing and other essentials and amenities that otherwise would not have been realized.

Coalitions, Incorporation, and Changing Policy Issues in the 1990s

Overall, the political incorporation and policy influence of African Americans is about the same today in these ten cities as in the late 1970s; Latinos and Asians are somewhat more numerous in some of these cities and are considerably more active politically, more strongly incorporated, and more influential than they were earlier.

Political mobilization of African Americans is generally less unified, less tightly organized, and less focused on electoral coalitions with whites in the 1990s than it was in the 1960s and 1970s. Electoral slates are less common than they were, but biracial/multiracial governing coalitions are well established, stable, and strong in several cities. As African-American leaders became multiterm officeholders in some cities and liberal coalitions institutionalized their political power, the necessity for highly unified mobilization decreased, and the progression of issues and competi- tion for leadership opened up divisions between "progressive" and "liberal" coali- tions with blacks and whites in both camps.

Political incorporation and policy influence have been institutionalized in the practices of some city governments, though of course unevenly from city to city. Af- firmative policies, deliberate inclusion, and fairness taken for granted in some cities are still not on the governmental agenda in others. Nevertheless, city government employment of previously excluded groups is closer to parity even in cities where they have still not achieved much political incorporation.

The structure of explanation for differences among these cities in racial/ethnic politics is much the same in the 1990s as it was in the 1960s and 1970s. Political or-

TABLE 1.2   Incorporation and mobilization, 1960s to 1995 (alphabetical within categories)

Incorporation and Mobilization	1960s–1970s	1995
Established to very strong	Berkeley Richmond Sacramento San Francisco	Berkeley Oakland Richmond Sacramento San Francisco San Jose
Weak mobilization and incorporation	—	Daly City Hayward Stockton
Protest and exclusion	Oakland San Jose Stockton	—
Weak mobilization and exclusion	Daly City Hayward Vallejo	Vallejo

ganization and coalitions and the political incorporation of the three groups—blacks, Latinos, and Asians—are strongest in cities where (a) the group is largest and (b) supportive members of other groups—liberals or left-of-liberal progressives—are most numerous. These resource factors constitute both the incentive frame for political action and limits on what can readily be achieved in a city with respect to coalition formation and challenge to conservative power holders.

We can summarize patterns of mobilization, coalition, and incorporation of these groups by comparing our classification of cities in the early part of the 1960–1979 period with our classification now (Table 1.2). The classification of cities in the earlier period stemmed almost entirely from the activity and success of African Americans—they were by far the most strongly mobilized and incorporated; now it refers to the combined activity and incorporation of all three groups.

The most important difference is that exclusion is far less common, and in six of the ten cities, including all the largest cities, these groups are, overall, well established, politically important, and strongly incorporated. A second difference is that protest, common in the 1960s, is not a defining aspect of politics in these cities now; it is nevertheless employed from time to time in several cities, with determination and some success even if with less defiance.

We would no longer use the term *co-optation* to characterize coalitions led by liberal whites in the 1960s.[4] The white leader of such a coalition in Sacramento now sits in the state legislature; he has been succeeded as mayor and leader of the coali-

---

[4] See Browning, Marshall, and Tabb (1984, 1990).

tion by a long-time Chicano activist, Joe Serna. In San Francisco, black, Latino, and Asian members of the board of supervisors (city/county council) work together in shifting coalitions with liberal and progressive whites on many issues. In San Jose, a newly elected black council member who made what many interpreted as racist remarks about Latinos and Asians was quickly recalled by a multiracial coalition effort. *Co-optation* does not capture the autonomy, strength, and diversity of political leadership and alliance in these cities, even where whites lead a controlling coalition.

New issues have come to the fore, and the absolute necessity of maintaining unity on every issue and in every election is no longer present in most of these cities. In Berkeley, two black council members are united on some issues but support opposing coalitions on others; one of the coalitions is led by traditional liberals, the other by "progressives" who support rent control, a larger city budget and higher taxes, and a determined effort to build more low- and moderate-income housing and to provide expanded services for the homeless. In many cities, black, Latino, and Asian voters and activists, and their white allies, are less willing now to support candidates for their color only; they insist on candidates whose views they support on many issues.

New aspirations have also made their mark. Whereas biracial coalitions mobilized to challenge conservative power holders in the 1960s and 1970s, Latinos and Asians and women have since engaged in their own mobilization, insistently and effectively though with less attention. Years in which African-American men have been mayors of Berkeley, where the population was about 20 percent African American, have been followed by terms of two white women as mayors. Has this in itself damaged the political incorporation of black people in Berkeley? As we scored incorporation in earlier work, holding the mayor's position counted a good deal. But in Berkeley, loss of control of the mayor's office and of the city council by the progressive coalition, with the mayor's office passing from one white woman to another, was more important for city government policies across the board and could not be correctly understood as a threat to the strongly felt and widely shared concerns for fairness held generally by politically active people in Berkeley.

The fact is that with the success of their political incorporation in most of these cities and the achievement of sought-after gains, African Americans and all these groups now express a greater diversity of interests than heretofore. We see a progression of issues that divide people along different lines. On property tax and rent control issues, for example, the interests of black homeowners and property owners are simply different from the interests of progressives and low- to moderate-income renters.

In short, within groups, including whites and African Americans, somewhat greater diversity of interests has appeared, not with respect to rights but on issues such as rent control, levels of taxation, encouragement of economic growth, and regulation of the urban environment. All these groups are typically represented both in progressive and in moderate (traditional liberal) coalitions in cities such as San Francisco, Oakland, and Berkeley, where progressive coalitions are active and significant political forces. Coalitions between groups, including liberal or progressive whites, are more likely to be organized around particular and diverse issues than before rather than fixed in electoral slates centered on the issues of fairness in housing, employment, and services that formerly defined racial liberalism.

One issue that has attained prominence recently is the rise of anti-immigrant sentiment manifested in the passage of Proposition 187 (the "Save Our State" initiative), approved by the California electorate in November 1994. Proposition 187, now under review in federal court, would deny welfare and other services to undocumented aliens and their families. It was widely seen as directed especially against Latinos. The conflict surrounding this issue might eclipse the continuing concerns of African Americans.

DID MINORITY INCORPORATION MAKE GOVERNMENTS MORE RESPONSIVE?

To the question of whether minority incorporation has made governments more responsive, some commentators have answered in the negative, arguing that the protest of the 1960s and a few black and Latino officeholders in the 1970s did not really make much difference in what city governments did. Cities are, after all, severely constrained by economic pressures and by the limits and mandates of federal and state governments (Peterson 1981). The politics of city governments are also strongly influenced by a formidable array of local forces including the rules and operating procedures established by bureaucrats (Levy, Meltsner, and Wildavsky 1974; Lineberry 1977). Under such limitations, how can we expect demonstrations, the efforts of a few minority officeholders, or even a change of dominant coalitions to have much impact?

The simple and true answer is that minority incorporation did make city governments more responsive, and Figure 1.3 provides a simple demonstration. Here we have charted the averages of city government responses to minority demands in four key areas: establishment of civilian police review boards, appointment of minority members to city boards and commissions, provisions for minority shares of city contracts, and minority employment in city government. Figure 1.3 shows a close relationship between these average responsiveness values and black political incorporation. City governments in which blacks had achieved strong incorporation were more responsive on this measure, and for the most part, *only* such governments were responsive.

At its strongest, the governmental response to minority interests extended across the programs and agencies of city government and permeated routine decision making and service delivery. At its weakest, the response was sporadic, halfhearted, undertaken only under duress, and limited to verbal assurance and an occasional, isolated action.

Across a wide range of issues and routine actions that never became issues, the responsive governments were pervasively different. Economic development funds were channeled to minority business districts. Several of the most highly incorporated cities, like Berkeley, Richmond and Oakland, have established elaborate housing rehabilitation programs as a way of maintaining housing affordability. Sen-

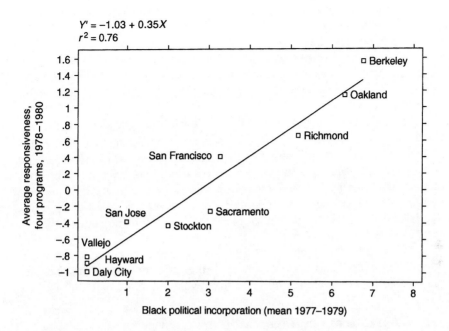

$Y' = -1.03 + 0.35X$
$r^2 = 0.76$

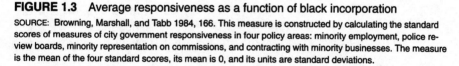

FIGURE 1.3 Average responsiveness as a function of black incorporation

SOURCE: Browning, Marshall, and Tabb 1984, 166. This measure is constructed by calculating the standard scores of measures of city government responsiveness in four policy areas: minority employment, police review boards, minority representation on commissions, and contracting with minority businesses. The measure is the mean of the four standard scores, its mean is 0, and its units are standard deviations.

ior centers were deliberately located in minority neighborhoods, which were also beneficiaries of programs for street tree planting, sidewalk repairs, and the relocation underground of utility lines and poles. City-supported and minority-oriented health services, such as sickle-cell anemia and blood-pressure control programs, were located in minority neighborhoods. Funding for homeless services including emergency shelters, transitional housing, independent living, and related services increased markedly. Though the federal government has decreased funding for employment programs, Berkeley and Oakland in particular have continued to fund and refine a series of existing employment and social services programs that focus on reducing the level of poverty in the city and particularly in minority areas. Major parks were developed or improved in minority districts. Support was given to dozens of community-based organizations that offered employment, health, educational, social, and cultural services to residents. Even city libraries developed responsive programs, such as the tool-lending office behind the South Berkeley Branch, where residents of low-income neighborhoods were able to borrow tools for nothing or at modest cost. Major city projects such as housing and redevelopment were developed with minority participation in the more responsive cities.

Although the picture was uneven from city to city, it is clear that demand-protest produced some responsiveness and that very strong incorporation, as in

Berkeley and later in Oakland, could produce across-the-board change at the highest levels of city government and significant changes in the allocation of neighborhood improvements; the prevention of unwanted change in minority neighborhoods; the provision of new social services; the redistribution and reorientation of traditional city services, including police protection; and minority employment. Where minority incorporation was less potent, substantial gains were made in at least some of these areas.

The presence of people of color on councils changed decision making to include them as a matter of course and sensitized whites to their concerns. Blacks and Latinos talked about how different it was to be "on the inside," to attend council meetings and see minority representatives on the council, and to be able to call them on the telephone. Council members talked about a new atmosphere and new pressure on the council once minorities were members. As one city official said, "When minorities talk to the city council now, council members nod their heads in agreement rather than yawn."

Measured by the standards of the dream of integration and an end to poverty, these gains still fall short. They were nevertheless of enormous importance to people of color and dramatically different from what had gone before.

City Government Employment in the 1990s

Employment discrimination generally and city government employment of people of color in particular was at the center of group demands in the 1960s and of governmental responsiveness in the 1970s. Research showed that the rate of gain in black employment especially was closely related to the political incorporation of African Americans (Browning, Marshall, and Tabb 1984, ch. 5). How do these groups fare now in this respect?

The easiest way to see the relevant relationships is to assess employment in relation to percentage of adult (voting-age) population. Figure 1.4 shows the relationship for African Americans and their share of city government employment overall.

Note first in Figure 1.4 the wide variation in African-American populations among these cities, ranging from 4.5 percent of voting-age population in San Jose to 41.3 percent in Oakland and Richmond. For various reasons, including locus of original migration in the 1940s and 1950s and discrimination in housing, African Americans tend to be concentrated in a few cities.

Second, note the line of parity—the line of equal percent employment and percent of the voting-age population. Parity is a commonly accepted target for minority-group employment. In *all* of the cities, total black employment in city government is close to parity. Berkeley and San Francisco, well above parity, had already made black employment a high priority by the mid-1960s; no city is disastrously below parity, even those where blacks are not strongly incorporated. African Americans *are* strongly incorporated in Berkeley and San Francisco, given their share of the populations of those cities, and their record speaks to the importance of political incorporation; but the achievement of parity even in cities where they are not strongly incorporated speaks clearly to the diffusion of nondiscrimination in gov-

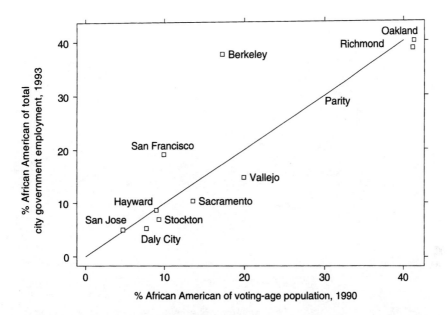

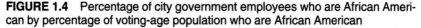

FIGURE 1.4 Percentage of city government employees who are African American by percentage of voting-age population who are African American

ernment employment. Nowhere do we see the sort of exclusion—near-zero employment—that was still common in the 1960s.

Latino populations are more evenly distributed in these cities than black populations, ranging from 7.4 percent in Berkeley to 23.8 percent in San Jose (Figure 1.5). They are diffusing more rapidly than African Americans to the many cities that ring the San Francisco Bay Area, perhaps in part because of economic mobility and less severe discrimination in housing.

Latino employment displays a pattern similar to that of blacks, without the markedly higher-than-parity rates of employment found for blacks in Berkeley and San Francisco. City government employment is closely related to the size of the Latino population, and most of the cities are only slightly below parity. That is the main message: close-to-parity has been achieved regardless of whether Latino political incorporation is particularly strong.

The pattern of Asian employment (Figure 1.6) looks different from the Latino and black patterns partly because people of Asian origin are rather evenly distributed among these cities; therefore, the Asian populations cluster in the range between 10 and 20 percent—except for San Francisco, with a large Chinese population of long standing, and Daly City, with a Filipino population that has been increasing rapidly in recent years. Of the three groups, Asian Americans have experienced the most rapid economic mobility in recent years and the least discrimination in housing.

In San Francisco, the greater-than-parity Asian share of city government employment is a reflection of a long-established population, high levels of education,

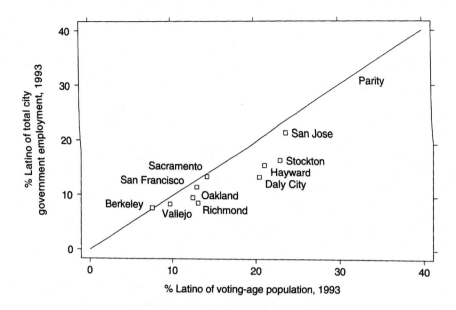

FIGURE 1.5 Percentage of city government employees who are Latino (1993) by percentage of voting-age population who are Latino

and political strength. In other cities, the *lag* of employment behind population probably reflects the rapid suburbanization of Asian-American populations as a recent phenomenon. In no city is Asian employment so low as to suggest exclusion.

How do the groups compare? Overall, African Americans have done somewhat better in city government employment than Latinos—the cities in Figure 1.4 are generally closer to the line of parity than those in Figure 1.5. Also, in Berkeley and San Francisco, black employment is substantially above parity. Comparing Figures 1.5 and 1.6, Latinos appear to have done better than Asians.

"Done better" is a simple assessment of a multifaceted situation, however. Although we can look at governmental employment simply as a piece of the pie for which groups will compete, a group's success in city government employment may mask more general problems—it is no advantage to reside in a city where city government employment of your group is relatively high if overall unemployment is also high. The extent to which a group pursues city employment may reflect the lack of employment opportunities in the private sector, or it may reflect widely shared group expectations of the necessity of governmental help that grow out of the same historical experience of discrimination in employment and education that in the 1960s led African Americans to mobilize first and most strongly, then Latinos, then Asians. Government employment is a consequence not only of a group's success but also of historical experience, shared group preferences, and the conditioned choices of job seekers.

Higher-level employment in city government presents a partly different, partly similar picture. Graphs for group shares of employment of officials and administra-

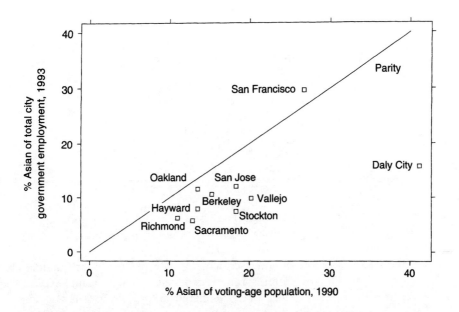

FIGURE 1.6 Percentage of city government employees who are Asian by percentage of voting-age population who are Asian

tors in city government suggest that blacks, Latinos, and Asians are excluded nowhere. Their employment is well above parity in a few cities; it is positively related to population shares, but it is typically at somewhat lower levels than total city government employment. African and Asian Americans have typically gained shares of official/administrator employment at substantially higher rates than Latinos. Differences in group political incorporation make a greater difference for group shares of the employment of officials and administrators than for group shares of total employment. For example, in cities where Latinos are not strongly incorporated and fairness in hiring is not a high priority, their share of the employment of officials and administrators falls far short of parity.

We can certainly still see the effects of high levels of political incorporation: biracial and multiracial coalitions that controlled city governments did significantly elevate city government employment of nonwhite groups, especially African Americans, and incorporation still has a substantial impact, especially for employment of officials and administrators. But in addition, we are seeing a widespread reduction of discrimination in city government employment, even in cities where the groups do not have the advantage of strong political incorporation. For example, Vallejo is the only one of these cities without either a black or a Latino council member, yet total government employment of blacks and Latinos in Vallejo is not far from parity. Early, strong political incorporation did make a difference—city government employment of blacks and Latinos approached or exceeded parity in the middle and late 1970s in Berkeley, San Francisco, Sacramento, and San Jose, much earlier than in other cities (Browning, Marshall, and Tabb 1984, 173), and it is considerably

TABLE 1.3   Black incorporation and civilian police review boards

Police Review Board	Black Incorporation, 1994		
	Weak	*Moderate*	*Strong*
Yes	—	San Francisco San Jose	Berkeley Oakland Richmond
No	Daly City Hayward Stockton Vallejo	Sacramento	—

higher than parity in Berkeley and San Francisco still. But fairness in hiring has continued to spread somewhat even to cities where group political incorporation has not changed much.

The reduction of employment discrimination, the rise of a black middle class, and the upward mobility of people of color generally is a significant success story, and government employment has played a significant role in it. It is also true that the success has been selective, it is still uneven, and too many have not benefitted.

Police Review Boards

Civilian police review boards have been one of the instruments African Americans have used to exert control over police departments and reduce the level of police violence against them. Other tools in this continuing effort include the appointment of black police chiefs in cities where black political incorporation is strongest; hiring and promotion of black police officers, sometimes using the courts to force departments to do it; and protest.

The establishment of police review boards was clearly related to black political incorporation in 1979, but only Berkeley and Oakland had created them. By 1994, five cities had them, including the three largest, and their establishment was closely related to black political incorporation (Table 1.3).

POLITICAL ECONOMY

In the Introduction, we noted that the overarching structure of capitalism exerts profound effects on cities; in addition, powerful economic elites may dominate the local political process and the governing coalition. Those forces can shape or nullify the acts of political leadership, coalition formation, and elections.

The political economy of a region affects

- the power of government relative to investors—cities that are attractive to investors will be able to extract concessions from them; cities that are not will have to grant concessions to attract investment

- the power of government relative to particular employers—a single large employer determined to preserve its advantages can be very powerful because the city's prosperity depends on it, whereas many smaller employers in a diversified economy will be less able to dominate city government
- the nature of the population—a highly educated work force is likely to be significantly more tolerant on racial issues and sensitive to environmental concerns

These ten cities have had significant political-economic advantages. The San Francisco Bay Area has experienced rapid growth—consider the electronics industry in "Silicon Valley" and its impact on the region—and has been enormously attractive for investors, thus increasing the power of city governments somewhat in relation to investors. Not blue-collar manufacturing firms but public agencies, universities, hospitals, and the military are among the largest employers. Public investment in services and administration on this scale diversifies local economies, attracts highly educated people and private investment in services and research, and reduces the potential power of private investors and employers.

Not all the political-economic determinants have been favorable. Heavy manufacturing and other blue-collar employment was concentrated during World War II in San Francisco, Oakland, Vallejo, and Richmond, producing rapid growth of black populations in those cities, attracted by job opportunities. As industry shrank in the postwar period, San Francisco was able to stay prosperous on the shoulders of a growing tourism industry and service sector, including education, health, banking, and legal services. Oakland and Richmond, and their black and Latino populations in particular, experienced persistently higher unemployment.

The presence of large numbers of highly educated and highly skilled people had direct political implications in many of these cities. As we have noted, support for black candidates and interests was crucial to the formation of racially liberal coalitions that were able to take control of city governments in the 1960s and 1970s. Figure 1.7 shows that the level of such support varied widely among cities and was closely related to their levels of white-collar employment, which we take as a rough indicator of the size of a well-educated professional class.

Historically, these ten cities experienced distinctive patterns of economic development. Distinctive economic development led to distinctive clustering both of racial/ethnic minority groups and of educated whites. The resulting characteristics of economy and population made it likely that some of these cities would be relatively responsive to the civil rights movement and the movement to gain access to city government, and relatively autonomous in relation to investors and local economic elites.

The historical political development of San Francisco also predisposed people of the major cities of this region generally to respond favorably to the civil rights politics of the 1960s and the gay politics of the 1970s to the present. The city is famous both for its tolerance of alternative lifestyles and for the left-liberal cast of its politics, and has been so since the mid-nineteenth century. These conditions continue to attract like-minded people.

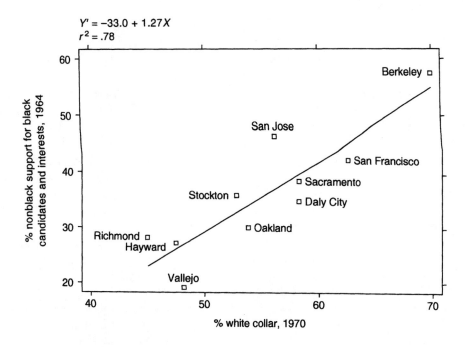

$Y' = -33.0 + 1.27X$
$r^2 = .78$

FIGURE 1.7 Nonblack support for black candidates and interests by percentage of white-collar employees

PRESENT PROBLEMS AND EMERGING THREATS

To shift our vision from the restricted sphere of local government to the problems of these groups is to bring into focus a different set of concerns. At the core of poverty, unemployment, and crime, and of some drug abuse leading to poverty, must be lack of skills, the loss of hope and community, and rage. These in turn might be addressable in part through education, but education is not in the sphere of general local government in California. Although some of these cities invest in youth and drug programs, low- and moderate-income housing, and health programs directed toward particular neighborhoods and groups, still the core interest of education cannot be addressed through these city governments in which so much political effort has been invested.

We do not understand in a systematic way the effect of group political efforts aimed at urban schools. We do know that citizens' groups in many of these cities have vigorously pursued their interests at neighborhood and school district levels. But there are no overarching coalitions that make education a foundation of their programs and work in a unified way in both the education and city government arenas.

In California as a whole, the success of antitax, anti-expenditure forces beginning in 1978 means that schools and local governments generally are severely restricted in their funding options. The tax and spending limits now part of the state constitution by initiative drag down the level and scope of public spending for state government and for all local governments and school boards. However, the structure of tax and spending limits does not totally eliminate variation among localities in what they can do. The cities in which African Americans and Latinos, in particular, are most strongly incorporated are also the cities that do best in the struggle to bend or circumvent the taxing and spending limits and maintain relatively high levels of spending for public education.

The spreading anti-immigrant sentiment manifested in the passage of California Proposition 187 in 1994 in one sense competes with and takes the spotlight from African Americans and claims they might press. The reaction to immigration, both legal and not legal, does present new moral and political claims, but the issues are also clearly broader than immigration. In California, the reaction to affirmative action in education rises and intensifies in the politics of the presidential election campaign, in the so-far successful effort to end affirmative action in University of California admissions, and in the furor over the so-called Civil Rights Initiative on the California ballot in 1996, which would end affirmative efforts throughout state government and public higher education. Because both blacks and Latinos see such efforts as essential to the education of their young people and because many immigrants are justifiably afraid of the wave of anti-immigrant feeling, we are seeing a new push for citizenship among Latinos and Asians, renewed efforts to mobilize voters, and a coming together of the now well-organized leadership of these diverse groups. The unity lost in the historical (though partial) success of separate efforts may be regained to meet the threat of the reactionary challenge. Political incorporation in localities will not directly win these battles, but it will provide a much stronger base from which to mount a countereffort.

REFERENCES

Browning, Rufus P., Dale Rogers Marshall, and David H. Tabb. 1984. *Protest Is Not Enough*. Berkeley: University of California Press.

Browning, Rufus P., Dale Rogers Marshall, and David H. Tabb. 1995. Mobilization, Incorporation and Policy: Ten California Cities Revisited. Paper prepared for the annual meeting of the American Political Science Association, New York.

Browning, Rufus P., Dale Rogers Marshall, and David H. Tabb, eds. 1990. *Racial Politics in American Cities*. White Plains, N.Y.: Longman.

Levy, Frank, Arnold Meltsner, and Aaron Wildavsky. 1974. *Urban Outcomes*. Berkeley: University of California Press.

Lineberry, Robert L. 1977. *Equality and Urban Policy: The Distribution of Municipal Public Services*. Beverly Hills, Calif.: Sage.

Nathan, Harriet, and Stanley Scott, eds. 1978. *Experiment and Change in Berkeley*. Berkeley: Institute of Governmental Studies, University of California.

Peterson, Paul E. 1981. *City Limits*. Chicago: University of Chicago Press.

part **II**

Biracial Coalitions

chapter **2**

Post-Incorporation Politics in Los Angeles

Raphael J. Sonenshein

Editors' Note

In the study of minority incorporation, Los Angeles stands as the leading big city example of the political success of minority incorporation through biracial electoral coalition. Despite a black population that has never exceeded 17 percent of the city (now reduced to 14 percent), blacks won a major share of power at city hall under the five-term leadership of African-American mayor Tom Bradley.

In this chapter, Raphael J. Sonenshein traces the special circumstances and leadership techniques that made this extraordinary coalition successful in the face of widespread beliefs that interracial politics were dead. He highlights the roles of shared ideology, common political interests, and creative leadership in the development of cross-racial coalitions.

Yet even in Los Angeles, the general decline of such alliances has been severely felt. In 1993, Republican Richard Riordan defeated Bradley's ideological heir, and the black community found itself out of power. Coalition lines fell into disrepair, and Latinos and Asian Americans chafed at the notion of a solely black-white politics. Sonenshein discusses the decline of the coalition and the dramatic rise of a Republican mayor in the Democratic city.

This chapter explores the Riordan era in Los Angeles politics, both in politics and economics, as well as the requirements for a resurgent progressive movement. Sonenshein argues that while there is still a basis for coalition politics, its practitioners must walk a fine line between a politics of diversity and black-white politics, and must also propose a policy agenda that cuts more deeply into the economic needs of the city's residents than occurred under the previous model of minority incorporation.

In their 1984 book *Protest Is Not Enough*, Browning, Marshall, and Tabb contended that biracial coalitions are powerful vehicles for achieving minority incorporation in the political life of cities. Their relatively optimistic view of biracial and multiracial coalitions contrasted strikingly with the more common pessimism about cross-racial politics. Racial polarization in such major cities as New York and Chicago (as well as in a number of medium- and smaller-size cities) fed the belief that the black protests and white backlash of the 1960s doomed biracial politics.

In that light, the success of biracial coalition politics in Los Angeles was extremely significant. In Los Angeles, the urban center of traditionally conservative Southern California, a small black community won a major share of political power through membership in a biracial coalition with white liberals. Under the leadership of African-American mayor Tom Bradley, this liberal coalition dominated city politics for two decades, between 1973 and 1993. Latinos, who significantly outnumbered blacks in the city, were junior partners in the coalition and were less successful than blacks in winning political incorporation. Asian Americans, allies of Bradley since his first election to the city council, were also important, if secondary, members of the Bradley mayoral coalition (Sonenshein 1993).

But by the mid-1990s, the Los Angeles coalition was on its last legs, torn asunder by racial and class conflicts. After the videotaped beating of Rodney King in 1991 and the massive civil unrest of April 1992, the city seemed to be careening out of control. Bradley chose not to run for a sixth term in 1993. He was replaced by a white Republican businessman, Richard Riordan. And the question for the future was not the relationship between blacks and whites that had so animated city politics for decades but the stresses and strains among the city's many diverse groups.

What do these changes mean for the theory of political incorporation set forth by Browning, Marshall, and Tabb? More specifically,

1. What demographic and economic factors underlay the development of a winning biracial coalition and then its demise?
2. What benefits were gained for minorities through the strong political incorporation achieved by the biracial coalition? What has been the fate of those changes under its conservative successor?
3. What is the future of minority politics in the puzzling new world of Los Angeles? What are the prospects for the development of multiracial coalitions?

BACKGROUND

Los Angeles is the prototype of the newer western city. Its expansion began in the 1880s and continued well beyond World War II, as its population rank among cities rose from 135 in 1880 to 2 in 1982. Los Angeles grew another 10 percent in the 1980s. During the period of its greatest growth, the city was dominated and shaped by white Protestant migrants from the Midwest who hoped to create an urban model of the heartland lifestyle (Fogelson 1967). Their explicit intention was to avoid the political "fate" of the big eastern and midwestern cities, dominated by Catholic immigrants, labor unions, and minority groups.

Midwestern values helped create and sustain the nonpartisanship of California cities. In both formal structure and actual practice, Los Angeles has been a strongly nonpartisan city (Adrian 1959). As a result, party organizations have been virtually nonexistent. Despite a clear majority in party registration, Democrats failed for many years to take over city hall (Mayo 1964; Carney 1964) until the rise of the liberal coalition in the early 1970s.

Unlike many big cities in the East and Midwest, but more like the sunbelt of which it was a part, Los Angeles was dominated by its business leaders for the first half of the twentieth century. It was very much an "entrepreneurial political economy" as defined by Elkin (1987, 61):

> All entreprenurial cities have in common a relatively unimpeded alliance at work composed of public officials and local businessmen, an alliance that is able to shape the workings of city political institutions so as to foster economic growth. In each, moreover, electoral politics is organized so that businessmen play an important role, and urban bureaucracies are adept at organizing their domains so that they are neither dominated by elected officials nor in the service of local businessmen.

The homogeneous community ideal of the midwesterners' new city implicitly excluded such minority groups as blacks, Jews, Mexicans, and Japanese. However, the steady migration of minorities into Los Angeles before and after World War II slowly eroded the predominance of conservative whites. The city's economy also dramatically changed, as Greater Los Angeles became the most important aircraft production center in the nation. Los Angeles rapidly industrialized, and thousands of black workers migrated from the South for highly desirable industrial jobs (Smith 1978).

It took several decades for these wartime economic changes to generate political effects, but by the 1950s and early 1960s the growing black community was actively organizing for political power. The much less economically grounded Latino community was also growing in numbers but developed politically at a much slower pace. Asian Americans were even farther from the more active political role they were to assume in later years.

During the same decades, the Jewish community had also grown by leaps and bounds (Vorspan and Gartner 1970). Economically adaptable, Jews moved steadily from the downtown area through mid-city and out to West Los Angeles, and then a large group moved over the mountains into the San Fernando Valley. Jews responded to their exclusion from the business world of white Protestants by building their own economic power centers away from downtown (Davis 1991). The social provincialism of the city's Protestant economic leaders therefore helped divide and weaken their dominance of city life. Indeed, the election of maverick Sam Yorty as mayor in 1961, despite the near-total opposition of the business community, suggested that the downtown alliance of corporate leaders and the *Los Angeles Times* was not an unbeatable monolith (Carney 1964).

Jews (included in the white category by the Bureau of the Census) have been an important and distinctive group in the city, representing about 6 percent of the population in 1990. Highly mobilized, Jews composed an estimated 15 percent of the local electorate in 1973. Twenty years later, Jews cast an astonishing 19 percent of the votes in the mayoral runoff. Los Angeles Jews have remained Democratic in very large numbers. Private polling in the mid-1990s indicated that more than three-quarters were Democrats (Fairbank, Maslin, Maullin, and Associates, various dates).

THE RISE OF A BIRACIAL COALITION

The political and cultural exclusion of Jews from the homogeneous community in the first half of this century suggests that despite their economic success, they experienced the feeling of being an out-group (Vorspan and Gartner 1970, ch. 5). They combined this sense of being left out with their liberalism and activism to establish the basis for a political coalition with blacks. Blacks and Jews were drawn together by liberal *ideology* as well as shared political *interests*. In the early 1960s, Jewish liberals and blacks formed a powerful coalition able to challenge both the rigidities of the downtown establishment and the conservative reactionaries led by Mayor Sam Yorty. In 1973, this coalition elected a black mayor, Tom Bradley, and dominated city politics for the next two decades.

With Bradley's election, racial minorities had attained strong incorporation. Before 1973, minority incorporation had been minimal in Los Angeles, in a pattern similar to that found by Browning, Marshall, and Tabb in ten northern California cities. For the first half of the twentieth century, blacks and Latinos were largely invisible in city politics, to a much greater degree than in the East and Midwest where party organizations sometimes provided partial incorporation. The first minority council member, Edward Roybal, a Latino, was elected in 1949, and until 1962 there were no black city council members.

In 1962 and 1963, blacks organized with remarkable effectiveness to elect three members to the 15-seat council, a 20 percent proportion they have held to this day (Sonenshein 1993, ch. 3; Patterson 1969). In the process, Latinos lost their one seat to blacks, not to attain another of their own until 1985. The black gains on the council were diluted, however, by the extreme hostility of the incumbent mayor Sam Yorty. Elected mayor in 1961 with strong minority support, Yorty became a relentless foe of minorities and progressives, backing the hated Police Chief William Parker and using racist appeals to defeat Bradley's strong challenge in 1969. At best, minorities had some representation prior to 1973 but very little incorporation.

The biracial coalition gained its first great success with the election of Bradley to the city council in 1963. In a district only one-third black, Bradley's black and Jewish allies built a powerful biracial alliance that overwhelmed the conservative white appointee to a vacant council seat. As the central focus of these interracial efforts, Bradley became well known citywide and soon made plans to challenge Yorty for the mayoralty.

In 1969, Bradley made a stunning showing in the nonpartisan primary, far out-distancing Yorty with 42 percent to 26 percent of the vote. But Yorty's blatantly racist appeals dominated the runoff campaign, and the mayor succeeded in portraying the moderate Bradley as the tool of black militants and white leftists. To the profound dismay of his followers, Bradley lost. He had, however, set a record for major American cities, winning more than one-third of the white vote (Hahn, Klingman, and Pachon 1976).

In 1973, Bradley again challenged Yorty and utilized a highly effective campaign organization that had matured significantly since the 1969 crusade. Dominating the media with powerful television commercials and keeping Yorty on the defensive, the Bradley forces reversed the outcome of 1969 and solidly defeated the three-term mayor. Bradley's allies were also dominant in the city council, providing a strong base for a moderately progressive mayoralty.

With Bradley's election as mayor in 1973, minorities—especially blacks and their liberal Jewish allies—gained strong incorporation. Three council seats were held by blacks, and the biracial coalition controlled a majority of the council. The mayor appointed allies to city commissions and boards, and the coalition's electoral fortunes were assured with the solid support of highly mobilized blacks and Jewish liberals.

The biracial coalition was built on a foundation of shared liberal ideology; common political interest; and strong, trusting leadership. Contrary to the point of view presented in Carmichael and Hamilton's *Black Power* (1967), self-interest was not the only or even the main guiding force of the coalition. Liberal ideology among whites, particularly Jews, was essential to Bradley's majority coalition. This role for ideology confirmed the analysis by Browning, Marshall, and Tabb. But neither view explains the full, human dimensions of coalition success, which ultimately depended on leadership.

Bradley's coalition was immeasurably strengthened by the close political and personal ties among the black and white liberal activists who had worked together since the early 1960s. Trust among leaders is an underrated element of coalition development (Hinckley 1981), and the Bradley coalition showed its value in 1979 when the controversy over the forced resignation of United Nations Ambassador Andrew Young led to black-Jewish conflicts in numerous cities. Only in Los Angeles was the preexisting leadership group able to find a way to defuse the potentially deadly controversy (Sonenshein 1993, ch. 8).

The role of Latinos was less clear. Courted by Yorty, Latinos came over to the Bradley coalition in his 1973 election (Hahn, Klingman, and Pachon 1976). Over the years, Latino voters strongly backed Bradley's reelection. They were well rewarded with commission posts. But it was 12 years into Bradley's mayoralty before they regained council representation with Richard Alatorre's election in the eastside Fourteenth District. The next year, Gloria Molina was elected in the neighboring First District, created only after a lawsuit against the city by Latino activists. In 1993, Richard Alarcon was elected in the Seventh District of the San Fernando Valley. By the time Bradley left office in 1993, the council was 40 percent black and Latino, half from each group.

Asian Americans gained greater political representation through the Bradley coalition, especially in appointments to city commissions. The first Asian-American city council member, Michael Woo, was elected in 1985 and became a Bradley ally. In fact, when the city council tried to redistrict Woo out of his new district in 1986, Bradley saved Woo's seat by his veto of the ordinance.

DID MINORITIES BENEFIT FROM THE BIRACIAL COALITION?

Minorities gained important benefits from the political incorporation they enjoyed during the heyday of the biracial coalition. The main benefits came in four areas: representation, city hiring, federal aid, and police accountability (Sonenshein 1993, ch. 9).

Representation

Bradley brought an entirely new body of people into Los Angeles city government. Whereas Yorty's appointees had tended to be older white businessmen, apolitical minorities, and wives of prominent politicians, Bradley appointed a diverse array of politically active men and women from minority and white communities. Tables 2.1 and 2.2 show the Bradley style in appointments to city commissions compared with Mayor Yorty's appointees. On key commissions, such as public works and civil service, the Bradley appointees aggressively pursued an agenda that was favorable to minority interests.

Affirmative Action in City Hiring

With the help of his appointed civil service commissioners, Bradley aggressively increased minority hiring at city hall, both in overall percentage and in the higher ranks of job categories. Significant gains in city hiring were obtained by blacks, Latinos, Asian Americans, and women (Tables 2.3–2.6). All four groups registered solid gains in the two most desirable categories: officials/administrators and professionals.

TABLE 2.1 Minority representation among Yorty commissioners, 1973

	%	N
Blacks	6	11
Latinos	9	12
Asian Americans	1	5
Jews	11	15
Women	17	23
Total N		133

SOURCE: *Los Angeles Times*, 8 August 1973.

TABLE 2.2   Minority representation among Bradley commissioners, 1973, 1984, and 1991

	1973		1984		1991	
	N	%	*N*	%	*N*	%
Blacks	21	15	23	19	42	20
Latinos	13	9	19	16	34	16
Asian Americans	10	7	11	9	28	13
Women	43	32	40	33	99	47
Total appointments	140		120		213	

SOURCE: 1973—*Los Angeles Times*, 8 August 1973; 1984—*Los Angeles Times,* 2 August, 3 August 1984; 1991—Office of the Mayor.

TABLE 2.3   Composition of city government workforce, 1973 and 1991

	1973		1991	
	N	%	*N*	%
Whites	26,681	64.1	21,088	46.0
Blacks	9,135	21.9	10,286	22.4
Latinos	3,879	9.3	9,112	19.9
Asian Americans	1,659	4.0	3,452	7.5
Women	6,660	16.0	11,705	25.5

SOURCE: Comparative analysis of data from City of Los Angeles, Numerical Progress, 1973–1991.

TABLE 2.4   Job classifications of Latino, Asian American, and women city employees, 1973 and 1991 (percentage of group)

	Latinos		Asian Americans		Women	
	1973	*1991*	*1973*	*1991*	*1973*	*1991*
Officials	0.2	0.5	0.2	1.5	0.1	0.8
Professionals	6.8	10.1	27.8	37.3	10.3	21.2
Technical	8.2	8.3	17.5	13.9	7.0	4.9
Protective services	15.4	24.2	2.0	7.6	3.0	13.0
Paraprofessionals	0.8	1.2	0.4	1.4	1.0	2.0
Service	23.2	18.4	6.6	3.4	2.2	4.0
Skilled	23.3	18.8	14.3	14.3	0.1	1.0
Clerical	22.1	18.5	31.2	20.7	76.3	52.8

SOURCE: Comparative analysis of data from City of Los Angeles, Numerical Progress, 1973–1991.

TABLE 2.5   Minority representation in top-level city jobs, 1973 and 1991 (percentage of jobs)

	Officials and Administrators		Professionals	
	1973	*1991*	*1973*	*1991*
Whites	94.7	70.9	81.4	54.9
Blacks	1.3	10.5	5.0	12.0
Latinos	2.6	7.5	4.6	11.1
Asian Americans	1.3	8.0	8.0	15.4
Women	3.0	14.9	11.9	29.9

SOURCE: Comparative analysis of data from City of Los Angeles, Numerical Progress, 1973–1991.

TABLE 2.6   Blacks in low-level city jobs, 1973 and 1991 (percentages)

	1973	1991
Share of service and maintenance jobs held by blacks	57.6	42.6
Share of jobs held by blacks that were service and maintenance jobs	40.0	23.5

SOURCE: Comparative analysis of data from City of Los Angeles, Numerical Progress, 1973–1991.

Even though blacks were declining as a share of the city's population, they were holding their position in city hiring. Despite a lower degree of political incorporation, Latinos and Asian Americans were markedly improving their positions. In a quiet way, the regime did a respectable job of developing a secure and upwardly mobile occupational base for some elements of minority communities.

Federal Aid

Again in stark contrast to Yorty, Bradley sought to improve city services through the search for federal and state assistance. He became an outstanding mayoral grants-person, bringing tens of millions of dollars into the city for physical improvements and social services (Saltzstein, Sonenshein, and Ostrow 1986).

The pressure to make redistributive choices was anticipated and eased by an emphasis on increasing overall resources. In this sense, the federal funding boom of the 1970s was a godsend. Using federal money, the city undertook a wide range of new social service programs, hardly tapping the city treasury. Many, although not all, of these programs were in poor and minority communities. A study of grants in the Bradley era indicated that overall they had the effect of redistributing resources downward (Ross 1980).

Using federal and private dollars, the administration pursued a major economic development program. Bradley's Los Angeles received a greatly increased share of federal economic development funds and millions of dollars were invested in the redevelopment of downtown.

Police Accountability

Progress was exceedingly slow in reforming the highly entrenched Los Angeles Police Department. Although Bradley's police commissioners were often perceived as antagonists by police officials, reformers frequently felt that the Bradley group was too cautious. Even so, the Bradley forces won some important battles, including some limits on police shootings and a tighter rein on the police budget and pension fund. But it was the videotaped beating of black motorist Rodney King in 1991 that set off the climactic battle between the biracial coalition and the department.

From March 1991 until the summer of 1992, liberal and conservative forces were locked in mortal combat. Bradley's allies on the police commission tried to remove Police Chief Daryl Gates but were overruled by the city council. Bradley's appointed Christopher Commission had more success. The commission's report was exhaustive and dramatic, and the city council placed most of its recommendations for police reform on the June 1992 ballot as Proposition F. The most important recommendation was that the police chief no longer have civil service protection.

Perhaps the greatest victory achieved by the Bradley coalition was the voters' approval of Proposition F in 1992, even in the wake of the civil disorder several months before. The biracial coalition shone through one more time as black voters joined with white liberals and Latinos to carry Proposition F to an easy victory (Table 2.7).

Although the Bradley forces had won a great victory, the political damage to Bradley was fatal. His support among white voters fell so dramatically that his biracial base could no longer deliver for him, and he decided not to seek a sixth term.

Economic Policy

Minorities obtained only mixed benefits from the biracial alliance in neighborhood economic development. In the area of economic policy, the Bradley coalition was

TABLE 2.7 Proposition F vote and margin in four key council districts, 1992

		Yes (%)[a]	No (%)[a]	Margin (N)
5th	White liberal/Jewish	71.1	28.9	22,645
8th	Black	92.0	8.0	24,024
12th	White conservative	46.3	53.7	−3,420
14th	Latino/moderate white	65.4	34.6	6,408

[a]Percentage of all votes cast on Proposition F.

SOURCE: Analysis of data from County of Los Angeles. Registrar-Recorder.

unquestionably committed to a downtown development strategy. With the close ties between the mayor and the Community Redevelopment Agency (CRA), the administration embarked in 1975 on one of the grandest downtown building programs of any American city. Within the next decade, the Los Angeles skyline grew dramatically, and downtown was filled with gleaming skyscrapers. Tax increment financing made the massive project self-sustaining, as the increased property values generated tax revenue that was plowed back into development.

The downtown building boom helped cement the economic alliance between the Bradley regime and downtown business and labor (Regalado 1991) in uneasy coexistence with the minority-liberal coalition that sustained its electoral success. But it also increased the alienation of poor, minority neighborhoods, which continued to deteriorate as Los Angeles became a global city with a world reputation.

While Bradley ceaselessly pursued programs to draw business into the inner city, it was only near the end of his mayoralty that he invested substantial political capital in programs that would ease bank lending practices in poor and minority neighborhoods. In those later years, he developed a program to use redevelopment funds to provide after-school care in the city schools and supported council efforts to push banks to increase their lending in the inner city.

One Bradley critic set forth the paradox of Bradley's economic policy:

> Critics who accuse the Bradley administration of "killing Southcentral L.A." usually ignore its achievements in integrating the public workforce. . . . It may be equally true that Black political leadership in Los Angeles County has sponsored significant economic advance and contributed to the community's benign neglect at the same time. (Davis 1991, 304)

Thus, the Bradley regime generated substantial political and social benefits for minority communities. At great political cost, some police accountability was achieved. Even in South Central Los Angeles, many families owed their livelihoods to affirmative action programs in city hiring and to federally funded projects pursued aggressively by Bradley. But the economic development of the inner city languished alongside the shining towers of Los Angeles. As thousands of young men roamed the streets without work, the potential for civil violence was plain to see (Morrison and Lowry 1994).

THE DECLINE AND FALL OF THE BIRACIAL COALITION

The steady obliteration of the city's industrial base and the rise of a globally based service economy, sustained by massive immigration, ultimately changed the foundations of the city's life. As with the industrial economy before it, the political effects of this new economy were not immediately felt. But it helped seal the doom of the biracial coalition and sent the political system into its current period of confusion and conflict. Ironically, Tom Bradley's dream to create a world-class city was coming true, but with consequences he would never have imagined.

It was not the changing economy alone that spelled the end of the coalition; there were many political factors as well. For example, increasing conflict between blacks and Jews had a chilling effect on the elite ties that had been essential to the coalition's success. When Louis Farrakhan came to town in 1985, the leaders of the Bradley coalition were unable to surmount the intergroup divisions that resulted. The increasing fear of crime among middle-class whites made it extremely difficult for progressive candidates to build majority coalitions crossing race and class lines.

But economic changes made a big difference. The downtown growth boom sustained by the Bradley coalition alienated disparate groups. Inner-city blacks and Latinos felt that their neighborhoods had been shortchanged in the midst of an economic restructuring. At the same time, whites in West Los Angeles and in the San Fernando Valley felt that there had been too *much* growth in their areas—too much traffic, too many stores, too big a jump in home costs. Few in either area felt that the quality of their lives had been improved by Los Angeles's growth machine. And the divergent complaints and conflicts of interest provided little ground for coalition building.

The immigration issue also significantly weakened coalition politics. In the diverse global city, there were increasingly cross-cutting conflicts at the street level. In South Central Los Angeles, citywide issues of black and white were replaced by localized conflicts between blacks and immigrant Latinos for construction jobs, and between blacks and Korean-American storeowners (Oliver and Johnson 1984; Johnson and Oliver 1989; Sonenshein 1996).

Less visibly, but crucially, the immigration issue was leading to a wide concern among whites (and many blacks) that the city was changing in an unpredictable and uncomfortable direction. The strands came together in 1994 when the white conservative and black areas voted on the same side for Proposition 187, while Latinos and white liberals voted against it. Immigration was one of the few issues that seemed capable of fracturing the basic structure of Los Angeles politics.

The new global economy was not creating the sorts of jobs that had sustained the political activism of an up-and-coming black community after World War II. Although immigrant Latinos in South Central Los Angeles were employed at high levels, they were not earning high wages (Pastor 1995). Most were not citizens and were struggling to make ends meet. Unlike the workers in World War II Los Angeles, those who were doing the hard work of the city were not in a position to build a foundation for future civic involvement. Indeed, they were virtually invisible in the city's politics, unenfranchised, formally represented by black elected officials, and often ignored by Latino elected officials with their own districts to represent.

The city's population was changing rapidly (Table 2.8). Until the 1980 census, whites had been a majority of the city's population. By 1990, whites represented less than 40 percent of the city's nearly 3.5 million people. The single largest group were Latinos, who had increased in number significantly from 1980.

But the city's political system was becoming a much narrower version of the "lived" city. Table 2.9 below contrasts the actual population of the city with the politically eligible and active.

TABLE 2.8   Population of Los Angeles by race/ethnicity, 1990

	%	N
Whites	37.3	1,299,604
Blacks	14.0	487,674
Latinos	39.9	1,391,411
Asian Americans	9.8	341,807
Total		3,485,398

Note: Percentages total more than 100 because of rounding.

SOURCE: Census data.

TABLE 2.9   Population versus registration, Los Angeles (in percentages)

			Votes for Mayor (%)	
	Population	Registration	*1993 primary*	*1993 general*
Whites	37.3	65	68	72
Jews	7.0 (est.)	15	16	19
Blacks	14.0	15	18	12
Latinos	39.9	11	8	10
Asian Americans	9.2	4	4	4

SOURCES: Population, U.S. Census; registration, summary of various estimates; vote in 1993 from *Los Angeles Times* exit polls.

For all the dramatic demographic changes that Los Angeles had experienced, the city's political system continued to resemble what it had been for decades—politics in black and white. In the 1993 mayoral runoff, 84 percent of all votes were cast by these two groups. Blacks and Jews, the core groups of the biracial alliance, alone cast nearly one-third of all the runoff votes. The gap between Latino population and Latino participation is truly astonishing—four times as many people as their share of the vote.

Table 2.10 reveals the components of this participation gap. Compare the highest and lowest participation districts among the 15 council districts. The First is a low-income, largely Latino district on the east side. The Fifth is the principal westside liberal district, nearly 40 percent Jewish and heavily Democratic.

Table 2.10 clearly shows the hole in the electorate. Age opens up one important gap; the Latino community is much younger. But the huge drop is citizenship, reducing the potential voting bloc in the First District to only one-third of the Fifth. Then registration and voting bring the First down to only one-fifth of the Fifth District's vote per population. Standard turnout figures obscure this difference. Whereas about one-third of the registered voters turned out in each district in the April primary, there were more than five times as many voters in the Fifth.

TABLE 2.10   The mobilization gap between two council districts, 1992–1993

Population		18 yrs of age and older	Citizen 18 yrs of age	Reg. Voters	Votes Cast 4/93
1	228,695	160,576	58,547	36,804	10,118
5	236,423	203,451	174,199	151,020	53,018

SOURCE: Pactech Consultants. Report to the Los Angeles City Council. "1992: Votes Cast," from city clerk election division.

Indeed, despite the enormous demographic changes in Los Angeles, the political community in the mid-1990s looked remarkably similar to what it was when Bradley fought Yorty in 1969 and 1973: a white majority, a stable one-sixth black base, and a significant but surprisingly small Latino bloc.

In this context, the 1992 civil disturbance and the 1993 election of Mayor Richard Riordan represented two sides of a coin: the appearance or reappearance of characters in the drama of Los Angeles politics. The violence came from the poor and unaffiliated, to a far greater degree than the more political Watts riot of 1965 (Sears 1994). Alienated poor people had not been much of a presence in the upwardly mobile, middle-class biracial coalition, and they were out in inchoate force, even burning down such landmarks of the minority movement as the Watts Labor Community Action Center. Latinos on the more established eastside displayed little inclination to participate, but Latinos in South Central and Koreatown represented a core component of the violence.

A year later, white conservatives, long marginalized under the Bradley regime, burst back into the politics they had dominated in the era of Sam Yorty. They voted in a large bloc, with a very high turnout, for a Republican candidate who promised a tough and businesslike approach.

With both the minority poor and white conservatives out in force, Los Angeles politics were certain to become more diverse, more polarized, and more unpredictable than they had been under the long and stable rule of the Bradley coalition. In that context, how did the rollback of minority incorporation occur, and what have been its consequences?

THE RISE OF A CONSERVATIVE COALITION

In the 1993 Los Angeles municipal elections, the long era of strong minority incorporation ended. City councilman Michael Woo, a Chinese American associated with the progressive ideal of multiracial politics, was soundly defeated by Republican businessman Richard Riordan. In a city two-thirds of whose registered voters are Democrats and where whites represent less than 40 percent of the population, how did this occur? How did a Woo aide's confident prediction that "Los Angeles will never elect an old, rich, white Republican" turn out to be 1993's epitaph for Los Angeles liberalism?

The first explanation has already been presented: the electoral system in to-day's Los Angeles has little to do with the census figures. Whites represent two-thirds of the voters, and in that sense nothing much has changed. But that is only the first part of the answer, as a liberal coalition had triumphed five consecutive times behind Tom Bradley by drawing off large blocs of Latinos and liberal and moderate whites, especially Jews.

As an Asian American drawing on a multicultural constituency, Woo came to symbolize the uncertain future of a city becoming more diverse but also more con-fusing and even threatening. The declining popularity of the Bradley coalition com-bined with the gloomy outlook held by the great majority of the city's voters made the road for a liberal candidate rocky indeed. Los Angeles is a moderately liberal city with a strong Democratic majority. Winning progressive alliances join the left and the center. But Woo found himself largely on the left, with little appeal to the center.

There had arisen a vast new level of *interest* conflicts among the various groups likely to form a progressive multiracial coalition. Some were neighborhood based—such as the interminority battles in an increasingly diverse South Central—while others concerned the distribution of resources and power between the inner city and the more affluent parts of the community. And there was a serious decline in the leadership capabilities of the liberal forces, compared with the Bradley coali-tion in its heyday.

Woo's runoff opponent, Republican businessman Richard Riordan, seemed an easy target in a city of Democrats. But he had a personal fortune, from which he spent freely, and a simple and compelling pledge: "Tough enough to turn L.A. around." Riordan quickly staked out the highest ground on the two key issues: pub-lic safety and the economy. He promised to hire 3,000 more police officers and to remove barriers to private investment in Los Angeles. Woo's private polling showed that on most indicators of leadership, the voters preferred Riordan by a wide margin (Fairbank, Maslin, Maullin, and Associates, various polls). Even those who eventu-ally voted for Woo were only "mild about Mike." In areas of Woo's greatest strength, the turnout was significantly lower than in his weakest areas (Sonenshein and Va-lentino 1995).

Riordan held a near-monopoly of elite support across party lines. To many of the city's leaders, Riordan was a *mensch*, a real grownup with weight. To city coun-cil president John Ferraro, his colleague Woo was "a snot-nosed kid." Woo was not widely liked or respected on the council, and leaders flocked to Riordan's cam-paign. Even President Clinton, in his tepid endorsement of fellow Democrat Woo, praised Riordan. Riordan was certainly no Yorty-style populist, but neither did he draw his support only from business elites. He gained endorsements from Latino council member Richard Alatorre, and from J. Stanley Sanders, the leading black candidate in the mayoral primary.

In the election, the traditional patterns of the city's coalitions held firm. Woo, the liberal candidate, had the great share (86 percent) of the black vote, due to his prominent role in opposing Chief Gates. He won handily among white liberals and won bare majorities among Jews and Latinos. He won the great majority of Asian-

American votes. In a city that only a year before had witnessed assaults on Asian-American stores by black and Latino rioters, Woo managed to craft a strong rainbow coalition.

But he was crushingly defeated among white non-Jews and his support among Jews and Latinos was well below Tom Bradley levels. Most remarkably, Riordan won a solid majority of the Fifth council district, the most liberal, most Jewish, and most participatory of all 15 council districts. It had been a pillar of the Bradley coalition. Clearly, the liberal side of Los Angeles politics, although still competitive, was less unified, less enthusiastic, and less able to hold the center than in its glory days.

MINORITY INCORPORATION IN THE RIORDAN ERA

Under Richard Riordan, minority influence has significantly declined at city hall. After enjoying 20 years at the head table in the mayor's office, black voters saw the top executive job go to a person who was backed by fewer than 15 percent of African-American voters, and by a minority of Latinos and Asian Americans.

In his first year in office, Riordan's consensus, power-brokering style allowed him to isolate and marginalize liberal and minority opposition. Three blacks and three Latinos serve on the 15-member council, but their influence is uncertain. Among Latinos, Mike Hernandez was a liberal critic of the mayor, but Richard Alatorre strongly backed the mayor. Among African Americans, both Rita Walters and Mark Ridley-Thomas frequently criticized the mayor, but Nate Holden was relatively supportive.

Liberals were not defeated in city council campaigns before and after 1993. What changed was that those liberals who were on the council, or who joined the council, once the key to the political prosperity of the Bradley majority, became somewhat less liberal than before. They were more likely to be described as "moderates," with the possible exception of the more liberal Jackie Goldberg (13th CD). They were unlikely to form a coalition with the minority members against Riordan.

Indeed, in his first year Riordan had substantial support in the broad center of the council. To the extent that there was a liberal coalition on the council it was a cross-racial bloc of Ridley-Thomas, Walters, Hernandez, and the newly elected Goldberg, the city's only openly gay elected official.

The current era in Los Angeles politics is one of partial, inconsistent incorporation by minority groups, certainly a far cry from the full incorporation of the Bradley era (1973–1993), although more positive than the earlier Yorty era (1961–1973).

With a white conservative Republican businessman as mayor, minorities lost the full incorporation they had enjoyed under Tom Bradley. Elected with the Sam Yorty coalition of Valley conservatives and a minority of Latinos and Jews, in the face of the near-unanimous opposition of blacks, Riordan could be expected to roll back many of the gains made for minorities under the previous regime.

But in his first year, Riordan was a surprise to many observers. To those who knew him well, it was hardly surprising at all. Riordan had been a Bradley commissioner and had been an active campaign donor to such Democrats as Bradley. Many of his closest associates have been Democrats, and his campaign operatives were mostly retreads from the 1992 Clinton campaign in California. State Republicans derisively referred to Riordan as R.I.N.O. (Republican in Name Only).

In his first months in office, Riordan seemed to ally himself with the city's new black police chief, Willie Williams, and with Democratic president Bill Clinton. He flew to Washington to lobby Congress for Clinton's crime bill, and in 1994 he went against his party to back Democratic Senator Dianne Feinstein for reelection.

Riordan made a major commitment to the revitalization of South Central Los Angeles, attempting to bring corporations into the inner city through streamlined city regulations and other methods. He worked aggressively to keep existing companies in the city. Applying for federal empowerment zone funds, Riordan seemed to be pledging more economic development for the inner city than had the Bradley administration. This would certainly have never been a program of a Sam Yorty.

In fact, Riordan's ability to meet his campaign pledges was almost entirely dependent on the success of the Clinton administration's policies on crime and economic development. Riordan counted on the crime bill to help him meet his pledge of adding 3,000 police officers to the city's force. In addition, his strategy of investment in the city became heavily tied to the Clinton administration's empowerment zone program. Oddly, one thing that would have seriously hurt Los Angeles's Republican mayor would have been the ability of congressional Republicans to gut both programs in the name of the private sector that Riordan held up as the city's salvation.

Riordan's appointments to city commissions were eclectic and surprising. Although they did not follow the coalition pattern of the Bradley years, these appointments placed a number of progressive Democrats in very important positions. Police and fire commissioners included several members very willing to confront the departments on minority hiring and promotion. In fact, Riordan's fire commission took on the department's popular chief on this very question, far more publicly than Bradley's people had (*Los Angeles Times*, 3 January 1995).

Riordan's appointments to city commissions were substantially less oriented toward minorities and skewed more to the Valley, to Republicans, and to mobile economic elites than were those of Bradley (*Los Angeles Times*, 9 September 1993, 29 November 1993). More striking was Riordan's selection of commissioners with less visible stakes in city politics. Half the members of Riordan's transition team did not live in Los Angeles (*Los Angeles Times*, 16 June 1993).

Schockman (1996, 68–9) found that a surprising number of Riordan's commissioners live far beyond the city's borders and that they disproportionately represent affluent white areas. Despite a significant degree of racial and economic diversity in commission appointments, Schockman concluded that Riordan had assembled a "neo-rainbow coalition, based on class, not on race."

On police reform, Riordan sent a mixed message. As a private citizen, he had supported Proposition F for police reform in 1992. But his mayoral campaign received critical help from the Police Protective League, a largely white union profoundly hostile to police reform. His campaign promise to hire 3,000 new police officers without raising taxes placed him on a potential collision course with the equally costly and popular policy of community-based policing championed by Chief Williams. Some of his police commissioners were highly committed to reform, but the mayor himself seemed to define reform as manpower expansion. Not surprisingly, Riordan's early support for Williams soon evaporated, and they entered a long period of conflict.

How to explain the survival of even some of the minority agenda in the post-incorporation era? It is testimony to the long-run impact of strong minority incorporation that a new victor at city hall does not simply dismantle all of its successes. The difference lies in the gap between Sam Yorty and Richard Riordan. Their electoral coalitions are similar, but their mayoralties have been worlds apart.

Riordan has been more than acceptable to Democrats and has provided relatively nonpartisan leadership thus far. While he was elected without black support, he has continued to pursue economic development in the inner city. His image is "tough," but only "tough enough," an important distinction for white moderates and even white liberals. On social issues important to white liberals—gay rights and abortion—Riordan has been unthreatening. In fact, shortly after he took office, Riordan marched in the Gay Rights Parade and was photographed hugging a participant.

In the policy areas examined in the discussion of Bradley's administration, Riordan has made substantial changes in political representation to the detriment of minority incorporation, affirmative action in city hiring has remained steady, police accountability has been a mixed picture, and on economic development Riordan has the potential to be more successful in helping minority communities than Bradley.

In his second year in office, however, Riordan began to wander from his central message of crime fighting and economic revival, and from centrist moderation. His relations with the Clinton administration were damaged by the city's failed application for empowerment zone funds, and his conflict with Police Chief Willie Williams became a major issue at city hall.

The city council, which had been a bedrock of support for the mayor, found itself baffled by his shifting moves. A stunning city report in October 1995 found that after two years of strenuous effort to increase the police force, there were no more officers on the street than when Riordan was elected. Mayor-council conflict developed over mayoral appointees to city commissions, and the council rebuffed the mayor several times, including a highly contentious struggle over Chief Williams. Backed by advisers who favored a strong mayoral role, Riordan became angered at what he perceived to be council interference. With the increased rancor at city hall, the voters found less reason to believe that the mayor was making progress in creating a safer and more prosperous city.

As a result, Riordan's overall popularity declined to 46 percent in 1995, compared to 59 percent in 1994, according to the *Los Angeles Times* poll (2 July 1995). His support fell most dramatically in the largely white and Latino San Fernando

Valley while it held steady on the westside. Oddly, the Republican Riordan was becoming more dependent on the generally liberal and moderate white westside.

Then, the O. J. Simpson trial in 1995 reopened the racial wounds that had been barely sealed in Los Angeles. Without much skill at intergroup relations, Riordan became nearly invisible, and his rival Willie Williams became the city's voice as it sought to pass through the racial divisions opened by the Fuhrman tapes and the Simpson verdict.

In the short term, the anger over the Simpson acquittal helped Riordan because it so bitterly divided westside liberals from African Americans. But in the face of the severe racial divisiveness of the verdict, progressive forces in the city soon took the opportunity to greatly increase the intensity of their meetings. On October 24, 1995, councilman Mark Ridley-Thomas sponsored a Day of Dialogue at one hundred sites throughout the city. Such meetings could be a first step toward restoring some of the frayed leadership ties in Los Angeles.

Where Riordan's approach has been most disturbing (and at times successful) has been his belief in business as the salvation of the city's economy. As a venture capitalist with broad ties to the city's economic elite, Riordan has demonstrated a belief that business methods can turn the city around. For those communities without political power in Los Angeles, Riordan's approach has been troublesome.

Because of profound demographic and economic changes, the issues that will affect the daily lives of minority communities have changed. They are more economic, more down-to-earth, and more practical. These issues will force minority coalitions to confront issues of class and economics that were less crucial to the era of minority political incorporation. They will also increasingly cross the line between the city and county of Los Angeles. And Riordan's role has been mixed in these issues, reflecting the upper-class definition of his coalition.

BUS FARES AND LIQUOR STORES

The end of the era of biracial coalition power at city hall has meant that issues that concern minorities have become seriously fragmented. At one time, the city's warring factions were divided clearly into two main groups: those who sided with minorities against those who were unfriendly to minorities. That is no longer the case. The issues that once defined minority progress were well known: affirmative action in city hiring, the obtaining of federal funds, and police accountability. Nothing like that clarity exists in today's Los Angeles, where the old biracial alliance shares space with angry white conservatives, assertive minorities, and the often inchoate demands of the urban poor.

With governing coalitions less dominant, problems have seemed caught in a netherworld of power. The confusion between city and county becomes important, as issues threaten to fall through the cracks. And community groups, in this confusion, move into the breach to seek to expand opportunity for minorities. Two remarkable examples are bus fares and liquor stores.

Unlike the situation in New York City, where public transportation is widely and democratically shared, the poor in Los Angeles take the bus, the upper-status commuters take the train, and everybody else drives. As a result, the bus system, which is essential to the working lives of thousands of city residents, has little political protection. When the Rapid Transit District was joined to the County Transportation Authority to create the Metropolitan Transportation Authority (MTA), many feared that the buses would be drained to pay for expensive subsidies to build train lines. That is exactly what occurred.

The MTA is one of the ugliest spectacles in Los Angeles politics, as rail interests pay large campaign contributions to county supervisors and city council members, and then expect expensive rail lines to be financed by the taxpayers. Its business largely conducted outside the public eye, the MTA has favored affluent train riders over the half-million poor and working people, disproportionately minorities, who ride the buses.

Overextended by rail investment, the MTA sought in 1994 to raise the bus fare yet again and were stopped only by the order of a federal judge. There seem to be no elected officials, minority or white, willing or able to take the bus riders' case as their own. They are all too busy trying to get the rail lines into their own districts. And Riordan, himself an investor in a consulting firm involved with the MTA and holding four votes on the MTA board, has been in the thick of things without ever raising a voice on behalf of the bus riders.

In 1995, the county of Los Angeles faced a severe crisis in health services, leading to calls for the closing of many health clinics and hospitals. When the state of California seemed prepared to authorize the use of county MTA funds to keep the hospitals open, Mayor Riordan blocked the transfer. Riordan was bailed out by President Clinton, who averted a damaging health crisis by agreeing to a large federal aid package for the county.

For another example, an intense battle has been going on between black, and, to some extent, Latino residents of South Central Los Angeles and Korean-American liquor store owners. Yet there have been serious attempts to channel the conflict in ways that deemphasize its racial and ethnic components (Sonenshein 1996). A community group has had great success blocking the rebuilding of liquor stores damaged or destroyed in the 1992 violence, placing the city's pro-business and pro-order mayor in a political bind. Does he support the community's effort to clean itself up, or the property rights of minority business owners?

WHITHER MINORITY POLITICS IN LOS ANGELES?

Minority incorporation in Los Angeles politics has obviously been significantly rolled back. Minorities are not part of the mayor's coalition, and the liberal members represent a minority of the city council. Minorities and their liberal allies have a smaller share of commission posts than they enjoyed under Mayor Bradley. Yet the long-term impact of minority incorporation has been deep and powerful. The mayor, while awkward in his dealings with minority communities, has not been implacably hostile to the economic aspirations of minorities.

To a remarkable degree, the city's political system has remained stable in the face of huge demographic changes. Once Los Angeles's politics was black and white; to a shocking degree, it still is. And that represents a serious problem for democratic governance.

Although the electoral structure of the city has not changed much despite massive demographic shifts in the city's population, resurrecting the old biracial coalition will be no small matter. Those who built that coalition are slowly moving out of Los Angeles politics and have yet to be replaced by another generation of coalition builders. In both the black and Jewish communities, there has been an inward turning that may lead to stronger coalitions in the future, but that makes bridge building harder in the present.

Within the Latino community, there is continuing debate over whether to pursue coalition politics or to go it alone with a reliance on demographics and the actuarial tables. The Latino community is deeply divided by nationality, citizen status, and class. Proposition 187 and other anti-immigrant actions have spurred a strong citizenship and voter registration effort among Latinos; if their political potential were to increase, the minority politics of Los Angeles would be fundamentally altered.

The Asian-American community, long quiet in city politics, is now beginning to carve out a political role. The Woo mayoral campaign was a remarkable achievement for an Asian-American community whose voice has been much quieter in Los Angeles than, for example, in San Francisco. Woo nearly recreated a successful version of the Bradley coalition in very tough times.

The civil unrest of 1992 devastated the Korean-American community, but it also generated an enormous push toward political involvement. Younger Korean Americans have brought new lobbying skills to city hall and have begun to examine the tactical value of targeted campaign contributions. Coalition efforts in the city now have a strong Asian-American component, to a far greater degree than before the civil unrest.

But with all the interminority conflicts and the emergence of each group in its own right, the city is a long way from being the site of a multiracial coalition that is ready for prime time.

The political difficulties, largely self-inflicted, that have characterized the Riordan mayoralty after a very promising beginning, suggest that conservative leadership is unlikely to dominate Los Angeles permanently. But liberal forces are a long way from resolving the issues that caused them to lose the support of an electoral and governing majority. The principal difficulty is the conflict between rainbow and interracial politics.

At the heart of the matter is the potential role that both minorities and whites might play in the future of minority politics in Los Angeles. If minority activists choose to go it alone, they will be consistently outvoted. If minority activists choose a white-oriented strategy, their ability to bring about serious changes in the city's life will be compromised. Once again, the dilemma is as it has always been: how to pursue an activist agenda for minority equality while responding to the legitimate needs and interests of whites. No matter how confused the Riordan agenda has become, the liberal, multiracial alternative has not yet demonstrated its ability to master that challenge. And even if it does, the issue of equality has become more complicated than it was during the heyday of minority incorporation.

A biracial or multiracial coalition, whether in power or as a challenger to power, must cut more deeply into the city's economic problems than the Bradley coalition was able to do.

Any challenge from the left or from minority communities would need to readdress itself to the problems of the communities they want to represent. There was a lesson in the low turnout Woo received from these very communities. Are there new ways for political leaders to address the economic issues facing poor neighborhoods while still building citywide coalitions?

At the neighborhood level, in fact, there is much greater attention these days to resolving interminority conflicts than to building citywide electoral majorities. In South Central Los Angeles, the three-cornered conflict among long-time black residents, new Latino immigrants, and Korean-American storeowners is more about the management of conflict than traditional coalition building.

Such negotiations offer promising evidence that in the unstructured, multicentered politics of today's Los Angeles, there are still people who can draw on the tradition of coalition politics to solve problems. There is still a question, however, of whether enough political communication exists between minority communities and whites, who make up two-thirds of the registered voters.

Even if all minority groups settled their conflicts with each other, they would still be outvoted by whites. The key to the Los Angeles biracial coalition was to divide whites by ideology and to build cross-racial, cross-city alliances. A very sad outcome of today's politics would be a city politics in which whites control the elections and minorities negotiate agreements with each other. Government simply controls too many resources for minority and progressive activists to cede power over it. How can the interests and beliefs of groups be tied together, and by which leaders? These political questions cross the boundaries between electoral politics and economics and will set the stage for the minority and majority politics of the next Los Angeles.

REFERENCES

Adrian, Charles R. 1959. A Typology for Nonpartisan Elections. *Western Political Quarterly* 12: 449–458.

Browning, Rufus P., Dale Rogers Marshall, and David H. Tabb. 1984. *Protest Is Not Enough: The Struggle of Blacks and Hispanics for Equality in Urban Politics.* Berkeley: University of California Press.

Carmichael, Stokely, and Charles V. Hamilton. 1967. *Black Power: The Politics of Liberation in America.* New York: Random House.

Carney, Francis M. 1964. The Decentralized Politics of Los Angeles. *The Annals of the American Academy of Political and Social Science* 353: 107–121.

Davis, Mike. 1991. *City of Quartz: Excavating the Future in Los Angeles*. London: Haymarket Press.

Elkin, Stephen L. 1987. *City and Regime in the American Republic*. Chicago: University of Chicago Press.

Fairbank, Maslin, Maullin, and Associates. Various dates. Public opinion poll reports (unpublished). Santa Monica, Calif.

Fogelson, Robert M. 1967. *The Fragmented Metropolis: Los Angeles, 1850–1930*. Cambridge, Mass.: Harvard University Press.

Hahn, Harlan, David Klingman, and Harry Pachon. 1976. Cleavages, Coalitions, and the Black Candidate: The Los Angeles Mayoralty Elections of 1969 and 1973. *Western Political Quarterly* 29: 521–530.

Hinckley, Barbara. 1981. *Coalitions and Politics*. New York: Harcourt Brace Jovanovich.

Johnson, James, Jr., and Melvin Oliver. 1989. Interethnic Minority Conflict in Urban America: The Effects of Economic and Social Dislocations. *Urban Geography* 10: 449–463.

Mayo, Charles G. 1964. The 1961 Mayoralty Election in Los Angeles: The Political Party in a Nonpartisan Election. *Western Political Quarterly* 17: 325–337.

Morrison, Peter A., and Ira S. Lowry. 1994. A Riot of Color: The Demographic Setting. In Mark Baldassare, ed., *The Los Angeles Riots: Lessons for the Urban Future*, 19–46. Boulder, Colo.: Westview Press.

Oliver, Melvin L., and James H. Johnson, Jr. 1984. Inter-ethnic Conflict in an Urban Ghetto: The Case of Blacks and Latinos in Los Angeles. *Research in Social Movements, Conflict, and Change* 6: 57–94.

Pactech Consultants. 1992. Report to the Los Angeles City Council for the Redistricting Process.

Pastor, Manuel, Jr. 1995. Economic Inequality, Latino Poverty, and the Civil Unrest in Los Angeles. *Economic Development Quarterly* 9 (August): 238–258.

Patterson, Beeman. 1969. Political Action of Negroes in Los Angeles: A Case Study in the Attainment of Councilmanic Representation. *Phylon* 30: 170–183.

Regalado, James. 1991. Organized Labor and Los Angeles City Politics: An Assessment in the Bradley Years, 1973–1989. *Urban Affairs Quarterly* 27 (September): 87–108.

Ross, Ruth. 1980. *The Impact of Federal Grants on the City of Los Angeles*. Federal Aid Case Studies Series, paper no. 8. Washington, D.C.: Brookings Institution.

Saltzstein, Alan, Raphael Sonenshein, and Irving Ostrow. 1986. Federal Aid to the City of Los Angeles: Implementing a More Centralized Local Political System. In Terry Clark, ed., *Research in Urban Policy*, vol. 2, 55–76. Greenwich, Conn.: JAI Press.

Schockman, H. Eric. 1996. Is Los Angeles Governable? Revising the City Charter. In Michael Dear, H. Eric Schockman, and Greg Hise, eds., *Rethinking Los Angeles*, 57–72. Thousand Oaks, Calif.: Sage.

Sears, David O. 1994. Urban Rioting in Los Angeles: A Comparison of 1965 with 1992. In Mark Baldassare, ed., *The Los Angeles Riots: Lessons for the Urban Future*, 237–254. Boulder, Colo.: Westview Press.

Smith, Alonzo Nelson. 1978. Black Employment in the Los Angeles Area, 1938–1948. Ph.D dissertation, University of California, Los Angeles.

Sonenshein, Raphael J. 1993. *Politics in Black and White: Race and Power in Los Angeles*. Princeton, N.J.: Princeton University Press.

Sonenshein, Raphael J. 1996. The Battle over Liquor Stores in South Central Los Angeles: The Management of an Interminority Conflict. *Urban Affairs Review* 31: 710–737.

Sonenshein, Raphael J., and Nicholas Valentino. 1995. A New Alignment in City Politics? Evidence from the 1993 Los Angeles Mayoral Election. Paper presented at the annual meeting of the Western Political Science Association, San Francisco.

Vorspan, Max, and Lloyd P. Gartner. 1970. *History of the Jews of Los Angeles.* San Marino, Calif.: The Huntington Library.

chapter **3**

After the First Black Mayor: Fault Lines in Philadelphia's Biracial Coalition

Richard A. Keiser[1]

Editors' Note

Like Los Angeles, Philadelphia is a case of black political success. Like Chicago, Philadelphia is a large, old, eastern city with partisan elections and a history of machine politics. Yet Philadelphia presents many contrasts to both. Blacks constituted more than twice the proportion of the population in Philadelphia than in Los Angeles, but the election of a black mayor came a full decade later—Wilson Goode in 1983.

Why such a long delay? Richard Keiser shows that a liberal reform movement that had displaced a long-lived Republican machine began the job of black political incorporation, but a rejuvenated Democratic party halted this progress. During periods when the alliance of white liberals and blacks temporarily overcame the machine, black incorporation progressed. Even when the organization politicians governed the city, the biracial, reform alliance dampened the efforts of the machine to roll back black political gains. Eventually, a moderate, biracial, reform coalition elected a black city council president and a black mayor. Keiser's account of the origins and evolution of this coalition is worth studying for the light it sheds on the displacement of conservative coalitions, the linkages between electoral competitiveness and the emergence of political leadership, the nurturing of trust, and the avoidance of the extreme racial polarization that we observe in Chicago.

The problem for Philadelphia and other cities in the period after the first black mayor leaves office is maintaining the unity of the dominant coalition. Divisions be-

[1] I would like to thank Carleton College for a Faculty Development Grant that provided leave time for writing this chapter.

tween powerful black leaders that were papered over in the effort to elect the first black mayor now have emerged. The election of a white mayor, Ed Rendell, indicates an antiblack backlash to some, even though Rendell has long been part of the white liberal faction. Finally, the fact that in the 1991 mayoral elections neither white nor black voters acted as if they had to elect anyone but a member of the other race presents a sharp contrast to the "anybody but Harold" politics of white ethnic Chicago and is testimony to the legitimacy black leadership has earned through the process of political incorporation.

INTRODUCTION

In 1983, Wilson Goode was elected the first black mayor of Philadelphia. Goode was one among a cadre of prominent black politicians in Philadelphia who gained legitimacy and could garner votes in both the black and white communities. In Philadelphia, black leaders had been participating in biracial coalitions that had delivered incremental political incorporation for quite some time. This chapter presents a history and analysis of the formation of the biracial, reform-oriented alliance in Philadelphia that was the forerunner of the coalition that elected Wilson Goode as mayor in 1983. This chapter discusses the origins of the biracial reform coalition and its intermittent success in gaining the political incorporation of blacks. We examine the opposition that a biracial coalition dedicated to an incrementalist strategy faces from within the black community and from whites. After discussing the election of Goode, I review the Goode administration, focusing particularly on the extent to which his administration enhanced the status and furthered the political incorporation of blacks and Hispanics. I also discuss the current biracial coalition that is headed by a white Democrat with liberal credentials and suggest that biracial alliances are no longer limited to the reform variety. Finally, I compare the evolution of Philadelphia's biracial coalition with the patterns found in some of the other cities examined in this book.

In addition to Browning, Marshall, and Tabb's argument that black incorporation is a product of alliances with white liberals who are motivated by ideological concerns and an affinity of interest in empowering subordinated groups, this chapter provides evidence for the structural hypothesis that closely contested or competitive elections create the circumstances within which subordinated groups such as blacks can wrest concessions and win incorporation (Keiser 1993). To take advantage of these circumstances, black leadership must recognize the nature of this opportunity and gain a commitment from other coalition members, liberal or otherwise, that incremental steps of black incorporation will be exchanged for delivery of a bloc of votes that appears decisive to election outcomes. Without denying the general effect that ideology has on proclivities for coalition partners, in Philadelphia both the reform and regular factions recognized that black voters were not wedded to either faction and that they could be a decisive electoral bloc. The white factions acted accordingly and frequently engaged in small-scale bidding wars for black votes.

INCREMENTAL CONSTRUCTION
OF A BIRACIAL ALLIANCE

In the late 1940s, Philadelphia government was rocked by scandals that disgraced the formerly dominant Republican party, a party that had governed Philadelphia since 1881 and had rebuffed all efforts by blacks to gain political power. Joseph Clark, a reformer who promised "good government" in the wake of this corruption, led a coalition that ushered in a period of Democratic party domination of the city's politics when he was elected mayor in 1951. This new coalition included the Greater Philadelphia Movement (GPM), an umbrella business organization that mobilized the city's business leadership against their former GOP allies, the Americans for Democratic Action (ADA), home of the city's liberal activists, as well as significant aspects of the black community. Since then, politics in Philadelphia has been characterized by competition between (1) an amalgam of white liberal activists and "good-government" reformers, including many of the city's business leaders, and (2) the regular organization ethnic politicians of the Democratic party, many of whom defected, with their neighborhood ties intact, from the discredited Republican organization. The reformers and the organization politicians have battled largely within the confines of the Democratic party (for example, in primary elections); however, when either the reformers or the ethnic pols have been defeated in such battles, they have not hesitated to shift their support to Republicans and to use this otherwise moribund party as an alternative front for the ongoing battle. One of the major battle lines in this competition has been for the votes of the expanding black electorate. These conditions of electoral competitiveness made black voters a potentially decisive force in electoral outcomes and gave black political leaders leverage with which they could bargain for group political incorporation or more particularistic benefits.

Seeking to put machine-style politics out of business, the reformers instituted a new city charter that included a rigid civil service system for the awarding of city jobs. Because of private sector discrimination, an especially well-educated pool of blacks was available to take the examinations and win city employment (Lowe 1967; Weiler 1974). The crucial contribution that black votes made to the reform coalition was recognized and blacks were rewarded in a number of ways for their defection from the GOP to the reformers. The Commission on Human Relations declared that discrimination in private sector employment would no longer be tolerated and that companies would be penalized if they failed to "tak[e] affirmative steps to guarantee and promote equal employment opportunities" (Lowe 1967). Additionally, Mayor Clark and his reform-minded successor, Richardson Dilworth, began the incorporation of blacks into city government by backing black community leaders, especially clergymen, for elected and appointed offices that heretofore had not been held by blacks. Blacks affiliated with the reform movement were elected as city council members, recorder of deeds, and commissioner of records, and were appointed to prominent positions in such agencies as the civil service commission and as assistant district attorneys. The reform administrations eschewed high-rise public housing in favor of a program targeted at middle-income blacks that included redevelopment of extant housing (Lowe 1967). Mayor Dilworth, specifically seeking to remedy police brutality against blacks, created the first civilian police review board in the nation (Rogers 1971). Aside from this latter benefit, the value of which should not be gainsaid, poorer blacks received little other than the vicarious satisfaction of seeing better-educated members of the race employed in city government (Reichley 1959). But this intangible reward would not prove sufficient to maintain the loyalty of poor blacks to the reform wing of the Democratic party.

Rollback and Response:
The Resilience of the Reform Alliance

When Democrat George Leader was elected governor in 1955, the weak Philadelphia Democratic organization finally obtained the means to compete effectively with the reformers for control of the party and the city government. Leader strengthened the organization by placing nearly 3,000 patronage jobs at its disposal. The organization cultivated a mass base of support among low-income blacks by distributing patronage jobs, albeit those with the lowest salaries (Reichley 1959; Strange 1966). In 1958 the organization coopted a prominent black councilman, who had until then been allied with the reformers, by promising him the next available judgeship. That same year the organization further increased its black support by slating the first black Philadelphian elected to the U.S. Congress, Robert N. C. Nix. Hence the regular organization (not just white liberal reformers) deserved some credit for early advances of black incorporation, and the impetus for this was the imperative of competing for black votes in order to win competitive elections.

Even after an organization ward leader and councilman, James Tate, was elevated to the mayor's office in 1962 (because of Mayor Dilworth's resignation to run unsuccessfully for governor) and elected in 1963, the organization wing and the reform wing of the Democratic party remained highly competitive. The organization did not crush the reformers and come to dominate the city's politics as some have erroneously argued (Banfield 1965). The organization was weakened by the death of its "boss," Congressman William Green, in 1963. More devastatingly, Republican governors were elected in 1963 and 1967, depriving the Democratic organization of its intergovernmental source of patronage. Evidence that the regular organization had not vanquished the reformers and that politics in Philadelphia remained competitive can be found in the data for the mayoral elections of 1963 and 1967. Although Clark and Dilworth had not faced primary challenges in their terms, Tate faced challengers backed by disgruntled Democratic reformers in both 1963 and 1967. Tate defeated his 1963 Republican opponent by the narrow margin of 61,000 votes, about half the margin of his Democratic mayoral predecessors. In 1967, Tate's 11,000 vote margin barely enabled him to defeat Republican District Attorney Arlen Specter (a Jewish former Democrat supported by the GPM and the ADA), whose victory in the district attorney's race two years earlier was another indication of the weakened condition of the Democratic organization. Finally, in 1969 the Democratic candidates for district attorney and controller, were defeated by Republican candidates who received strong support from the white reformers.

That politics in Philadelphia remained highly competitive is significant because it meant that Tate and the regular Democratic organization were forced to court black voters at the same time they were trying to keep the blue-collar white ethnic vote from defecting to the GOP, as was the case in the 1968 presidential election of Richard Nixon. In classic machine fashion, Tate developed a political organization in black neighborhoods by creating new leaders to administer the federally funded antipoverty program and placing patronage jobs at their disposal so they could mobilize others in their neighborhoods (Peterson 1967). In both mayoral elections, Tate's victory came on the strength of the black vote, largely from poorer black wards (*Philadelphia Bulletin* 1965; Ekstrom 1973). Tate had earned this support by delivering about 39 percent of the city's jobs (more than 11,000) to blacks. These were entry-level jobs or menial labor, but for most of the recipients the alternative was to remain in what we refer to today as the underclass (Ershkowitz and Zikmund 1973, 58).

Note that although Tate used particularistic rewards to ensure that blacks remained the nucleus of the Democratic organization's *electoral coalition,* blacks were not part of the *governing coalition,* nor had they been with the liberal reformers. Blacks who aspired to leadership positions within the organizational structure of the party were rebuffed (Strange 1969). Moreover, blacks were not slated for visible public offices, as they had been under the reformers, from which they could influence the formation of policy. Consequently, policy emanating from city hall was less responsive to their needs. For instance, blacks in the party organization and middle-class black leaders who were not beholden to the Democratic organization (such as ministers and lawyers) were for most of the 1960s unsuccessful in their efforts to lobby city hall to end discrimination in the school system, halt police brutality and punish the offending officers, enforce housing codes created under Clark and Dilworth that would have raised the quality of housing in black ghettos, and enforce existing contract provisions prohibiting discrimination in city building projects.

The growing unresponsiveness to demands of the black middle class by Tate and the Democratic organization was part of their attempt to halt massive electoral defections by the white ethnic working class (Ekstrom 1973; Edsall and Edsall 1991). White voters who viewed black advancement as threatening had been defecting to Republican candidates like Specter who promised to "get tough on crime." To increase the party's lagging support among these voters, Tate promoted a charismatic policeman, Frank Rizzo, to the post of chief of police. Additionally, Tate moved to shore up white ethnic support by eliminating the city's civilian police review board. Tate was betting that black levels of electoral support for Democratic party candidates could be maintained even as the party adopted a less sympathetic view toward the policy concerns of blacks (*Philadelphia Bulletin* 1974).

In response to city hall's inattention to their substantive policy concerns, blacks began a protest movement under the leadership of Cecil Moore, the president of the National Association for the Advancement of Colored People (NAACP). Moore led demonstrations against the discriminatory practices of labor unions that were awarded contracts with the city (Fonzi 1963). He also led the battle to force an all-white orphanage held in trust by the city to open its doors to black children. Moore and the protest movement that he led did win some battles and provoked a few brutal responses by the police, yet city hall remained largely unresponsive to black policy demands.

Moore also sought to expand his power through the electoral process by promoting black separatism. He argued that only blacks—and preferably militant blacks—could electorally represent black constituencies; cooperating in political alliances with whites was inherently bad and those "so-called Negroes" who did were branded "tools of the white power structure" (Strange 1969, 1973). But Moore's separatist approach and antibiracial coalition rhetoric was contradicted by the successes that moderate blacks continued to achieve through biracial cooperation, even though white liberal reformers no longer occupied city hall.

After a group of 400 black ministers led a series of well-coordinated boycotts against selected Philadelphia businesses that failed to respond to requests that they hire more blacks, Philadelphia's business community seemed to require no further prodding. It began major efforts to create employment and employment training programs specifically for the black community (Strange 1973). One concerted, well-funded effort to provide employment and training was the Urban Coalition. More than $1 million was pledged to the Urban Coalition by Philadelphia's business community. Together with $4.7 million from the federal government, these monies created the Philadelphia Employment Development Corporation, which provided job training for the hard-core unemployed. In announcing this initiative, Philadelphia's premier business leadership organ, the Greater Philadelphia Movement, echoed the pragmatism for which Atlanta's business leadership has become known by candidly admitting that their motivation for the project was to preclude an escalation from peaceful boycotts to violent riots: "Most of greater Philadelphia's business and industrial leaders realized that unless the plight of the Black Americans became the central concern for all Americans, there will be no racial peace in this nation for possibly generations to come" (*New York Times* 1968).

The most notable example of cooperation between the black leadership and the business community was the Opportunities Industrialization Center (OIC). OIC was created in 1964 by the Reverend Leon Sullivan and his Zion Baptist Church to provide job training and business skills for blacks. After a year of success, local business leaders and the Ford Foundation began contributing money, training machinery, and program guidance. These are some of the most significant organizational vehicles by which the biracial reform alliance begun under Mayor Clark was continued in the period of rollback that this alliance faced in the Tate/Rizzo years; this alliance was further strengthened by the tenure of Mayor Frank Rizzo, discussed below.

By the close of the 1960s, three distinct political segments existed among Philadelphia's black community: a group linked to Mayor Tate and the Democratic organization through patronage; a group that followed Moore on a radical, protest path that condemned any biracial alliances; and a third group that sought electoral and civic alliances with white liberal reformers that was led by black ministers and business people.

Rizzo Unifies the Opposition:
The Reform Black Alliance of the 1970s

Because Mayor Tate was prevented by the city charter from running for a third consecutive term, the 1971 Democratic primary became a pivotal contest. Frank Rizzo
entered the campaign with the endorsement of Tate and the Democratic organization. Also running were black state Representative Hardy Williams; Congressman
Bill Green, Jr. (son of the former party leader), who had broken with the organization and staked out a position as an independent, reform Democrat; and liberal
Councilman David Cohen. Green, Williams, and Cohen were all competing for the
votes of the biracial reform coalition. Green convinced Cohen to withdraw and lend
him his support, but he was unable to convince Williams that dividing the anti-
Rizzo vote ensured a Rizzo victory. With 48 percent of the vote, Rizzo won, while
Green captured 35 percent, Williams won 12.5 percent, and Cohen received the remainder even though he had withdrawn.

In the general election Rizzo faced Thacher Longstreth, executive vice-president of the Philadelphia Chamber of Commerce. Rizzo confined his appearances to
working-class white neighborhoods. He promised the residents of these neighborhoods no unwanted public housing projects, opposition to busing children to
schools for purposes of racial balance, no tax hikes, and a get-tough attitude toward
crime that he boasted "would make Atilla the Hun look like a faggot." Though
Rizzo did no campaigning in any black wards, he predicted, "I will win every black
ward with the exception of maybe one" (Daughen and Binzen 1977).

Longstreth campaigned tirelessly throughout the city. He had the support of
the Republican organization, much of Philadelphia's business and civic leadership
including the Greater Philadelphia Movement (GPM), former mayors Clark and Dilworth, and the endorsement of the *Bulletin*. However, this was not enough. With a
record turnout of 77 percent of the city's registered voters, Rizzo defeated Longstreth by just under 50,000 votes.

Frank Rizzo's 1971 mayoral campaign catalyzed a previously unseen degree of
mobilization in the black community. In the primary, black voters demonstrated a
greater willingness to support a white liberal who could win rather than a black
who was relatively unknown to white voters. Bill Green won 51 percent of the vote
in predominantly black wards while Williams captured only 37 percent (Keiser
1989). In retrospect Williams's candidacy has been viewed as a milestone in independent black politics both because it represented a first black mayoral candidacy and because a young housing activist named Wilson Goode was the campaign manager. Williams, however, was the wrong black for the job of mobilizing a
united black vote to take advantage of the split in the white vote and, quite significantly, the majority of black voters recognized this. The Reverend Leon Sullivan and
Charles Bowser had much greater name recognition and legitimacy in both the
black and white communities.

In the general election, white liberals and blacks had chosen neither to stay at
home nor to passively accept defeat and vote for their party's candidate. Instead
they unified behind Longstreth and came close to defeating Rizzo. This was most
noteworthy for black voters because it represented their first massive defection from

the Democratic party to join in alliance with white liberal reformers. In the ten wards in which more than 90 percent of the registered voters were black, Rizzo won only 23 percent of the vote. Sixty-four percent of the city's registered black voters cast ballots and Rizzo was rejected by an amazing 77 percent of the voters in predominantly black wards. That Tate had captured approximately 70 percent of the vote in these black wards four years earlier indicates that the black vote represented a "sophisticated" defection from the candidate of the Democratic party. If contrasted to Chicago where Mayor Richard J. Daley consistently won more black votes than any candidate he faced, including white liberal and black challengers, this demonstration of black independence from the Democratic party seems particularly significant.

As mayor, Rizzo continued to foster black unity. In addition to condoning a policy of police brutality against blacks that ultimately led to a federal investigation of the police force, Mayor Rizzo systematically waged war on the city's black leadership (Keiser 1990). Even so, in 1975 Rizzo defeated Republican Thomas Foglietta and Charles Bowser, a black who ran as an independent candidate in the mayoral election. With two candidates dividing the anti-Rizzo vote, the election was really a contest for second place. Rizzo won with 57 percent of the vote, Bowser garnered 25 percent, and Foglietta received 18 percent. Yet, it is most significant that voters in the city's white reform wards demonstrated their willingness to support a qualified nondivisive black candidate by giving Bowser 41 percent of their vote. Even in the face of certain defeat, black and white leaders who favored a moderate, biracial coalition continued to work together to preserve the trust and norms of mutual support created under Clark and Dilworth and reaffirmed in the Longstreth campaign.

ELECTORAL MOBILIZATION AND THE FORMATION OF A DOMINANT BIRACIAL COALITION

Because of the prohibition in the city's home rule charter against more than two consecutive mayoral terms, Rizzo began a campaign to amend the charter to eliminate this limitation. To protect the charter, "good government" business leaders including the GPM, liberal activists from the ADA and similar groups, and black reformers organized, financed, and provided the leadership for a coalition that also included many diverse neighborhood groups.

When Mayor Rizzo followed a strategy of attempting to divide the city along racial lines by calling on white citizens to "vote white," the city's civic leadership joined with the black community in unequivocally condemning and repudiating such tactics. After this blatant attempt to foster racial polarization, Rizzo was constantly on the defensive (*Philadelphia Inquirer* 1978). The election results suggest—and interviews conducted by the author confirm—that the wide spectrum of leaders who condemned Rizzo's polarizing strategy produced an anti-Rizzo coalition broader than any he had ever faced before, or since. Sixty-seven percent of the voters voted against changing the charter. The winning coalition comprised blacks, reformers, liberals, and Jews (Featherman and Rosenberg 1979). Displaying unprecedented unanimity, voters in predominantly black wards cast 96 percent of their ballots against Mayor Rizzo's proposal to change the charter.

Perhaps even more significant than black unanimity was the degree of mobilization in the black community. The voter registration drives in the black community were hugely successful and raised the black proportion of total registered voters by six points to 38 percent. The rate of turnout in predominantly black wards was 63 percent. Only three years before, when Charles Bowser ran as an independent mayoral candidate, blacks made up 31 percent of the city's registered voters and the rate of turnout in the black wards was 54 percent. Bowser's mayoral candidacy had not succeeded in getting unregistered black voters to register nor in getting enough registered black voters to vote for him. However, Rizzo's blatantly racial appeal did succeed in catalyzing massive black voter registration and turnout against him. Commenting on the decade-long effort to fight Frank Rizzo through the ballot box, Wilson Goode said, "Biracial coalitions and reformers were dominant forces in city politics. No longer regarded as an anomaly, black and liberal white voters were now taken seriously and had often become pivotal in deciding the outcome of close elections" (Goode 1992).

In the race to fill the vacuum left by the removal of Frank Rizzo from the 1979 mayoral race, Congressman Bill Green, Jr., jumped out to an early lead. Green, who narrowly lost to Rizzo in the 1971 Democratic primary, aimed his appeal at the biracial coalition of white reformers and blacks. Within the black community, however, there were leaders who argued that after the massive registration and turnout of blacks precipitated by the charter referendum, a black mayor could be elected even with minimal white support. They convinced Charles Bowser to be their candidate. Seeking to remobilize the additional 100,000 blacks who registered to vote against the charter change, Bowser shifted from the moderate tenor of his 1975 campaign and relentlessly attacked Bill Green whom he tried to equate with the Rizzo gang. Green, however, refused to be provoked into confrontation and spoke only of healing the wounds left from Rizzo's tenure.

Green captured 53 percent of the vote and defeated Bowser (44 percent) in the Democratic primary. Bowser won every black ward and two predominantly white wards, but he was not able to mobilize the degree of support in the black wards that was necessary for victory. Turnout in the thirteen predominantly black wards was only 54 percent, which, although high for a primary election in Philadelphia, was lower than the 63 percent black turnout in the charter referendum.

Green faced Republican David Marston in November. Marston immediately began to try to build support in the black community. He publicly pledged that, if elected, he would name a black as the city's managing director (city manager), the second most powerful post in the city government. Marston also initiated a dialogue with Bowser and attempted to win his endorsement.

Arguing that a third party black candidate would have a better chance in the general election against the two white candidates, Marston and Green, than Bowser had in the primary head to head with Green, Councilman Lucien Blackwell entered the mayoral race. Green recognized that Bowser's attacks had diminished the support Green could expect from blacks, especially against Blackwell and Marston. Such considerations led Green to strike a deal, in which, in exchange for the endorsements of Bowser and black senior statesman Samuel Evans, Green matched Marston's promise (in a written agreement) to appoint a black as managing director. Again competition for the pivotal black vote produced a major step forward in the complete incorporation of blacks into the dominant political coalition.

Green emerged victorious with 53 percent of the vote to Marston's 29 percent and Blackwell's 17 percent. Green waged an especially vigorous campaign in the black community and an analysis of the 13 wards in which at least 90 percent of the registered voters were black shows that Green and Blackwell evenly split the black vote (Keiser 1989). The rate of turnout in predominantly black wards was 55 percent.

Bowser's endorsement was a watershed event that gains significance when compared with other cases in the literature on urban minority politics. Many of the city's black leaders followed Bowser and endorsed Green over Blackwell, thereby preempting the possibility of a polarizing campaign based on dividing the white vote and mobilizing a black bloc. Because of the history of mutually advantageous cooperation and coalition formation between middle-class white liberals and blacks, lining up behind Green was not perceived by blacks to be "selling out." Rather, it yielded a black managing director and brought blacks one step closer to the mayor's office. The man Mayor Green named as managing director was Wilson Goode. Bowser, Evans, and the other black leaders who consummated this deal on behalf of black constituents were sharply criticized by the Blackwell camp, yet charges of "Uncle Tomism" were not perceived as credible and did not stick. The iterative process of biracial cooperation that had historically yielded incremental black empowerment provided legitimacy for this historic step.

When Green took over the reins of Philadelphia's government, the city was in the midst of a fiscal disaster, facing a $167 million deficit and a declining municipal bond rating. To attack this deficit, Green increased taxes, laid off more than 1,200 city employees, including more than 700 police officers, and denied city employees a first-year wage increase. At the end of the first fiscal year of the Green administration, the city reported a small surplus.

Within Green's first two months, he delivered on what was undoubtedly the most pressing issue for the black citizenry, their fear of harassment and brutality from Frank Rizzo's police department. A black aide to Congressman William H. Gray, III, said, "I used to warn my own son, 'If a cop stops you, smile, do everything he tells you, and pray he doesn't kill you.' It was very real" (Paolantonio 1993). The Green administration issued new rules for the use of firearms by police officers, mandating that use of a gun should come only after all other methods of suspect apprehension were exhausted. The police rank and file were livid about this new policy, which made them subject to a panel of Monday morning quarterbacks. But after only two years of this policy, the incidence of police shooting civilians was halved (Paolantonio 1993). Although this procedural reform produced diffuse support for Green among black citizens, the black political leadership had a much more ambitious agenda.

So too did the leaders of the Democratic organization, the unions, and black leadership, all of whom were disappointed that the mayor was more committed to the tenets of reform and efficiency than to rewarding his allies. Ultimately these groups pressed their particularistic agendas over the objections of the mayor. Acting on behalf of the city's unionized workforce, the city council ignored the wishes of Green and city business leaders and enacted the nation's first city-level plant closing legislation in 1982. The law required firms employing 50 or more to give 60 days of notice prior to closing (Portz 1990). Green clashed with black leaders over an affirmative action hiring program for black police officers. In 1980, only 17 percent of Philadelphia's police force was black, although 39 percent of the population was black. Even so, Mayor Green opposed legislation to redress this balance because earlier in his administration he had laid off policemen and did not want to hire new officers. Councilman Blackwell and others argued that blacks deserved preferential treatment from Green, not only to remedy an unjust system built on past discrimination initiated by then Police Commissioner Rizzo but also because as crucial members of the mayor's electoral coalition they had earned such rewards. Blacks and white liberals on the city council also clashed with Mayor Green over set-aside legislation to aid minority-owned firms in winning city contracts on a range of services from construction to consulting. The legislation called for minority-owned businesses to get 15 percent of the city's contracts. Green vetoed this bill, but the city council overrode the mayor's veto. In both these instances, black elected officials were in a position to advance the progress of black empowerment through their domination of the city council. This development came as a result not only of black electoral mobilization but also of scandals produced by a federal sting operation that forced three conservative Rizzocrats to resign and gave blacks and white liberals a dominant coalition in the city council. Students concerned with the subservience of urban regimes to capital should note that the successes on plant closing and set-aside legislation came over the opposition of the city's business community.

Besides the appointment of Goode and the better service delivery that he brought to all neighborhoods and the decisive actions to reform the police department—in which the office of District Attorney Edward Rendell also played an important role—the Green administration did little else to advance the political incorporation of blacks. Before the emerging split between Green and his black supporters could splinter the biracial coalition, Green shocked everyone in Philadelphia by announcing that he would not be a candidate for mayor in 1983. Attention immediately focused on two men: Green's predecessor, Frank Rizzo, who had long been hinting that he would run again, and Green's right-hand man and natural successor, Wilson Goode.

Wilson Goode is part of the moderate, reformist black political leadership group that captured biracial legitimacy. This legitimacy has long existed in cities like Philadelphia and Atlanta and distinguishes them from a city like Chicago, which has not fostered a moderate black political cadre (Keiser 1993). Like many in this group,

Goode has strong ties to the black clergy, having long been a deacon in his church. He also has worked closely with the business community and many black neighborhood activists as the president of a nonprofit agency that built low-income housing. Goode was also a familiar face to the city's liberal activists having been for years a member of Americans for Democratic Action. He was an early member of the Black Political Forum, a group of reformers dedicated to black political empowerment. In 1978, Governor Milton Shapp appointed Goode to the public utilities commission. There Goode gained attention for his skillful handling of the Three Mile Island nuclear facility disaster. From there he went to the most powerful post in Philadelphia government aside from the mayor—the office of managing director. Here he earned a sterling reputation for effective, nonpolitical service delivery in the black community and beyond (*Philadelphia Daily News* 1982).

ELECTING THE FIRST BLACK MAYOR

To the surprise of almost every observer, the campaign between Rizzo and Goode was almost totally free of overt racial divisiveness. What had changed since 1978 when Rizzo had mobilized his base of support with a call for them to "vote white"? Rizzo's campaign had an amicable, nondivisive tenor because that was the most expedient strategy for being elected mayor in the Philadelphia of the 1980s. Given an electorate in which blacks made up 39 percent of the registered voters, a Rizzo victory hinged on three factors: ensuring a large turnout of white, ethnic, blue-collar voters; winning some black votes; and minimizing his losses among white, middle- and upper-class reformers. Blacks and white liberal reformers previously had turned out and voted against Rizzo in heavy numbers because of his racially divisive tactics. Therefore, to Rizzo and his campaign strategists, the way to diminish the turnout and anti-Rizzo voting of blacks and liberal whites was to avoid the race issue. In short, although a "vote white" strategy would be successful nationally for George Bush when he used Willie Horton to defeat Michael Dukakis in 1988, it would not work in a city with a 40 percent black population.

Goode understood the political environment in much the same way that Rizzo did. The failure of blacks and white liberals to unify in 1971 produced a Rizzo victory that lasted eight years. Conversely, in 1978, Rizzo was stopped by a coalition of registered, mobilized black voters in alliance with the business community and liberal white voters. Goode reached the same conclusion as Rizzo: the road to victory was not to be found in an overtly racial appeal to blacks, which might polarize the electorate, but in an inclusive, reformist appeal to white liberals and the business community. Neither the black vote nor the white, ethnic, blue-collar vote was big enough to win alone.

Goode's campaign was a position-paper campaign, not a racial crusade. Goode's major campaign themes were the problems of unemployment, the imperatives of creating and maintaining jobs in the city, and the need for the city to attract and retain mobile employers. He also discussed the need to create and refurbish public and private housing and reform of the criminal justice system, often adding that there was no black or white way to deliver such city services. And he criticized Rizzo *as an administrator*.[2] He reminded voters of the corruption that existed in the Rizzo years, the cronyism in city hall, the huge tax hikes in the second Rizzo term, and the fiscal disaster that the Green administration inherited. When the newspapers did allude to the race factor in the campaign, the discussion was almost always about the striking absence of racially divisive rhetoric (*New York Times* 1983).

Goode was very successful in galvanizing the business community to make a strong effort on his behalf (*Philadelphia Inquirer* 1983a). Among Goode's backers in the business community, which included the Greater Philadelphia Partnership (the new name for the former GPM), two themes were consistently evident. First, the business and banking leadership believed that electing Goode would improve the city's position in the economic competition for new and relocating capital. Second, Goode would "unify the city" and be fair to all neighborhoods as well as to the downtown interests (*Philadelphia Inquirer* 1983b).

Goode also had strong ties to community groups and liberal organizations. As managing director of the city, he had demonstrated a genuine desire to improve the conditions of the city's neighborhoods. He had approached representatives of more than 30 neighborhood groups seeking to familiarize them with ways that they could influence city hall to improve program and service delivery in their neighborhoods. In meetings throughout the city, Goode explained how the budget was formulated, where the money went, the effects of federal government funding cutbacks, and how citizens could make the city government more accountable to their demands. An agenda that included the issues most commonly raised throughout the city was presented to Mayor Green and the city council (Schwartz 1982; *Philadelphia Daily News* 1982). Because of Goode's historic ties to liberal activism and his pervasive presence as a problem solver while he was managing director, he received substantial support from white liberals.

Goode won the primary, capturing 53 percent of the vote, whereas Rizzo received 43 percent. Goode's general election victory would turn out to be a virtual replay of the primary vote. In the primary, black turnout was 69 percent whereas about 70 percent of registered whites voted. In predominantly black wards, Goode won 91 percent of the vote in the primary and 97 percent in the general election. Goode won about 18 percent of the white vote in the primary and 23 percent in the general election against Republican John Egan, a successful businessman, and independent candidate Thomas Leonard, formerly a Democrat and the city's controller. Rizzo's nondivisive campaign failed to win over liberal, upper-class voters in Chestnut Hill and Center City. In those wards (which Bowser had failed to win in the 1979 primary against Green), Goode captured 70 percent of the vote. In addition, Rizzo won only 44 percent of the vote in West Philadelphia/Overbrook and in the Logan Circle area, both of which were largely white (65 percent of the registered voters), middle-class areas with growing black populations.

---

[2] Goode had impressive credentials for discussing government administration. He had earned a master's degree in government administration from the University of Pennsylvania's Wharton School in 1968.

Who Got What? Evaluating Goode's Record

Evaluating the performance of Goode and his administration is a contentious issue. Goode and his supporters argue that he has compiled a record of accomplishments that, if compared to those of his predecessors or mayors in other cities, would inspire praise. Yet Goode's record has been eclipsed by the MOVE disaster in which the mayor gave the order to drop a bomb on a neighborhood that ultimately killed eleven people, including five children, and destroyed 61 homes. MOVE is a radical, back-to-nature group that has existed in Philadelphia since the 1970s. In Mayor Rizzo's second term, an armed confrontation between the police and MOVE led to the death of an officer. MOVE had received virtually no sympathy or support from Philadelphians of any stripe; in the areas where MOVE has settled, they have quickly alienated their neighbors. In May of 1985, after members of the group refused to evacuate a house they were occupying, a Philadelphia police helicopter dropped a bomb on the house. The bomb started a fire that killed 11 MOVE members and burned two city blocks of the surrounding black neighborhood.

This outcome shocked and outraged even the most passionate enemies of MOVE and the mayor drew sharp criticism from a blue ribbon investigative commission. Much ink has been spilled regarding the MOVE disaster, and space limitations preclude our examination of any of the issues. One thing is certain, however; the basis for Goode's political appeal beyond his black base, Goode's reputation as an effective administrator and manager, was damaged beyond repair in the episode.

Aside from the MOVE debacle, the mayor's supporters claim that his performance has been measured, especially by the media, against the lofty and, given constraints on mayoral leadership, unrealistic expectations people had of him. One example of this concerns the quality of city services. The Goode administration argued that it was unfairly blamed for the numerous potholes in the city streets because this condition has existed for at least 30 years and no mayor has been able to address it except in an ad hoc fashion (*Christian Science Monitor* 1986; *Philadelphia Inquirer* 1987a). Moreover, decline in the quality of city services in Philadelphia has more to do with the dramatic cuts in federal funding that the city suffered than with who sits in the mayor's office. During Frank Rizzo's second term, the mayor used Comprehensive Employment and Training Act (CETA) funds to pay the salaries of 4,442 city workers. During Mayor Goode's two terms in office, the Reagan administration's attack on urban America fully eliminated CETA funds. Overall, federal aid to the city fell during the decade Goode was managing director and mayor from more than $250 million to only $54 million (*Philadelphia Inquirer* 1987b; Adams 1991).

A second example of the unfair treatment Mayor Goode received is his being blamed for failing to solve problems when the blame should have been shared with the city council. This was most notable in the city's inability to solve its expensive garbage disposal crisis, a problem that had stymied the Green administration as well. The city was paying enormous sums to bury its garbage in landfills outside the city limits. Both mayors and the business community agreed that the best policy was to build an incinerator in the city that would burn trash and use the steam produced in the process for energy needs. The city council basically took a "not-in-my-backyard" approach to location of an incinerator that some feared was an environmental hazard and potential producer of carcinogens. No location for a trash-to-steam facility could be agreed on by the city council and the bill for landfill dumping continued to drain the city budget. During the Green years, the city council deservedly received the blame for this stalemate. In the Goode years, the mayor was accused of lacking the political skills to forge a compromise; although accurate, this charge constituted only half the explanation: The city council remained an obstructionist body.

The fiscal crisis that engulfed the city in Goode's second term is a third failure that is unjustly put on Goode's balance sheet. Certainly as chief executive of the city during the crisis, Wilson Goode must share in the responsibility and blame. Yet as with most fiscal crises, the seeds of the problem were sown long before his term as mayor. One of the most significant aspects of Frank Rizzo's reelection strategy in 1975 was his granting of a 12.8 percent pay increase to municipal unions, a raise that was three times the 4.2 percent increases the unions had enjoyed in each of the prior two years. Rizzo was running without the party endorsement and this whopping increase (along with the sweetening of their benefits package) no doubt contributed to Rizzo's ability to defeat the organization's candidate in a party primary. The fact that Frank Rizzo was President Richard Nixon's favorite mayor ultimately contributed to the city's fiscal crisis as well. Federal revenue sharing funneled money into Philadelphia at a time that other cities were beginning the belt-tightening process. According to Paolantonio, "The city got double per capita more than Chicago, reaping $65 million, or about 10 percent of the city's operating budget, in the first 18 months of the program. It enabled the city to balance the budget. In Philadelphia, an inevitable fiscal crisis had been forestalled" (Paolantonio 1993, 154). During Goode's administration, he was unable to gain the cooperation of Democratic state legislators in his efforts to address the city's mounting debt and its inability to borrow in municipal bond markets because of its junk bond status. To a significant extent, the failure of the Democratically controlled state legislature to rescue the state's largest Democratic stronghold occurred because the speaker of the house wanted to be elected governor. He saw the danger of appearing to be the orchestrator of a bailout of the city that many nonurbanites saw as a repository for victims of acquired immune deficiency syndrome (AIDS), welfare recipients, and the homeless. Meanwhile, the two most powerful black city councilmen, without whom no budget legislation could be passed, refused to offer cooperation or alternative leadership. Lucien Blackwell did not want to support any tax increases because he was planning to run for mayor in 1991 when Goode stepped aside. Appropriations committee chair John Street wanted to become city council president first (he was the heir apparent but would not be elected until after the 1991 election cycle) and then take as much credit as possible for solving the city's fiscal crisis.

Finally, although Goode took credit for resolving a long-standing impasse that blocked the legislation necessary for establishing cable TV franchises in the city, the politics behind the resolution of this issue indicates some of the constraints that a technocratic reformer like Goode faces (and black mayors increasingly have technocratic backgrounds). Mayor Green believed that the licenses and contracts for cable television service should go to the one company that made the best offers on the basis of cost per customer and extent of service. Members of the city council wanted multiple cable vendors to serve different parts of the city. Goode was expected to come in as a strong mayor and force the city council to be a vehicle for "good government." Instead, he balked at confronting the council. Goode chose to cede to city council control in awarding four separate contracts (with four different opportunities for council oversight and potentially corrupting relationships) and thereby satisfy the demands of the citizenry for cable television service.

But two other issues that Goode promised to resolve—the future plan for trash disposal in the city and construction of a major convention center—languished in the city council because the mayor, in his own words, refused to "do the kind of political trading that goes with that. . . . We simply can't afford to satisfy the insatiable appetite of members of Council if you're going to base votes on political trading" (*Philadelphia Inquirer* 1987c). The mayor offered a number of sound proposals to resolve these issues, yet he could not proceed without the approval of the city council. Goode's administration faltered in much the same way as Green's. Neither mayor was enough of a politician (and Goode was too much the technocrat) to "go along to get along" with the city council's dominant coalition of bipartisan, patronage-minded, neighborhood representatives. The reformist, public-regarding faction (mostly blacks aligned with Congressman William Gray, III) were too few to pass legislation in the city council. Both mayors were also good-government advocates; they would not threaten to use their power to punish the constituents of their opponents as a tactic for expanding their coalitions. Goode's discussion of this factional split within the black community is worth quoting at length (Goode 1992):

> Over the years black politicians had gained significant power. Bill Gray was now majority whip in Congress. . . . Our reform movement had broken down the racial barriers, but it was threatening to create others as these new "bosses" sought to solidify and hold on to their power, not through merit, but by political control.
>
> Essentially, they were saying they didn't like the way the first wave of reformers had played the political game. It was too altruistic, they didn't like this "community good" stuff—working primarily for the best interests of the community rather than themselves. Basically, they wanted now to play politics the same way the "old boy" establishment had played. Their goal was not to reform politics, but to change the complexion of who was in charge.
>
> Realizing this, I knew the only way I could get some things passed by the council in my final administration would be to work on behalf of their interests. I was out of the equation. So I started strategizing, doing things like getting Blackwell to see that by supporting some of my reforms he wasn't helping me, but painting a favorable portrait of himself as future mayor in the eyes of the people and the business establishment. I made

similar suggestions to Street as he pursued his desire to become council president. (pp. 279–280)

When the Philadelphia Eagles professional football team threatened to leave the city for financial reasons, Mayor Goode personally negotiated with the team's ownership and carved out an agreement. Goode received heavy criticism because he agreed to have the city pay the costs—and receive partial rental rights—for deluxe corporate skyboxes to be built atop the stadium. But by September 1987, when the Eagles wanted to buy back the skyboxes because of their popularity, Goode appeared to have scored a coup that promised financial gains for the city. This is but one example of the successes that the mayor has had in convincing mobile capital to remain in Philadelphia and in attracting new companies to the city because of his personal involvement. The dramatically changed appearance of center city Philadelphia, with numerous office towers framing the statue of William Penn atop city hall, is testimony to the service Goode performed on behalf of the growth coalition (Summers and Luce 1987). Goode deserves more credit than he has received for facilitating Philadelphia's belated movement into the corporate era, yet he has been criticized for being too subservient to capital (Jennings 1992), another criticism his defenders consider unfair. A mayoral aide said, "Scholars are always talking or writing about the tragic consequences of suburban competition with cities. Yet when our mayor takes steps to compete with suburbs and attract good jobs, he is criticized as a lackey for the business elite."[3]

It would be inaccurate to view the Goode administration simply as a corporate-centered regime. Goode believed that job creation was the number one issue in the black community (*Philadelphia Magazine* 1984). The vast majority of the city's blacks continued to support Wilson Goode in his successful reelection bid of 1987, not only because he was the city's first black mayor and not only because he brought blacks into many positions of real power and responsibility (discussed below), but also because Goode delivered on his promise by creating 37,000 new jobs (*Philadelphia Inquirer* 1987a).

In the area of executive appointments, where the mayor of Philadelphia is given nearly total discretion by the city's charter, Wilson Goode was the only black appointed to Mayor Green's four-man cabinet. In Goode's six-person cabinet, there were three blacks, including one black female, and three whites (two female), marking a doubling of the proportion of blacks in the cabinet. In 1980 the census reported that 39 percent of the city's population was black. Goode's appointments went beyond parity for blacks; 60 percent of the commissioners heading city agencies in the Goode administration were black; in the Green administration the comparable figure was 30 percent. In 1987, after a number of top-level reorganizations, 43 percent of these executive appointments were black. In 1988, Goode appointed the city's first black police commissioner, Willie Williams, capping a restructuring of the police force that was begun by Mayor Green and District Attorney Edward Rendell and continued by Goode.

---

[3] Personal interview, July 1986.

The Green administration also did not enthusiastically attack the problem of racial and gender discrimination in the awarding of contracts with the city. After the city council overrode a mayoral veto of set-aside legislation, the Green administration awarded only a total of $2.4 million to minority and female-owned firms. In contrast, in 1984, the Goode administration awarded $43 million worth of contracts to such firms (32 percent to female-owned firms), and in 1985, $63 million worth of contracts went to minority-owned firms and $27 million went to female-owned firms. This amount still represented only 26 percent of the city's aggregate contract expenditures. When the U.S. Supreme Court struck down set-asides in the Croson case of 1989 (*Richmond v. Croson,* 1095, Ct. 706), Goode refused to modify the city's plan. When a U.S. district judge struck down the city's minority set-aside plan in April 1990, Goode signed an executive order mandating a new set-aside plan.

Critics point to some blemishes in Goode's record regarding black employment, although defenders would be quick to point out that Goode's actions were designed to protect the tenuous economic position of the city rather than to advance any narrow interests, such as those of growth barons. For instance, Goode has been criticized for opposing a measure that called for affirmative action hiring preferences for city residents, minorities, and women in construction jobs funded even partially by the city. But Goode was not alone in his opposition to this bill; the city council's two most prominent black leaders also opposed it. Beauregard (1989) concluded that Goode's argument against the legislation was sound. The opposition believed it would produce similar retaliatory legislation by surrounding suburbs that would hurt Philadelphia construction workers who, in the aggregate, were successful in finding employment outside the city.

Goode's efforts to restore fiscal discipline to the city led him to refuse the demands of the public employees union and withstand a 20-day strike by predominantly black sanitation workers. Goode eventually endorsed plans for reduction of the size of trash collection crews from three or four to two. This decision seemed reasonable considering the design of modern trash trucks; nevertheless, it promised to eliminate the jobs of about 1,500 workers (Paolantonio 1993).

With respect to affirmative action in the municipal work force, the record of the Goode administration also is noteworthy. According to Equal Employment Opportunity (EEO) reports filed by the city with the federal government, in the last year of Mayor Green's administration (1982–1983) blacks represented 28 percent of the municipal workforce, Hispanics 1 percent, and whites 70 percent. By the end of Goode's second term, blacks held about 45 percent of the jobs in the city government. The Goode administration was not satisfied with simply raising aggregate numbers of minorities in city jobs. It increased the proportion of blacks in the top three EEO job classifications from 24 percent under Mayor Green to 28 percent by 1987 and 31 percent by 1991.

In the neighborhoods, the Goode administration used the meager trickle of federal Urban Development Action Grant funds to supplement private capital and bring to fruition efforts to revitalize neighborhood shopping areas. This move created construction jobs as well as permanent service industry jobs, in addition to upgrading the quality of life in the neighborhoods. Though these projects developed throughout the city, the Goode administration, unlike its predecessors, did not ignore the low-income black and Hispanic sections of North Philadelphia where private capital has been least willing to invest. Goode spent one-half of the city's $60 million block grant on low-income housing rehabilitation in predominantly black North Philadelphia, yet these efforts were considered disappointing because of the high expectations engendered by Goode's previous involvement with housing issues. Importantly, the Goode administration was responding to pressure from an activist neighborhood organization headed by city councilman John Street and his flamboyant brother, Milton. Protest is not enough, but without it, resources probably would have been less forthcoming.

The Goode administration did not ignore the city's poor. The single largest shift in spending in the budget ($2 million in the first year of the program) was to programs that provided shelter and provisions for the homeless of the city, a program that earned national recognition (U.S. Conference of Mayors 1987). Unfortunately, in the midst of the national recession of 1990–1992 and impending municipal bankruptcy, spending on the homeless and on AIDS treatment was dramatically cut (*New York Times* 1989). With the city's bonds rated at junk bond status and the city council refusing to enact adequate tax increases, services were cut across the board. Wages of municipal employees were also targeted.

Does this suggest that Goode failed to deliver to the poorer segment of the black community or that the mayor and the black city council members who passed his budget were puppets of a growth coalition (Jennings 1992)? This is a conclusion that can be reached only by those who divorce theorizing from empirical realities and exigencies. Although the question of who gets what in black mayoral administrations requires additional case study data such as are presented in this book, it is clear that the Goode administration did not limit political and economic advancement to the middle class beneficiaries of affirmative action and minority business set-aside programs. Less-educated, less-skilled blacks also won a greater share of low-skill city jobs, the likes of which are disappearing in the private sector. As well, the mayor's efforts improved employment prospects in the private sector. Goode improved the quality of life in poor neighborhoods that were largely ignored in the past and his administration temporarily took steps that represented a comprehensive, humanitarian response to the problems of homelessness and AIDS. Although there is certainly much more that needs to be done for the city's disproportionately black poor, the scope of the problems goes far beyond what even a united mayor and city council can do. Federal aid to the cities has declined dramatically, as we have noted. The national epidemic of family breakup that has been correlated with poverty exacerbates the problems of Philadelphia's poor as well; by 1988, "about 45% of the city's black families and 13% of its white families were headed by single women" (Adams 1991, 31). As the economy of Philadelphia and the greater metropolitan area changes in step with domestic and international rearrangements, demand for a better-educated workforce grows while wages for low-skilled service jobs decline. By the 1980s, according to Adams (1991, 31), "three quarters of the black men who had not finished high school were out of the workforce." Educational initiatives should be at the top of the agenda for all big city mayors as should strategies for linking employable blacks to jobs in the suburbs.

Hispanics in Philadelphia

In contrast to some of the other chapters in this volume, discussion of the Hispanic population of Philadelphia has been conspicuously absent. This is because Hispanics have until recently played a very minor role in the city's politics. According to Census Bureau data, in 1970 only about 2 percent of the city's population were Hispanics; by the 1990 census almost 6 percent were Hispanic, with nearly three-quarters of these being Puerto Rican. Even with the small numbers they represent, however, the competitiveness of the city's politics has forced politicians seeking citywide offices to give attention to the political demands of Hispanic voters.

Wilson Goode did this assiduously and, under Goode, black empowerment initiated Hispanic incorporation. In his initial mayoral campaign, Goode listed liberal lawyer Angel Ortiz on his sample ballot for an at-large seat on the city council. Ortiz was not elected, but he came very close to winning. As mayor, Goode appointed him to the post of commissioner of records, the first Hispanic to head a city department. Due to the death of a councilman, Ortiz ran in a special election and won, with Goode's support, becoming the first Hispanic to serve on the city council.

Wilson Goode received strong electoral support from the Hispanic community. He received approximately 66 percent of the vote in predominantly Hispanic precincts in the 1983 Democratic primary against Frank Rizzo and 77 percent of their votes in the general election. In the 1987 general election, Ortiz, who was again elected to an at-large seat on the city council, campaigned vigorously for Goode against Republican candidate Frank Rizzo, warning that a Rizzo victory would mean a "return to slavery . . . and racism." Goode won about 75 percent of the Hispanic vote in his narrow victory over Rizzo. Because he was elected at large, Ortiz has not been able to devote himself solely to Hispanic community concerns. For instance, Ortiz was a leader in the fight for domestic partnership benefits for gay and lesbian city employees.

The most pressing issue for the Hispanic community seems to be police brutality. Only 3 percent of the police force are Hispanic, and in 1994 none held a rank higher than lieutenant. Mayor Edward Rendell's black police chief has promised to find ways to bring more Hispanics (and Asians, who represent half the numbers of Hispanics) into the department to foster equity and to reduce the likelihood of brutality. Hispanics have also been vociferous in their demands for a strong, independent civilian police review board that would punish and deter brutality. Mayor Rendell (introduced below) had originally sought to create a weak, advisory police review board, but a high degree of pressure from black city council members and Hispanic activists forced the mayor to accede completely to community demands (see *Philadelphia Inquirer* 1993, 1994a; and *Philadelphia Inquirer Magazine* 1994a).

AFTER THE FIRST BLACK MAYORAL ELECTION:
THE FUTURE OF BIRACIAL POLITICS IN PHILADELPHIA

Following Frank Rizzo's announcement that he was switching to the GOP to challenge Wilson Goode's reelection, approximately 50,000 of his most ardent supporters gave up their Democratic registration and became Republicans. This increased the black proportion of registered Democrats so that for the first time in the city's history, blacks outnumbered whites in the Democratic party. Yet Rizzo's switch to the Republican party did not divide the city and make the Democrats a "black" party.

It is important to recognize that even with the MOVE incident overshadowing the mayor's accomplishments and sullying his reputation, political divisions did not produce racial polarization in Philadelphia. Goode's opponents never attacked him for favoring blacks in appointments nor have they condemned black politicians in general for the mistakes of the mayor. In the Democratic mayoral primary, Goode won 57 percent of the vote and defeated Edward Rendell, the very popular former district attorney. Rendell had previously enjoyed the backing of the biracial reform coalition and had been an ally of Goode. But in 1987, Rendell was vigorously opposed by the city's black clergy who claimed that in exchange for black support for his unsuccessful 1986 gubernatorial bid he had promised not to challenge Goode. Rendell received the support of many of the white liberals and business executives who had supported Goode in 1983 as well as both the city's newspapers, which had endorsed Goode in 1983. In personal interviews, these reform-minded former supporters of Mayor Goode indicated that although they were backing away from a mayor whom they perceived to be incompetent, they had not lost faith in the ethos of biracial, reform coalitions. Some already were looking toward 1991 and the opportunity to vigorously support another black reformer.

Even Goode's staunchest supporters were not optimistic about the potential for accomplishments by a second Goode administration, largely because they felt that the MOVE disaster had irreparably diminished the mayor's political capital. Still, the continued support for Mayor Goode from both liberal activists and business leaders against Rendell and even more so against Republican mayoral candidate Frank Rizzo—and the stated intent to support black reformers in future mayoral races—indicated that the incremental incorporation of blacks in a biracial, reform coalition has made and will continue to make a difference in the way political alliances are evaluated in Philadelphia.

But the persistence of the biracial reform coalition is not the only reason that party and race do not overlap in Philadelphia. The white ethnic and labor leadership of the Democratic party did not defect from Wilson Goode in 1983 or 1987, even though many of their constituents did. The Democratic party organization, largely because of the unifying leadership of ward leader and former union leader Robert Brady, has also been able to reach accommodations with Mayor Goode and even more so with black leaders in the city council (*Philadelphia Inquirer Magazine* 1994b). Although there had been rumors anticipating defections of white Democratic politicians to Rizzo and the Republicans, none materialized. Only one of the city's 28-member Democratic delegation to the state house and senate defected to the Rizzo team. Credit for Goode's 1987 mayoral victory goes foremost to blacks, who turned out at a rate of about 70 percent and gave Goode 97 percent of their votes. Among whites, Goode received 18 percent of the vote. The mayor received diminished but significant support from those living in the city's upper-income reform areas, who gave Goode 54 percent of their votes. But Goode could not have eked out his 18,000-vote victory without the support of Democratic party ward leaders, who persuaded their friends, families, and city job holders to vote for Goode. Even though most of these ward leaders and voters had been lifelong supporters of Rizzo, a significant minority remained loyal to the party's candidate. Party loyalty and precinct level organization were crucial ingredients in Goode's reelection, suggesting that while his electoral coalition was biracial, it was no longer unequivocally liberal or reformist.

Brady and the Democratic ward leaders of course had pragmatic reasons for reelecting Goode. Goode had appointed Brady to head the party in 1986 and knew what he was getting. He gave control over patronage jobs in the court system and Parking Authority to Brady (Balchunis 1992). In addition Brady amassed patronage jobs by becoming a board member of the Pennsylvania Turnpike Authority, the city Redevelopment Authority, and the Delaware River Port Authority. A Republican administration would have been a major setback to the resurgent Democratic organization, regardless of the race of the mayor. But more significantly, these white leaders of the Democratic organization believed that in 1991 they might elect a black Democrat who was not a reformer and was amenable to their machine style of politics, a position Goode was already moving toward. They still believe they will accomplish this in the near future.

Fault Lines after the First Black Mayor

In the post-Rizzo era, the city council shifted from an arena in which Rizzocrats fought the white reform/black coalition over the issue of political incorporation to one in which a biracial coalition of politicians who favor a machine style of politics are in conflict with a biracial reform coalition allied with the city's good-government reform elements. The business community seems comfortable with both coalitions so long as corruption scandals are avoided by the regular organization, and environmentalists and preservationists are not allowed by the reformers to impede development. Black leaders such as former Councilman and Congressman Lucien Blackwell, state Representative Dwight Evans, and City Council President John Street are now powerful figures within the Democratic organization that once tried to subordinate them. Issues of patronage, the dispensation of city contracts, the selection of candidates for political offices, and spoils for their supporters are all areas in which they can align with conservative white ward politicians and party leaders (including Republicans). But other black leaders, many of whom are political disciples of former Congressman William Gray, Jr., and former Councilman John F. White, remain committed to the good government tenets they share with the city's white liberal and business communities. In short, two biracial coalitions now exist in Philadelphia. Mayor Goode walked the line between both groups, and depending on the issue, was a champion or a disappointment to either group. In October 1986, even before the campaign had begun, the leaders of these black factions unanimously endorsed Goode for a second term. They stated that they did not want the city "to go the way of Cleveland"—a city where an incumbent black mayor lost to a white challenger. But in 1991, the black vote divided between Blackwell and an Ivy League–educated black reformer, Councilman George Burrell. Maintaining unity in the election of a second black mayor represents a major crisis point in black political development, as other cases in this book also illustrate.

As with New York's Rudolph Giuliani and Chicago's Richard M. Daley, Edward Rendell's election in 1991 replaced a black mayor with a white mayor. Although the three mayors may share certain policy strategies—for instance, privatization of some city services—scholars should not assume that this position represents a backlash against black mayors and reassertion of white political power. That has not been the case in Philadelphia. Councilman Lucien Blackwell was the leading mayoral contender in the black community and although he had high negative ratings among white voters, he would have won the Democratic party primary, in which blacks were a majority of the registered voters, *if he had been the only black candidate*. He would have received strong support from the black clergy, including good-government clergy, because of their opposition to his leading opponent, Ed Rendell. He probably would have also won the general election because the Democratic party organization would have had little trouble turning out a sizable minority of white voters willing to support this patronage-oriented, former union leader (as they did for Goode in 1987). The business community would have settled for Blackwell because he had engineered the consent of the fractious city council on a number of major development projects, a task for which they could not count on Mayor Goode. Congressman William Gray, III, was characteristically two steps ahead of the unfolding events. For personal and ideological reasons, Gray and Blackwell had long been opponents. Even if blacks would be at the front of the line that included machine-style politicians of both parties, Gray and his biracial reformist allies could not support a candidate who would turn the city's coffers into a spoils trough. Perhaps more important, Gray and his black clergy allies feared that Blackwell's abrasive style and the overlaid racial and class resentments he shared with his working-class and poor constituents regarding white privilege would foment racial polarization in the citizenry. The efforts that Gray's predecessors and contemporaries had made to demonstrate to whites that they could work harmoniously with blacks, particularly middle-class blacks, for mutual development and advancement would be jeopardized by a Blackwell mayoralty. Gray persuaded one of his city council protégés, George Burrell, to enter the race early and to declare that under no circumstances would he withdraw. Gray twisted the arms of other black ministers either to support Burrell or remain uncommitted. Either Burrell would be the one black candidate, in which case he would cruise to victory, or the black vote would be divided. A term or two with the mayor's office occupied by Ed Rendell or Republican Frank Rizzo (or the other leading GOP candidate) would not do damage comparable to a Blackwell victory. Rendell would likely hand the mayoral baton to a moderate black (as Bill Green had done), whereas Rizzo would unify and rejuvenate the black-white liberal alliance as he had always done. Even after revelations about Burrell's finances and ethics devastated his candidacy, he refused to withdraw. The black vote divided and Rendell easily won the Democratic primary. Rizzo captured the GOP nomination, but he died soon after and his replacement was unable to mount a serious campaign.

Rendell has liberal reformer credentials because he broke into politics by defeating an incumbent district attorney who was using the office for personal enrichment. He had the support of the ADA, the *Philadelphia Inquirer,* and the black community. However, he has admitted that this image was an accident, that he was only interested in making the district attorney's office work effectively and "didn't care about making a statement and beating the machine" (Rottenberg 1994). He earned support in the black community, in part because of his aggressive actions against police brutality, and this support was not dramatically eroded by the virulent opposition he faced from black clergy who believed he had promised not to run against Goode in 1987. Rendell has become the most esteemed mayor in the nation because in his first year he produced a small budgetary surplus in a city that had a junk bond rating and a $250-million-dollar cumulative deficit. Not only is he a friend of Bill Clinton, he is also a poster boy for the *Wall Street Journal, The Economist*, and the conservative Manhattan Institute because he rolled back union benefits and froze wages to save $78 million annually. He has also persuaded the state legislature to underwrite some of the city's continuing economic development efforts. The entire budgetary process in his first two years smoothly sailed through the city council because council president John Street has received at least half the credit for everything. Rendell heads a biracial coalition and Street is his closest advisor aside from the mayor's chief of staff. Rendell has been a charismatic cheerleader for the city and has capitalized on the fiscal crisis environment to divide the city's municipal unions against other unionized workers (whose high taxes pay for the salary and benefit packages that Rendell slashed); he has taken only a few meager steps toward privatization. He has given no indication that he plans to govern as a reformer and root out patronage, corruption, or abuse of power. Rendell strongly supported a number of changes to the city charter (which failed) that would have increased either the power of the mayor or the president of city council at the expense of independent boards and commissions. When the local Democratic party was implicated in a plot to tamper with and falsify absentee ballots in a crucial state legislative race, the mayor refused to treat the episode as anything deserving of concern, let alone a cause for a thorough housecleaning of the party he now heads. Hence, although the mayor heads a biracial coalition that continues to advance black incorporation, that coalition is neither liberal nor reformist.

That Rendell is much more of a pragmatist than a reformer has significant consequences for the future of black politics in Philadelphia. In turn, the future of black politics in Philadelphia has significance for theorizing about black political incorporation. At this point, a second Rendell term seems highly likely. If the mayor can complete his two terms without a serious scandal, one of his black allies like John Street or Happy Fernandez could easily follow him and receive the backing of a party that is replenishing its patronage stock and learning to divide the spoils of government equitably between blacks and whites.[4] If the Rendell administration is tripped up by a corruption scandal, however, the door will reopen for the more liberal reformers in the black leadership including Councilwoman Marian Tasco, former state official C. Delores Tucker, or two others who may be able to bridge the gap between reformers and organization politicians and garner support among white ward leaders, Congressman Chaka Fattah and newly elected Councilman Michael Nutter. Fattah stands out as the black politician with the brightest political future should he choose to leave the Republican-controlled House of Representatives. White liberals would be willing to support any of these candidates; their negative appraisal of Wilson Goode has not soured them on other black mayoral contenders.

Yet regardless of who occupies the mayor's office, that person will be operating under some constraints that will make the economic empowerment of blacks difficult. With Republican control of the Congress, the outlook for cities, particularly eastern and midwestern cities dominated by Democrats, is not good. Federal dollars that in a variety of ways have a positive impact for city residents appear likely to dry up. Moreover, while the suburbs that encircle Philadelphia rebounded economically in 1993 and added 12,000 jobs, employment continued to fall in the city (*Philadelphia Inquirer* 1994b).

Philadelphia's Biracial Coalition in Comparative Perspective

One of the questions that Browning, Marshall, and Tabb do not address is how liberal coalitions that produce minority incorporation emerge in cities where stable conservative coalitions are comfortably ensconced. The Philadelphia case furnishes an insight to this question of regime change. The conservative Republican coalition that survived the New Deal and blocked black political incorporation was displaced by political scandals. Like the Seabury investigation scandals that toppled Mayor Jimmy Walker's Tammany Hall and enabled Fiorello La Guardia to instigate Italian and Jewish political incorporation, like the parking meter scandals that led to the suicides of some of Mayor Edward Koch's close party organization allies and enabled David Dinkins to displace (at least for one term) the Koch coalition and vigorously advance black incorporation, in Philadelphia scandals brought down the Republican machine and opened the way for a reformer-led business coalition that included middle-class blacks who found no place in the GOP. The leaders of fledgling biracial reform coalitions would be wise to recognize that political scandals create propitious circumstances for expanding their ranks.

The role that the business community played in Philadelphia's biracial coalition was quite considerable and on a par with the role of liberals. The Greater Philadelphia Movement was formed by businessmen who personally encountered difficulty in attracting new firms to the city because of its reputation for corruption (Lowe 1967). These leaders of the business community realized that the prevailing climate

---

[4] Both Lucien Blackwell and William Gray, III, are no longer active players in Philadelphia politics.

of race relations was also an important aspect of the city's image and attractiveness for investors, and this led them to strike an alliance with middle-class black leaders. Browning, Marshall, and Tabb specify the role of liberal Democrats in biracial coalitions, but the business communities in their mostly Republican California cities made little positive contribution to black incorporation. Yet, Philadelphia, and more than any other city, Atlanta, suggest that business leaders seeking a stable environment for growth can be a positive force for minority incorporation.

But urban coalition formation and policy making cannot be reduced to being the products of efforts by city leaders to advantageously position themselves in economic competition with other cities. In Philadelphia as well as in New York and Los Angeles, the biracial coalition included an organized, vibrant liberal-reform community that, among other issues, was opposed to the political and economic subordination of blacks. Their basis for participation was ideological, having little to do with economic competition among cities. With social and economic dynamics very similar to those of post-Lindsay New York, Philadelphia's biracial coalition suffered a rollback of its power in the Tate-Rizzo era. But the political response of the participants in the biracial coalition was very different in the two cities. In New York, liberal Jews parted ways with their former black allies after the Ocean Hill–Brownsville school crisis and increasingly moved toward an alliance with conservative whites (Rieder 1985). In Philadelphia, both liberal reformers and the business leadership maintained and further solidified their alliance with black leaders in an eight-year rearguard experience as the opposition, minority coalition. Certainly the fact that the alternative to the biracial coalition was an alliance with Mayor Frank Rizzo helped to maintain the unity of the biracial coalition, but efforts such as the business–black "Urban Coalition," the joint defection of blacks, liberal Democrats, and the GPM to the Longstreth candidacy, and the victory of the biracial coalition against the 1978 charter change referendum have more to do with the political trust that was a product of the Clark-Dilworth era and that has been maintained because of the continued electoral viability of this alliance.

The historical alliance within which this political trust was developed has been facilitated by the weakness of the regular Democratic organization that has allowed the factionalization of the traditional urban Democratic party coalition. Politics in Philadelphia has been less like that of Chicago and, to a lesser extent, New York, where strong Democratic party organizations have persisted, and more like the intraparty factionalism of New Orleans as well as the fluid nonpartisan politics of Atlanta and Los Angeles. In Philadelphia, partisan loyalties have not been strong enough to preclude a biracial reform coalition of traditionally Democratic white liberals and blacks, with broad support from the business community, from engaging in intra and interparty competition against traditionally Democratic conservative whites.

The election of Edward Rendell signified the victory of a man with a liberal-reformist reputation who was one of the most popular white candidates in the black community. His election was not a repudiation of liberal, biracial politics, although most black voters would have preferred either Blackwell or Burrell. Mayor Rendell's first term indicates that his administration does not represent a rollback of black political incorporation. More data are necessary before we can conclude whether his administration represents a regime change from a liberal, good-government biracial coalition to a biracial form of machine-style politics that unites whites and blacks who are interested in reviving a regular Democratic organization. But it is clear that these two coalitions, with blacks in leadership positions of both, are likely to battle for the future control of the city of Philadelphia.

REFERENCES

Adams, Carolyn Teich. 1991. Philadelphia: The Slide toward Municipal Bankruptcy. In H. V. Savitch and John Clayton Thomas, eds., *Big City Politics in Transition*. Urban Affairs Annual Reviews, Vol. 38. Newbury Park, Calif.: Sage.

Balchunis, Mary Ellen. 1992. A Study of the Old and New Camapign Politics Models: A Comparative Analysis of Wilson Goode's 1983 and 1987 Philadelphia Mayoral Campaigns. Unpublished Ph.D. dissertation, Temple University.

Banfield, Edward. 1965. *Big City Politics*. New York: Random House.

Beauregard, Robert A. 1989. Local Politics and the Employment Relation: Construction Jobs in Philadelphia. In Robert A. Beauregard, ed., *Economic Restructuring and Political Response*. Urban Affairs Annual Reviews, Vol. 34. Newbury Park, Calif.: Sage.

Christian Science Monitor. 1986. Goode's bright promise beset by MOVE, strike. July 22.

Daughen, Joseph, and Peter Binzen. 1977. *The Cop Who Would Be King: Mayor Frank Rizzo*. Boston: Little, Brown.

Edsall, Thomas, and Mary Edsall. 1991. *Chain Reaction: The Impact of Race, Rights, and Taxes on American Politics*. New York: Norton.

Ekstrom, Charles A. 1973. The Electoral Politics of Reform and Machine: The Political Behavior of Philadelphia's "Black" Wards, 1943–1969. In Miriam Ershkowitz and Joseph Zikmund II, eds., *Black Politics in Philadelphia*. New York: Basic Books.

Ershkowitz, Miriam, and Joseph Zikmund II. 1973. *Black Politics in Philadelphia*. New York: Basic Books.

Featherman, Sandra, and William L. Rosenberg. 1979. *Jews, Blacks and Ethnics: The 1978 "Vote White" Charter Campaign in Philadelphia*. Philadelphia: American Jewish Committee.

Fonzi, Gaeton. 1963. Cecil Storms In. *Greater Philadelphia Magazine*. (July).

Goode, W. Wilson, with Joann Stevens. 1992. *In Goode Faith*. Valley Forge, Penn.: Judson Press.

Jennings, James. 1992. *The Politics of Black Empowerment*. Detroit: Wayne State University Press.

Keiser, Richard A. 1987a. Amicability or Polarization? Patterns of Political Competition and Leadership Formation in Cities with Black Mayors. Paper presented at the annual meeting of the Midwest Political Science Association, Chicago.

Keiser, Richard A. 1987b. Why Biracial Coalitions Matter: Patterns of Black Leadership and the Election of Black Mayors in Chicago and Philadelphia. Paper presented at the annual meeting of the American Political Science Association, Chicago.

Keiser, Richard A. 1989. Black Political Incorporation or Subordination? Political competitiveness and leadership formation prior to the election of Black mayors. Unpublished Ph.D. dissertation, University of California, Berkeley.

Keiser, Richard A. 1990. The Rise of a Biracial Coalition in Philadelphia. In Rufus P. Browning, Dale Rogers Marshall, and David H. Tabb, eds., *Racial Politics in American Cities*. New York: Longman.

Keiser, Richard A. 1993. Explaining African-American Political Empowerment: Windy City Politics from 1900 to 1993. *Urban Affairs Quarterly* 29 (1): 84–116.

Lowe, Jeanne. 1967. *Cities in a Race With Time*. New York: Random House.

New York Times. 1968. Philadelphia Poor Pledged $1 million by Business Group. May 12.

New York Times. 1983. Race is a Muted Issue in Philadelphia. April 12.

New York Times. 1989. 50% Cutback in Funds for Homeless is Fiercely Protested. September 15.

Paolantonio, S. A. 1993. *Frank Rizzo: The Last Big Man in Big City America*. Philadelphia: Camino Books.

Peterson, Paul E. 1967. City Politics and Community Action: The Implementation of the Community Action Program in Three American Cities, ch. 4. Unpublished Ph.D. dissertation, University of Chicago.

Philadelphia Bulletin. 1965. Parties Court Negroes, Who Hold Key to Power. January 24, sec. A, p. 3.

Philadelphia Bulletin. 1974. Tate Felt a Rizzo Win Would Save Democratic Control. January 23.

Philadelphia Daily News. 1982. Wilson Goode: He Transformed the Job. November 30, p. 6.

Philadelphia Inquirer. 1978. City's Religious Leaders Censure Racial Rhetoric. September 30.

Philadelphia Inquirer. 1983a. Business Leaders Give Less to Goode for this Campaign. October 31, sec. B, p. 1.

Philadelphia Inquirer. 1983b. Philadelphia Was Also a Winner in the Primary. May 22.

Philadelphia Inquirer. 1984. Strong Start, Few Fumbles for the Mayor. April 22.

Philadelphia Inquirer. 1986. Goode's Re-election Is a Dilemma for Blacks, Also. November 27.

Philadelphia Inquirer. 1987a. Goode Pulled Black Vote for a Range of Reasons. May 24.

Philadelphia Inquirer. 1987b. Many on Green's Team Help Rendell. April 25.

Philadelphia Inquirer. 1987c. For Goode, a Year of Recovery. January 4.

Philadelphia Inquirer. 1993. Marching Side by Side along a Divide. September 27.

Philadelphia Inquirer. 1994a. Police Accused of Beating Up Latinos. January 15.

Philadelphia Inquirer. 1994b. After Years of Losses, Area Jobs Up. April 7.

Philadelphia Inquirer Magazine. 1994a. Response Time. February 6.

Philadelphia Inquirer Magazine. 1994b. The Soul of an Old Machine. April 17.

Philadelphia Magazine. 1984. The No-Frills Mayor. December.

Portz, John. 1990. *The Politics of Plant Closings*. Lawrence: University Press of Kansas.

Reichley, James. 1959. *The Art of Government: Reform and Organization Politics in Philadelphia*. New York: The Fund for the Republic.

Rieder, Jonathan. 1985. *Canarsie: The Jews and Italians of Brooklyn against Liberalism*. Cambridge: Harvard University Press.

Rogers, David. 1971. *The Management of Big Cities*. Beverly Hills: Sage.

Rottenberg, Dan. 1994. Ed Rendell: The eternal sophomore as America's mayor. *The Pennsylvania Gazette* (May).

Schwartz, Edward. 1982. The Philadelphia City Council: From ABSCAM to Activism. *Ways and Means* (September-October).

Strange, John Hadley. 1966. The Negro in Philadelphia Politics: 1963–1965. Unpublished Ph.D. dissertation, Princeton University.

Strange, John Hadley. 1969. The Negro and Philadelphia Politics. In Edward Banfield, ed., *Urban Government*. New York: Free Press.

Strange, John Hadley. 1973. Blacks and Philadelphia Politics. In Miriam Ershkowitz and Joseph Zikmund II, eds., *Black Politics in Philadelphia*. New York: Basic Books.

Summers, Anita, and Thomas Luce. 1987. *Economic Development within the Philadelphia Metropolitan Area*. Philadelphia: University of Pennsylvania Press.

U.S. Conference of Mayors. May 1987. *A Status Report on Homeless Families in America's Cities*. Washington, D.C.: U.S. Conference of Mayors.

Weiler, Conrad. 1974. *Philadelphia: Neighborhood, Authority, and the Urban Crisis*. New York: Praeger.

part **III**

Barriers to Coalitions

chapter 4

New York: The Great Anomaly

John Mollenkopf

Editors' Note

New York is the largest city in the United States. More than half its population is black, Latino, or Asian. Blacks and Latinos have a long history of sophisticated political participation and at times have formed an alliance with a sizable, politically active, liberal white population. Knowing these facts makes it easy to predict that blacks, Latinos, and white liberals have formed a strong and durable governing coalition.

Easy, but wrong. As John Mollenkopf shows, blacks and Latinos have been politically much weaker in New York than we would expect. The contrast to other cities with nonwhite majorities is striking. It did not elect a black mayor until 1989, long after Los Angeles, Chicago, and Philadelphia had done so, and that mayor served only one term. Both before and after, white mayors held sway, playing to a white, middle-class coalition with relatively conservative programs that stressed fiscal prudence and fighting crime. Moreover, until redistricting in 1991, both blacks and Latinos were substantially underrepresented on the city council. Neither group can be said to be part of the current governing coalition.

Why have blacks and Latinos been so weak in New York? Read Mollenkopf's *explanations as a sourcebook of barriers to minority incorporation: the persistence of regular Democratic party organizational influence; the divisions among and competition between white liberals, blacks, and Latinos; and the absence of independent means for these groups to form a durable coalition. These barriers are not unique to New York, but they come together with special intensity to deter minority political empowerment in that city.*

In their admirable *Protest Is Not Enough*, Rufus Browning, Dale Marshall, and David Tabb argue that minority protest alone did not cause city governments in ten California cities to become more responsive to minority interests (Browning, Marshall, and Tabb 1984). Instead, the nature of a city's governing coalition mediated the relationship between protest and policy. Only when insurgent liberal, biracial coalitions displaced more conservative, white coalitions did cities adopt policies that promoted minority interests; this was especially so when blacks or Latinos led the challenging coalitions. Where conservative white coalitions remained in power, city governments resisted policy changes despite minority protest.

Whether biracial coalitions could win office depended, in their view, on the overall extent of minority political mobilization and the degree to which white voters were willing to support minority political advancement. The former depended in turn on the relative size of the minority population and whether it had capable leaders. Raphe Sonenshein built on this framework by arguing that white support for minority advancement turned not only on ideological liberalism among whites, but also on whether minority empowerment advanced the political interests of white liberals. In Sonenshein's view, biracial coalitions were more likely to form where potential coalition participants had long-term personal ties with one another (Sonenshein 1993). In short, biracial coalitions should succeed where sizable black and Latino populations have mobilized for protest and electoral politics, where these minority populations have produced strong leadership, and where these leaders formed a mutually beneficial long-term alliance with white liberals.

From this perspective, New York City should be an early and leading case of successful biracial coalition building and minority incorporation. Instead, it emerges as a triple anomaly: minority political empowerment came late to New York, it was quickly defeated, and yet city government still pursued policies that Browning, Marshall, and Tabb thought would flow only from a politically successful biracial coalition. This paper explores these anomalies with an eye toward extending and improving on the theoretical work begun by Browning, Marshall, and Tabb.

NEW YORK AS AN ANOMALOUS CASE

New York City has long had the political raw materials that Browning, Marshall, and Tabb say will enable a liberal, biracial coalition to win office and bring about minority political incorporation. New York's non-Hispanic black, Hispanic, and Asian populations accounted for 37 percent of the total in 1970, growing to 57 percent by 1990.[1] They have a robust history of mobilization for electoral politics and protest. Its white voters are more liberal than those of other cities and the nation as a whole (Goldberg and Arian 1989; Gifford 1978). Finally, white liberal, black, and Puerto

---

[1] In the 1990 census, New York's population of 7.3 million was 25.2 percent non-Hispanic black, 24.4 percent Hispanic, and 6.7 percent non-Hispanic Asian. References to black, Asian, and white populations exclude those of Hispanic origin, who are grouped together as Latino throughout this paper. For an overview of demographic change in the 1980s, see Mollenkopf 1993.

Rican leaders have a lengthy record of working with each other through electoral politics, trade unions, social service agencies, and civic organizations.

Black and Latino political mobilization dates to the Depression and World War II. Democrat Adam Powell and Benjamin Davis, a Communist, became the city's first black elected officials when they won city council seats in the 1941 and 1943 elections, conducted under proportional representation. The first Puerto Rican assemblyman was elected on the Republican and American Labor party lines in 1938. Black and Puerto Rican political representation grew steadily, though not without setbacks, after World War II. It reached one peak in 1969, when minority voters helped elect Herman Badillo, who was a reform-oriented Puerto Rican, to the office of Bronx borough president, and helped win the office of Manhattan borough president for Percy Sutton, an African American. Minority voters also played a key role in the reelection of Mayor John V. Lindsay (Kimball 1972, 170). Though these individuals had all moved on by 1974, the city's growing black and Latino populations and the influence of the Voting Rights Act on redistricting enabled a new generation of minority legislators to win office in the 1980s. By 1992, blacks and Latinos had come to hold 21 of the 53 seats on the city council, six of the city's 14 congressional seats, six of 25 state senate seats, and 24 of the 60 assembly seats. (Republicans control the redistricting of senate seats and Democrats, the assembly seats. Jointly they determine congressional districts.)

Black and Latino protest also has a long and turbulent history in New York City. Highlights include the black boycott of white merchants along 125th Street in Harlem in the 1950s, the civil disturbances and school decentralization protests of the 1960s, and marches led by the Reverend Al Sharpton and others in the late 1980s and early 1990s. On both electoral and protest counts, then, New York has clearly experienced the black and Hispanic political mobilization that Browning, Marshall, and Tabb say is one major determinant of success for biracial political coalitions.

Equally important, a third of New York City's white voters call themselves liberals and have cast ballots for minority mayoral candidates; three-fifths typically cast ballots for white candidates who openly seek minority support. Although whites gave little support to minority candidates who opposed whites in the 1974 and 1977 Democratic mayoral primaries, white voters gave a larger share of their votes to David Dinkins in 1989 than whites had done in any other city for a first-time race by a black mayoral nominee—except for Tom Bradley in Los Angeles (Arian, Goldberg, Mollenkopf, and Rogowsky 1991). These electoral alignments are based on the close working relationships that white, black, and Latino political leaders have developed over a long period within the Democratic party county organizations and various other arenas.

Based on these antecedent conditions, Browning, Marshall, and Tabb's theoretical framework leads us to expect that a liberal, insurgent biracial coalition would have been victorious in New York City politics by the early 1970s and that minority political empowerment would have become deeply embedded in the New York City political system. The election of John V. Lindsay as mayor in 1965 and 1969 and the slow accretion of minority legislative representation suggested this might happen. In fact, however, it did not. If we define minority incorporation as black and Latino involvement as key participants in the electoral and governing coalitions of the mayor and legislative majorities, minority incorporation in New York City can at best be termed weak and subordinate. Instead, except for David Dinkins's single term, since 1972 New York has been governed by relatively conservative mayoral administrations elected largely by white voters which ceded little influence to minority political leaders.

The failures of the two major thrusts toward minority incorporation, the Lindsay and Dinkins mayoralties, demonstrate the tenacity of this pattern. The Lindsay administration offered the nation a model for liberal, biracial coalition politics between 1965 and 1973. It sought to incorporate minorities not only by traditional means, like welfare and public employment, but also through innovations like the Office of Neighborhood Government and community development corporations (Pecorella 1994; Katznelson 1981; Yates 1973). But this experiment failed politically in the wake of political turmoil over such issues as the establishment of a civilian complaint review board and community control of the school system (Morris 1980; Shefter 1985). It was succeeded by the white, ethnic clubhouse politics of Mayor Abraham Beame (1973–1977), the fiscal crisis (1975–1977), and the conservative administration of Mayor Edward I. Koch (1977–1989). Mayors Beame and Koch both reduced the share of redistributive spending in the city budget and used programs originally designed to promote minority interests to keep minority politicians in line (Katznelson 1981; Mollenkopf 1985, 1994; Shefter 1985; Brecher and Horton with Cropf and Mead 1993).

Similarly, although the election of David N. Dinkins as New York City's first African-American mayor in 1989 was widely heralded as a breakthrough for minority empowerment, Rudolph W. Giuliani, an Italian-American, Republican former prosecutor, defeated Dinkins after only one term (Mollenkopf 1994). Facing a budget crisis almost as severe as that of the mid-1970s, Mayor Giuliani has terminated affirmative action programs, cut social spending, increased the size of the police department, and cracked down on "quality of life" problems like homeless people and panhandling. Today, New York has neither a liberal biracial governing coalition nor broad political support for the spending and distributional priorities such regimes put in place.

By Browning, Marshall, and Tabb's measures, minorities are weakly incorporated in New York City. Although black and Latino legislative representation finally began to approach parity after the 1990 round of redistricting, four of the five borough presidents, the speaker of the city council, the mayor, and the two other city-wide elected officials are white. Most crucially, Mayor Giuliani won a closely contested election in 1993 with few black or Latino votes. Instead, he tends to view blacks as the opposition, as Mayor Koch did in the 1980s. Despite running on the liberal line and seeking support from white Democratic defectors, the Giuliani administration cannot be called liberal. Like Mayor Koch, Giuliani has been criticized for being insensitive to the black community. He has included only one black and one Latina within his inner circle. Many of the budgetary measures and shifts in the patterns of letting contracts to nonprofit service providers have had adverse effects on blacks and Latinos.

Minority legislators have not exercised much influence within the various decision-making bodies that shape city policy. Historically, the Board of Estimate was the key legislative body within city government; the mayor, comptroller, and city council president, as citywide elected officials, each cast two votes on this body, while the five borough presidents cast one. Between 1977 and 1991, when the board was abolished, it had only two minority members: David Dinkins, Manhattan borough president between 1985 and 1989, and Fernando Ferrer, Bronx borough president since 1987. At their strongest, minorities thus cast two of the board's 11 votes. Even then, Dinkins and Ferrer were wary of each other and did not much constrain Mayor Koch, though each influenced decisions affecting his borough. Most of this period, however, there were no minority votes on the board.

Between 1977 and 1991, minorities were also substantially underrepresented on the 35-member city council. Because it was overshadowed by the Board of Estimate, some called it "worse than a rubber stamp because it leaves no impression." By the end of the 1980s, only seven blacks and three Latinos held council seats (28.6 percent of the total), though blacks and Latinos made up 42 percent of the voting-age citizen population and 46 percent of the 1989 Democratic mayoral primary electorate. Seven of these minority council persons were on the losing side of the 1986 factional fight that made Peter Vallone the council speaker.

In 1989, in the wake of court rulings that had declared the board's voting scheme unconstitutional, voters adopted a new city charter that abolished the board, enlarged the council to 51 members, and gave the council new powers as of the 1991 election. In 1991, the council was also redistricted to increase the number of minority districts. As a result, its minority membership increased dramatically to 41.2 percent of the total (Macchiarola and Diaz 1993; Gartner 1993). Council Speaker Vallone nevertheless continues to direct the business of the council through a central staff and to punish individual council members who challenge his policies. Black and Latino members do constitute a potential bloc of votes, but generally they shore up the speaker's leadership. Although minority members of the state assembly have a more active caucus, a strong speaker also runs that body's affairs. With the possible exception of Congressman Charles Rangel, none of the city's minority legislators wield great influence within their bodies.

Though minority elected officials extract rewards from the white leaders of the political establishment, they do not exert a strong collective influence on the overall allocation of public benefits. Established white leaders secure their cooperation with relatively low levels of patronage, contracts, and similar benefits. This subordinate position persisted, except for the Dinkins administration, because the white political leaders of the Board of Estimate, the city council, and the state legislature did not have to depend on black and Latino votes. Consequently, white leaders have incorporated minority interests in a dependent, controlled, and numerically underrepresented manner. The result is a surprisingly low score on Browning, Marshall, and Tabb's index of political incorporation.

New York departs from Browning, Marshall, and Tabb's predicted path in a second way in that minority empowerment was quickly rolled back after its initial victory. While Browning, Marshall, and Tabb concede that the Reagan and Bush administrations threatened minority gains during the 1980s in the cities studied by the trio, none of the biracial coalitions that governed in some of these cities experienced defeat. Prompted by the fiscal crisis of the mid-1970s and the priorities of the Reagan and Bush administration, the Koch administration governed against the Lindsay tradition and undid the spending patterns of the Lindsay years (Brecher and Horton 1991). Similarly, the Giuliani administration, acting in response to the severe local recession of 1989–1991 and the state budget adopted after the 1994 elections, also reduced funding for programs designed to incorporate minority interests that had expanded under Dinkins.

New York is also anomalous in a third way. Despite the electoral failure of biracial coalitions and the low degree of minority political incorporation, New York City government still produces policy outputs that favor minority interests. Browning, Marshall, and Tabb measure policy responsiveness through minority public employment, the existence of a police review board, minority appointments to commissions, and Community Development Block Grant (CDBG) funding for minority areas and contractors. On these indicators, New York City does well. Minority employees now make up over half the civil service in New York. Mayor Koch was proud of appointing blacks or Latinos to 18 percent of his managerial positions, including the offices of police commissioner and several deputy mayors. While he rejected an independent police review board, he added civilians to a departmental review board.

Even the Giuliani administration, in which few blacks have been appointed, has made an effort to appoint Latino commissioners. While Giuliani has also opposed a civilian review board and an independent prosecutor for the police department, the city council moved independently to establish them over the mayor's veto. The Koch and Giuliani administrations both opposed racial quotas and set-asides, but the Koch administration used community development funds, city capital funds, and other sources of creative financing to launch an ambitious $5.2 billion program to rehabilitate abandoned properties for use as subsidized housing. Though the Giuliani administration has reduced funding for this program, it continues to support it, as did the Dinkins administration.

Although deriving exactly analogous measurements to those used by Browning, Marshall, and Tabb is difficult, New York City would thus seem to compare well with the ten California cities in terms of policy responsiveness. New York's minority public employment may be above the extrapolated current median for the California cities (Browning, Marshall, and Tabb 1984, 172). Certainly, the Koch and Dinkins administrations' record of minority managerial hires compares well with records of the California cities, except for Oakland, though the New York figure may have fallen under the Giuliani administration.

Browning, Marshall, and Tabb acknowledge that external factors like federal regulations and local demographics can contribute to local policy responsiveness, and the Koch, Dinkins, and Giuliani administrations may have had little choice but to hire minorities as welfare department case workers or traffic enforcement agents. Yet Mayor Koch went beyond necessity in maintaining employment and contracting patterns that benefited blacks and Latinos, despite the weak, controlled, and divided nature of minority political incorporation in New York.

These three anomalies prompt us to revise and extend the analysis presented in *Protest is Not Enough*. Why, given New York's liberal image, was the biracial political impulse so slow to develop in that city? Why did a conservative white coalition defeat a biracial (or more properly multi-ethnic) coalition when it did finally succeed with the election of Mayor Dinkins in 1989? Why, despite the weakness of minority political incorporation and Dinkins's defeat in 1993, has New York nonetheless persisted in measures that suggest policy responsiveness? Finally, what does the experience of New York and the other large cities where white mayors have succeeded black mayors tell us about the future of biracial coalition building?

WHY NEW YORK IS AN ANOMALY: MACHINE POLITICS, THE DECAY OF WHITE REFORM, INTERETHNIC COMPETITION, AND CO-OPTATION

Possible explanations for why the biracial impulse has been comparatively weak in New York City and why the dominant coalition has nonetheless paradoxically responded to minority interests may be found in three ways that New York City differs from the ten California cities studied by Browning, Marshall, and Tabb. First, New York City retains a strong "machine" political culture compared to the reformed political cultures of California cities (Shefter 1983). Machine politics has tended to slow the pace of minority empowerment across American cities. A one-party system influenced by regular Democrats deprives those who wish to construct an insurgent coalition of the means to realize this end. Regular Democrats also learned to use tools originally invented by urban reformers to promote minority empowerment to deter minority electoral challenges.

Second, white liberalism lost its vitality more rapidly in New York than in the California cities. New York's political establishment absorbed white reformers while deindustrialization and racial change undermined the white leaders of the labor movement and the old left. Over time, however, minority political empowerment became less sure to advance the interests of white liberals. To the contrary, in some arenas, such as the leadership of public employee and social service unions, minority advancement might threaten the white liberal establishment. Equally important, New York's African Americans and Latinos are more divided and competitive than appears to be the case in the ten California cities.

Though political scientists and some local observers classify New York as a reformed city, New York undeniably partakes of the eastern urban political culture characterized, to use Wolfinger's distinction, by machine politics if not by political machines (Wolfinger 1972). Regular county party organizations, which locals call "the machine" or "the regulars," exert a strong and persistent, if incomplete, hold on politics in New York's five boroughs.

Certainly, these organizations are not what they once were (Ware 1985; Peel 1935; Adler and Blank 1975). There are fewer political clubs across the city's assembly districts; they have fewer members and are less vigorous than in the 1950s. The county party organizations are less able to mobilize voters and were rocked by political scandal in the mid-1980s when the Queens county leader committed suicide, the Bronx leader went to jail, and the former Brooklyn leader was also convicted of a felony (Newfield and Barrett 1989).

At the same time, the county party organizations remain strong in certain respects (Mayhew 1986). They exercise considerable control over access to the ballot for and election to lesser offices. They determine who will serve as judges in the state supreme court. Most members of the city council and state assembly are allied with the regular Democratic county party organizations. Legislative staff, funded by the state, perform many of the campaign and constituency service activities formerly done by political clubs (Gerson 1990). Some clubs, such as Assemblyman Anthony Genovese's Thomas Jefferson Democratic Club in Canarsie, remain powerful campaign organizations. From their position on the city's periphery, the regular Democratic organizations thus exercise considerable power in the city and state's decision-making centers and constrain Manhattan-based reformers.

The persistence of regular organizations in the outer boroughs is particularly important. Many observers do not realize that most New Yorkers, including its largest and fastest growing minority communities, live outside Manhattan. The Brooklyn, Queens, and Bronx regular Democratic organizations have coped with racial and ethnic transition by promoting the careers of loyal minority politicians and absorbing minority insurgents. Black and Latino machine politicians and their clientele helped Mayor Koch pull more votes against black challengers in the 1985 and 1989 mayoral primaries than in similar districts represented by minority reformers. Minority regulars have also defeated or made life extremely difficulty for insurgent opponents in legislative elections. Through these means, white regulars can often command substantial support in black and Latino districts. Although Manhattan's county Democratic organization is considered to be "reformed," that borough's black elected officials continue to exhibit the "regular" traits so skillfully deployed by J. Raymond Jones, the "Harlem Fox" (Walter 1989).

Regular Democrats used the tools of minority political incorporation to retard and absorb insurgent minority politicians. They used appointments to community boards, city jobs, and legislative member item budget allocations to reward political supporters and undermine potential challengers. Even as he reduced the growth rate of spending on public assistance, Mayor Koch appointed blacks and Latinos to senior positions and initiated contracts with community organizations to consolidate his electoral base. Even when community organizations won contracts "on the merits," they needed political sponsors to protect them and knew that an overt challenge to the mayor would cost them their funds.

It is worth noting that white regular Democrats achieved their influence over minority political mobilization by being more liberal than similar politicians in other eastern cities, like Frank Rizzo of Philadelphia. While Rieder's analysis of Canarsie accurately describes Italian-American and Jewish unease over racial change and school integration, it does not give sufficient weight to how Canarsie's Thomas Jefferson Democratic Club, perhaps the city's premier regular Democratic club, worked against the school boycott, supported liberal Democrats for state and national office, and has produced leaders like former Assembly Speaker Stanley Fink and Assemblyman Tony Genovese who strongly support social spending measures (Rieder 1985).

New York resembles V.O. Key's description of the South before the rise of the Republican party: It is a one-party Democratic system with a strong tendency toward factionalism and a politics of personalism and invidious distinction (Key 1949, ch. 14). The ten California cities studied by Browning, Marshall, and Tabb had Republican mayors in the late 1950s, as did Los Angeles, even when their systems were nominally nonpartisan. White Democrats had an incentive to mobilize all politically excluded groups to challenge these mayors. The tables are turned in New York. The hegemony of regulars makes the Democratic party an unsuitable vehicle for organizing an electoral challenge, whereas the Republican party has forsaken its traditional role as the organizational kernel of reform.

Second, compared to the situation in California cities like Berkeley, Oakland, and San Francisco, the vitality of New York's white liberal reform movement has ebbed over the last two decades. At times, white reformers have certainly matched or exceeded the regular organizations' ability to influence citywide election campaigns and have elected reform candidates, especially on the "Upper Left Side" of Manhattan and in brownstone Brooklyn. Since the early 1970s, however, the "movement liberalism" of well-educated baby boomers who favored civil rights and opposed the Vietnam war and the "old liberalism" of unionized, blue-collar, and lower-middle-class Jewish constituencies have both atrophied in New York.

On the one hand, the national and local cycles of fiscal retrenchment and political conservatism made "Lindsay-type" ideological liberalism unfashionable. Moreover, many of its proponents have been absorbed into the incumbent establishment: White reform insurgents who won election to the assembly and council have slowly been melded into the regular-dominated hierarchy while the young innovators of the Lindsay administration have gone on to pursue their careers. As Sonenshein notes, the group advancement of New York's liberals no longer depends on challenging and overturning the establishment. Leaders such as Manhattan Borough President Ruth Messinger and campaigns such as that of David Dinkins in 1989 periodically reinvigorate this constituency, but it lacks causes or passions as intense as those of the civil rights movement or the Vietnam war. The same can be said about black and Puerto Rican reformers.

The forces of change have also squeezed the old liberal, unionized, blue-collar or lower-middle-class Jewish constituency that so distinguished New York from other eastern cities. As Shefter has shown, this process began in the 1950s with the destruction of the American Labor Party as the admission price that the Democratic establishment forced Jewish activists to pay (Shefter 1986). In the 1960s, the traumas of racial succession in neighborhoods and labor markets pushed them further right (Rieder 1985). Finally, deindustrialization, generational change, and ethnic succession have weakened the trade unions and other organizations that served as the base for this old left perspective.

While it vastly oversimplifies matters to say that New York became more conservative when racial conflict led Jews to abandon their alliance with minorities and embrace white Catholics, this dictum contains an element of truth. This shift is tempered by the commitment of regular and reform Democrats to spending patterns that favor public service providers (such as the public employee unions) and public service recipients. The alliance bonds white, often Jewish, professionals in the "helping professions" with minority rank and file workers and service recipients. Thus the Jewish former president of a teamsters' local representing public employees supported Jesse Jackson's 1988 campaign in New York, and the Jewish woman who heads the teachers' union is married to a black man. Despite such ties, however, most white voters, including two-thirds of the Jewish voters, defected from the Democratic party in 1989 and 1991 to support a white Republican.

Third, black and Latino political leaders often compete with each other, and their electoral constituencies differ significantly (Falcon 1988). The post-1965 wave of immigration has made broad categories increasingly less descriptive of both constituencies. West Indians and Dominicans are asserting political interests that are distinct from, and in some instances may challenge, those of native born African Americans and Puerto Ricans. Browning, Marshall, and Tabb note that similar tensions exist in the California cities, but they conclude that black incorporation strengthened Latino incorporation. The same cannot be said for New York.

The relatively similar size of the black and Latino populations contributes to the tension between them. When candidates of each background are running in the same race, there tends to be considerable polarization between the two groups. Moreover, there is a history of discord among the most prominent leaders of the two groups. An attempt to select a consensus minority challenger to Mayor Koch in the 1985 mayoral primary foundered because black elected officials, banded together as the Coalition for a Just New York, refused to support Herman Badillo. Even though they could not identify a strong black candidate of their own, the officials withheld their support because Badillo had not withdrawn in favor of the first black candidate for mayor, Percy Sutton, in the 1977 Democratic primary. Instead, they ran a weak black candidate. In their turn, Puerto Rican leaders fear that blacks will always put them at the end of the line of political succession, and they resent what they perceive to be black leaders' implicit belief that blacks have a historic and political claim to lead any minority coalition.

Political fragmentation among Latinos exacerbates this problem. Most Puerto Rican New Yorkers feel that blacks and Latinos are equally discriminated against and two-thirds feel that they should work together. But most also feel that Puerto Rican elected officials are "more interested in their own careers than in serving the community" (Velazquez 1988, 11). More than four out of five Latino New Yorkers identified themselves racially as white or "Other" in the Census, not as black. Because most Latinos are Catholic and more describe themselves as conservatives than in any other ethnic group, Latinos are open to appeals from white Catholic politicians, making the road to an effective black-Latino alliance something of a minefield.

Blacks and Latinos are both heterogeneous groups, divided by ancestry and nativity. Increasingly, native born African Americans and Puerto Ricans are experiencing a net outmigration from New York; their populations are stable only because births exceed deaths. Instead, immigration from the Anglophone West Indies, Haiti, the Dominican Republic, Mexico, and Central America is driving the growth of the city's black and Latino populations. In the main, native born African Americans and Puerto Ricans have not sought to mobilize and incorporate these groups. Instead, they have developed their own leadership, with one Dominican-born and two Jamaican-born members joining the city council since 1991. West Indian and Dominican leaders tended to support David Dinkins in 1989 and 1991, but the underlying tensions between and within the black and Latino communities provide fertile territory for those who would peel minority voters away from a coalition led by a native-born African American.

The persistence of machine politics, the decline of white liberalism, the division among minorities, and the absence of a mechanism for dialogue and coalition formation among them reinforce each other. Many other cities have tensions between natives and immigrants, between different ethnic groups, between blacks and Latinos, and among white professionals, minority service workers, and unionized white ethnics, making it hard for them to talk with each other. In the California cities, white liberals, minority groups, public employees, and others were all political outsiders, as was the Democratic party, at the beginning of the period examined by Browning, Marshall, and Tabb. Not only did they have a political incentive to coalesce, but the Democratic party had an interest in helping them to do so. The Democratic party does not serve this purpose in New York, nor does any other institutional mechanism. Instead, New York City's political system plays on these divisions. In this setting, it is less surprising that minority empowerment is weak than that it happened at all.

HOW NEW YORK ELECTED A BLACK MAYOR AND WHY HE WAS DEFEATED

The 1983 victory of Mayor Harold Washington in Chicago prefigured—and to some degree inspired—the election of Mayor David Dinkins in New York in 1989. According to informed observers, the Washington victory was preceded by racial polarization, the alienation of black leadership from the regular Democratic organization, a consensus-based candidate recruitment process, an upsurge in minority turnout in which Latinos joined black voters, and a division among regular Democrats. Many of these same trends developed in New York City during the latter 1980s.

According to Barker, Chicago's black leaders used a survey to unearth the names of 90 possible candidates for mayor, 20 of whom were submitted to a meeting attended by a thousand grassroots leaders. The participants overwhelmingly endorsed Washington (Barker 1983). A grassroots surge was also crucial: Preston reports that registration increased 29.5 percent in black wards, that the lowest general election turnout in a black ward was 73 percent, and that Washington won 73 percent of the black vote in the primary and 97 percent in the general election (Preston 1983; Kleppner 1985, 149). Furthermore, Washington won over 50 percent of the Latino votes in the general election, though he received only 20 percent in the primary. Peterson argues that blacks gradually accumulated political resources within the Cook County regular Democratic party organization and then capitalized on a division among white regulars to elect Washington (Peterson 1983).

For most of the 1970s and 1980s, New York City offered a sharp contrast to these conditions. In 1985, the closed-door deliberations of the Coalition for a Just New York led to a weak black candidate in preference to a liberal white woman and a potential Puerto Rican candidate. This candidate got just 41 percent of a low black vote, even though the 1984 Jesse Jackson presidential campaign had increased black registration. The candidate also received only 12 percent of the Latino vote, whereas Mayor Koch got 70 percent. Mayor Koch was able to hold the allegiance of many black and Latino regular Democratic officials. New York's black leaders could not coalesce around a mayoral candidate who could mobilize black voters, much less build the necessary biracial alliances.

This situation started to change in 1988 when Jesse Jackson won a plurality of New York City's votes in the Democratic presidential primary and showed that a black candidate might be able to win a Democratic mayoral primary in 1989. His 1984 race produced a groundswell of black registration and turnout but did not mobilize Latinos. Jackson's 1988 candidacy did not further increase black mobilization, but in this campaign he did win 61 percent of the Latino vote and 15 percent of the white vote, gaining a 43.5 percent plurality in the city. This included 9 percent of the Jewish vote despite Mayor Koch's assertion that Jews would have to be crazy to vote for Jackson (*New York Times* 1988).

Washington's 1983 and 1985 victories in Chicago and Jackson's 1988 victory in New York inspired Mayor Koch's black, white, and Latino opponents; however, other circumstances made David Dinkins's victory possible. A corruption scandal in 1986 and 1987 led to the suicide of one borough president, the conviction of another, and the resignation of three commissioners and numerous other senior appointees, all of whom were closely tied to Mayor Koch. These events caused Koch's approval rating to plummet, opening the way for well-known, well-financed candidates to challenge him in the 1989 primary.

David Dinkins, who played a leading role in the 1988 Jackson campaign, united the previously divided black leadership and won over many Latinos and white liberals. Like the Jackson campaign, the Dinkins campaign had an organizational base in public sector trade unions and reform political clubs. Having gotten his political start in Harlem clubhouse politics, Dinkins had drawn broad support from whites in his 1985 race for the Manhattan borough presidency and had used this position to establish his independence from the mayor. The scandal-bred weakening of the county party organizations freed regular Democratic black leaders from Brooklyn, the Bronx, and Queens to back Dinkins in 1989. Jackson's ability to gain greater support among Latino voters in 1988 set the stage for greater black-Latino cooperation.

Finally, a series of polarizing events reawakened concern over race relations in 1988 and 1989. A fatal mob attack on three blacks in Howard Beach, a "wilding" assault by black teenagers on a white woman jogging in Central Park, and the murder of a black in the conservative Italian neighborhood of Bensonhurst sharply worsened racial tensions in the months leading up to the 1989 mayoral primary. Combined with frequent pronouncements from Mayor Koch that observers interpreted as insensitive and racially polarizing, these events increased black and Latino dissatisfaction with the mayor and convinced many white voters to consider other options.

In the 1989 primary, Dinkins received virtually unanimous support from black voters, about half the white liberal vote, and a substantial minority of Latino votes to win a majority of the primary votes and defeat Mayor Koch and two other white candidates. He then narrowly beat Rudolph W. Giuliani, a Republican former prosecutor, in the general election by maintaining his position with blacks and white liberals, increasing his Latino support, and retaining a quarter of the white Catholic and Jewish Democratic vote.

Crucial to these victories was the unity and mobilization of the black electorate, mirrored in virtually unanimous support from black elected officials. The promise of electing the city's first African-American mayor yielded major turnout gains in the primary and general elections, making blacks the single largest component of the Democratic vote at about 34 percent. Equally crucially, half the white liberals and a quarter of the white ethnic Democrats were willing to support a black nominee (Arian, Goldberg, Mollenkopf, and Rogowsky 1991; Mollenkopf 1994).

Dinkins could not convert his electoral triumph into a durable governing coalition, however. New York City experienced a severe recession between 1989 and 1993, which put great strain on the city's budget. While Dinkins managed his fiscal difficulties without losing control to the Financial Control Board, itself an accomplishment, the board made it difficult for him to deliver benefits to his core constituencies among public employee unions and social service producers and consumers.

Dinkins also faced a media-driven opinion panic over street crime and the continuation of racially polarizing events. In 1991, the largely black Crown Heights community erupted in a riot when an auto in the entourage of the Lubavitcher Hassidic Rebbe struck and killed a black child, and Hispanic Washington Heights nearly erupted in violence over the death of a Dominican man at the hands of the police in 1992. Dinkins also failed to halt a long-running boycott of a Korean merchant in Flatbush, Brooklyn, by black nationalists working on behalf of a Haitian woman who was treated roughly by its owner. In response to these events, Dinkins used all his degrees of budgetary freedom to expand the city's police force. Unfortunately, this did not quell public doubts about his ability to restore harmony to the city nor did it keep white ethnic voters in his corner.

On November 2, 1993, David Dinkins narrowly lost his rematch with Rudolph Giuliani and became the nation's first breakthrough black mayor to lose office after one term. More than half the margin of change since 1989 came from middle-class white Catholic and Jewish election districts (Mollenkopf 1994). They not only gave Dinkins less support but they also turned out in increased numbers, particularly in

Staten Island where many such voters were drawn to the polls by a referendum on whether that community should secede from New York City. The increased mobilization of relatively conservative white voters was enough to make the difference for Giuliani.

In addition, however, black voters turned out in lower numbers; Latinos both turned out in lower numbers and defected from Dinkins, and white liberals defected. The relative demobilization among Latinos was greater than for any other group; exit poll data suggest they were disappointed that Mayor Dinkins did not do more to foster Latino advancement and address the extreme problems facing their community.

In short, the conditions that enabled a biracial coalition to elect an African-American mayor proved to be short-lived in New York City. Once again, regular Democrats showed a surprising ability to restore their organizations in the wake of the scandals of 1986 and 1987; by 1993, a number of Democratic political clubs in white ethnic areas declared for Rudolph Giuliani's candidacy. Despite the fact that most white regular Democratic officials endorsed Dinkins, they could not, or at any rate did not, deliver their constituencies for him. Dinkins was unable to manage public reaction to events like the Crown Heights riots or the Korean store boycott in ways that improved his support from white liberals. Finally, despite Dinkins's strong record on Latino appointments, black-Latino political relations also frayed over this period, especially with regard to the city council redistricting, in which some Latinos charged that the mayor's appointees to the districting commission had favored blacks over Latinos in the construction of minority districts.

LESSONS FOR THE THEORY AND PRACTICE OF BIRACIAL COALITION FORMATION

The sharp differences between the New York City experience and those of the ten relatively small California cities studied by Browning, Marshall, and Tabb suggest the need to revise and extend their theoretical approach in two basic directions (Browning, Marshall, and Tabb 1990, 1994). First, we need to develop a more complex model of the process of racial and ethnic succession in urban politics. Their evidentiary base led Browning, Marshall, and Tabb to make unexamined assumptions about this issue that the New York experience suggests we must critically reevaluate. In the California cities, except for San Francisco, native-born blacks or native-born Latinos, typically Mexican Americans, were gaining ground on the white population and might, as in the case of Oakland, ultimately become a majority of the electorate. This led Browning, Marshall, and Tabb to anticipate a unidirectional shift from white influence to preponderant influence by one or another minority group and a more or less permanent rise to power of a biracial challenging coalition.

The case of New York City shows that whereas a city can become less white, it does not necessarily become more black, and that while a biracial coalition may come to power, it may not be able to consolidate its position. More broadly, urban politics is no longer a simple matter of black and white, where black political leaders can consolidate minority empowerment primarily on appeals to black solidarity. Racial succession has already taken place in most of the large central cities where it will ever happen. In these cities, white minorities can influence competition between black factions. In other large cities, ranging from New York and Los Angeles to San Francisco, Boston, San Diego, Houston, and Miami, blacks will never become a majority of the electorate. Indeed, under the impact of immigration, the populations of these cities are becoming more diverse. Although declining, whites may remain the single largest group within an increasingly complex constellation of other constituencies, most of whom will not defer to black leadership of all "people of color." If racial division continues to mark these cities, and if the racial divide comes to be defined as "black/nonblack" instead of "white/nonwhite," the prospects for black-led biracial or multiethnic coalitions may actually worsen. In the future, therefore, the course of urban politics will depend on who can construct broader and more complex coalitions than the relatively simple biracial coalitions discussed by Browning, Marshall, and Tabb.

The New York experience also shows that real differences of interest divide the potential components of multiracial insurgent coalitions. Key elements of such coalitions—white liberals, native-born blacks, and Puerto Ricans—are on the wane. Given present economic and demographic trends, the white, professional stratum of New York and other large central cities is more likely to shrink than grow. Moreover, it is well ensconced and typically has no great incentive to join in risky political challenges. It shares an interest with more conservative white ethnic voters in reducing crime and taxes. So far, Mayor Giuliani and his mayoral colleagues Daley, Rendell, and Riordan have avoided being trapped into advocating socially conservative positions on abortion or gay rights that might push white liberals back toward a multiracial coalition.

Similarly, the native-born black population of New York City has been declining relative to other groups. More than Latinos or Asians, blacks rely on public sector and publicly supported nonprofit sector jobs. They have achieved proportionate legislative representation and are actually overrepresented within the Democratic party electorate. As a result, other groups view them as part of the political establishment. Caribbean immigrants and their children, most of whom cannot yet vote, provide most of the growth in the black population. Black incumbents, who represent safe seats, have no particular incentive to bring these new voters into the electorate. Puerto Ricans are in a similar if more disadvantaged position. Their numbers are also in relative decline; although Puerto Rican elected officials like to speak of representing Latino interests, they view the rapidly growing Dominican population as a potential threat. Native-born black and Puerto Rican elected officials have reacted negatively to the idea that foreign-born minorities should be allowed to vote in New York City elections even though they are the only source of long-term growth for the minority electorate.

In such an environment, even an initially successful biracial coalition faces major obstacles to institutionalizing its political position and preventing a subsequent rollback of its policies. New York joins Los Angeles, Chicago, and Philadelphia as cities where white voters have enabled relatively conservative white mayors to defeat minority candidates and replace black mayors. These mayors have succeeded in part by exploiting differences within liberal, multiracial coalitions.

Second, New York's experience suggests that we must give more theoretical attention to how a city's political system shapes the expression of group interests and allocates access and influence across them. These have a crucial impact on the feasibility of constructing a durable multiracial coalition. Even where the elements of a would-be insurgent coalition wish to overcome their divisions, they need an organizational framework through which to construct the necessary trust and cooperation. Browning, Marshall, and Tabb's California cities had reformed, nonpartisan political systems in which the Democratic party, or extra-party organizations, could unite out-groups. The entrenched nature of the Democratic party makes this problematic in New York and other large, old, eastern cities.

Other organizations that might help to forge such coalitions, like public employee unions, have also failed to perform this function. Though unions like District Council 37 or Local 1199 of the hospital workers represent all the different components of the potential liberal, multiracial coalition, they have been thrown on the defensive by the city's fiscal problems, are distracted by internal conflicts, and have been unwilling or unable to reach outside their ranks to give equal partnership to community organizations in forming a new liberal coalition. These aspects of how New York City's political system is organized explain much of the weakness of biracial coalition politics in New York City and other large central cities.

The news for urban liberals is not all bad, however. Just as they have not resolved the problem of constructing a durable political majority, the white mayors who have recently won office in New York, Los Angeles, Chicago, Philadelphia, and other majority-minority cities have also had difficulty in fashioning a coherent, majoritarian governing coalition. Jim Sleeper has suggested that these "Rainbow II" mayors built majority support by opposing racial preferences and ill-conceived liberal social policies and favoring lower taxes, negotiating tougher union contracts, fighting crime, and reinventing local government (Sleeper 1993). In his view, this platform has attracted votes from entrepreneurial Latinos, Asians, and other immigrants as well as from white ethnics, giving these mayors claim to an ethnically diverse base of support. In practice, however, many of these mayors' bases of support remain predicated on the unity of white support and the division of minority opponents. Moreover, a number of these mayors have managed to forge good relations with municipal employees' unions, despite their tough rhetoric.

Whether these mayors' political base will cohere over the long term is uncertain, at least in the case of New York City. Many of Mayor Giuliani's policies have generated opposition—for example, when his budget cutbacks had a disproportionate impact on services to black and Latino communities and when he cut off contracts to community organizations and shifted them to more supportive white, ethnic organizations. Although he has retained a good relationship with the largest municipal union by avoiding layoffs and providing sizable incentives for those who leave the payroll voluntarily, his tendency to draw lines in the sand has alienated many white liberals and minority politicians. Eventually, such actions may give minority leaders, community groups, and at least some public employee unions good cause to search for a political alternative.

To prevent this from happening, "Rainbow II" mayors must broaden their appeal, keep their opponents divided, and develop their own organizational base. Mayor Richard M. Daley of Chicago can rely on the traditions of regular Democratic organizational rule to keep many minority politicians in his orbit. Mayor Giuliani does not have an equivalent base in the Republican party; whether he succeeds in his attempt to keep public employee unions neutral and his Democratic opponents divided in the face of his budget and program choices remains to be seen.

In sum, New York City presents a far less optimistic picture of the future of biracial coalition politics and minority incorporation than the one Browning, Marshall, and Tabb offered us a decade ago. But if the goal of a more democratic, inclusive, and responsive city government has often proven elusive, that does not mean it is impossible. As Theodore Lowi (1964) once observed, the reform impulse has been a long-standing and creative force in the political development in New York and, by example, many other cities. New York teaches us now that progress toward this goal will depend on whether groups coming from highly diverse racial, ethnic, and geographic locations can find new ways to engage in political dialogue, define common purposes that enable them to transcend group differences, and cooperate in practical politics. In these respects, the 1997 mayoral primary and general elections will be a defining moment for New York City's liberal tradition.

REFERENCES

Adler, Norman, and Blanche Blank. 1975. *Political Clubs in New York*. New York: Praeger.

Arian, Asher, Arthur Goldberg, John Mollenkopf, and Edward Rogowsky. 1991. *Changing New York City Politics*. New York: Routledge.

Barker, Twiley. 1983. "Political Mobilization of Black Chicago: Drafting a Candidate." *PS* 16 (Summer): 482–485.

Brecher, Charles, and Raymond Horton. 1991. The Public Sector. In John Mollenkopf and Manuel Castells, eds., *Dual City: Restructuring New York*. New York: Russell Sage Foundation.

Brecher, Charles, and Raymond Horton with Robert A. Cropf and Dean Michael Mead. 1993. *Power Failure: New York City Politics and Policy since 1960*. New York: Oxford University Press.

Browning, Rufus P., Dale Rogers Marshall, and David H. Tabb. 1984. *Protest Is Not Enough*. Berkeley: University of California Press.

Browning, Rufus P., Dale Rogers Marshall, and David H. Tabb. 1994. Political Incorporation and Changing Perspectives on Urban Politics. Paper presented at the annual meeting of the American Political Science Association, New York, September 1–4.

Browning, Rufus P., Dale Rogers Marshall, and David H. Tabb, eds. 1990. *Racial Politics in American Cities*. White Plains, N.Y.: Longman.

Falcon, Angelo. 1988. Black and Latino Politics in New York City: Race and Ethnicity in a Changing Urban Context. *New Community* 14 (Spring): 370–384.

Gartner, Alan. 1993. Public Involvement in the Work of the New York City Districting Commission: An Insider's View. Paper presented at the annual meeting of the Western Political Science Association, San Francisco.

Gerson, Jeffrey. 1990. Building the Brooklyn Machine: Irish, Jewish, and Black Succession in Central Brooklyn, 1919–1964. Unpublished Ph.D. dissertation, Political Science Program, City University Graduate School and University Center, New York.

Gifford, Bernard R. 1978. New York City and Cosmopolitan Liberalism. *Political Science Quarterly* 93 (Winter): 559–584.

Goldberg, Arthur, and Asher Arian. 1989. The American Urban Electorate in the 1988 Presidential Election. Paper presented at the annual meeting of the American Political Science Association, Atlanta, August 31–September 3.

Katznelson, Ira. 1981. *City Trenches.* New York: Pantheon.

Key, V. O., Jr. 1949. *Southern Politics in State and Nation.* New York: Vintage.

Kimball, Penn. 1972. *The Disconnected.* New York: Columbia University Press.

Kleppner, Paul. 1985. *Chicago Divided: The Making of a Black Mayor.* DeKalb: Northern Illinois University Press.

Lowi, Theodore. 1964. *At the Pleasure of the Mayor: Patronage and Politics in New York City, 1896–1956.* New York: Free Press.

Macchiarola, Frank J., and Joseph G. Diaz. 1993. Minority Political Empowerment in New York City: Beyond the Voting Rights Act. *Political Science Quarterly* 108 (1): 37–57.

Mayhew, David. 1986. *Placing Parties in American Politics.* Princeton, N.J.: Princeton University Press.

Mollenkopf, John. 1985. The Politics of Racial Advancement and the Failure of Urban Reform: The Case of New York City. Paper commissioned for a colloquium at the Center for the Study of Industrial Societies, University of Chicago, April 25.

Mollenkopf, John. 1993. *New York in the 1980s: A Social, Economic, and Political Atlas.* New York: Simon & Schuster.

Mollenkopf, John. 1994. *A Phoenix in the Ashes: The Rise and Fall of the Koch Coalition in New York City Politics.* Princeton, N.J.: Princeton University Press.

Morris, Charles. 1980. *The Cost of Good Intentions.* New York: Norton.

New York Times. 1988. New York Times/CBS Exit Poll, Thursday, April 21, D25.

Newfield, Jack, and Wayne Barrett. 1989. *City for Sale: Ed Koch and the Betrayal of New York.* New York: Harper & Row.

Pecorella, Robert F. 1994. *Community Power in a Postreform City: Politics in New York City.* Armonk, N.Y.: M. E. Sharpe.

Peel, Roy V. 1935. *Political Clubs of New York City.* New York: Putnam.

Peterson, Paul. 1983. Washington's Election in Chicago: The Other Half of the Story. *PS* 16 (Fall): 712–716.

Preston, Michael. 1983. The Election of Harold Washington: Black Voting Patterns in the 1983 Chicago Mayoral Race. *PS* 16 (Summer): 486–488.

Rieder, Jonathan. 1985. *Canarsie: The Jews and Italians of Brooklyn against Liberalism.* Cambridge, Mass.: Harvard University Press.

Shefter, Martin. 1983. Regional Receptivity to Reform. *Political Science Quarterly* 98 (Fall): 459–483.

Shefter, Martin. 1985. *Political Crisis/Fiscal Crisis: The Collapse and Revival of New York City.* New York: Basic Books.

Shefter, Martin. 1986. Political Incorporation and the Extrusion of the Left: Party Politics and Social Forces in New York City. *Studies in American Political Development.* 1: 50–90.

Sleeper, Jim. 1993. The End of the Rainbow. *The New Republic,* November 1, 20–25.

Sonenshein, Raphael. 1993. *Politics in Black and White: Race and Power in Los Angeles.* Princeton, N.J.: Princeton University Press.

Velazquez, Nydia. 1988. Puerto Rican Voter Registration in New York City: A Comparison of Attitudes Between Registered and Non-Registered Puerto Ricans. Migration Division, Department of Labor and Human Resources, Commonwealth of Puerto Rico.

Walter, John C. 1989. *The Harlem Fox: J. Raymond Jones and Tammany, 1920–1970*. Albany: State University of New York Press.

Ware, Alan. 1985. *The Breakdown of Democratic Party Organization, 1940–1980*. New York: Oxford University Press.

Wolfinger, Raymond. 1972. Why Political Machines Have Not Withered Away and Other Revisionist Thoughts. *Journal of Politics* 34 (May): 365–398.

Yates, Douglas. 1973. *Neighborhood Democracy: The Politics and Impacts of Decentralization*. Lexington, Mass.: Lexington Books.

chapter **5**

An Examination of Chicago Politics for Evidence of Political Incorporation and Representation

Dianne M. Pinderhughes

Editors' Note

Chicago was well known for many years as a traditional machine city led by Mayor Richard J. Daley. The two decades after his death in 1975 were marked by challenges to the machine and by racial polarization and conflict. Even though blacks constituted more than one-third of the population, they did not gain substantial political power. In 1983, Harold Washington became the first black mayor of Chicago and fought rather successfully to reform the machine and move the city toward progressive politics and policy.

Dianne Pinderhughes puts that story in a larger context, emphasizing Chicago's adaptation to constant changes in ethnic politics over the years. She shows that Chicago's black activists used demand-protest to increase electoral mobilization and formed coalitions of organizations to unify black groups and to cross racial lines in building a winning coalition. However, it was difficult to translate the electoral coalition into a governing coalition and after Washington's untimely death, the conflicts within the coalition could no longer be resolved. Ironically, increases in the black population and black electoral success were followed by intragroup conflict. However, whites when they were defeated, unified their efforts in ways they had not been able to do when they were a larger proportion of the population. Unity among whites and competition among blacks led to the success in 1991 of a new stable electoral coalition led by Richard M. Daley, the first Mayor Daley's son. However, Pinderhughes suggests that Harold Washington's administration has had a lasting impact on black politics in Chicago and on the new electoral coalition.

INTRODUCTION

For nearly two decades, Chicago politics was synonymous with volatile racial and ethnic conflict expressed in the political system. Richard J. Daley's 1975 election as mayor (his last) marked the beginning of the era, and the reelections of his son Richard M. Daley in 1991 and 1995 suggest the reestablishment of a stable electoral coalition. In between, Harold Washington's mayoral elections in 1983 and 1987 marked the creation of a distinctive political alternative, which proved unstable and short-lived after his death. As that dynamic era has gradually subsided, several questions arise that serve as the focus for this examination of racial and ethnic politics in Chicago in the context of Browning, Marshall, and Tabb's conception of the entrance into politics of racial and ethnic groups. First, what impact has the Washington coalition had on Chicago politics? Has Mayor Richard M. Daley created a stable electoral and bargaining structure so as to constitute a new Chicago political regime? (This structure was characterized by Stone as "the informal arrangements by which public bodies and private interests function together in order to be able to make and carry out governing decisions" [Stone 1989, 6]). What role do race and ethnicity play in contemporary Chicago politics now that black mayoral candidacies no longer seem to be viable? Does the post-Washington city government incorporate blacks and Hispanics in decision-making and policy-making structures and processes?

To answer these questions framed by Browning, Marshall, and Tabb (1984) as political incorporation, group mobilization, coalition formation, incorporation, and responsiveness, I review several areas.

The chapter provides a demographic portrait of Chicago as of the 1990 census, summarizes the dramatic electoral representation changes it has undergone in the last two decades, and illustrates the political constraints and opportunities these changes provide politicians and groups. I describe the complex array of leadership coalitions offered and rejected by the voters. I address the fusion of demand protest and electoral mobilization and governing activities developed by black activists. I consider Harold Washington's administration and the incorporation of blacks and Hispanics into the city council and other governmental bodies during his years in office and after, and I compare the experience of Chicago and several other cities. Was another Mayor Daley the inevitable successor "after Washington?" (Gove and Masotti 1982). Finally, what is the role of blacks, in terms of positions and policy, in this new era?

I use the broader conceptual framework of the political participation model to discuss changes that occurred in Chicago during this era. The political participation model predicts a group's likelihood of winning political leadership in terms of external variables that arise from outside the group's behavior, such as the structure and organization of the electoral system, demographic factors, and internal variables that have developed from the group's own specific history (Pinderhughes 1987).

THE POPULATION OF CHICAGO[1]

Political structures in Chicago reflect its long-term group heterogeneity. Since the late nineteenth century, Chicago has had densely complex ethnic populations that increased until the immigration reforms of the 1920s closed the borders. After immigration reform in 1965 reopened the borders and ended preferences for European immigrants, Asian Pacifics, South and Central Americans, and Africans settled in the city. Others such as Puerto Ricans and Mexican Americans also increased their numbers through long-term migratory patterns.

Demographic changes significantly shape Chicago's political environment but in citywide politics the largest groups are not necessarily the electoral victors. Poles were the largest white ethnic bloc, but Polish candidates were unsuccessful in mayoral primary contests against Mayor Daley in 1963 and against Daley's successor, Bilandic, in 1977. Another large group, African Americans, offered challengers in the primary in 1975 and 1977, also unsuccessfully. The Irish, one of the smaller white groups, have dominated the mayor's office and the machine for much of the century.

At the ward level, group representation appears rapidly. The nature of Chicago's political life translates demography into politics. The city council, with a large number of small wards, is organized around group-based representation and is especially sensitive to new groups. The building blocks of political life tend to rest on the geographic and political organization of these groups within wards. When a group settles within a single ward, as little as 2 percent of the voting-age population can elect an alderman.

The city's population became dramatically more diverse during the years between 1970 and 1995 as new groups arrived and older groups left the city and the metropolitan region (see Tables 5.1 and 5.2). In 1970, two-thirds of the population was non-Hispanic white, and in 1980, this figure had grown to 43.6 percent. By 1990, however, non-Hispanic whites accounted for only about 37 percent. By 1980, the city's total population had contracted by 10 percent, and it had declined again by 1990. The largest change, however, occurred with the growth of the Hispanic population—from 7.3 percent of the total in 1970 to 14 percent in 1980 and to 19.2 percent in 1990. By 1990, the populations of the city and the metropolitan region had declined more, as had the white and black populations. In 1970, blacks represented about one-third of the city; their proportion peaked at 39.5 percent in 1980, dropping to 39 percent by 1990. Although blacks were the largest single group by 1990, they had also increased their outmigration to the suburbs from 1980 to 1990, with the result that the total black population declined by 10 percent. Only the numbers of Asian Pacific Islanders and Latinos grew during the 1980s. The proportion of Latinos in Chicago's population reached 19.2 percent. Asians increased their numbers by nearly one-third to 3.7 percent in the city and by even greater percent-

---

[1] This section and part of the next are based on Pinderhughes 1994; see especially pp. 39-43 and 48-54.

TABLE 5.1 Chicago population by race, ethnicity and Hispanic origin, 1970–1990

Groups	1970[a]	%	1980	%	1990	%
African American	1,102,620	32.7	1,187,168	39.5	1,086,389	39.0
Asian Pacific			70,970	2.4	104,141	3.7
Hispanic	247,343[b]	7.3	423,357	14.0	535,315	19.2
White	2,207,767	65.5	1,311,808	43.6	1,265,953	38.2
Other Race[c]	56,570	1.6	11,775	.39	320,482	11.5
Total	3,366,957	100	3,005,078	100	2,783,726	100

[a]Data for places of 50,000 or more: Chicago City.

[b]People of Hispanic origin may be of any race.

[c]In 1970, "Other Race" includes Asian Pacific Islanders and Native Americans; by 1990 the vast majority in this category had self-identified as of "Other Race."

SOURCES: 1970: U.S. Bureau of the Census, Illinois, Vol. 1, Part 15, Section 1, Chapter B, Table 23: 15–105. 1980: U.S. Bureau of the Census, Illinois, Vol. 2, Part 15, Chapter 1, Table 59: 15–52. 1990: U.S. Bureau of the Census of Population and Housing, Summary Tape File 3A.

ages in suburban Cook County, the Collar Counties (outside of Cook), and the larger metropolitan area (Chicago Urban League 1994, 6).

These broad identities are much simpler than the actual racial and ethnic categories. Whites, for example, include European ethnic groups who are third- or fourth-generation citizens in the United States; the largest groups in order of size are Poles, Germans, and Irish, followed by Italians, Lithuanians, Russians, and Czechs. Asian Pacific groups include, also in order, Filipinos, Chinese, Asian Indians, Koreans, Japanese, and others. Most studies of Latinos in Chicago emphasize the city's atypical pan-ethnic diversity, including Mexican Americans, Puerto Ricans, and Cubans as the largest and most significant groups (Casuo and Camacho 1985; de la Garza et al. 1992; Padilla 1987). The 1990 census showed Guatemalans had replaced Cubans in number rank, followed by smaller groups from Central and South America (U.S. Bureau of the Census, 1990).[2] The African-American population has declined but has also grown more diverse, with 10,231 sub-Saharan Africans, 10,291 blacks of Hispanic origin, and 7,795 West Indians.

These shifts in the demographic character of the city have directly affected political life. In the 1970s and 1980s, whites competed among themselves, but as their proportion in the city has fallen, they have reduced their intragroup conflict in order to sustain citywide political leadership and have associated themselves into a

---

[2] The census designations follow varying and often changing preferences of the populations in question. The long-term emphasis on race in the American group pantheon has arbitrarily required groups to be categorized by their relationship to whites. During early census years in the century, for example, Mexican Americans were moved into and out of the Caucasian category. In recent years, the census first used *Spanish speaking* as a category, then in 1980 shifted to *Hispanic*, in which the group in question might be of any race. Thus the percentages indicated in Tabel 5.1 may add to significantly more than 100 percent because the categories mix race and culture.

TABLE 5.2   Percentage of population change by race and by location in metropolitan Chicago, 1980–1990

	White	African American	Latino	Other	Total
Chicago	−17.9%	−10.1%	+29.3%	+7.6%	−7.4%
Suburban Cook	−6.2%	+53.4%	+92.0%	+11.8%	+3.2%
Collar Counties	+11.7%	+31.1%	+75.5%	+68.4%	+16.5%
Metro Total	−3.2%	−.7%	+44.1%	+45.8%	+2.2%

SOURCE: Chicago, Metro Chicago Information Center, and Northern Illinois University, *Metro Chicago Political Atlas— 1994* (Springfield: Institute for Public Affairs, Sangamon State University, 1994).

predominantly white, loosely affiliated coalition. Blacks forged an intragroup coalition in the early 1980s that served as a basis for the broader, multiracial coalition through which Harold Washington was elected, but both disintegrated after his death. Blacks and whites competed for political leadership in the city, partly as a result of the changes in the city's demographics and partly as a result of the differing character of the relationship of blacks to the city's political frame of reference. Although blacks and whites approximate each other in population size, other groups such as Hispanics now command political representation. Asian Pacifics command attention in the political arena although they have not yet elected a representative to public office. Redistricting efforts seem to have focused on limiting rather than enhancing their opportunities for elected office (Bush 1984; Padilla 1987; Torres 1991).

The size of racial and ethnic populations is not the same as their voting-age populations, their voter registration, or their actual voter turnout. Table 5.3 presents the composition of Chicago's voting-age population from 1950 to the present. Whites fell from the dominant position in the electorate in 1950 to less than half the total in 1990; blacks rose from less than one-tenth of the total in 1940 to 35.7 percent in 1990. The census has reported the Hispanic voting-age population only since 1970; by 1990 Hispanics were 16.8 percent (Chicago Urban League 1994). More than three-quarters of the city's total voting age population was registered to vote at the beginning of the 1980s and that proportion actually increased until the mayoral and presidential election years of 1983 and 1984, with 79.9 percent and 78.9 percent, respectively (Chicago Urban League 1990, 61). After a decline in the late 1980s, registration had risen to 84.2 percent in 1992 (Chicago Urban League 1994, 10). Table 5.3 shows that 72.5 percent and 73.6 percent of the total voting-age population were registered in 1988 and 1989. Of the 1.56 million registered voters in the city, 52.2 percent were white, 41.4 percent were black, 5.7 percent were Latino, and the rest a combination of groups.

Several factors explain the differences between a group's voting-age population and its voter registration. One reason is the somewhat older age of the white population relative to the black and the Hispanic populations. Citizenship, language, and literacy are others. Puerto Ricans are citizens of the United States; many

TABLE 5.3 Racial and ethnic composition of Chicago's voting-age population, 1950–1995

	White	African American	Latino	Other
1950	86.5	13.4	N.A.	N.A.
1960	79.7	20.2	N.A.	N.A.
1970	67.2	27.1	5.6	N.A.
1980	53.5	37.5	7.5	1.3
1990	43.5	35.7	16.8	4.0
1995[a]	40.9	34.8	20.0	4.3

[a]Projected population.

SOURCE: Chicago Urban League, Metro Chicago Information Center, and Northern Illinois University, *Metro Chicago Political Atlas—1994* (Springfield: Institute for Public Affairs, Sangamon State University, 1994), 9.

Mexican Americans are not citizens or legal residents of this country. The 1975 extension of the 1965 Voting Rights Act outlawed English literacy tests for voting, so illiteracy is not a formal barrier to political participation; it may, however, be an informal one, especially for non-English-speaking groups.

Electoral Representation

The city's racial and ethnic groups reside in distinct locations so that neighborhoods and wards are easily identifiable for political purposes. Chicago is also often noted as one of the country's most segregated cities (Massey and Denton 1988). Zikmund (1982), Kleppner (1985), and the atlas of the Chicago Urban League/Northern Illinois University (Chicago Urban League 1990) divide the neighborhoods into racial and ethnic political enclaves. These have shifted over the years as the black population has grown, the white has shrunk, and the Puerto Rican and Mexican groups have established distinct residential locations on the northwest and south sides, respectively, and have grown in size. The city's politicians use detailed knowledge of racial and ethnic group location in the decennial redistrictings of local, state, and national office boundaries to acknowledge growth in some groups; more often, however, they use it to maintain the power of those designing the districts.

Chicago politics has traditionally been based on small unit politics. Whereas reform movements attacked ward politics, Chicago emphasized this pattern and moved from a 35-seat city council to a 50-seat council early in the century. New York City recently reorganized its council in this fashion in the 1990s (Mollenkopf 1992, 1995). Wards are a small enough prize to attract the interest of small and large groups and to enable these groups to win access to the city council. The wards also become the electoral building blocks used to win the mayor's office. The ability to control these wards in significant numbers, to turn out the vote, or to turn out voters in the numbers and for the candidates the party leaders have selected is of continuing concern to the party. The demographic changes in the city and the policy issues that arose from them challenged the machine at the most fundamental level in recent decades.

THE SEARCH FOR AN ELECTORAL
AND GOVERNING COALITION

The Balance of Power:
Demographics and Partisan Politics

The size of the black population is a critical factor shaping the opportunities for blacks to win election to office and to maintain control over the political process (Karnig and Welch 1980, 64). Cities with majority black populations, especially those over 65 percent, are especially likely to have elected black mayors on a sustained basis. Examples are Detroit; Washington, D.C.; Atlanta; and Gary, Indiana. When the black population is below 65 percent, the coalition is much less secure and more likely to be subject to the vagaries of partisan politics and/or intragroup fission—for example, New Orleans after Mayor Ernest Morial's term expired and Chicago after Harold Washington's death. Cities with black populations above 40 percent and below 65 percent of the total population find it possible to win control of city hall if they can minimize conflict within the group. Where the black electorate is a minority or only a narrow majority, possibilities of internal conflict *may* be more easily controlled because the stakes are clearer. Even cities with minorities of 38 percent or less may elect a black mayor, as Charlotte, Hartford, Los Angeles, Kansas City, and New York have done. That individual, however, must rely on a significantly broader multiracial coalition to win election than would be needed with a larger black proportion of the population.

Chicago's African-American and European-American populations are each too small to control the mayor's office on their own and must seek broader support from each other and from Latino voters. In multiracial, multi-ethnic settings, one group may also be able to mediate among competing interests, whether they are divided along socioeconomic, religious, racial, ethnic, or language dimensions. For much of this century, Irish politicians have led or managed complex coalitions of groups.

Richard J. Daley was first elected mayor of Chicago in 1955 with strong support from the black population, but black voters began to break away from the machine in the 1960s (Pinderhughes 1987, 240; Grimshaw 1982, 62; 1992). Middle-class black voters became more independent, and Daley began to rely more strongly on support from white ethnic wards that had not supported him in his earlier administrations. In the 1970s, poor black areas shifted toward independent status as community organizations arranged voter registration drives and get-out-the-vote campaigns.

Although there were shifts from one group to another, the machine always had support from both black and white wards. Zikmund shows that despite these electoral shifts, the machine cultivated the loyalty of a continuing core of voters across all racial and ethnic groups: machine core, reform/northshore wards, black wards, southside white ethnics, Polish northwest, and northside ethnics. Richard Newhouse, Edward Hanrahan, and Dick Singer challenged Daley in the 1975 primary, and Washington and Pucinski challenged Bilandic in 1977. Yet the black wards still produced a mean of 47.2 percent of their votes for Daley in 1975, and 46.2 percent for Bilandic in 1977 (Zikmund 1982, 49). Table 5.4 ranks mayoral winners' total votes by number. Mayor Daley won the largest vote in the 1971 general

TABLE 5.4   Mayoral votes ranked by winner's total

Winner's Total Votes	Year	Winner	Election[a]	Percentage of Total Votes Cast
740,137	1971	Daley	G	70
671,189	1979	Byrne	G	83.6
666,911	1983	Washington	G	51.6
600,252	1987	Washington	G	53.7
586,941	1987	Washington	P	53.5
576,620	1989	Daley II	G	55.4
542,817	1975	Daley	G	79.5
485,182	1989	Daley II	P	55.3
475,169	1977	Bilandic	G	77.3
463,623	1975	Daley	P	57.8
450,155	1991	Daley II	G	71.1
424,122	1983	Washington	P	38.1
412,909	1979	Byrne	P	51.0
407,730	1991	Daley II	P	32.2
342,301	1977	Bilandic	P	49.3

[a]G = general election; P = primary election

SOURCE: Dianne Pinderhughes, "Racial and Ethnic Politics in Chicago Mayoral Elections." In George E. Peterson, ed., *Big City Politics*, 42. Washington, D.C.: Urban Institute Press, 1994.

election, winning 70 percent of the total. His share dropped significantly in the 1975 primary; but even with three opponents, he still won 57.8 percent of the primary vote and 79.5 percent of the general election vote, winning majorities of the vote of the machine core, southside white ethnics, northside white ethnics, and Polish northwest. He won less than a majority only in the black wards and the reform/lakefront areas (Zikmund 1982, 49).

Mayor Bilandic was first elected by the Chicago city council after Daley's death in 1975. He won the mayoral primary in 1977 with only a plurality of the vote and the *lowest* voter turnout of all but two primaries and general elections between 1971 and 1995. In the general election, he improved his total turnout and won with 77.3 percent of the vote, but this election showed the first evidence of white ethnic conflict. In comparison to Daley's experience in 1975, Bilandic's mean proportion of support was stable in the machine core, the reform/northshore wards and the black wards, but he lost modest support among southside and northside white ethnics, and 20.7 percent in the Polish northwest wards (Zikmund 1982, 49).

The challengers from 1975 through 1995 represented stronger or weaker component units within the racial and ethnic elements of the machine. (Daley, already challenged by the reform and black sectors of the machine by 1975, was nevertheless able to hold on to a substantial portion of the vote in these areas.) Bilandic retained the same level of support as Daley in black and machine areas, but lost support in the white ethnic areas to Pucinski. In 1977, Washington improved his showing over Newhouse in the 1975 mayoral primary but performed poorly in all the other areas. Pucinski won more than half the vote in the Polish northwest side, and 41.6 percent in the reform/northshore areas, but no more than 30.5 percent in the rest (Zikmund 1982, 44–50).

The representatives of the major groups—Bilandic, Epton, Byrne, Daley, Washington, Sawyer, and Evans—and their challengers—Haider, Vrdolyak—in the years between 1977 and 1989 typically mobilized votes by race in only one or at the most two of these ward groups. Put more simply, they were able to generate interest among some of the white ethnic groups or some sectors of the black population, but rarely were they able to cross racial lines or generate interest across a number of sectors—which by the end of the era also included the Hispanic population. Those who mobilized across racial lines were successful: Bilandic in 1977, Byrne in 1979, Washington in 1983, Daley in 1989; those who moved away from a multiracial coalition to concentrate on their own group were defeated after one term: Bilandic in 1979, Byrne in 1983. Those who sustained interest across racial lines were reelected: Washington in 1987 and Daley in 1991 and 1995. Only a few of the challengers seemed able to understand the heterogeneous and competitive composition of the electorate and to be able to plan electoral strategy based on that new demographic reality.

In 1979, Jane Byrne, for example, won 11 out of 12 black wards and all the reform/northshore wards, split the Polish areas, and took less than a third of the vote in the remaining white ethnic and racially mixed machine areas. In that year, Byrne won 83.6 percent, the second highest number of votes in this era in a general election, as is shown in Table 5.4. She then proceeded to alienate her strongest base in her effort to lure white voters, at a point when the demographic changes suggested this would probably not have been worth the investment.

Byrne competed with Daley for the white ethnic and machine vote in the 1983 primary, abandoning the black vote to Washington; Bernard Epton, a previous unknown, became the Republican candidate in the general election. In the 1987 primary, Byrne challenged Washington while Edward Vrdolyak and Donald Haider ran as independent and Republican competitors against him.

Alderman Eugene Sawyer was nominated by the city council to succeed Washington after his death in 1987. Blacks saw Sawyer as the candidate of white northside and machine forces, this perception produced internal conflict over succession. Blacks limited their focus to the black ward groups; and as white groups had competed in 1983 and 1987, blacks competed in 1989, 1991, and 1995 rather than offer a single candidate in the primary and general elections. Latino voters allied with Washington in 1983 and 1987, but when black alderman Tim Evans challenged former alderman Mayor Sawyer, they shifted their support to Daley by 1989.

DEMAND-PROTEST, ELECTORAL MOBILIZATION, AND GOVERNING COALITIONS

In the ten northern California cities studied by Browning, Marshall, and Tabb, electoral politics followed an era of demand-protest. Chicago's activists fused demand-protest with electoral mobilization rather than engaging in periods of protest separated from and/or followed by electoral mobilization. Chicago's earliest black city council representation occurred in the second decade of the twentieth century, whereas representation on the county commission had occurred even earlier. Membership in a dominant racially liberal coalition, it can be argued, occurred on a number of occasions, as when William Hale Thompson was elected mayor in 1915, 1919, and 1927 in an alliance comparable to the relationship Latinos had with Mayor Harold Washington in 1983 and 1987, as a small but loyal and decisive group.

Chicago's black grassroots community organizations had to create the energy, the strategy, and the political relationships to mobilize themselves to place substantive policy concerns on the city council's and mayor's agenda. African Americans were represented inside the machine but had no real influence over the substantial racial discrimination in the city, which effectively demobilized them from the 1930s through the 1970s. They created electoral remobilization in the 1980s as a form of demand-protest. Black organizations used conflicts over Mayor Byrne's appointments to the school board and public housing board as well as over ChicagoFest as a basis for protest—but protest that was specifically framed within and used as an engine to respond electorally. They emphasized these issues in the October 1982 voter registration drive, which laid the foundation for a strong Washington challenge in the 1983 primary.

Starks and Preston described how the creation of coalitions of organizations, combined with identification of a single enormously popular black candidate in the person of Harold Washington, framed a mayoral campaign. When the leaders of coalitions of organizations, the Task Force for Black Political Empowerment and Chicago Black United Communities, asked Harold Washington to run for mayor, he required them to increase voter registration by at least 50,000 and raise $250,000 (Starks and Preston 1990, 95). Washington had legislative experience at the state and national levels, characterized himself as an "independent machine politician" and had deep roots in the labor movement (Travis 1987). His 1983 mayoral primary campaign supported by a unified and mobilized black electorate was balanced and enhanced by the competition between Byrne and Daley. Washington won nearly 80 percent and 73 percent of the vote in the southside and westside wards, which, with a majority of the Latino vote and small support from whites, produced a 38.1 percent plurality in the primary and 51.6 percent in the general election.

The successful fusion of demand-protest with electoral goals and the conventional structure of interest organizations left the black community with a serious political problem after Washington's election. An electoral coalition and a governing coalition, as Mayor Washington and his supporters discovered very quickly, are two different things. Running a government and formulating policy were things the black community had not done previously. Chicago had no tradition of deliberative policy making by a broad popular coalition. Squires, Bennett, McCourt, and Nyden (1987) and Suttles (1990) note that there were no integrative, citywide public structures to manage such a process.

It is important to consider what structures were available for participation in that process, what types of organizations existed, what types of tasks had been engaged in previously, and with what tasks the organizations were most familiar. Several associations of organizations had grown into structures that mobilized and unified the black community for the mayoral campaign: the Task Force for Black Political Empowerment, Chicago Black United Communities, and VOTE as well as a complex array of neighborhood groups, professional organizations, social groups, religious bodies, even some ward organizations. Basically, most existing organizations that were not conventionally politically oriented were linked together and transformed into electoral mobilizing committees in support of Washington's election (Alkalimat and Gills 1984).

Traditionally, black organizations combine the sacred and secular, with churches often serving as umbrellas for secular activities. Black religious, social, and professional organizations also integrate activities that might be treated separately by white interest groups at the national level. Chicago's black political groups reflected similar patterns. Harold Washington played the role of a secular substitute for an electoral leader of the type represented by the late congressman and minister Adam Clayton Powell, or by the late Elijah Muhammad of the Nation of Islam. Washington, elevated above the mass united by organizations of organizations in singular, hierarchical fashion, articulated the political and material as well as the moral goals and interests of the black community to the larger white city (Morris 1984; Hamilton 1991).

This structure worked for blacks in pressing forward the civil rights movement and in winning control of the Chicago mayor's office; it also works especially well for managing crises, for meeting political challenge, for mounting protest, and for mobilizing voters. This structure has not, however, been used to develop or maintain grassroots interest in governing and policy making, in contacting and communicating with public officials, or in negotiating with or choosing among political leaders within the community.

During the election and for most of Washington's first term, the coalition protested, mobilized, and challenged the machine, which was controlled by white ethnic groups. Washington's election to office had not secured a voting majority in the city council or over city agencies; Washington's support of the Shakman decree recognizing civil service protection over city jobs weakened his control. In 1986, Washington's supporters defeated enough machine representatives in black or mixed wards to control the city council. Washington won the mayor's office in 1983 and was reelected in 1987; in his first term he eventually won a majority on the city council. He was to learn, however, that governing was quite different from winning elections.

Black Chicagoans differed by class, education, income, occupation, and their choices of leaders and policy. Mediating among the complex range of interests that were part of the Washington coalition was a major task even for Harold Washington. Differences appeared among African Americans and even among the organizations over how to identify economic policy, how to organize and manage the schools in light of poor student scores and rising deficits, how to judge environmental safety and other issues. At Harold Washington's death, the African-American community and therefore the city were immediately confronted with conflicts over leadership succession that were not resolved successfully within the black population.

The black political structure that elected Harold Washington was thus not organized for the governance process, for contacting public officials, for concentrating on specialized policy areas, and for developing sustained accountability. This problem is neither new nor unique to Chicago groups, but it reflects the long history of political, social, and economic discrimination and exclusion of African Americans from public life in the broadest terms.

In the fusion of protest and electoral mobilization leading to the Washington era, race and representation were increasingly linked by grassroots organizations, as much by the nature of the organizational structure and process as by the policies articulated by them. Washington's own preferences and understanding of the city's demographics meant that while he aimed at full mobilization of the black community, he also sustained his ties to labor and reached out to other racial and ethnic groups who would accept his leadership.

HAROLD WASHINGTON: LIBERAL TENDENCIES AND BLACK POLITICAL INCORPORATION

Political incorporation, group mobilization, coalition formation, and responsiveness are the core variables in Browning, Marshall, and Tabb's study. Chicago is the city with the political tradition that has demonstrated wide flexibility and creativity in its responsiveness to a series of racial and ethnic groups over the span of the twentieth century. Browning, Marshall, and Tabb also compare the demand-protest cycles they found in ten northern California cities with the era of electoral participation in which blacks and Hispanics began to elect representatives to city councils, and in some cases to mayor's offices.

New York City is the great anomaly, Mollenkopf argues, because it produced relatively liberal policies even though blacks and Latinos remained outside its structure of power. Atlanta's regime politics links the large economic interests and the city's political leaders; San Franciscans' electoral politics involves competition among three sources of left politics. Chicago presents another type of anomaly. Chicago's political structure produces routine, even swift, descriptive political representation, but blacks and other ethnic groups remain outside the substantive policy-making arenas and there is little competition over liberal policy. The city has small precincts and wards dominated by single racial and ethnic groups. The wards are joined together in the city council, but there are few other citywide arenas in which racial and ethnic groups operate. The city's large economic interests tend to interact directly with the mayor outside the ward-based city council. Racial and ethnic groups have limited impact on the mayoral-economic interest interaction, and liberal reform, therefore, rarely occurs (DeLeon 1992; Mollenkopf 1995; Stone 1989).

Before Washington, Chicago's politics over the last three-quarters of a century moved between unregulated, highly competitive group politics and highly centralized, regulated political monopoly. In neither case was policy making an expertise-based, deliberative policy process into which the racial and ethnic groups were drawn. The Washington administration moved the city away from the confines of the machine dimension onto another more deliberative continuum, which combined liberal policy, racial and ethnic interests, and ward politics.[3]

On the ethnic dimension-machine dimension, Washington's administration strengthened cross-group political alliances, continued the detachment of the civil service from the machine, created policy-based entitlements in the form of civil rights ordinances for relatively weak groups, and promoted greater recognition of political rights of several groups, including African Americans, gays and lesbians, women, and Latinos (Clavel and Wiewel 1991). On the policy-making dimension, Washington had to create policy-making infrastructures where none had existed and bend those in existence in directions in which they had not yet gone. In effect, he had to create constituency, institutional, and policy-making connections simultaneously—a gargantuan task.

Starks and Preston noted that African Americans had already achieved participation, substantial representation, and "modest" incorporation in Chicago government and within the Democratic party for some time prior to Harold Washington's election to the mayoralty. Nevertheless, Starks and Preston felt this gain was "sharply limited in its impact on policy" (1990, 92). The black population concluded, they argued, that "much more could be achieved if the reins of political power could be grasped by blacks as leaders of a multiracial coalition. Only in this way could government and party agendas be restructured so that black interests were protected and realized" (Starks and Preston 1990, 91).

Evaluations of political incorporation thus require examination of both these areas: the public electoral arena in which fierce racial and ethnic competition occurs, and the more cloaked policy-making arena in which large economic interests seek their concerns. Despite considerable challenges, the Washington administration made headway in both these areas.

Not only had the machine's white ethnic leaders not been responsive; they had been highly resistant to the demands and interests of the black community. Chicago's political regime differed from those found in most of the northern California cities in *Protest Is Not Enough,* except for Oakland in the 1960s and 1970s. Oakland was an industrial city with an industrial labor force and a strong and concentrated white power structure, capable of considerable political and economic resistance to minority challenges to the racial status quo. Oakland and Chicago were similar in that minority incorporation at the highest levels outlined by Browning, Marshall, and Tabb was considerably delayed: representation on the city council, representation within coalitions that controlled liberal reformist policy making on minority issues, and minority control of the mayor's office.[4]

---

[3] See Pinderhughes 1987, 39-48, for a more detailed discussion and conceptualizations of the evolution of competition and monopoly in Chicago politics. See also Keiser 1993.

[4] There were even similar reactions to their respective grass roots young male political activists; the Black Panthers in Oakland and Chicago and the Black Stone Rangers in Chicago were met with challenge, violence, and political repression by public officials. I think it can be argued that the Chicago response weas even more intense and decisive than that in Oakland, where some segments of the Panthers were left to offer candidacies for political office.

In Chicago, only Hyde Park and north Lakeshore harbored a genuine white liberal constituency; there was only a weak basis for a white liberal coalition taking control of city hall from the immigrant, industrially based population groups that controlled city hall after 1931. In fact, the black challenge to the segments of the traditional white ethnic machine's leadership was beneficial to white liberals and reformers. Within a black administration elected with the support of Latino voters, the white liberals had more space to influence policy than they had previously enjoyed.

Solving leadership succession crises and sustaining interest in policy making, even when the mayor in office represents black interests, is problematic. The literature on the Washington administration suggests policy reform of at least a modest sort. Pelissero and Holian (1994) show that minority mayors in 12 cities including Chicago increased general expenditures and also increased debt per capita in five of the six. Bennett (1993) shows that Washington distributed benefits to black wards, but in order to avoid being accused of favoritism, "he was careful to budget, if anything, a surplus of spending in anti-Washington wards" (432). Washington was not always able to balance the interests of his core black supporters and his Latino allies, according to Bennett's examination of hiring proportions, to the latter's satisfaction. "For Washington, effectively delivered city services were perfectly consistent with minority empowerment. . . . Although Washington shied away from welfare-state-style redistribution of resources, his administration's collaboration with community-based organizations helped stretch city resources and offered neighborhoods across the city—not just on Chicago's black south and west sides—enhanced access to city government" (Bennett 1993, 438).

CHICAGO AFTER HAROLD WASHINGTON

Citywide Politics

By his 1987 reelection Washington's electoral and governing coalition had solidified his political base to the extent that his voting majority in the city council shifted dramatically upward from a bare majority to 40 or more votes in designating committee appointments.

The 1987 mayoral election held within the city council immediately after Mayor Washington's death suggests that the black and white communities simultaneously polarized during the campaign (Hawking 1991). Whites and blacks preferred one candidate and came to see the other as the nominee of their enemies. The polarization identified Sawyer as the nominee of whites and Evans as the nominee of blacks. That split and the community's inability to compromise led to two black candidates in the 1989 special election and guaranteed internal competition among blacks, a group that was a minority of the population and the voting-age population. The 1989 pattern, which mirrored that among whites in 1983 and elected Harold Washington, was repeated in the 1991 and 1995 mayoral elections. A succession of black candidates competed against one white, Richard M. Daley, who was consistently supported by white voters, and against each other in the primary and in the general election, thereby strengthening rather than weakening the party's nominee.

After Washington's death in 1987 and Daley's election in 1989, Mayor Daley could easily reinvigorate the traditional relations of the varying sectors of the white community and begin incrementally to increase his support in the black sector. The strategy that failed with Sawyer and Evans was used again to Daley's electoral advantage in 1991. The black candidate in the mayoral primary from the West Side, Danny Davis, won only 198,000 votes. Eugene Pincham ran as an independent in the general elections in April and won 159,608 votes. In 1995, Mayor Daley was reelected; the black primary candidate Joseph Gardner, Metropolitan Water Reclamation District commissioner, won 164,969 votes, 29 percent of the vote, to Daley's 70 percent in the primary, but the turnout was only 40 percent of the city's registered voters. In the general election in 1994, black Democratic gubernatorial nominee Roland Burris, former comptroller and secretary of state, challenged the mayor as an independent and won 207,464 votes, 35.8 percent of the total turnout of about 41 percent of the registered voters. Miriam Santos, elected treasurer on the Democratic ticket, ran well ahead of the mayor by about 80,000 votes. The division in the black community grew more substantial when Senator Carol Moseley-Braun and Dempsey Travis endorsed Daley (*Chicago Tribune,* March 2 and April 6, 1995; *Washington Post,* February 26 and March 1, 1995). One might speculate, therefore, that there is some incorporation of the black population as a result of this protest–electoral mobilization cycle. Daley increased his support among black voters and won the Latino wards decisively. On the other hand, turnout dropped to about 40 percent in the primary and general elections, which suggests that some proportion of the population has withdrawn from participation.

The consolidation of a new Chicago electoral coalition took the following form: large turnout and high loyalty among white voters, combined with a small percentage of black voters, and strong majorities from the small but electorally significant Latino population. Several factors explain the change. First, African Americans lost focus and competed over goals and leadership at the polls. Where they had supported only Harold Washington in the primaries and general elections in 1983 and 1987, they offered multiple candidates in both contests in 1989, 1991, and 1995. The black electorate gradually demobilized and generated lower turnout. Second, European ethnic groups competed with Mayor Richard J. Daley in the 1970s and with each other with abandon in the early 1980s; after 1989, they constrained their disagreements and concentrated support on a single mayoral candidate in the primaries and in the general elections. Finally, Latino voters shifted from 70 percent and 80 percent support for Mayor Washington in the 1987 primary and general elections to 50 percent in the 1989 special elections; by the 1995 mayoral elections, more than 80 percent of Latinos supported Mayor Daley.

Daley consolidated his hold on the mayor's office with large white turnouts and high loyalty, reduced turnout but increasing proportions of black voters, and small turnouts but increasing support from Latino voters. The 1995 election confirmed this pattern. Mayor Daley was reelected again, making him the mayor with the greatest longevity "after Daley" (Gove and Masotti 1982).

Ward-Level Politics

At the ward level in Chicago's public life, African-American and Latino electoral representation is significant and subject to competition, bargaining, and lawsuits. On a 50-member city council, blacks hold 19 and Latinos hold seven seats. There are 20 majority black wards (in the Eighteenth, blacks hold a narrow majority and a white alderman represents it) and seven majority Latino. Representation of blacks on the council approximates their proportion of the population (39 percent), whereas Latinos are somewhat underrepresented in comparison with their total (14 percent). Among those racial and ethnic groups with city council representation, Latinos are the only one whose population increased in the 1990s. In 1991, blacks held 18 seats and Latinos four. Black representation increased when Fifth Ward alderman Larry Bloom entered the 1995 race for city treasurer, opening his seat to a win by Barbara Holt; the ward that includes Hyde Park and the University of Chicago had been majority black for some decades. Latinos gained three new wards in the redistricting necessitated by the 1990 census.

After the 1990 census, city council redistricting culminated in a 1992 citywide referendum on alternative redistricting proposals offered by administration versus independent aldermen. The mayor and administration aldermen proposed an "Equity Map" that preserved greater representation for whites—23 wards although there are 200,000 fewer whites in the city in 1990 than there had been in 1980—and 20 black wards. Black and white independent aldermen proposed the "Fair Map," which increased the number of black wards to 22, gave the Eighteenth a large majority, and reduced white wards to 21. Both groups proposed seven Latino wards, but white wards were preserved in the administration's proposal by stabilizing black and staunching Latino expansion. The alternative proposal split southeast side Hispanics into two wards.

The administration's map won 61 percent of the vote and reflected an electoral pattern that began with the 1989 mayoral election. Richard Daley and his allies turned out overwhelming proportions of white voters, about one-fifth of black voters, and at least three-quarters of Latino voters. Black aldermen turned out lower proportions of their supporters and won only about three-quarters to four-fifths of their votes. Latino turnout was low but directed primarily toward Mayor Daley's position.

Three lawsuits have since been filed in federal court charging discrimination in the equity redistricting plan. Independent aldermen in *Smith v. Daley* and *Barnett v. Daley,* and Latinos in *Bonilla v. Daley* sued the city for greater black (22 wards) and Latino (8 or 9) city council representation. The administration's allies include Latinos and blacks.

CONCLUSION

First, what impact has the Washington coalition had on Chicago politics? Has Mayor Richard M. Daley created a stable electoral and bargaining structure, a new Chicago political regime? What role do race and ethnicity play in contemporary Chicago politics now that black mayoral candidacies no longer seem to be viable? Does the post-Washington city government incorporate blacks and Hispanics in decision-making and policy-making structures and processes?

Harold Washington's campaigns and administration had a dramatic impact on African-American participation, mobilization, and incorporation. Although Chicago no longer has a black mayor, for the first time blacks now hold countywide and statewide positions; elections are not always polarized if voters can be mobilized by appeals simultaneously to race and to some other factors such as gender, their status as independent voters, or class. Carol Moseley-Braun was elected to the U.S. Senate in 1992, and John Stroger was elected chairman of the Cook County Board in 1994. Inside the city, elections remain highly polarized although portions of the black population, including opinion leaders like Senator Moseley-Braun and Dempsey Travis, have begun to support Mayor Daley. In the wards, competition for office remains intense and highly group oriented. Daley has placed some blacks in office in order to sustain his support in black areas. In policy-making areas Daley has moved away from the reforms initiated during the Washington era.

In the last 20 years, Chicago's voters have sampled different political leaders, substantive policies, and policy approaches. Mayor Daley's death offered the city the opportunity to consider leaders from an array of political coalitions, to consider different substantive policy emphases—such as economic development, physical infrastructure, school reform and housing—and to consider different strategies of resource distribution and fiscal policy. This chapter has examined the differing po-litical resolutions that successive mayoral elections offered and analyzed why they did or did not result in stable coalitions.

Some coalitions, such as the Bilandic and Evans solutions, were not tenable— that is, they were not workable. Others could not survive the death of their leader, Harold Washington. Others were tenable but could not survive, subject to coalition drift or unstable coalitions—namely the Byrne and Sawyer coalitions. Balancing the competing interests in political leadership of diverse groups that also interconnect with economic status, and increasingly with partisan differences, makes manage-ment of the city's political and economic life a complex challenge.

REFERENCES

Alkalimat, Abdul (Gerald McWorter), and Doug Gills. 1984. Black Power vs. Racism: Harold Washington Becomes Mayor. In Rod Bush, ed., *The New Black Vote: Politics and Power in Four American Cities,* 53–180. San Francisco: Synthesis.

Bennett, Larry. 1993. Harold Washington and the Black Urban Regime. *Urban Affairs Quarterly* 28 (March): 423–440.

Browning, Rufus P., Dale Rogers Marshall, and David H. Tabb. 1984. *Protest Is Not Enough: The Struggle of Blacks and Hispanics for Equality in Urban Politics.* Berkeley: University of California Press.

Bush, Rod, ed. 1984. *The New Black Vote: Politics and Power in Four American Cities.* San Francisco: Synthesis.

Casuo, Jorge, and Eduardo Camacho. 1985. Hispanics in Chicago, Conclusion. *The Chicago Reporter* 14 (April): 1–4.

Chicago Urban League and Northern Illinois University. 1990. *CUL/NIU Atlas: Chicago Politics 1990*. Chicago and DeKalb: Social Science Research Institute, Northern Illinois University and the Chicago Urban League.

Chicago Urban League, Metro Chicago Information Center, and Northern Illinois University. 1994. *Metro Chicago Political Atlas—1994*. Springfield: Institute for Public Affairs, Sangamon State University.

Clavel, Pierre, and Wim Wiewel, eds. 1991. *Harold Washington and the Neighborhoods: Progressive City Government in Chicago, 1983–1987*. New Brunswick, N.J.: Rutgers University Press.

de la Garza, Rudolfo O., Louis DeSipio, F. Chris Garcia, John Garcia, and Angelo Falcon. 1992. *Latino Voices: Mexican, Puerto Rican, and Cuban Perspectives on American Politics*. Boulder, Colo.: Westview Press.

DeLeon, Richard Edward. 1992. *Left Coast City Progressive Politics in San Francisco, 1975–1991*. Lawrence: University Press of Kansas.

Gove, Samuel K., and Louis H. Masotti, eds. 1982. *After Daley: Chicago Politics in Transition*. Urbana: University of Illinois Press.

Grimshaw, William. 1982. The Daley Legacy and Declining Politics of Party, Race and Public Unions. In Samuel K. Gove and Louis H. Masotti, eds., *After Daley: Chicago Politics in Transition*, 57–87. Urbana: University of Illinois Press.

Grimshaw, William. 1992. *Bitter Fruit: Black Politics and the Chicago Machine, 1931–1991*. Chicago: University of Chicago Press.

Hamilton, Charles V. 1991. *Adam Clayton Powell, Jr.: The Political Biography of an American Dilemma*. New York: Macmillan.

Hawking, Jim. 1991. We Have a Mayor. *Chicago Reporter* 20 (December): 3–5, 10.

Karnig, Albert, and Susan Welch. 1980. *Black Representation and Urban Policy*. Chicago: University of Chicago Press.

Keiser, Richard A. 1993. Explaining African-American Political Empowerment: Windy City Politics from 1900 to 1983. *Urban Affairs Quarterly* 29 (September): 84–116.

Kleppner, Paul. 1985. *Chicago Divided, the Making of a Black Mayor*. DeKalb: Northern Illinois University Press.

Massey, Douglas S., and Nancy A. Denton. 1988. Suburbanization and Segregation in U.S. Metropolitan Areas. *American Journal of Sociology* 94 (November): 592–626.

Mollenkopf, John Hull. 1992. *A Phoenix in the Ashes: The Rise and Fall of the Koch Coalition in New York City Politics*. Princeton, N.J.: Princeton University Press.

Mollenkopf, John. 1995. New York, The Great Anomaly. Paper prepared for presentation at the American Political Science Association, September.

Morris, Aldon M. 1984. *The Origins of the Civil Rights Movement: Black Communities Organizing for Change*. New York: Free Press.

Padilla, Felix. 1987. *Puerto Rican Chicago*. Notre Dame, Ind.: University of Notre Dame Press.

Pelissero, John P., and David B. Holian, II. 1994. Electing a Minority Mayor: The Impact on City Finances and Employment. Paper presented at the American Political Science Association, New York, September 1–4.

Pinderhughes, Dianne M. 1987. *Race and Ethnicity in Chicago Politics: A Reexamination of Pluralist Theory*. Urbana: University of Illinois Press.

Pinderhughes, Dianne M. 1994. Racial and Ethnic Politics in Chicago Mayoral Elections. In George E. Peterson, ed., *Big City Politics: Governance and Fiscal Constraints*, 37–62. Washington, D.C.: Urban Institute Press.

Squires, Gregory D., Larry Bennett, Kathleen McCourt, and Philip Nyden. 1987. *Race, Class and the Response to Urban Decline*. Philadelphia: Temple University Press.

Starks, Robert T., and Michael B. Preston. 1990. Harold Washington and the Politics of Reform in Chicago 1983–1987. In Rufus P. Browning, Dale Rogers Marshall, and David H. Tabb, eds., *Racial Politics in American Cities*, 88–107. White Plains, N.Y.: Longman.

Stone, Clarence N. 1989. *Regime Politics Governing Atlanta 1946–1988*. Lawrence: University Press of Kansas.

Studlar, Donley T. 1992. Review, Racial Politics in American Cities. *National Political Science Review* 3: 238–240.

Suttles, Gerald D. 1990. *The Man-Made City: The Land Use Confidence Game in Chicago*. Chicago: University of Chicago Press.

Torres, Maria de los Angeles. 1991. The Commission on Latino Affairs: A Case Study of Community Empowerment. In Pierre Clavel and Wim Wiewel, eds., *Harold Washington and the Neighborhoods: Progressive City Government in Chicago*, 165–187. New Brunswick, N.J.: Rutgers University Press.

Travis, Dempsey J. 1987. *An Autobiography of Black Politics*. Chicago: Urban Research Press.

Turner, Margery. 1991. *Opportunities Denied, Opportunities Diminished: Discrimination in Hiring*. Washington, D.C.: Urban Institute Press.

U.S. Bureau of the Census. 1990. Census of Population, Summary Tape File 3A, Illinois, Ancestry, Hispanic Origin. CD-ROM.

Zikmund, Joseph, II. 1982. Mayoral Voting and Ethnic Politics in the Daley-Bilandic-Byrne Era. In Samuel K. Gove and Louis H. Masotti, eds., *After Daley: Chicago Politics in Transition*, 27–56. Urbana: University of Illinois Press.

chapter **6**

Progressive Politics in the Left Coast City: San Francisco

Richard E. DeLeon

Editors' Note

    Many observers view San Francisco as the last outpost of urban liberalism among large U.S. cities. Richard DeLeon agrees but cautions that the city's liberalism has become too wide ranging and unfocused—a "politics of everything." One result has been a lack of attention to the still-unfinished struggle for racial equality. As shrinking numbers of African Americans try to defend hard-won gains from right-wing attacks at the state and national levels, the city's growing Asian and Latino populations are mobilizing to achieve electoral clout and political incorporation. DeLeon contends that multiracial coalitions are essential to political success in the city's hyperpluralistic system. His analysis of the "political chemistry" of coalition building shows how different combinations of group interest and ideology can attract or repel potential allies. He argues that African Americans, in particular, confront difficult obstacles in forging stable electoral alliances with Latinos, Asians, and white progressives. Liberal on economic issues but conservative on social and environmental issues, many African Americans have come to feel isolated and estranged from mainstream city politics. DeLeon concludes with an analysis of Willie Brown's victory over Roberta Achtenberg and incumbent Frank Jordan in the 1995 mayoral election. As San Francisco's first African-American mayor, Willie Brown promises to make his administration the most racially and ethnically inclusive in the city's history. Brown is a progrowth mayor inclined to think big about San Francisco's future; however, it remains to be seen whether he can advance racial justice without dismantling the city's slow-growth policies and alienating his white progressive support.

Even in San Francisco, a city renowned for its cosmopolitan diversity and political tolerance, the struggle for racial equality continues. Long shut out of city hall, Asians and Latinos have mobilized in recent years and are moving from the periphery toward the center of political power. African Americans, on the other hand, have lost ground in what could turn out to be the first stage of a process of political disincorporation—a process that might be reversed in the wake of Willie Brown's victory over incumbent Frank Jordan in the 1995 mayoral election. San Francisco's once-dominant white ethnic working class has shrunk into a few scattered neighborhood enclaves. The city's white professional middle-class liberals, having vanquished downtown business in the growth control wars of the 1980s, now control the Board of Supervisors and have the power both to help and hinder Mayor Brown. Highly educated and politically correct, many of these "white progressives" see themselves as the vanguard of a new politics for the twenty-first century. In matters of race, however, they have put first things last in their efforts to build a progressive urban regime.

LIBERAL OASIS

San Francisco not only survived the Republican onslaught that toppled Democrats from power in the 1994 elections but actually polished its image as the nation's capital of progressivism. The city's voters reelected all local Democrats holding seats in the state legislature and in the U.S. House of Representatives. In statewide races, huge majorities voted to keep Democrat Dianne Feinstein in the U.S. Senate and backed Democrat Kathleen Brown in her losing campaign against incumbent Republican governor Pete Wilson. Bucking the conservative tide, a mere 29 percent supported Proposition 187, the anti-illegal immigration measure that won 59 percent of the statewide vote. Only 42 percent joined the 3 to 1 statewide majority in passing the wildly popular "Three Strikes" anticrime initiative. San Francisco voters also retired the lone Republican (Annemarie Conroy) from the city's Board of Supervisors and elected two new Democrats (gay activist Tom Ammiano and career educator Mabel Teng), creating a solid liberal-progressive majority that would eventually obstruct Mayor Jordan's conservative initiatives and undermine his reelection campaign.

"Some people think of us as the United States of San Francisco," joked Mayor Jordan after the 1994 election. Supervisor Terence Hallinan, the most liberal of liberals on the board, commented: "We're conservative about being liberal. Our traditions are well entrenched. They're not subject to swings the way the rest of the state and country are" ("City's Liberal Reputation" 1994). Even with the formidable Willie Brown in charge at city hall, San Francisco's liberal leaders know that their isolated victories could prove short and bittersweet. The 1994 elections dramatically changed the state and national context of urban politics. The war against the cities being waged by Republicans and southern and suburban Democrats is accelerating (Davis 1993). The federal government's steady abandonment of cities (Caraley

1992) is turning into a full-scale retreat under President Bill Clinton. House Speaker Newt Gingrich and his new Republican majority began translating the GOP's Contract with America into a repressive approach to urban problems and the issues of race. Democrats at the national level now have much less power on committees to oppose draconian cuts in urban programs and attacks on the hard-won social and economic rights of urban communities of color. At the state level, Republican governor Pete Wilson continues to promote harsh restrictions on immigrants and the dismantling of affirmative action. Meanwhile, absent long-time Assembly Speaker Willie Brown, the Republican-controlled state legislature persists in its policy of urban neglect and its obsession with building prisons rather than schools. Its political defenses weakened, San Francisco remains an oasis of liberalism. But the desert creeps closer with each passing day.

THE PROGRESSIVE ANTIREGIME

As San Franciscans buckle in for the rough ride ahead in state and national politics, the critical challenge they face locally is how to build a progressive urban regime with the economic vitality and governing capacity needed to control their own destiny. An urban regime consists of the "informal arrangements by which public bodies and private interests function together in order to be able to make and carry out governing decisions" (Stone 1989, 6). A progressive urban regime is one that encourages an expanded role for local government in achieving distributive justice, limits on growth, neighborhood preservation, and ethnic-cultural diversity under conditions of public accountability and direct citizen participation (DeLeon 1992, 33).

After nearly two decades of mobilizing a grassroots community revolt against a business-dominated progrowth coalition, San Francisco's progressives in 1986 passed growth caps, linkage fees, neighborhood preservation policies, and citizen participation requirements that loosened the grip of capital on the city's physical and economic development (Wirt 1974; Mollenkopf 1983; Hartman 1984; DeLeon 1992). They followed that by electing liberal Art Agnos as mayor in 1987 and a liberal-progressive majority on the Board of Supervisors in 1988. These victories moved the city in the direction of a progressive regime. This movement came to a halt in 1991, however, when popular disenchantment with Mayor Agnos's abrasive personality and progrowth initiatives fractured the progressive coalition, sabotaged his reelection campaign, and ushered Frank Jordan into office.

The city now has an "antiregime" constituted of a loose network of environmental organizations, neighborhood groups, political clubs, and local government leaders. The antiregime coalition is easily mobilized to protect community from capital. It has succeeded in blocking large-scale projects and limiting their harmful effects. But it has failed thus far to harness capital to serve an ambitious social agenda (DeLeon 1992, 99). This stalement between community and capital will probably persist as long as both sides remain internally divided and politically disorganized.

San Francisco's extreme social and racial diversity, decentralized government, weak political leadership, and fragmented business elite all combine to undermine the capacity to govern (Wirt 1974; Savitch and Thomas 1991). The city's antiregime is good news for many white, middle-class environmentalists and neighborhood preservationists who cherish the city's "quality of life" and prefer to keep things more or less the way they are. It is bad news, however, for the city's nonwhite, working-class residents and the poor. Many fail to see how their own lives will be improved by scaring off big business investments, banning developments that generate jobs, and blocking demolitions in the neighborhoods that make room for affordable housing. In the domain of land use and development policy, these conflicts of interest and ideology between middle-class whites and working-class nonwhites obstruct the formation of a stable progressive urban regime.

THE POLITICS OF EVERYTHING

Over the last quarter century, consistent with its traditions of openness and political tolerance, San Francisco has earned its reputation as a "Sanctuary City." It is home to people of all races and classes, refugees and immigrants, gays and lesbians, beats and hippies, misfits and nonconformists, and more than a few counterculture McGovernites. To a significant degree, these varied groups and interests have achieved political voice and formal representation in San Francisco's highly decentralized governmental system. At a time when many anxious Americans have grown hostile toward social and racial diversity, San Franciscans continue to welcome and celebrate it.

The problem with such diversity is that it makes politics complicated, governance almost impossible, and democracy hard work. It engenders multiple and shifting lines of conflict, unstable coalitions and alliances, and an unfocused agenda for public policy debate. Cross-cutting cleavages, divided loyalties, and compound identities make political life interesting in San Francisco. But they can also corrode the bonds of shared values and grind things to a halt while diverse citizens struggle endlessly to define who they are and what politics should be about.

In San Francisco, politics is about everything; therefore, it is about nothing for very long. The politics of race must compete for public attention with gender politics, gay and lesbian politics, neighborhood politics, environmental politics, labor politics, and the politics of land use and development. Citizens find it hard to respond coherently to so many simultaneous appeals to racial, gender, turf, and class solidarities. And the politicians, like chameleons placed on plaid, contort themselves in trying to be all things to all people—anything to get elected. If San Francisco can be said to have a collective political mind, the only word to describe it is "confused."

San Francisco's white middle-class progressives have fanned out to engage in political battles over gay rights, reproductive choice, environmental justice, open space, growth limits, consumer protection, and other such causes. The city's non-white working-class liberals, on the other hand, have circled the wagons to protect modest gains in the areas of employment, housing, education, affirmative action, and social services from growing right-wing attacks. These conflicts over goals and priorities have been accompanied by expressions of anger, resentment, and a sense of betrayal on both sides.

The politics of everything is extremely frustrating for those who think politics should be more about race and who view a deracialized politics as benign neglect at best and racist at worst. That frustration is evident in the comments of Lulann McGriff, president of the San Francisco chapter of the National Association for the Advancement of Colored People: "To the outside world San Francisco touts itself as a very liberal city. My own perception is that it is probably one of the most racist cities in the country" (quoted in Gordon and Raine 1994, A1). In the recent afterglow of the city's triumphant liberalism, assessor Doris Ward (a black) charged, "This town is not as progressive as its image might suggest. When it comes to things that have nothing to do with ethnicity, we are progressive. But when it comes to race or cultural issues, we're not as progressive as Mississippi . . . and maybe Mississippi is better" (quoted in Johnson and Levy 1994, A1). "San Francisco is an anomaly, a real paradox," commented political scientist Steven Erie. "Here you have what is arguably the most liberal, vanguard progressive city in the nation, and it doesn't see liberalism in terms of race" (quoted in Johnson and Levy 1994, A1). The recent election of Willie Brown as mayor will blunt the sharp edge of such criticisms, but the underlying conflicts and tensions that gave rise to them are likely to remain.

An explanation for this paradox is that San Francisco's liberalism has two faces, not one. The older face of liberalism, more familiar to blacks and Hispanics in their struggle for equality, is fading. A new one is emerging that is still friendly but also more open to nonracial issues and agendas. This more ambitious yet unfocused brand of urban liberalism has reduced the political visibility and clout of some racial groups, especially blacks, and at just the wrong time.

RACIAL AND ETHNIC DIVERSITY

San Francisco's racial and ethnic composition has changed significantly since 1980. Table 6.1 shows that San Francisco is now a "minority-majority" city. Whites remain the dominant plurality, but their numbers are shrinking while those of Latinos and Asians continue to grow. Always a small minority, the city's black population is becoming even smaller as it loses ground, figuratively and literally, to other minority groups.

Since 1980, San Francisco's growing Chinese and Hispanic populations have spread out from Chinatown and the Mission district, respectively, into other parts of the city. In contrast, the city's declining African-American population has concentrated residentially in smaller enclaves in the Bayview–Hunters Point, Western Addition, and Ingleside districts. Their dwindling numbers and geographic confinement go far to explain why many African Americans feel increasingly embattled and isolated in city politics.

TABLE 6.1 Racial/ethnic composition of San Francisco population in 1980 and 1990

Racial/Ethnic Groups	1980 Number	%	1990 Number	%
Hispanic (all races)	85,840	12.63	96,258	13.30
Non-Hispanic				
White	358,200	52.70	339,452	46.91
Black	83,420	12.27	77,518	10.71
Chinese	82,120	12.08	127,269	17.59
Filipino	35,180	5.18	38,893	5.37
Japanese	12,720	1.87	11,231	1.55
Korean	3,620	0.53	6,597	0.91
Vietnamese	5,640	0.83	9,611	1.33
Other Asian/Pacific Islander	6,900	1.02	12,402	1.71
Other races	6,000	0.88	4,394	0.61
Totals:	679,640	100.00	723,626	100.00

SOURCE: U.S. Census 5% Public Use Microdata Samples (PUMS) for 1980 and 1990. All sample estimates are weighted.

Racial/Ethnic Group Differences in Needs and Resources

Table 6.2 reveals significant socioeconomic differences among and within San Francisco's major racial/ethnic groups. By nearly all indicators, the city's Anglos are better off on average than are members of other racial/ethnic groups. African Americans, Vietnamese, and Other Asians suffer the highest levels of poverty. Two out of three African Americans under the age of 16 live in single-parent households; next highest are Hispanics, with 34 percent. Vietnamese, Other Asians, and American Indians are predominantly renters and have the lowest home ownership rates. Among renters, Vietnamese and Other Asians pay more of their household income for rent. These two groups also experience the highest levels of overcrowding. Vietnamese and Chinese have the highest level of linguistic isolation. Among resident workers 21 years or older, Vietnamese and Hispanics have the smallest percentages with at least some college education.

As shown in Table 6.2, there are also large socioeconomic differences within the rapidly growing Asian and Pacific Islander population. For example, poverty rates vary from 5.7 percent for Filipinos to 38.9 percent for Vietnamese; overcrowding varies from 3.5 percent for Japanese to 53.4 percent for Vietnamese.

Race, Ethnicity, and the Local Economy

As a regional headquarters city and service economy, San Francisco specializes in advanced corporate services, finance, insurance, real estate, government, and hospitality and tourism. Despite considerable long-term growth in the number of both

TABLE 6.2 Breakdown of poverty rates, family structure, housing tenure, housing costs, overcrowding, linguistic isolation, and education by race and ethnicity: San Francisco residents, 1990

Race/Ethnicity	Percentage of Each Racial/Ethnic Group Who						
	Live Below 100% Poverty Line (All)	Live in Single-Parent Household (Under 16)	Are Renters (All)	Pay More Than 35% of HH Income for Rent (Renters)	Live in Overcrowded Housing Units (All)	Live in Linguistically Isolated Households (All)*	Have Completed at Least Some College (Workers 21+)
Hispanics (All Races)	17.5%	34.2%	67.2%	37.7%	23.6%	21.7%	39.0%
Non-Hispanics							
Whites	8.6%	21.9%	60.0%	30.5%	2.0%	3.0%	74.0%
Blacks	27.9%	67.3%	65.5%	36.8%	8.1%	0.5%	48.0%
Chinese	11.1%	12.4%	43.9%	34.9%	27.1%	47.5%	42.0%
Filipinos	5.7%	22.4%	47.6%	19.4%	27.8%	11.2%	61.0%
Japanese	10.3%	15.9%	57.5%	28.4%	3.5%	18.3%	65.0%
Koreans	19.9%	20.6%	69.0%	34.5%	22.9%	29.8%	57.0%
Vietnamese	38.9%	13.1%	82.7%	51.9%	53.4%	55.8%	35.0%
Other Asian/Pacific Is.	30.8%	18.9%	74.4%	48.3%	36.1%	24.6%	57.0%
Native Americans	17.4%	32.8%	74.4%	22.1%	17.7%	3.3%	65.0%
Other Races	19.5%	18.6%	67.1%	40.3%	30.0%	22.9%	55.0%

* In the 1990 census, a household was defined as linguistically isolated if no household member over the age of 14 could speak English. This table reproduces Table 2 of the following report: Richard DeLeon, Elisa Barbour, Kevin Carew, Will Aarsheim, and Jose Mauro Barron, *San Francisco's Changing Demography and Social Needs: Maps and Analyses for Community Development Strategic Planning* (San Francisco: Public Research Institute, San Francisco State University, 1995).

SOURCE: Analysis of U.S. Census 5% Public Use Microdata Sample (PUMS) data for San Francisco, 1990.

low-income and high-income service jobs, 30,000 net jobs of all types were lost between 1991 and 1993, and manufacturing jobs have declined by 15 percent over the last 20 years. Most of the new jobs created have gone to predominantly white nonresident commuters, whose numbers have swelled to over 45 percent of those holding jobs in the city (San Francisco Department of City Planning 1993).

Many San Franciscans, most of them nonwhite, are poor because they are unemployed or hold low-paying dead-end jobs in the dual labor market that undergirds the city's service economy. Even where job opportunities exist in the city or region, many residents lack the training and skills to qualify for them. John Kasarda (1985, 65) writes: "Cities that improve their social and physical environments and adapt to their emerging service-sector roles should experience renewed demographic and economic vitality. However, many urban residents who lack appropriate skills for advanced service-sector industries are likely to remain on the bottom rungs of the socioeconomic ladder. Indeed, their economic plight could further deteriorate." The combination of a sluggish economy, mismatch of jobs and skills, and rising housing costs has forced the exit of many would-be San Franciscans and for others has made continued residence in the city precarious at best.

Full citizenship in San Francisco increasingly means economic citizenship, and many of the city's residents are denied it. Access to jobs and business opportunities is linked to race and ethnicity. In the distribution of San Francisco's labor force by class of work, certain niches and specializations stand out. For example, relatively large numbers of Koreans are self-employed. Three out of ten African Americans are employed by government. Three out of four Vietnamese earn paychecks working for others in the private sector. In 1989, income derived from wage and salary income ranged from 69.6 percent for Anglos to 89 percent for Native Americans. Self-employment income ranged from 2.6 percent for Native Americans to 19.3 percent for Koreans. Anglos, Chinese, and Japanese received, on average, about a dime of every dollar in the form of interest, dividends, royalties, or net rent. Anglos alone received fully 79 percent of the city's total aggregate income from this source. Comparable stocks of income-generating capital were not available to Hispanics, Vietnamese, Koreans, African Americans, and other minority groups.

Although San Francisco is a mecca for small business enterprises, the city's African Americans and Filipinos, in particular, are not well placed to take advantage of such opportunities. Both groups possess little capital, have few self-employed members, and have a very large percentage of workers (37 percent in the case of blacks) holding jobs in the endangered government and nonprofit sectors. Further, despite continuing growth in the number of city-controlled contracts awarded to women and minority-owned firms (41 percent increase between 1991 and 1992), the lion's share went to firms owned by white males and only four-tenths of 1 percent went to black-owned firms (Oring 1993; Brazil 1993).

The structural linkages between race/ethnicity, class of work, sources of income, and business opportunities imply that different racial/ethnic groups have different levels of vulnerability to the employment impacts of corporate downsizing, government cutbacks, privatization, and global economic competition. One response has been a growing emphasis on economic development strategies (enterprise communities, empowerment zones, and so on) rather than government service programs as a solution to persistent inequalities.

Race versus Class

Compounded by cultural and language differences, San Francisco's race-related disparities in needs, resources, and economic opportunities challenge local leaders who wish to build a broad-based multiracial political coalition rooted in shared material interests and common goals. In particular, the class stratifications underlying and reinforced by the city's racial inequalities raise a strategic issue that many leaders engaged in mobilizing racial and ethnic solidarities do not want to confront. By making one type of social cleavage (racial/ethnic divisions) salient as a political resource for fighting injustice, they must often downplay or suppress other types of cleavage (such as class divisions) that have the potential to fracture and dissipate racial/ethnic consciousness. Ragin (1986, 199) writes that "class mobilization often is successful only when ethnic antagonisms within classes can be disregarded or, better yet, forgotten altogether. Similarly, ethnic mobilization may require a submergence of class antagonisms within an ethnically defined collectivity."

The choice of whether to mobilize around race or class is a particular issue for leaders of the city's extremely diverse Asian population. Yet it is also an issue even for African Americans who experience racial and class oppression as merely different manifestations of the same thing and who have chosen racial solidarity as the more efficient fuel for fighting political battles. The political opportunity costs of submerged class antagonisms are unsolved problems, unexploited resources, and unbuilt bridges across racial lines.

THE POLITICAL INCORPORATION
OF RACIAL AND ETHNIC MINORITIES

A leading theory of urban politics (Browning, Marshall, and Tabb 1984) asserts that protest in the form of demonstrations, boycotts, rallies and so on is not enough for disadvantaged racial and ethnic minority groups to succeed in their struggle for equality. Given sufficient population numbers, they must also mobilize electorally and form alliances with other disadvantaged groups and supportive white liberals to achieve political incorporation within the city's dominant governing coalition. Only then will they gain sustained political access to and responsive policies from local government on issues of most concern to them.

Political incorporation is key and involves a combination of formal representation and informal inclusion in the power centers that make policy. A group has achieved substantial political incorporation, argue Browning, Marshall, and Tabb, when it "is in a position to articulate its interests, its demands will be heard, and through the dominant coalition it can ensure that certain interests will be protected, even though it may not win on every issue" (1984, 27).

Although one can question whether San Francisco has either a "dominant coalition" or the governing capacity to respond effectively to minority group interests, we can at least provide some rough indicators in Table 6.3 of the degree of political incorporation achieved by each of the city's major racial/ethnic groups. These indicators cover not only the mayor's office and the Board of Supervisors but also the city's many boards and commissions and the departments and agencies they control. Until very recently, executive powers under San Francisco's 63-year-old city charter were divided between the mayor and the chief administrative officer (CAO). In the November 1995 election, voters approved a charter amendment that will place the CAO's office under the mayor's authority. The semi-autonomous boards and commissions, however, will continue to oversee the operations of what one scholar has accurately characterized as "government by clerks" (Wirt 1974, 13). The tip of the policy-making iceberg is very small in San Francisco; most of it is submerged.

As shown in Table 6.3, Anglos comprise 64 percent of the eleven-member Board of Supervisors, 58 percent of the members of the city's 32 boards and commissions, 55 percent of the members of "power" boards and commissions (those judged by the author to control large agencies, large budgets, and/or significant policy decisions), 56 percent of the presidents of boards and commissions, and 63 percent of the presidents of power boards and commissions. All these percentages exceed the 46.6 percent that Anglos represent in the city's population, as reflected in parity ratios that range from 1.18 to 1.36. Although Anglos claim only 39 percent of local government jobs, they occupy 55 percent of all official/administrator and professional (O/A&P) positions. Virtually identical rates are found for recent new hires: 39 percent of all new hires, 54 percent of O/A&P new hires.

With the recent election of Susan Leal, Latinos now have one representative on the Board of Supervisors, 9 percent of the total membership. Latinos make up 7 percent of the members of the city's 32 boards and commissions, 7 percent of the members of power boards and commissions, and zero percent of the presidents of boards and commissions. All these percentages are less than the 13.9 percent that Latinos represent in the city's population, as reflected in parity ratios that range from zero to .65. Although Latinos hold about 13 percent of all local government jobs, they occupy only 9 percent of the O/A&P positions. Despite the fact that new hires have slightly increased both these rates (14 percent of all new hires, 10 percent of O/A&P new hires), Latinos have achieved the lowest level of political incorporation of the four major groups compared here.

Following the recent resignation of Doris Ward (now city assessor), Willie Kennedy is the only remaining African American on the Board of Supervisors, 9 percent of the total membership. African Americans make up 14 percent of the members of the city's 32 boards and commissions, 15 percent of the members of power boards and commissions, 9 percent of the presidents of boards and commissions, and 6 percent of the presidents of power boards and commissions. Except for the last, these percentages are close to or exceed the 10.5 percent that African Americans represent in the city's population. The parity ratios range from .60 to 1.39. African Americans hold nearly 19 percent of all local government jobs and about 12 percent

TABLE 6.3 Representation of San Francisco's racial and ethnic groups on the board of supervisors, on commissions and boards, and in local government employment

Indicator (Commissions & Boards)	Anglos	Latinos	Blacks	Asians/PI	Other	Total %
(1) Pct of 1990 Total Population	46.6	13.9	10.5	28.4	0.6	100
(2) Pct of Board of Supervisors (N=11)	63.6	9.1	9.1	18.2	0.0	100
(3) Parity Ratio (2)/(1)	1.36	0.65	0.87	0.64	0.0	N/A
(4) Pct Members Boards/Commissions (N=246)	57.7	6.5	13.8	19.5	2.5	100
(5) Parity Ratio (4)/(1)	1.24	0.47	1.31	0.69	4.17	N/A
(6) Pct Members "Power" Bds/Commissions (N=96)	55.2	7.3	14.6	21.9	1.0	100
(7) Parity Ratio (6)/(1)	1.18	0.53	1.39	0.77	1.67	N/A
(8) Pct Presidents Bds/Commissions (N=32)	56.3	0.0	9.4	31.3	0.0	100
(9) Parity Ratio (8)/(1)	1.21	0.00	0.90	1.10	0.00	N/A
(10) Pct Presidents "Power" Bds/Coms (N=16)	62.5	0.0	6.3	31.3	0.0	100.1
(11) Parity Ratio (10)/(1)	1.34	0.00	0.60	1.10	0.00	N/A

Indicator (Local Government Employment)	Anglos	Latinos	Blacks	Asians/PI	Other	Total %
(12) Pct of 1990 Total Population	46.6	13.9	10.5	28.4	0.6	100
(13) Pct of 1990 Labor Force (16+ yrs)	50.4	12.2	9.7	27.1	0.6	100
(14) Pct of Local Government (LG) Jobs	39.2	12.7	18.6	28.8	0.7	100
(15) Parity Ratio (14)/(13)	0.78	1.04	1.92	1.06	1.17	N/A
(16) Pct of Professional/Managerial LG Jobs	54.7	9.4	12.4	23.0	0.5	100
(17) Parity Ratio (16)/(13)	1.09	0.77	1.28	0.85	0.83	N/A
(18) Pct of Total New Permanent Full-time (PFT) Hires by S.F. County & City FY 93	39.5	13.5	15.5	31.1	0.5	100.1
(19) Pct of New PFT Hires of Officials, Administrators, and Professionals FY 93	54.1	9.6	10.3	25.2	0.8	100

SOURCES: Indicators 2–11: Analysis of data from *Almanac of San Francisco Politics 1993* (San Francisco National Organization for Women, 1993). "Power" Boards and Commissions are defined by author as Airports Commission, Civil Service Commission, Fire Commission, Health Commission, Housing Authority, Parking and Traffic Commission, Board of Permit Appeals, City Planning Commission, Police Commission, Port Commission, Public Utilities Commission, Public Library Commission, Recreation and Parks Commission, Redevelopment Agency Commission, Residential Rent Stabilization Board, Social Services Commission. Indicators 1., 12–17: Analysis of U.S. Census 5% Public Use Microdata Sample (PUMS) data for San Francisco, 1990. Indicators 18–19: S.F. County & City Employees 1993 (EEO–4 Summary Sheet Government Information, 1994). N/A means not applicable.

of the O/A&P positions, yielding parity ratios of 1.92 and 1.28, respectively. Recent new hires show a decrease in both these rates (16 percent of all new hires, 10 percent of O/A&P new hires). On the whole, by these measures, African Americans have achieved a fairly high level of political incorporation in the city's policy-making bodies and bureaucratic apparatus. As indicated by the decline in new hire rates, however, these gains are starting to erode. Although African Americans should fare well under the new Brown administration, the long-term trend is clear, and there are limits to what Mayor Brown can accomplish in the face of demographic shifts and competing demands from Latino and Asian constituencies.

With liberal Mabel Teng joining moderate Tom Hseih on the Board of Supervisors, Asians now claim 18 percent of the total membership. (Ms. Teng, a Chinese American, was the first Asian candidate to be elected to the board without first having been appointed by the mayor.) In an important recent development, Mayor Jordan and the Board of Supervisors appointed Chinese American Bill Lee as the new chief administrative officer, replacing the retiring Rudy Nothenberg. Asians make up 20 percent of the members of the city's 32 boards and commissions, 22 percent of the members of power boards and commissions, 31 percent of the presidents of boards and commissions, and 31 percent of the presidents of power boards and commissions. Asians hold 29 percent of all local government jobs and 23 percent of the O/A&P positions, yielding parity ratios of 1.06 and .85, respectively. Recent new hires show an increase in both these rates (31 percent of all new hires, 25 percent of O/A&P new hires). Relative to the 28.4 percent they represent in the city's population, Asians (particularly Chinese) have made major strides toward achieving political incorporation. If demographic trends continue along with the recent upsurge in political mobilization, Asians may soon rival Anglos as the dominant players in San Francisco politics.

THE POLITICAL CHEMISTRY
OF MULTIRACIAL COALITIONS

Demographic realities dictate the necessity of building multiracial coalitions to achieve power and influence in San Francisco politics. The city's minority leaders face difficult strategic and tactical choices in selecting allies, negotiating agendas, and organizing campaigns. Those choices are complicated by the city's social diversity and political fragmentation. Electoral majorities tend to disintegrate rather quickly in the city's highly fissionable political culture. Many electoral coalitions are theoretically possible but only a few have prospects of stability and success. Which coalitions are feasible, and which are not? What holds them together? What tears them apart? What price must be paid to participate in such coalitions, and is it worth it?

According to Raphael Sonenshein, the "glue" that holds coalitions together is a mixture of group self-interest and shared ideology. "The optimists focus on the role of ideology and emphasize the enduring and solid character of biracial coalitions based on common beliefs. The pessimists tend to see interest as the glue of coalitions and to view biracial coalitions as at best short-lived tactical compromises between self-centered groups" (Sonenshein 1990, 195). He stresses the importance of leadership in forming stable coalitions that have the capacity to govern after elections are won. "The art of building biracial electoral coalitions calls for leaders who can link the interests and ideologies of groups together in order to win elections, enact policies, and offer benefits" (208).

Sonenshein's analysis of the role played by interest, ideology, and leadership in building biracial electoral coalitions in Los Angeles illuminates many aspects of multiracial coalition building in San Francisco. What follows is a summary (visually aided by graphs) of the political chemistry that appears to govern the mutual attraction and repulsion of potential coalition partners in San Francisco's multiracial political universe.

Materialist Left versus Postmaterialist Left

Postmaterialism is a term used by Ronald Inglehart (1990) to describe a new political polarization found increasingly in advanced industrial societies. It is a value-based political cleavage that cuts across traditional class divisions. It is focused on social and environmental issues relating more to the meaning and quality of life than to its materialistic basis in property and economic growth.

At the level of the city, postmaterialist values encourage political initiatives in such areas as environmental protection, neighborhood preservation, urban aesthetics, individual liberties, and citizen participation. Conflicts around these kinds of issues cross-cut those originating from class-based materialist values emphasizing jobs, housing, education, health, and physical safety.

Ideologically, San Francisco's "progressives" pursue a wide range of economic, social, and environmental initiatives through local government policies and programs. The city's "conservatives" resist such initiatives across the board. As defined here, the city's "traditional liberals" support redistributive economic programs but tend to oppose libertarian social policies and environmental regulations. In contrast, the city's "quality-of-life liberals" oppose local government redistribution but tend to support social tolerance, environmental regulation, and neighborhood and historical preservation (cf. DeLeon 1992, 32–34).

Case 1: Affordable Housing versus Growth Control

Illustrating the relative positions of San Francisco's major racial/ethnic groups within this two-dimensional (materialist/postmaterialist) ideological space, Figure 6.1 plots the 1990 precinct vote on Proposition H against the precinct vote on Proposition J. Proposition H was a successful local ballot initiative that banned the building of waterfront hotels and mandated citizen participation in the waterfront planning process. Proposition J was a failed local ballot initiative that would have earmarked city revenues for an affordable housing fund. In the graph space, the "P" plotting symbol identifies white progressive precinct electorates, "C" white conservative precincts, "B" black precincts, "A" Asian precincts, and "H" Hispanic pre-

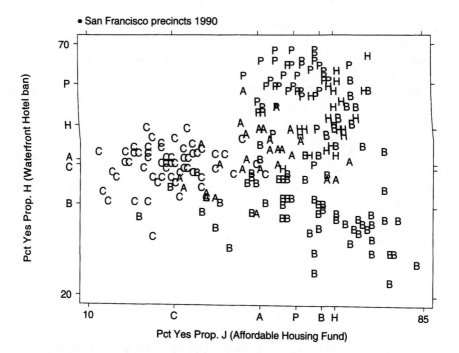

• San Francisco precincts 1990

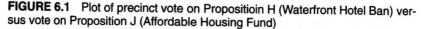

Pct Yes Prop. J (Affordable Housing Fund)

FIGURE 6.1 Plot of precinct vote on Propositioin H (Waterfront Hotel Ban) versus vote on Proposition J (Affordable Housing Fund)

The "P" plotting symbol identifies white progressive precinct electorates, "C," white conservative precincts, "B," black precincts, "A," Asian precincts, and "H," Hispanic precincts. Labeled tick marks on both axes show the median percent yes vote for each initiative cast by precinct electorates of each type. (Also see footnote 1.)

cincts. These same symbols are used with tick marks on both axes to show the median percent yes vote for each initiative cast by precinct electorates within each racial/ethnic group.[1]

Figure 6.1 shows that white progressive and Hispanic precinct electorates strongly supported both ballot measures. White conservative precincts slightly opposed Proposition H and strongly opposed Proposition J. Black precincts strongly supported Proposition J and strongly opposed Proposition H. Asian precincts occupy a middle position on both axes in this graphical molecule. The overall triangu-

---

[1] White conservative precincts are defined as those in which at least 75 percent of the population is white and scored below the 25th percentile on DeLeon's progressivism index, as described in DeLeon, 1992. White progressive precincts are those in which at least 75 percent of the population is white and scored above the 75th percentile on DeLeon's progressivism index. Classification of majority Hispanic, Asian, and black precincts is based on 1980 census tract data measured on precincts included in tracts. Other white majority precincts and those with no racial majority are not plotted. Sources: Statement of Vote from the San Francisco Registrar of Voters and 1980 census tract data on race.

lar pattern observed has been replicated in dozens of similar graphs on many other issues.

The tick marks on each axis summarize much of the story of this graph. Focusing on the materialist Proposition J vote, we see that black and Hispanic electorates were closely aligned in supporting this measure, with help from white progressives. White conservative precincts voted against it, and Asian precincts as a group scored near the middle. Focusing on the postmaterialist Proposition H vote, we see that white progressive and Hispanic electorates were fairly closely aligned in supporting this measure. Black precincts voted against it, and white conservative and Asian precincts scored near the middle. Moving from the Proposition J scale to the Proposition H scale, black precincts jump ideologically from Left to Right. The other groups of precincts stay fairly consistently Left, Middle, or Right on both scales. Indeed, if the Bs were erased from this graph, the two-dimensional ideological space it describes would collapse into a single Left-Right continuum. African Americans are an important part of the real world of San Francisco politics, however, and the result is a strategic and tactical challenge for coalition-oriented politicians.

Case 2: Voting for White Conservative and White Progressive Candidates

Figure 6.2 provides another graphical molecule for study, this one plotting the racial/ethnic group vote in 1992 for two white candidates for the Board of Supervisors. The white conservative candidate, local radio personality Barbara Kaufman, ran her victorious campaign as a progrowth moderate and fiscal conservative. She received strong support and lavish funding from downtown business. The white progressive candidate, gay activist Cleve Jones, ran his losing campaign with an emphasis on AIDS prevention, environmental protection, and neighborhood preservation. He received particularly strong support from the city's progressive political clubs and the gay and lesbian community. The plotting symbols are the same as those used in Figure 6.1, although the classification measures are different.[2]

As shown in Figure 6.2, white progressive precinct electorates strongly supported Jones and strongly opposed Kaufman. White conservative precincts strongly supported Kaufman and strongly opposed Jones. Hispanic precincts aligned with white progressives in supporting Jones and opposing Kaufman. Asian precincts, once again, took the middle position on both candidates, although with a more conservative drift in voting on Jones. Consistent with their materialist Left and postmaterialist Right positions on most issues, voters in black precincts joined white

---

[2] White conservative precincts are defined as those in which at least 75 percent of the population is white and scored in the bottom tenth in voter support for Barbara Boxer's 1992 campaign for the U.S. Senate. White progressive precincts are also at least 75 percent white but scored in the top tenth in voter support for Boxer. Other white majority precincts and those with no racial majority are not plotted. Sources: Statement of Vote from the San Francisco Registrar of Voters and 1990 census data on race for precincts.

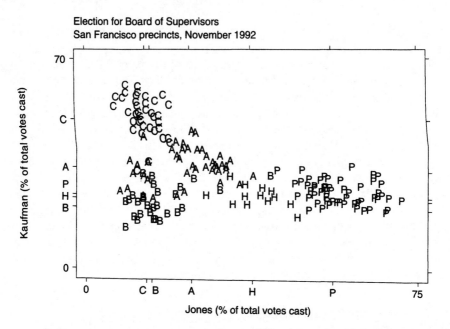

Election for Board of Supervisors
San Francisco precincts, November 1992

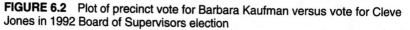

Jones (% of total votes cast)

FIGURE 6.2 Plot of precinct vote for Barbara Kaufman versus vote for Cleve Jones in 1992 Board of Supervisors election

The "P" plotting symbol identifies white progressive precinct electorates, "C," white conservative precincts, "B," black precincts, "A," Asian precincts, and "H," Hispanic precincts. Labeled tick marks on both axes show the median percent yes vote for each initiative cast by precinct electorates of each type. (Also see footnote 2.)

progressives and Hispanics in rejecting Kaufman and joined white conservatives and Asians in rejecting Jones.[3]

Based on these illustrative analyses and other research (DeLeon 1991, 1992), the following generalizations can be made about the political chemistry involved in building multiracial electoral coalitions in San Francisco politics.

1. Two distinct Left-Right axes structure San Francisco's ideological space. There is a "materialist" Left and Right and a "postmaterialist" Left and Right. San Francisco voters can be classified as Left on both, Right on both, or Left on one and Right on the other.
2. White progressive voters are Left on both; white conservative voters are Right on both.

---

[3] To some extent, the withholding of votes reflects the practice of bullet voting for black candidates only in the city's at-large elections. This tactic works to a point in denying votes to rival candidates, but it also wastes votes and in the long run can provoke a backlash from resentful voters in other racial/ethnic groups.

3. Hispanic voters align with white progressives on most issues and with black voters on issues involving jobs, housing, and similar concerns.
4. Asian voters align with white conservatives on many issues but occupy an overall middle position in the city's two-dimensional ideological space. They appear to be strategically located to play an important mediating and brokering role in building future multiracial coalitions.
5. African-American voters align with white progressives and Hispanics on materialist issues and with white conservatives and Asians on postmaterialist issues. Ideologically, as a group, they are both Left and Right, and which it will be at a given time depends on the issue. In this sense, African Americans are an anomaly in San Francisco politics. Pursuing Sonenshein's glue metaphor, they don't "stick" very well or for very long with coalition partners that are consistently Left-Left or Right-Right in their goals and priorities. This apparent volatility undermines prospects of forming stable alliances or coalitions with such groups.
6. San Francisco's two-dimensional ideological space is somewhat warped and wrinkled by the forces of group self-interest, especially in candidate races for elective office. Even in this more competitive and zero-sum arena of politics, however, a substantial amount of coalition building takes place consistent with each group's ideological position.

Black Liberals and White Progressives

In a remark that has direct relevance to San Francisco's racial politics, Sonenshein notes that building multiracial coalitions is harder for blacks than for others—especially if there is competition with other nonwhite groups and a dependence on white liberals for electoral support. "Racial ideology blocks off access to potential allies who share interests. When separated by interest conflict from those who share beliefs, blacks face exclusion. Dependence on liberalism undoubtedly adds to the inherent tension in any coalition" (1990, 106).

As their population base shrinks, some African-American leaders blame gays and lesbians, Latinos, and especially Asians for their declining political fortunes. Supervisor Willie Kennedy, for example, remarked that "for years we were considered *the* minority. Then everyone else became a minority, and we started to get pushed back." Blacks "ought to be further advanced than these other groups," she stated, "because we got here first" (quoted in Redmond 1986, A1). More recently, Supervisor Kennedy challenged the nomination of a black lesbian activist for a commission seat on grounds that she was likely to favor homosexuals over members of her own race. "I want someone who is black all the way!" Kennedy reportedly exclaimed (Zachary 1995, A1).

Tensions between the socially conservative African-American community and the socially liberal (and predominantly white) gay and lesbian community continue to flare up from time to time. For example, outraged gay and lesbian leaders pressed Mayor Jordan to fire the Reverend Eugene Lumpkin from the city's Human Rights Commission after the African-American clergyman publicly defended his scriptural exegesis condemning homosexuality as an abomination. Unpleasant memories of this incident were stirred recently when Willie Brown included the Reverend Lumpkin on his platform while announcing his candidacy for mayor of San Francisco.

Similar tensions have surfaced repeatedly in the relationship between African Americans and the city's white middle-class environmentalists and growth control advocates. In mobilizing opposition to a major growth control initiative in 1986, for example, the Reverend Cecil Williams attacked the "so-called conservationists who seem to conveniently forget and openly exclude the survival of poor people in our city" and who "take a self-righteous position on keeping the environment clean but ignore the pollution of conditions in our poor communities" (quoted in Adams 1986, A1). These kinds of recurring conflicts between black liberals and white progressives over social and environmental issues have complicated the task of building alliances to support the shared economic goals and political aspirations of both communities.

African-American residents and their leaders continue to defend their hard-won gains in political representation and incorporation. And they continue to push an economic development agenda that emphasizes provision of decent jobs, business opportunities, affordable housing, basic health services, and quality education for the city's have-nots in general and blacks in particular. Many African-American leaders will be understandably wary of heeding the advice to coalesce with "white liberals" in pursuing this agenda. The city's many white middle-class progressives support liberal programs as part of their own broader agenda, of course, but that support is often diluted or even undermined by their equally vigorous support of anti-growth initiatives and social policy innovations opposed by many African Americans.

From the perspective of political actors who have developed a consistent and locally coherent Left-Right stance on most issues, the apparent flip-flopping of blacks between conservative and progressive positions is unnerving, frustrating, and a sure sign of tactical self-interest and political instability. This attitude toward black leaders has gained strength in recent years, particularly among the city's white progressives. In turn, many black leaders have come to resent being viewed as political pariahs and have voiced objections to the insensitivity, neglect, and racism they see operating in the white progressive establishment.

One symptom of the growing estrangement of blacks from mainstream city politics is a rise in the level of racially charged demand-protest activities. An example is the demonstration of black leaders organized by the Reverend Amos Brown demanding millions of dollars in "reparations" from the city's redevelopment agency for bulldozing their community out of the Filmore district 20 years earlier (Adams 1993). Another symptom is the practice of encouraging bullet-voting by blacks for black candidates only in at-large elections for the Board of Supervisors. In general, the city's African Americans have felt increasingly isolated politically and forced to go it alone without partners or allies (Baca 1992).

Despite these disturbing trends, the political disincorporation of blacks is not inevitable. Other recent developments point to a brighter future. First and foremost is Willie Brown's election as mayor. His victorious campaign revived the hopes and aspirations of many African Americans and dramatically revived their flagging interest in local politics. Second, a younger generation of progressive black activists has emerged to challenge the more conservative black establishment for leadership roles. One of them, Steven Phillips, defeated rival Amos Brown in winning a school board seat in 1992 with the strong support of white progressives, Latinos, and younger African Americans. A third reason for optimism is the heightened militancy of San Francisco labor unions in organizing service workers of all races and in responding to the social problems and employment needs of disadvantaged neighborhood communities. Fourth, the Earth Island Institute and other local environmental organizations have begun to work with African Americans and other minority groups in mounting toxic cleanup campaigns and fighting different forms of environmental racism.

These kinds of movements will help to bridge the gap between materialist and postmaterialist value priorities. A final encouraging development to note here is the growing support within the African-American and Latino communities for preference voting and similar electoral reforms. These alternatives to the current at-large system of electing supervisors are not only more likely to secure minimal representation in government but also to promote cooperation rather than competition in building multiracial political coalitions.

THE 1995 MAYORAL ELECTION AND BEYOND

The 1995 race for mayor was a watershed event in San Francisco's turbulent political history. After surviving a vigorous challenge from Roberta Achtenberg and other white progressive candidates in the November "primary" election, Willie L. Brown, Jr., went on to defeat Frank Jordan in the December runoff to become the city's first African-American mayor.

Serving four years as a conservative mayor of a progressive city took its toll on Frank Jordan. His prospects for reelection looked dim. Jordan's upset victory over Art Agnos in 1991 was viewed by some observers as a historical accident occasioned by intense anti-Agnos sentiment and factionalism on the left. Plagued by lingering economic recession, declining federal and state assistance, repeated revenue shortfalls, ill-chosen staff appointments, and opposition from a liberal-progressive Board of Supervisors, the politically inexperienced Jordan had little to show for his four years as "citizen mayor." His controversial "Matrix" program had failed to solve the homeless problem, businesses and jobs continued to flow out of the city, and fear of crime remained widespread despite improving statistics. Jordan's successes in balancing budgets and resolving labor disputes were invisible to most voters, and his earlier major victory in preventing the San Francisco Giants baseball team from moving to Florida was a fading memory. Rather shy and reserved as a public figure, Jordan failed to develop a dynamic leadership style or an inspiring vision for the city's future. If liberals and progressives had learned from their fiasco in 1991 and could get their act together in 1995, Jordan's days as mayor were numbered.

In his last term as state assemblyman, Willie L. Brown, Jr., retired early from his powerful role as speaker to run for mayor. Flamboyant and charismatic, Brown was a major player in state and national Democratic party politics. Despite his long track record as a paid lobbyist for virtually every large corporation and developer in the Bay Area, and despite his freely acknowledged eagerness as speaker to accept huge campaign donations from anybody and everybody willing to pay to keep Democrats in power, Brown commanded impressive support from within the city's liberal-progressive community. Even his detractors conceded that Brown had used his position of power in the assembly to channel millions of state and federal dollars into the city, to defend civil rights and individual liberties, to expand educational and economic opportunities for blacks and other disadvantaged minorities, and to protect the "left coast city" from wrathful and intolerant right-wing attacks. Christened by many local observers as the front-runner in the race for mayor, Brown organized a formidable campaign operation under the direction of consultant Jack Davis, who had masterminded Jordan's upset victory over Art Agnos in 1991.

If Willie Brown was the quintessential black liberal, his major rival on the left, Roberta Achtenberg, was the quintessential white progressive. Openly gay, Achtenberg earned broad-based community support working as an attorney for lesbian rights and other social causes. After being elected to the Board of Supervisors in 1990, she established her reputation as a civil rights advocate, environmentalist, and defender of neighborhoods and the quality of life. Achtenberg became a national celebrity in 1993 by accepting President Clinton's invitation to run the fair housing division of the Department of Housing and Urban Development. She squeaked by a tough Senate confirmation vote marred by personal attacks on her sexual orientation and liberal beliefs. After resigning from that position to run for mayor, she endured a barrage of criticism charging that her entry into the race would detract from Brown's campaign, exacerbate long-standing tensions between the African-American and gay and lesbian communities, and provoke the same kind of factionalism on the left that allowed Frank Jordan to win in 1991. Despite her campaign's slow and bumpy start, polls conducted just prior to the November election showed her gaining on Brown and Jordan in the race for mayor.

As the November 7 election day approached, the betting odds were that Jordan would survive this first hurdle to face either Brown or Achtenberg in the December 12 runoff. Under this scenario, the critical test of progressive coalitional politics would be whether Achtenberg's predominantly middle-class gay and lesbian followers could be persuaded to support Brown in the runoff or whether Brown's working-class and African-American constituents could bring themselves to support Achtenberg rather than vote for Jordan or sit out the election. An even more dramatic scenario, one that some observers regarded as a win-win situation for the left but others saw as potentially divisive and volatile, would pit Brown against Achtenberg in the runoff.

After the ballots were counted on November 7, Willie Brown came out on top with 33.6 percent of the votes, followed by Frank Jordan with 32.1 percent and Roberta Achtenberg with 26.8 percent. Brown and Jordan would now face each other in the December 12 runoff election. In the runoff election campaign, Frank Jordan faced one of the state's most accomplished politicians, the entire Democratic party leadership establishment, and the unified opposition of the city's liberals and progressives. Any last hopes for a replay of the left's self-destruction in 1991 were dashed when Achtenberg urged her supporters to close ranks and vote for Brown. By adding her endorsement to those of Calvin Welch, Susan Hestor, Susan Bierman and other well-known environmentalists and neighborhood activists, Achtenberg secured the last hold-out white progressive votes needed to clinch Brown's victory. On December 12, Willie Brown defeated Frank Jordan 54 percent to 46 percent to become San Francisco's mayor-elect.

Following his inauguration on January 8, 1996, Mayor Brown took charge of city hall with electrifying zeal. On day one he appointed African-American Robert Demmons as fire chief and Chinese-American Fred Lau as police chief, thus acting on his promise to take immediate steps to make his administration the most racially and ethnically inclusive in the city's history. He also signaled that a very high priority will be given to economic development, business growth, and job creation, particularly in the working-class neighborhoods located in the long-neglected southern and eastern parts of the city. Thus, San Francisco's traditional liberals and racial minorities have good reasons for expecting that Mayor Brown will be responsive to their needs, interests, and aspirations in the years ahead.

For those very same reasons, however, the city's white progressives and quality of life liberals should brace themselves for a new assault on their hard-won growth limits and neighborhood preservation policies. Recently christened "Da Mayor" by his admirers, Willie Brown is inclined to think big when envisioning the city's future, and "big" is a bad three-letter word in the political vocabulary of many San Franciscans. Barely hours after the runoff election, for example, owners of the San Francisco Giants left skid marks in launching their latest proposal for a new baseball park to be built in the city's China Basin neighborhood. Following suit, Catellus Corporation executives lost no time in responding to Mayor Brown's call to accelerate development of the long-dormant Mission Bay Project. Speaker Brown served Catellus for many years as a private consultant and lobbyist, prompting the predictions of slow-growth critics that Mayor Brown will cater to unreasonable developer demands. Further, by announcing that Pacific Gas & Electric executive Tapan Monroe and commercial real estate tycoon Doug Shorenstein will serve as co-chairs of his forthcoming "economic summit," Mayor Brown laid out the welcome mat for downtown business leaders and set off alarms among neighborhood preservationists and small business advocates.

It is doubtful that Willie Brown's inclusive governing coalition can stretch far enough to embrace the full range of groups, interests, and ideologies found in San Francisco. Putting first things first in the struggle for racial equality may require the city's postmaterialist left to take the back seat while the materialist left moves forward under Mayor Brown's leadership. All roads point to the left in the Left Coast City, however, and if a progressive urban regime is possible, it will eventually happen here.

REFERENCES

Adams, Gerald D. 1986. Black Ministers Meet to Defeat Anti-Growth Plan. *San Francisco Examiner,* August 28, A1.

Adams, Gerald D. 1993. Blacks Seek "Reparations" for Filmore. *San Francisco Examiner,* January 13.

Baca, Kathleen. 1992. Clash on the Left: The Broad-Based Coalition behind the Success of Progressives in San Francisco Is on the Verge of Blowing Up along Racial Lines. *SF Weekly,* November 25.

Brazil, Eric. 1993. Black Firm Sues City over Losing Big Contract. *San Francisco Examiner,* February 23.

Browning, Rufus P., Dale Rogers Marshall, and David H. Tabb. 1984. *Protest Is Not Enough.* Berkeley: University of California Press.

Caraley, Demetrios. 1992. Washington Abandons the Cities. *Political Science Quarterly* 107 (1): 1–30.

City's Liberal Reputation Intact in Elections. 1994. *San Francisco Chronicle,* November 12.

Davis, Mike. 1993. Who Killed L.A.?: The War against the Cities. *CrossRoads* 32 (June): 2–19.

DeLeon, Richard E. 1991. The Progressive Urban Regime: Ethnic Coalitions in San Francisco. In Byran O. Jackson and Michael B. Preston, eds., *Racial and Ethnic Politics in California.* Berkeley: Institute of Governmental Studies, University of California.

DeLeon, Richard E. 1992. *Left Coast City: Progressive Politics in San Francisco, 1975–1991.* Lawrence: University Press of Kansas.

Gordon, Rachel, and George Raine. 1994. Blacks Charge Racism in Naming of Health Chief. *San Francisco Examiner,* January 13, A1.

Hartman, Chester. 1984. *The Transformation of San Francisco.* Totowa, N.J.: Rowman and Allanheld.

Inglehart, Ronald. 1990. *Culture Shift in Advanced Industrial Society.* Princeton, N.J.: Princeton University Press.

Johnson, Clarence, and Dan Levy. 1994. Minorities Find Power is Elusive. *San Francisco Examiner,* October 31, A1.

Kasarda, John. 1985. Urban Change and Minority Opportunities. In Paul Peterson, ed., *The New Urban Reality.* Washington, D.C.: The Brookings Institution.

Mollenkopf, John H. 1983. *The Contested City.* Princeton, N.J.: Princeton University Press.

Oring, Sheryl. 1993. City Contracts Up 41% for Women, Minorities. *San Francisco Business Times,* January 8.

Ragin, Charles. 1986. The Impact of Celtic Nationalism on Class Politics in Scotland and Wales. In Susan Olzak and J. Nagel, eds., *Competitive Ethnic Relations.* Orlando, Fla.: Academic Press.

Redmond, Tim. 1986. Behind the Bitter Lobbying of Declining Power. *San Francisco Bay Guardian,* May 14, A1.

San Francisco Department of City Planning. 1993. *Summary Findings: Commerce and Industry Inventory,* July.

Savitch, H. V., and John Clayton Thomas. 1991. Conclusion: End of the Millenium Big City Politics. In H. V. Savitch and John Clayton Thomas, eds., *Big City Politics in Transition.* Beverly Hills, Calif.: Sage.

Sonenshein, Raphael J. 1990. Biracial Coalitions in Big Cities: Why They Succeed, Why They Fail. In Rufus P. Browning, Dale Rogers Marshall, and David H. Tabb, eds., *Racial Politics in American Cities.* White Plains, N.Y.: Longman.

Stone, Clarence N. 1989. *Regime Politics: Governing Atlanta 1946–1988.* Lawrence: University Press of Kansas.

Wirt, Frederick. 1974. *Power in the City: Decision Making in San Francisco.* Berkeley and Los Angeles: University of California Press.

Zachary, G. Pascal. 1995. Who Needs Oprah? San Francisco Has Board of Supervisors. *Wall Street Journal,* February 2, A1.

part IV

Class and Leadership in the South

chapter 7

Atlanta and the Limited Reach
of Electoral Control

Clarence Stone and Carol Pierannunzi

Editors' Notes

African Americans constitute two-thirds of the population in Atlanta and have held a substantial majority of the elected positions in the city—excluding the office of mayor—for more than 20 years. Incorporation would seem to be well established. What more is there?

Plenty, according to Clarence Stone and Carol Pierannunzi. They argue that black *political power is limited by white economic power. Control of city hall provides severely limited leverage in a regional political economy in which private actors make most of the investment decisions. In the view of Stone and Pierannunzi, electoral incorporation is only one foundation for inclusion in a governing coalition.*

The incorporation picture in Atlanta is further complicated by the different positions of middle- and lower-class African Americans. For the middle class, Stone and Pierannunzi suggest, race is "the" obstacle, and to the extent that affirmative actions, formal and informal, overcomes that barrier, opportunities are available and can be taken. Thus electoral incorporation saw the opening up of jobs and contracts to many African Americans. But, Stone and Pierannunzi maintain, minority members of the lower class face more substantial barriers. Simply lowering the racial bar is not enough. Stone and Pierannunzi contend that, in an economy in which education credentials have assumed great importance, a more far-reaching program of human investment is needed. This approach is more long term and carries with it risks and uncertainties.

Socially embedded disadvantage is not easily overcome, and the challenge of doing so attracts few takers. It is not an undertaking to which the middle class is strongly attracted. Stone and Pierannunzi remind us that when jobs and business opportunities become available, the members of the middle class are eager not only to seize those opportunities but also to protect them. Also, what is within the reach of the middle class is not necessarily accessible to the lower class. So a protective approach to newly opened opportunities may not serve well those who are in need of more basic change. Thus Stone and Pierannunzi argue that the terms of incorporation for middle- and lower-class minorities differ. What benefits one does not necessarily serve the other.

African Americans hold governmental power in Atlanta. They have a strong majority on the city council and have held the mayor's office since 1974. Moreover, African Americans are a substantial presence in the civic life of Atlanta. They have held the presidency of the Chamber of Commerce and have for years been among the members of every important board and commission in the public life of the community, including the Atlanta Committee on the Olympic Games.

How such a seemingly strong form of incorporation came about is in part a familiar story. Key facts in the city's political history are widely known:

1. In 1946, Georgia's white primary was invalidated. A voter registration drive in the black community brought 20,000 new voters onto the rolls, making the black community more than a quarter of the city's electorate (Bacote 1955).
2. Atlanta's mayor at the time, William B. Hartsfield, saw the potential for including Atlanta's black community as junior partners in a coalition built around the themes of economic growth and racial moderation. He and his successor, Ivan Allen, Jr., profited electorally from that coalition over the next 20 years (Jennings and Zeigler 1966; Hornsby 1982).
3. Atlanta's black community entered a new and more assertive phase in 1960 as direct-action protests brought an end to an era of quiet accommodation between established black and white leaders (Walker 1963a).
4. The 1970 census showed a black majority in the city, and in 1973, Maynard Jackson was elected Atlanta's first black mayor. Atlanta's mayors have been African American since that time. By 1990, the city's population had reached two-thirds African American.
5. Concurrent with the 1970s shift in electoral power, white school enrollment declined to less than a quarter of the total student body in the city school district. A federal district judge appointed a biracial group to negotiate an alternative to busing, and in 1973 the resulting agreement provided for a black superintendent and an increased black presence in the upper level of the school system's administrative structure (Fleishman 1980).

African Americans have thus been part of the governing coalition in Atlanta for a half century, and in that time their steadily growing electoral power has enhanced their role within that coalition. As electoral power has grown, the earlier period of mainly symbolic benefits has given way to a situation in which African Americans have made substantial gains in municipal employment and in the receipt of city contracts (Eisinger 1980).

Electoral mobilization was a key element in black incorporation, and incorporation as a voting majority was central to the ability of the black community to achieve significant policy responsiveness. Clearly elections matter, and majority voting pays real dividends in governmental decisions.

What more is there to say? A great deal, it turns out. As we shall see below, incorporation is a complex phenomenon, shaped by many factors. The ideology of the governing coalition is one, but ideology is not the only factor at work. The initial incorporation of African Americans into Atlanta's governing coalition occurred under a mayor who held many of the segregationist views prevalent in the Deep South of that time (Martin 1978, 49), but Atlanta's Mayor Hartsfield was first and foremost a pragmatist. He also had strong ties to members of Atlanta's business elite—he was, for example, a former schoolmate and lifelong friend of Coca-Cola executive Robert Woodruff. Hartsfield professed deep faith in the enlightened self-interest of top business leaders to act in ways that would promote the city's well-being, and he looked to them for cues about what was acceptable and unacceptable.

Although many of Atlanta's prominent businessmen themselves held traditional southern views on race, they also were pragmatic. They aspired to see Atlanta grow, become the dominant city in the Southeast, and reach national prominence. Hence they cared about Atlanta's image in the larger world. The last thing they wanted was for Atlanta to be seen as a backwater defender of an old way of life.

The conventional wisdom of the time held that the white working class was the backbone of segregationist resistance to social change and that the educated white middle class, including Atlanta's business elite, was, although not especially liberal on racial matters, at least amenable to a policy of moderation. Certainly throughout the 1950s and 1960s, Atlanta's white electorate divided along class lines, as predicted by this conventional wisdom (Walker 1963b; Jennings and Zeigler 1966). But education and social class were not necessarily in themselves key factors. A supporter of the Hartsfield coalition observed:

> I've found that one of the best ways to anticipate how a man will vote is to ask him where he was born and grew up. If he comes from South Georgia or somewhere else in the Black Belt you can bet he will be against us, but if he's from the Piedmont area or grew up in Atlanta or outside the South, chances are he's with us. (Quoted in Walker 1963c, 46)

The traditional southern views on race, V. O. Key (1949) argued, were politically rooted in the old plantation areas of the Deep South—what is known as the Black Belt. According to Key, what sustained the Jim Crow system was not the racial attitudes of uneducated whites. Instead, it was the political power and leadership of propertied elites in the rural and small-town South, particularly in the Black Belt. Their position rested on perpetuating a system of racial subordination.

Atlanta's business elite operated on a much different basis. In their drive to promote Atlanta, they came into conflict with the tradition minded in Atlanta, who were less educated, less affluent, and who perhaps felt somewhat threatened by change. In the post–World War II period, the Atlanta business elite also came into conflict with stand-patters in statewide politics, the agrarian elite Key talked about.

As mayor, Hartsfield could see the possibility of a change-oriented coalition built around the twin themes of economic growth and racial moderation. Atlanta's electorally mobilized black community provided the numbers for swinging the balance of city voting power toward the forces of change. The state struggle was a different and more complicated matter.

When black college students began their sit-ins protesting segregation in Atlanta in 1960, the reaction of the mayor and the governor were diametrically opposed. Hartsfield characterized the statement of the students as "the legal aspirations of young people throughout the nation and the entire world" (*Atlanta Journal*, March 9, 1960). He immediately sought a negotiated settlement. The governor, Ernest Vandiver, characterized the student statement as "anti-American propaganda" and as a "left-wing statement . . . calculated to breed dissatisfaction, discontent, discord, and evil" (*Atlanta Journal*, March 9, 1960). In the face of a threatened student march to the state capitol grounds in Atlanta, Governor Vandiver deployed state highway patrolmen, who were armed with nightsticks, tear gas, and fire hoses—a preview of the coming confrontation in Alabama (Walker 1963c, 88).

Whether or not the political incorporation of minorities occurs, what kind of incorporation takes place and when it occurs are matters influenced by the particulars of the community setting. In postwar Atlanta, a key element was the congruence of black interests and the white business interests around the policies of change in land use. To be sure, there were conflicting interests between these two segments of the community as well, but Mayor Hartsfield was skillful in minimizing the conflicts that otherwise would have made the coalition difficult. Furthermore, black business and professional leaders were simply asking that doors closed on a racial basis be opened. They were seeking to use, not challenge, the strategically important place that the white business elite held in the political economy of the city and the state.

Achieving electoral influence is significant, but popular control of elected office is only one element in the actual governance of a city. The need for private investment in business activity makes control of economic institutions a second element of great consequence. Governance comes out of the *interplay* between electoral and economic power. Neither stands alone (Elkin 1985). Governance, then, consists not simply of city hall operating in isolation. It requires cooperation and accommodation among a network of institutions, especially political and economic ones. These arrangements form what is called an *urban regime* (Stone 1989).

In Atlanta, with its black electoral majority and its still preponderantly white control of economic institutions, the dual character of the urban regime is plainly visible, and black political incorporation occurs in that context. Joint membership in Atlanta's regime rests on the fact that African Americans have numbers and substantial voting power but limited economic resources. The business elite controls enormous economic resources but lacks numbers. That African Americans could supply needed numbers paved their way into incorporation initially, and as those numbers reached an electoral majority, they took on added weight.

As we probe the nature of urban regimes, we see that governance is shaped by a political economy in which many valued resources, including control of most investment decisions, are in private hands. In addition, associational life and social connections enjoy autonomy as well. Full incorporation is thus no simple matter of gaining elected office. It is a matter of becoming a part of a governing coalition *and obtaining a place in a web of relationships*. In analyzing a regime, it is not enough to identify the partners in the governing coalition. It is also necessary to know what each brings to the coalition and how they are related to one another (Mollenkopf 1992; Stone 1989).

COMPLEXITIES IN POLITICAL INCORPORATION

Incorporation has never meant simply holding office. In their original work, Browning, Marshall, and Tabb presented it as a matter of being "effectively represented in policy making." The incorporation of minorities thus could be assessed by "the extent to which they were represented in coalitions that dominate city policy making on minority-related issues" (1984, 25). By introducing the concept of urban regime, this chapter moves the discussion beyond the question of coalitions within the city council to the issue of the governance of the community and how various groups are related in that process.

Atlanta is particularly fitting for this wider examination. It is a city in which minority influence grew from a modest beginning as a voice in electoral contests between two white factions (but initially no office holding by African Americans themselves) to a position of electoral dominance in a city with a clear black majority. In some cities the issue is how much voice minorities have in the winning electoral coalition. Atlanta passed that point and has had black control of city hall since 1973. Despite intermittent episodes of discord, city hall and the business sector operate with a large measure of cooperation and goodwill. At the center of this informal partnership is a continuing devotion to economic development, especially in and around the central business district.

In assessing the change in electoral control of city hall, one observer put it succinctly when he said that black officeholders were committed mainly to "guaranteeing for blacks a more equitable share of existing governmental benefits and services within existing priorities" (Jones 1978, 99). At this writing, the partnership has been particularly centered on Atlanta's hosting of the 1996 Olympic Games. Black leaders have claimed a major part in those plans and projects without offering a competing set of priorities.

There is a fault line within the African-American community between haves and have-nots, but its reflection in electoral politics is quite weak (Clendinen 1986; Pierannunzi and Hutcheson 1990). More notable is the low level of voter participation, especially among the younger generation of African Americans (Affigne 1995). Atlanta's urban regime is therefore built around accommodations principally between the black middle class and white business elites. It is a regime that addresses some issues but not others.

We examine this matter below, first by looking at development policy and then turning to education. We do this by asking the question: "Who is being incorporated into what?" The "what" part of the question is a way of asking about the leverage that electoral control of city hall provides. In examining development issues, we can see that for this arena the real policy-making entity is the political economy of the metropolitan region, not simply city government.

The "who" part of the question is a way of questioning the assumption that African Americans in Atlanta have uniform interests. The nature of group interests for minorities is a complicated matter. For racial groups that have experienced nearly total exclusion, gains by any individual member are symbolically important for the entire group. But as individual gains accumulate and positions of power come into the hands of members of the racial group, more complex issues emerge—issues of how opportunities are made available to others.

Far from always being homogeneous, a racial minority can experience different interests along several lines—class, gender, religion, and recency of migration among them (Anyon 1995; Johnson 1995). In Atlanta's African-American community, class is a conspicuous divide, and the policy arena of education brings this divide into the spotlight. The city's school system is under the direction of middle-class professionals whereas nearly three-quarters of the students in that system are poor.

WHO IS INCORPORATED INTO *WHAT:*
THE CASE OF DEVELOPMENT

Background

A regime perspective reminds us that government, especially local government, is quite limited in what it can do on its own. One recent assessment of the Atlanta experience concludes that "local government is not nearly so powerful as state government, federal government, or the private sector in affecting broad social, economic and educational problems" (Orfield and Ashkinaze 1991, 24). Former mayor Andrew Young (1991) adds: "It is important to understand how little a mayor or a school superintendent can do about expanding opportunities to the truly needy." Economic competition among localities constrains even further what city governments can do (Peterson 1981). Yet, while local officials have little capacity to act alone, they are a significant part of the regime.

The present policies and practices in Atlanta came about through a process of conflict and negotiation, and that process continues. Always at issue is the set of terms under which a governing coalition operates. Holding local office is only part of the picture. City government is subject to federal mandates. It needs business cooperation (and business needs government cooperation). City government is a legal creature of state government but also a partner with state government.

Atlanta's regime rests on multiple relationships, the most obvious of which is the local government/business relationship. So when the black community initially gained an electoral voice and later electoral control of city hall, what it gained was a position in a complex of relationships—not a position from which it could exercise much in the way of an independent form of power, certainly not in the arena of development. Given this reality, black leaders were concerned that the benefits of economic growth would not be shared widely enough. When Maynard Jackson, the city's first black mayor, launched his campaign in 1974, he used various metaphors—"a place at the table," "a piece of the pie"—to indicate his determination to see benefits come to African Americans and others who had been largely left out.

The white business community for its part searched for ways to buffer investment activity from such demands, even activity subsidized by the city and other levels of government. Evolving over time, the strategy of the white business elite has had several parts. As it became clear that the city would have a black electoral majority, an effort was made to bring the black middle class into the mainstream of the civic life of the Atlanta business community. There was, after all, a long history of negotiation and accommodation between the white business elite and the black middle class.

In the late 1960s, two new organizations—Leadership Atlanta and Action Forum—were formed to provide means through which black and white business people could be brought together to consider various civic issues and seek common ground. The Chamber of Commerce also moved to integrate African Americans into its membership and activities. At the same time, although black demands for affirmative action were initially resisted, the white business community did not reject those demands totally. Subsequently it came to accept the idea that city employment and city contracts would carry affirmative action guarantees.

While making these moves of conciliation, business leaders sought to promote development and the public subsidy of development in ways that were insulated from city hall control. Examples of the kinds of arrangements the business community has promoted include the issuance of tax-free development bonds by an independent authority (the Atlanta Downtown Development Authority) and a nonprofit corporation to direct Underground Atlanta, the city's entertainment district.

Over time, the white business elite has thus made use of varied strategies to see that major parts of economic development activity would be insulated from city hall control. Therefore, while African Americans have achieved a strong form of electoral incorporation, their control is over a limited sphere of development—even though much of that activity is publicly subsidized.

Two Atlantas

To some in the black community, development policy may look like a well-coordinated conspiracy to perpetuate black economic disadvantage. Yet no single group is in command. Especially at the level of the metropolitan region, somewhat autonomous parts pursue their separate agendas, mostly unmindful of the larger whole that they construct.

Beginning with an expanded power of eminent domain for urban renewal, Atlanta business leaders have sought state resources and state authority to advance their development agenda. They have transformed the business district and have gotten state and local governments to build expressways and an arc of public facilities to provide a buffer zone between this transformed business district and low-income areas nearby.

For its part, the state of Georgia has seen the Atlanta economy as the dynamo of state economic growth. With city and business encouragement, the state has been willing to build a huge convention facility (the Georgia World Congress Center) and an adjoining domed stadium. In preparation for the Olympic Games it created a new entity, the Metropolitan Atlanta Olympic Games Authority, with the power to condemn land, issue bonds, and approve construction contracts.

At the same time that the state bolsters Atlanta's economy and through it the regional economy as well, the state of Georgia leaves intact a government structure designed in a much earlier era—a structure that separates Atlanta's booming suburbs from the city and its problems. The city now has only 14 percent of the metropolitan area's population, but it has 40 percent of the area's children below the poverty line.

State transportation policy encourages metropolitan fragmentation, expanding expressways to accommodate "edge city" development to the north while leaving the city-centered mass transit system confined to an inner core (Garreau 1988). This is not a result altogether favored by downtown businesses, but they accept it as an outcome backed solidly by suburban voting power.

The regional economy reaches far beyond the central city, and may well be said to have created two Atlantas, one predominantly black and the other heavily white. A recent study found that over a five-year period, "the five predominantly black [subregions] had a less than five percent rate of job growth while the seven [subregions] within metropolitan Atlanta with a greater than ninety percent white population had an average growth rate more than fourteen times higher" (Orfield and Ashkinaze 1991, 17).

Electoral control of city government thus falls far short of full incorporation into the making of development policy, which is centered in the private sector but involves significant public activities as well. The renewal of Atlanta's business district illustrates the point. Over a period of many years, the major downtown firms worked to have public office buildings (federal, state, and local) concentrated in the lower part of the business district and provide the infrastructure to move the financial district to an area north of the old business district, an area now known as "Midtown." This area was deemed desirable because it is close to the city's Northside, a predominantly white and affluent residential area.

The shift of the financial district northward never surfaced as a public issue and was treated as a purely private decision even though a series of public actions facilitated it. And it was made at a time when public rhetoric favored the black community's aim of promoting Southside development—that is, development in the area of black concentration, This aim, however, never was converted into a concrete program of action.

Discussion

Decisions overlie one another. So, while former mayor Andrew Young and other black elected officials proudly cite the 1,200 minority contractors involved in building various projects under city and state auspices (Orfield and Ashkinaze 1991, vii), these projects in reality contributed to an overall pattern of development that perpetuates the two Atlantas. Development comes through a combination of public and private actions, and electoral office confers only limited leverage over the total process, especially if officeholders are mainly focused on the particulars of who receives various contracts.

In one sense, the incorporation of African Americans into the Atlanta regime amounts to more than electoral control of city hall. It extends into the business and civic life of the city, but this incorporation is limited. Business interests make key decisions in the privacy of the boardroom, not in the more racially inclusive circles of Atlanta's civic life. State agencies, such as the department of transportation, make critical decisions as well, and they also operate without much voice from Atlanta's black leaders.

Incorporation is not an all-or-nothing matter. The action of a governing coalition rests not just on who has membership but also on the terms of involvement. Jobs and contracts were the main terms of black incorporation into economic development, and they were the principal harvest from a succession of electoral victories. Rhetoric about Southside development addressed a real concern, but black officials had neither the means nor the inclination to convert words into a plan of action. Bargaining for a general aim such as Southside development had less immediate appeal than seeking to increase the share of jobs and contracts going to the black community.

WHO IS INCORPORATED INTO WHAT: SCHOOLS AND SCHOOLING

In the economic arena, the pursuit of a broad aim like Southside development runs into the largely private character of the regional political economy. Education appears to be a different kind of arena. Although subject to state regulations, Atlanta's school system nevertheless enjoys considerable autonomy. Formal control appears solidly black. The Atlanta school system is an independent district, with its own taxing power. The school board and the school administrators have the authority to formulate an educational policy and seemingly the means to carry it out. On the face of it, education should be an arena in which collective purpose thrives. However, Atlanta's experience suggests that education is as complex in its own way as economic development is in its particular way. The path toward the broad aim of educational improvement for Atlanta's school children has proved to be filled with pitfalls.

Optimism, however, pervaded the first stage of black political incorporation in education. In 1973, with a federal judge's concurrence, a biracial committee negotiated an agreement known as the "Atlanta compromise" (Fleishman 1980). The heart of this agreement provided for black political and administrative control of the city's public school system in exchange for relinquished pursuit of busing either on a metropolitan basis or within the city (the city's school enrollment was about three-quarters African American at this point). Urban League Director Lyndon Wade, chair of the committee, stated, "I have always believed that if you could ever achieve equity in the administration of the school system, then it would improve the chances of black kids getting a better education" (quoted in Orfield and Ashkinaze 1991, 110).

The "compromise" laid the foundation for appointing a black superintendent, and subsequently African Americans came to control most of the key positions in the education arena. Currently two-thirds of the school board members are African American, as are holders of nine of the top 11 administrative posts, including the office of superintendent. African-American enrollment now exceeds 90 percent. Per-pupil expenditure is relatively high, and the city pays its teachers a slightly higher salary than do the surrounding suburbs (Orfield and Ashkinaze 1991, 141; Pierannunzi, Pedescleaux, and Hutcheson 1994). Yet the performance of the school system has been disappointing.

The hope was that "black administrators would understand the needs of black children and would *find* ways to make segregated, low-income, inner-city schools equal to middle-class white schools" (Orfield and Ashkinaze 1991, 109). Early on, however, some were skeptical that changing the race of the school superintendent would have a transforming effect. In a 1970s study of the Atlanta school system, one respondent complained that "school administrators, almost regardless of their background and certainly regardless of whether they are white or black, tend to be autocratic and bullheaded about their professional prerogatives" (Gittell 1980, 187). Moreover changing race did not change class perspective. Another respondent disapproved of the superintendent's "middle-class orientation," citing administration opposition to a school breakfast program because the superintendent thought "it disrupts an important part of family life" (Gittell 1980, 184).

Nevertheless, in the early days of black incorporation, hope ran high and public criticism was sparse. Hopefulness, however, proved short-lived. Test scores initially indicated significant gains, but these improved scores turned out to be based on manipulations of the test data. When the state began to release scores comparing school districts on the same data base, Atlanta school children fared poorly. Early elementary gains did not carry over to high school, and by ninth grade, Atlanta students' scores were below those for "the state's poor, rural majority-black districts" (Orfield and Ashkinaze 1991, 121).

Manipulating test data was by no means unique to the Atlanta system (Finn 1991, 100–104). Still, the effort "to maintain an aura of success" deflected attention from facing the problem of persistent low achievement and high dropout rates (cf. Sussman 1977, 225). Only gradually has the issue of educational performance gained public attention.

For the black community, gaining control of the school system posed a dilemma. Academic achievement rests not only on educational practices but is also embedded in social and economic conditions over which the school system has little control. Yet for school officials to talk openly about low test scores and high dropout rates might only highlight weaknesses in student performance and could even contribute to further flight from the system (Orfield and Ashkinaze 1991, 7, 25). Although the roots of student achievement are far deeper than school system performance, the public has little appreciation of such subtleties. Many citizens would simply say that schools should do better, and, indeed, schools that have high expectations and give close personal attention to students can make a difference. This approach, however, could mean a heavy concentration on the classroom, and a minimal number of administrative and nonteaching positions (Bryk, Lee, and Holland 1993; Meier 1995). In short, it could result in scaling back the opportunities for career advancement by an administrative route. Moreover, any new approach is likely to take time to have an impact (Comer 1980).

In Atlanta in the 1970s, the situation was further complicated by the high expectations surrounding black control of the school system. To acknowledge publicly that low academic achievement was not amenable to the quick fix of a change in the racial control of school administration would be risky; administrators might be seen as admitting failure. As it turned out, not acknowledging the problem and instead promoting "an aura of success" carried an even greater hazard—that of breeding cynicism and opportunism within the school system.

After the "Atlanta compromise," the school board and its agenda were initially controlled tightly by the superintendent (Gittell 1980, 200). With time, however, the school board became heavily involved in the details of administration and the rendering of services and jobs to constituents. One observer described the board "as an employment agency of last resort" (Tucker 1993). Allegations of corruption and mishandling funds surfaced, with one member being convicted of receiving a $200,000 kickback from a contractor (Pierannunzi, Pedescleaux, and Hutcheson 1994). A report from Atlanta Clark University found the school board to be the "most criticized and ridiculed" body in city government (Holmes 1993).

Though the school board was a symbol of black political control and though one of its most controversial members defended his actions as "best for blacks," the rhetoric of racial solidarity ceased to provide protective cover (Holmes 1993). In 1993, a biracial coalition came together to elect a new school board majority and move toward greater concern with educational performance. Yet when the new superintendent assumed office, he focused primarily on more efficient internal operations and took up the economizing measure of school closings.

Discussion

In writing about black regimes, Adolph Reed observes that "discourse about and within black political activity posits the racial collectivity as its central agency and racial discrimination as its main analytical category. Within that discourse a benefit that accrues to any member of the group is a benefit to the entire group" (1988, 157). Reed criticizes this form of discourse for downplaying class differences within the black community and muffling a needed debate over how policy alternatives affect various segments of the population (see also Barnes 1994).

The Atlanta experience shows that, as Reed argues, gains for some do not necessarily contribute to the advance of all. What benefits the individual may not benefit the larger group, except in a vaguely symbolic way. Jobs and contracts that are open to members of the middle class may offer little to the lower class. Moreover, as individual officeholders strive to gain allies and protect their position, these actions may work against attention to larger group aims. In education, a rhetoric of black solidarity was used to advance the same kind of policy evident in the development arena—jobs and contracts for adults, not expanded opportunity for the city's children and youth.

Improving education for those from nonaffluent backgrounds is no easy task. The school system has not achieved it under either black or white control. Recently, former president Jimmy Carter sought to enlist Atlanta's volunteer sector in combating poverty, and one task force dealt with education. But success was limited, even on such a modest goal as tutoring in the public schools (Bailey 1995). Long-term volunteer commitments to sustain tutoring are difficult to obtain. The most successful efforts have been small, focused groups, like 100 Black Men of Atlanta with its mentoring program, and these groups operate outside Carter's Atlanta project.

What the recently mobilized biracial education coalition will produce remains to be seen. New members of the school board and a new superintendent are only a first step toward fundamental change. The term "incorporation" implies that there is a ready capacity in place and that disadvantaged groups need only gain an inside position to secure policy gains. Experience suggests otherwise.

School systems are large enterprises that control substantial benefits in the form of jobs, fringe benefits, and various business and professional opportunities. Those in a position to distribute such benefits have a narrow path to follow—control what is available and keep enough insiders and their allies content to perpetuate that control. Preoccupation with that strategy, however, diverts attention from the alternative of adopting new approaches and creating a different set of arrangements for addressing problems long neglected. The latter is an uncertain path with unknown risks and not always appealing to those who have electoral or professional positions to protect.

To understand how policy paths come to be followed, it is necessary, as Adolph Reed has suggested, to look beyond the race of officeholders and those receiving jobs and contracts. Who is involved in the governing coalition is only the first-level concern. The deeper question involves the terms on which they are part of the governing structure and the policy aims to which they are devoted.

Black interests, as Reed points out, do not constitute a monolithic whole. Atlanta's experience makes that point forcefully. In a move from disestablishing the Jim Crow system to the challenge of expanding opportunity, especially for the city's poor and near-poor, the complexity of the task has increased greatly. Changing employment and contract procedures proved to be only a first step. The aim of expanded opportunity for the group can give way to the pursuit of specific gains for particular individuals. Rewarding an ally with a lucrative appointment as school board attorney is readily achievable. Altering a long-standing pattern of weak student performance is not, especially where pessimism and cynicism have taken hold. In a world where achieving broad group progress appears to be a herculean task, it is tempting to choose something easily doable, like favors for friends and constituents.

CONCLUSION

If incorporation were only a matter of electoral influence and its benefits, the Atlanta story would be simple. With the demographic balance shifting to an African-American majority in the 1970s, black control of city hall and the Atlanta school system became a reality. However, control of public office is only part of the foundation for a governing coalition. Electoral outcomes are an incomplete guide to the nature and composition of a city's governing coalition. Why?

A political economy perspective provides one answer. Public officeholders find themselves in the position of needing to promote business activity but lacking control of it. They can encourage it by putting public money into transportation, police protection, and other services. They can build convention centers and host major events. But these public actions are only a small part of the picture. Private ownership places many important decisions beyond the reach of electoral politics.

Furthermore, with money, prestige, connections, and an organizational capacity at their command, business executives can play a big role in city affairs, especially if they act as a cohesive force as they have in Atlanta. The business sector in Atlanta has pulled city hall toward its agenda. It can make things happen and produce visible results. With the added enticement of jobs and contracts that come from large development projects, the city's African-American political leadership finds this alliance very attractive. The black middle class and the white business elite have accumulated a long history of successful and backstage negotiations. It is an alliance that works. It has members who have learned the lessons of bargaining and accommodation. A local observer, in citing the city's "mercantile ethic," said that a room full of black and white leaders in Atlanta "is nothing but a roomful of people trying to cut a deal" (*Atlanta Constitution*, August 11, 1987).

Wanting to cut a deal is, however, not enough to forge a cohesive coalition. Distrust is to be expected among those unaccustomed to interacting with one another (Hardin 1982; Axelrod 1984). But Atlanta provides a situation in which interaction across racial lines is a deep and constantly renewed tradition. Newcomers learn from old hands, and organizations such as Action Forum are structured to maintain that tradition. Although the habit of trust does not come easily, the leaders in Atlanta's governing coalition realize that; and they take deliberate steps to preserve the city's tradition of biracial cooperation. This tradition makes possible an accommodation between the city's economic sector and its political-electoral sector. Tight cross-sector cooperation has enabled the Atlanta regime to carry out an active development agenda.

Although Atlanta has had close and continuing cooperation between the two sectors, not all cities experience that same level of cooperation. In some, it is a more episodic form of cooperation, and Atlanta could move in that direction if corporate leaders take a less active role in the future. Atlanta has had tight collaboration because the business sector has enjoyed unity around an ambitious redevelopment agenda and has been able to gain the support of the black middle class through the city's ethos of "let's cut a deal." Accommodation around a less particularistic set of policy transactions might have been much more difficult and might also have produced fewer minority jobs and contracts.

Education presents a further complexity. Why didn't putting the schools under black political and administrative control bring about the high level of performance for the city's poor children once hoped for? Why have jobs and contracts been central concerns? These questions lead us to ask about the nature of the educational task and how officeholders see and react to that task.

Control of top positions in a school system and the ability to determine school policy do not assure educational results, especially in the short run. School board members and administrators thus have little opportunity to coalesce around a policy capable of producing results that are quick, substantial, and highly visible. With the large role that family and community influences play in the academic performance of children, educators can produce substantial improvements only by enlisting these forces or creating effective surrogates for them. In either case, the process is long term and uncertain.

Given that the general public is somewhat naive about the extent of effort needed to improve student performance and, in any event, tends to view it as strictly a matter of school responsibility, school board members and administrators see a long-term and uncertain process as politically unappealing. If there is no broad and immediate program success to provide political cover, then those in top positions are quite vulnerable. They might well choose to build support by rendering favors, making alliances around quick-return opportunities, or touting a succession of superficial "innovations."

In both development policy and education, black interests turn out to be quite complex. There is a group stake in opening jobs and contracts to members of the African-American community, but group access to those benefits fails to alter the disadvantage suffered by the city's lower class. Indeed, the competitive scramble for middle-class jobs and contracts may even divert efforts from the expansion of opportunities for the larger population. In any case, the scramble does not assure attention to policy questions of special relevance to the lower class.

What lessons do we draw from the Atlanta experience? We have long looked on democratic politics as the process that equalizes opportunities and redresses imbalances. Yet, numbers alone amount to little. That the black community electorally controls city hall leaves open the question of which policy concerns are represented and how different segments of the black community are affected by various actions and inactions. Electoral power is not a key that by itself unlocks the door to policy success. It is only one of several keys. The capture of elected and administrative positions can yield immediate and particular benefits. But it is no guarantee that broad efforts at problem solving will be undertaken.

REFERENCES

Affigne, Anthony D. 1995. The Urban Regime's Shaky Foundation. Paper presented at the annual meeting of the National Conference of Black Political Scientists, Baltimore, March 8–12.

Anyon, Jean. 1995. Racial, Social Class, and Educational Reform in an Inner-city School. *Teachers College Record* 97 (Fall): 69–94.

Axelrod, Robert. 1984. *The Evolution of Cooperation*. New York: Basic Books.

Bacote, C. A. 1955. The Negro in Atlanta Politics. *Phylon* 16 (4): 333–350.

Bailey, Anne L. 1995. Critical Report Leads Jimmy Carter's Atlanta Anti-Poverty Drive to Make Changes. *Chronicle of Philanthropy*, March 9, 8.

Barnes, Claude W., Jr. 1994. Black Mecca Reconsidered. In Marilyn E. Lashley and Melanie Njeri Jackson, eds., *African Americans and the New Policy Consensus*. Westport, Conn.: Greenwood Press.

Browning, Rufus P., Dale Rogers Marshall, and David H. Tabb. 1984. *Protest Is Not Enough*. Berkeley: University of California Press.

Bryk, Anthony S., Valerie E. Lee, and Peter B. Holland. 1993. *Catholic Schools and the Common Good*. Cambridge, Mass.: Harvard University Press.

Clendinen, Dudley. 1986. In Black Atlanta, Affluence and Sophistication Are for the Few. *New York Times*, January 20, 10.

Comer, James P. 1980. *School Power*. New York: Free Press.

Eisinger, Peter K. 1980. *The Politics of Displacement*. New York: Academic Press.

Elkin, Stephen L. 1985. Twentieth-Century Urban Regimes. *Journal of Urban Affairs* 7 (Spring): 11–28.

Finn, Chester E. 1991. *We Must Take Charge*. New York: Free Press.

Fleishman, Joel L. 1980. The Real against the Ideal—Making the Solution Fit the Problem. In Robert B. Goldman, ed., *Roundtable Justice*. Boulder, Colo.: Westview Press.

Garreau, Joel. 1988. *Edge City*. New York: Doubleday.

Gittell, Marilyn. 1980. *Limits to Citizen Participation*. Beverly Hills, Calif.: Sage.

Hardin, Russell. 1982. *Collective Action*. Baltimore: Johns Hopkins University Press.

Holmes, Robert. 1993. *The Status of Black Atlanta, 1993*. Atlanta: Southern Center for Studies in Public Policy, Clark Atlanta University.

Hornsby, Alton, Jr. 1982. A City Too Busy to Hate. In Elizabeth Jacoway and David R. Coburn, eds., Southern Businessmen and Desegregation. Baton Rouge: Louisiana State University Press.

Jennings, M. Kent, and Harmon Zeigler. 1966. Class, Party, and Race in Four Types of Elections: The Case of Atlanta. *Journal of Politics* 28 (May): 391–407.

Johnson, Valerie, 1995. The Political Consequences of Black Suburbanization: Prince George's County, Maryland, 1971–1994. Unpublished Ph.D. dissertation, University of Maryland.

Jones, Mack H. 1978. Black Political Empowerment in Atlanta: Myth and Reality. *Annals of the American Academy of Political and Social Science* 439 (September): 90–117.

Key, V. O., Jr. 1949. *Southern Politics in State and Nation*. New York: Knopf.

Martin, Harold H. 1978. *William Berry Hartsfield: Mayor of Atlanta*. Athens: University of Georgia Press.

Meier, Deborah. 1995. *The Power of Their Ideas*. Boston: Beacon Press.

Mollenkopf, John H. 1992. *A Phoenix in the Ashes: The Rise and Fall of the Koch Coalition in New York City Politics*. Princeton, N.J.: Princeton University Press.

Orfield, Gary, and Carole Ashkinaze. 1991. *The Closing Door*. Chicago: University of Chicago Press.

Peterson, Paul E. 1981. *City Limits*. Chicago: University of Chicago Press.

Pierannunzi, Carol, and John D. Hutcheson, Jr. 1990. Electoral Change and Regime Maintenance. *PS: Political Science and Politics* (June): 151–153.

Pierannunzi, Carol, Desiree Pedescleaux, and John D. Hutcheson, Jr. 1994. From Conflict to Coalition: The Evolution of Educational Reform in Atlanta. Unpublished report for the Civic Capacity and Urban Education Project.

Reed, Adolph, Jr. 1988. The Black Urban Regime. In Michael P. Smith, ed., *Power, Community and the City*. New Brunswick, N.J.: Transaction Press.

Stone, Clarence N. 1989. *Regime Politics*. Lawrence: University Press of Kansas.

Sussman, Leila. 1977. *Tales out of School*. Philadelphia: Temple University Press.

Tucker, Cynthia. 1993. Ousting School Board May Not Be So Simple. *Atlanta Journal and Constitution*, January 20, A13.

Walker, Jack L. 1963a. Protest and Negotiation: A Case Study of Negro Leadership in Atlanta, Georgia. *Midwest Journal of Political Science* 7 (May): 99–124.

Walker, Jack L. 1963b. Negro Voting in Atlanta, 1953–1961. *Phylon* 24 (Winter): 379–387.

Walker, Jack L. 1963c. Protest and Negotiation: A Study of Negro Political Leaders in a Southern City. Unpublished Ph.D. dissertation, State University of Iowa.

Young, Andrew. 1991. Foreword to *The Closing Door* by Gary Orfield and Carole Ashkinaze. Chicago: University of Chicago Press.

chapter **8**

The Evolution and Impact of
Biracial Coalitions and Black Mayors
in Birmingham and New Orleans

Huey L. Perry[1]

Editors' Note

How much difference do leaders make? How do their styles and strategies shape black-white politics? This chapter documents the astonishing change from white and more or less racist regimes in two cities of the Deep South to regimes in which blacks play leading roles. But the chapter demonstrates also that black leadership may unfold in quite different ways in spite of regional and developmental similarities. As Huey Perry shows, Richard Arrington, mayor of Birmingham, Alabama, is a consensus builder who established cooperative relations with business and gained control over city council elections. In contrast, Ernest Morial, mayor of New Orleans from 1977 to 1985, was unsuccessful in controlling council elections, and had a more confrontational style.

Perry credits both Arrington and Morial with progressive actions and policies for blacks in executive appointments, municipal employment, and minority business programs. Have their different styles led to significantly different governmental outcomes? When two black candidates for mayor run against each other, as in New Orleans, what difference does it make for the structure and policy commitments of their competing coalitions? Finally, how do these cities compare with other southern cities with large black populations and black mayors? The reader might ask whether black successes have been greater in these two cities than in Atlanta (ch. 7), or whether the

---

[1] I am enormously grateful to Katherine Penn, my former senior research assistant, for the first-rate research assistance she provided in the revision of this chapter. I am also grateful to three other former research assistants—Tamisha Green, Adrian Lewis, and Aegeda Davis—for the valuable assistance they provided in the revision of the chapter.

marked difference in the assessment of black regimes in chapters 7 and 8 reflects different evaluational criteria of the authors.

Birmingham, Alabama, and New Orleans, Louisiana, have both had black mayors long enough to assess their impact—Birmingham since 1979 (Richard Arrington), New Orleans since 1977 (Ernest Morial, followed by Sidney Barthelemy in 1985 and Marc Morial in 1993). In both cities, developing biracial coalitions exerted significant influence in city politics during the late 1960s and early 1970s. By the mid-1970s, these coalitions were the governing coalition in the two cities. They were responsible for the election of Arrington and Morial. The biracial coalitions that elected these mayors evolved in different ways, with different consequences for the programs and policies of the two city governments and for their black populations.

This chapter analyzes the development of black politics and biracial coalitions in Birmingham and New Orleans. The overall trend in this regard is the rapid strengthening of black political organizations and the steady rise of black politicians since the 1960s. Within that common trend, the focus of this chapter is on the impact of different mayoral styles and strategies on the evolution of coalition politics and the actions and policies of city governments, especially with regard to the allocation of benefits to blacks. The impact of mayoral governance on governmental outputs is assessed with respect to police treatment of citizens, municipal employment, executive appointments, and minority business assistance.

Significant black political participation in both Birmingham and New Orleans, as is the case with most localities in the South, is a post-World War II development. In both cities, the push for blacks' inclusion in the political process was orchestrated by black political organizations. In Birmingham, the organization principally involved in this regard was the Jefferson County Progressive Democratic Council (JCPDC). JCPDC was formed in 1936 to work for the end of white supremacy in Alabama. The leaders of JCPDC filed a lawsuit in federal court, successfully contesting the exclusion of blacks from participation in the Democratic party in Alabama. The lawsuit, the formation of a state black political party (the National Democratic Party of Alabama), and pressure from the national Democratic party resulted in blacks' winning the right to participate in politics in Birmingham and in the rest of Alabama within the structure of the Democratic party.

Blacks in Birmingham in the 1950s and early 1960s encountered substantial resistance from whites to their desire to participate in the political process. Whites' resistance to blacks' demands for political rights was more severe in Birmingham than in any southern city of comparable size (Strong 1972, 443; Perry 1983, 206–207). However, the number of black voters began to increase appreciably during the early 1960s, and as their numbers increased, blacks, in coalition with middle-class whites, began to exert a greater impact on electoral outcomes. The growing black vote in Birmingham played an increasingly important role within the structure of the biracial coalition in electing seriatim the city's first racially moderate white mayor, first racially liberal white mayor, and first black mayor (see Table 8.1).

The growing black vote in Birmingham also played an important role in electing over several city elections a more racially progressive city council, a process that

TABLE 8.1 Percentage of total voter registration and political incorporation by blacks in Birmingham and New Orleans

	Birmingham		New Orleans	
Key Elections	Year	% Black Voters	Year	% Black Voters
	1960	10	1960	17
	1967	36		
	1970	40		
Racially liberal mayor	1975	41	1969	30
	1970	40		
	1977	33	1973	36
Black mayor (first time)	1979	45	1977	43
	1980	36	1980	43
	1981	37	1981	45
Black mayor (second time)	1983	51	1982	46
	1985	54	1985	51
Black mayor (second generation)			1986	51
			1989	
			1990	56
			1991	59
Black mayor (third generation)			1993	59
			1994	61
Black mayor (third term)	1987	55		
	1989	59		
	1990	59		
Black mayor (fourth term)	1991	60		
	1993	61		
	1994	62		
Black mayor (fifth term)	1995			

SOURCE: Registration data for this table were provided by the Registrar of Voters, Parish of Orleans, State of Louisiana, and the Registrar of Voters, County of Jefferson, State of Alabama.

eventually resulted in the election of a black majority to the council. Black voters over the last two decades have also played a significant role in passing bond measures that have allowed the city to dramatically improve its infrastructure and educational system and to increase other public amenities, such as libraries, important to the quality of life. Black voters have benefited as recipients of these resources through the governmental allocation process. These developments make up what Browning, Marshall, and Tabb refer to as political incorporation, which is "the extent to which" minorities "have achieved not only representation but positions of influence in local policy making" (1984, 12).

The emergence of the biracial coalition has played a critical role in shaping political life and policy outcomes in Birmingham. The coalition first emerged in the election of 1962 with a successful effort to change the type of government from the commission form to the mayor-council form. The basis of the coalition was the development of a consensus among blacks, a small number of liberal whites, and members of the business community that Police Commissioner Eugene "Bull" Connor had become a liability to the city. The leaders of these groups decided that as Connor had approximately two years remaining in office, the best way to remove him from office was to change the form of government. The strategy was successful. The government was changed from a commission form to a mayor-council form, and because of the change, Connor and the two other commissioners were removed from office (Perry 1983, 207). The next major point in the development of the coalition was the mayoral election in 1967, in which the biracial coalition was responsible for the election of George Seibels, the city's first moderate mayor. The coalition consisted of a large number of blacks, a somewhat smaller number of liberal and moderate whites, and a small number of people from the business community.

The third major point in the development of the coalition involved the mayoral election of 1975 when blacks and liberal whites helped to elect David Vann, the city's first liberal mayor. At this point, the coalition consisted of a significant black minority and a white majority. The 1975 election represented the greatest racial mixture of the coalition. The fourth major point in the development of the coalition consisted of the election of Richard Arrington as the first black mayor in 1979. The composition of the biracial coalition that elected Arrington in 1979, and which has reelected him in 1983, 1987, 1991, and 1995, is different from the composition of the coalition that elected Vann. The composition of the Arrington coalition is a large black majority with a small but significant proportion of liberal whites and businesspersons.

After several years of increased black voter registration and officeholding, a split emerged in the Jefferson County Progressive Democratic council and another organization was formed—the biracial Citizens Action Coalition. The split was basically generational. Younger black leaders grew uncomfortable with the leadership style of the older black leaders. Arrington provided the central leadership in the formation of the Coalition in 1983. The Coalition soon became the ascendant political organization in the city. It presently is the single most important organizational forum in Birmingham for the discussion of political issues in reference to blacks, the development of the black political agenda, the recruitment of blacks to public office, and the election of both blacks and whites to public office.

In New Orleans, the organization most prominently associated with the emergence of black political participation was the Orleans Parish Progressive Voters League (OPPVL). OPPVL was formed in 1949 to push for increased black political participation in New Orleans. As was the case with JCPDC in Birmingham, the influence of OPPVL eventually began to wane and its role as the organizational leader of black politics in the city was successfully challenged by another black political organization.

The evolution of black political empowerment in New Orleans and Birmingham can be attributed in part to changes in the total population and in the percentage of black registered voters since 1960. In New Orleans, from 1960 to 1990, the total population steadily declined as the proportion of black voters increased. In

1960, the total population was 627,000 and blacks represented 17 percent of the registered voter population. In 1970, those figures were 560,000 and 40 percent; in another ten years, they were 515,000 and 43 percent. By 1990, the total New Orleans population had declined to 497,000 and the registered black voter population had increased to 56 percent of the registered voter population.

A similar situation can be charted in Birmingham. In 1960, Birmingham had a total population of 341,000 and blacks accounted for 10 percent of the registered voter population. By 1970, these numbers were 276,000 and 40 percent; ten yers later they were 284,000 and 36 percent. In 1990, Birmingham's total population had declined to 266,000 and the percentage of registered black voters had increased to 59 percent of the registered voter population.

Like blacks in Birmingham, a growing number of black voters in New Orleans in coalition with middle-class whites played an increasingly important role in the election of the city's first racially moderate white mayor, first racially liberal white mayor, and first black mayor (see Table 8.1). Also, as in Birmingham, the growing black vote in New Orleans was central to the election of a more racially progressive city council and eventually a black majority council.

A key dissimilarity in the strength of the governing biracial coalitions in Birmingham and New Orleans had to do with their ability to pass bond issues and other revenue-enhancing proposals. Whereas in Birmingham blacks as part of the biracial coalition have played a consistently pivotal role in passing bond issues that have improved municipal services, in New Orleans, revenue-enhancing proposals have generally been rejected by the voters. In New Orleans, the biracial coalition that made Morial the first black mayor in the city's history in 1977 and reelected him in 1982 repeatedly broke down on revenue-enhancing proposals. Both Mayor Morial and Mayor Barthelemy failed in their efforts to convince voters to pass revenue-enhancing proposals. This difference has important implications for the quality of life enjoyed by residents of the two cities, as discussed later.

Another difference in the politics of the two cities concerns city council elections. In Birmingham, Mayor Arrington, working through the Citizens Action Coalition, virtually controls city council elections. Arrington's control over city council elections resulted in the election of a majority black council in 1987 and the selection of a black president by the council, both events occurring for the first time in the city's history. The New Orleans experience has been just the opposite of that of Birmingham, despite the fact that in 1987, New Orleans also elected its first majority black city council and the first black was chosen president of the council by the council members. Mayor Morial was unsuccessful in his efforts to control elections to the city council.

DIFFERENCE IN MAYORAL STYLE

The difference between the accomplishments of the mayors of the two cities is of such magnitude that a close examination is warranted. One possible explanation is the difference in personal style between Morial and Arrington. Morial's style during his eight-year mayoral tenure was confrontational—a style developed during his tenure as a civil rights activist. Another factor that may have contributed to Morial's governance problem, in addition to his personal style, was the poor state of the New Orleans economy. At the time of Morial's first election as mayor, New Orleans was overwhelmed with problems. These ranged from "low income and poverty, maldistribution of income, unemployment and subemployment to low educational attainment" (Schexnider 1982, 223). According to James R. Bobo, the crux of New Orleans's economic problem was not growth but inadequate economic development:

> The local economy has experienced economic stagnation tendencies since the mid and late 1950s, with chronic and severe stagnation since 1966, not because there was an absence of economic growth, but because economic development did not provide adequate employment opportunities for an expanding labor force. . . . Employment opportunities have been inadequate since 1966 . . . consequently, unemployment has increased both absolutely and as a percentage of the labor force since 1966, reaching 9.0 percent in 1975. (Bobo 1975, 1–2)

Many believe that the main reason for Morial's limited success in his mayoral leadership was his problematic relationship with the business community. However, Morial asserted that he was pro-economic development. According to Morial, he had no problem with the business community in its entirety, only with certain individuals in the business community. Morial by and large thought he had a fairly good relationship with the business community. According to Morial, the problem with certain individual business leaders involved whether the city should play a substantive role in economic development or let the private sector handle it. Additionally, Morial blamed the press rather than the business community itself for creating the friction between himself and the business community. Morial indicated that he only wanted to ensure that the city received some of the benefits from economic development activities, and certain members of the business community did not want the city to benefit in that way.[2]

In Birmingham, Arrington's style is that of a consensus builder. Arrington has cooperative relationships with the business community whereas Morial's relationship with the business community was tenuous at best. As a consensus builder, Arrington makes whites feel comfortable with a black political leadership majority in Birmingham whereas Morial made whites feel uncomfortable with majority black political leadership in New Orleans.

Throughout his mayoral tenure, Arrington has demonstrated a genuine willingness to cooperate with the business community and to make the business community a part of the governing coalition. An important symbolic manifestation of this approach is the monthly breakfast meetings Arrington holds with business leaders.

---

[2] Personal interview with Ernest "Dutch" Morial, former mayor of New Orleans, Louisiana.

Moreover, he made economic development the key policy objective of his second term and this emphasis continued during his third and fourth terms. The principal beneficiary of this policy initiative has been business interests. Even when the city's leading banks failed to give Arrington his highest priority request, a Minority Enterprise Sector and Business Initiative Cooperation program, Arrington refused to terminate accounts the city had with some of those banks.

This difference in personal style influences the ability of a black mayor to establish a political power base. To the extent that a consensus builder like Arrington can win the trust of whites generally and the business community in particular and still exert influence over blacks, he can exert tremendous influence over city council elections and thus over the success or failure of his policy and programmatic initiatives. Arrington controls not only the routes to office, particularly to the city council, but also the substantive agenda of city government, perhaps more than any other contemporary big city mayor. In this respect, Arrington is probably the most powerful urban mayor since Mayor Richard J. Daley of Chicago during the zenith of his political power in the 1960s.

The difference in mayoral leadership between Arrington and Morial is primarily one of style rather than issues. The overriding issue facing both cities during Arrington's and Morial's administrations was basically the same: how to maintain city services in the face of dramatically reduced support from the federal government and a declining tax base. However, Morial had an additional problem that Arrington does not have: Morial's policy and programmatic initiatives were constantly opposed by the second most powerful black in city government, then City Council President Sidney Barthelemy, who later became mayor. Barthelemy's opposition to Morial's policy and programmatic initiatives weakened the support of the black community for these and made it easier for other interests to oppose Morial's initiatives.

Not only did Morial have a problem with Barthelmy; he had a problem with the entire city council. Morial was not on the council when he was elected mayor. He was something of an outsider in New Orleans black politics, but he tried to build rapport with the city council. As a symbolic gesture, he had private brunches for the members of the city council and their wives. According to Morial, some city council members expected his support for traditional patronage politics in exchange for their support of his policy initiatives, but he was opposed to conducting the city's business that way. As a result of his refusal to play patronage politics, Morial believes, many of his proposals were killed by the council. The relationship between Morial and the city council was not what he had wanted it to be in either term and that was his biggest disappointment.[3]

To a large extent, the difficulty Morial had in translating proposals into public policies is explained by city council opposition. A majority of the council generally opposed Morial's proposals. The New Orleans city council comprises eight members, of whom five were black and three were white during Morial's mayoral ten-

---

[3] Personal interview with Ernest "Dutch" Morial, former mayor of New Orleans, Louisiana.

ure. The city council in Birmingham has nine members; six were black and three were white during Arrington's third and fourth terms. Morial was not nearly as successful as Arrington in shaping the council to support his proposals. Arrington achieved this objective as a result of his influence over city council elections. He was successful in helping elect a council majority that felt some political allegiance to him. By contrast, Morial was able to rely on only two of the seven council members for consistent support. Whereas black politics in Birmingham under Arrington is unicentered in the mayor's office, black politics in New Orleans under Morial was dual centered—in the mayor's office and the city council. These competing forces in black politics in New Orleans have severely limited the ability of black political participation to produce benefits for blacks.

THE IMPACT OF BLACK POLITICAL INCORPORATION ON GOVERNMENTAL ACTIONS AND POLICIES

Black political incorporation generally has meant that blacks in both cities have favorably influenced governmental actions and policies. This section assesses the impact of black political incorporation on governmental actions and policies in four categories of public sector activity: police treatment of citizens, municipal employment, executive appointments, and minority business assistance.

Police Treatment of Citizens

Historically, the relationship between blacks and the police has been problematic, fluctuating from being mildly strained to being openly confrontational. One study of police abuse of citizens in selected major cities by the U.S. Department of Justice found that police brutality in New Orleans is a major problem (U.S. Department of Justice 1991). New Orleans was rated number one out of more than one hundred cities in the study in the number of police brutality complaints made to the Department of Justice. A study for the New Orleans Human Relations Commission examined data on brutality complaints filed against the New Orleans Police Department (NOPD) in 1990, 1991, and 1992 (Perry and Delmas 1992). According to the study, 140 complaints were filed against black officers by black complainants, and 16 complaints were filed against black officers by white complainants. Also, 86 complaints were filed against white officers by black complainants and 19 against white officers by white complainants (Perry and Delmas 1992, 23). These findings lead to two major conclusions: blacks are significantly more likely than whites to file police brutality complaints, and white officers are much less likely than black officers to be the subject of black complaints (Perry and Delmas 1992, 22). The latter conclusion stands out in stark contrast to the popular perception that blacks are frequently subjected to abuse by white police officers.

The situation regarding police treatment of citizens in Birmingham is entirely different from that of New Orleans. In fact, Birmingham could be a model for New

Orleans and other cities in this regard. Mayor Arrington's efforts to eliminate police brutality in Birmingham is an excellent example of how mayors can substantially improve the relations between black citizens and the police. During the 1950s, 1960s, and 1970s, Birmingham had a widespread problem of white police officers abusing black citizens. The professionalization of the police department was a high priority for Arrington during his first term. His efforts were very successful; police officers used less force in making arrests, and charges for resisting officers and assaults decreased. In fact, police brutality complaints dropped by 75 percent during Arrington's first term (Franklin 1989).

Police brutality continued to decline in Birmingham beyond Arrington's first term. Table 8.2 presents data on excessive force by race of complainants for the city of Birmingham between 1973 and 1991. The table presents annual data on excessive force complaints in addition to two-year averages. The importance of the two-year averages is that these averages produce a better determination of trend lines given wide fluctuations in the annual data. In terms of total number of excessive force complaints, the annual data generally reveal that the number of complaints decreased between 1973 and 1982 and increased between 1982 and 1991. The two-year averages reflect this general trend but place it in starker relief. Between 1973 and 1982, the two-year averages show that the total number of excessive force complaints declined by 45 percent, although there was an 11 percent increase between 1974 and 1976. The two-year averages also show that between 1982 and 1988, the number of excessive force complaints increased by 122 percent, with a 9 percent decrease by 1990.

Table 8.2 also presents annual data on black and white excessive force complaints and two-year averages of the annual data for the years between 1975 and 1985. The annual data show that between 1975 and 1985, black excessive force complaints declined substantially over the period to less than half the number at the beginning of it. White excessive force complaints declined more than black excessive force complaints between 1975 and 1985. Extraordinarily, Mayor Arrington reported in 1990 that police brutality simply did not exist in Birmingham (Perry 1992). This optimistic assessment belies the data presented in Table 8.2.

Municipal Employment

The capacity of increased black political participation to produce an increased share of municipal employment has received much attention in the scholarly literature on black politics (Eisinger 1980, 1982; Perry 1983, 1990a, 1990b, 1992; Browning, Marshall, and Tabb 1984; Stein 1986; Perry and Stokes 1987, 1993; Stein and Condrey 1987; Mladenka 1989a, 1989b; McClain 1993). Earlier research has confirmed the strength of that relationship in Birmingham and New Orleans (Perry 1983; Perry and Stokes 1987; Perry 1990a, 1990b, 1992).

In Birmingham, by 1985, blacks had succeeded in integrating the city's workforce at all occupational levels, although they were disproportionately employed in service/maintenance and office/clerical categories. Table 8.3 presents municipal

TABLE 8.2 Excessive force complaints by race of complainants for the city of Birmingham, 1973 to 1991

Year	Total Number of Complaints	Total Two-Year Avg.	Black			White		
			No.	%	Two-Year Avg.	No.	%	Two-Year Avg.
1973	27		—	—		—	—	
1974	39	33	—	—		—	—	
1975	54		34	63		20	37	
1976	19	36.5	13	68	23.5	6	22	13
1977	33		15	45		18	55	
1978	—		—	—		—	—	
1979	26		17	65		9	35	
1980	35	30.5	21	60	19	14	40	11.5
1981	18		11	61		7	39	
1982	18	18	11	61	11	7	39	7
1983	39		26	67		13	39	
1984	15	27	10	67	18	5	33	9
1985	21		15	71		6	29	
1986	39	30	—	—		—	—	
1987	37		—	—		—	—	
1988	43	40	—	—		—	—	
1989	34		—	—		—	—	
1990	39	36.5	—	—		—	—	
1991	45		—	—		—	—	
Totals	581		173	*62		105	*38	

* This percentage is based on the total number of complaints for the period between 1975 and 1985, which is 278.

SOURCE: Data on the number of complaints provided by the Birmingham, Alabama, Police Department.

employment data for Birmingham for 1993 by race, using an index of representation[4] to indicate the extent to which blacks and whites were under- or overrepresented in the standard Equal Opportunity Office occupational classifications. The table confirms the pattern of the 1985 data. Although blacks remained fully integrated into the city's workforce, they were still overrepresented in low-skilled, low-wage classifications (service/maintenance and paraprofessionals). Table 8.3

[4] The index of representation is a standard statistical technique for determining the extent to which target groups are under- or overrepresented in certain classifications, using their percentage in the general population or the labor force as a baseline. The index of representation is computed by dividing a group's percentage in a target classification by the group's percentage in the baseline category. A quotient of 1 indicates perfect representation. A quotient of less than 1 indicates underrepresentation. A quotient of greater than 1 indicates overrepresentation.

also shows that blacks were underrepresented in the higher-scale, higher-paying occupational classifications (professionals, technicians, skilled craft workers and officials/administrators). For whites, Table 8.3 shows the exact opposite pattern, except for the paraprofessional classification in which blacks and whites are virtually equally represented.

Although the tendency for blacks to be employed in low-scale, low-wage occupational classifications reflects a limitation on black political participation, it is possible to interpret this pattern in a way that reflects quasi-positively on black political participation. The employment of blacks in low-scale, low-wage classifications is important because the jobs in these classifications are significant sources of employment for low-income blacks. This is an important consideration because an increasing criticism of black politics is that the benefits produced by increased black political incorporation have gone to members of the black middle class who possessed the education, occupational, and social skills necessary to take advantage of the new opportunities. There is considerable validity to this criticism. The irony is that the increased black political participation and influence in cities in the 1970s and 1980s is in large part a result of the entry of a significantly larger proportion of the black lower class into electoral politics, and their political awakening was often stimulated by the prospect of electing a viable black candidate to a high-level political office. By increasing employment opportunities for blacks in the office/clerical and especially the service/maintenance classifications, black politics in Birmingham has produced significant benefits for members of the black working class.

Although blacks in Birmingham have clearly not achieved an equitable proportion of municipal employment commensurate with their approximately 55 percent of the city's population, they have made significant progress in increasing their representation in municipal employment. In addition to strong representation of blacks in the service/maintenance and office/clerical categories, blacks, as Table 8.3 shows, were also well represented in the middle-level occupational classifications, which generally consist of jobs that require more skills and pay better than the service/maintenance and office/clerical classifications. These classifications include skilled craft workers, paraprofessionals, protective services, and technicians. Blacks made up 37 percent of skilled craft workers, 64 percent of paraprofessionals, 42 percent of protective services workers, and 37 percent of technicians. Blacks were also well represented in the two high-skill, high-wage categories: professionals (33 percent) and officials/ administrators (39 percent). As a result of black political empowerment in Birmingham, the representation of blacks in municipal employment has increased. One of the strongest relationships in the black politics literature is the relationship between increased black political participation and blacks' obtaining increased municipal employment (Eisinger 1980; Stein 1986).

Increases in black political employment in New Orleans have been similar to those in Birmingham. Between 1960 and 1985, the last year of the mayoral administration of Ernest Morial, New Orleans's first black mayor, the black proportion of the New Orleans municipal work force increased from a small percentage to 53 percent. The bulk of that increase occurred during the eight-year mayoralty of Moon Landrieu, the city's first white liberal mayor. Table 8.4 provides data on municipal

TABLE 8.3 Full-time employees for the city of Birmingham by race, 1993

Occupation Classification	Black			White			Other		
	No.	%	IOR*	No.	%	IOR*	No.	%	IOR*
Officials/administrators	13	39.39	0.61	17	51.51	1.45	3	9.09	13.56
Professionals	116	32.95	0.51	231	65.62	1.84	5	1.42	2.11
Technicians	168	37.25	0.57	281	62.3	1.75	2	0.44	0.65
Protective services workers	615	42.18	0.65	839	57.54	1.62	4	0.27	0.4
Paraprofessionals	83	64.36	0.99	45	34.88	0.98	1	0.77	1.15
Office/clerical workers	236	58.7	0.91	165	41.04	1.15	1	0.24	0.36
Skilled craft workers	90	37.19	0.57	151	62.39	1.75	1	0.41	0.61
Service/maintenance workers	703	76.66	1.18	214	23.33	0.65	0	0	0
Totals	2024	50.8	0.78	1943	48.77	1.37	17	0.42	0.62

*Index of representation.

SOURCE: Data on the number of full-time employees provided by the City of Birmingham, Alabama.

employment for the city of New Orleans by race for 1993, also using the index of representation as the critical measure of the representation of blacks in city employment. The index of representation in this table indicates the same general pattern as that for Birmingham: blacks were overrepresented in the low-scale, low-paying occupational classifications, and underrepresented in the higher-scale, higher-paying occupational classifications.

Executive Appointments

Executive appointments include appointments by the mayor of his top personal executive staff and heads of departments of city government. Previous research has shown that increased black political participation and influence in both Birmingham and New Orleans have resulted in a significant increase in black representation in these key executive positions. In Birmingham, black representation in key executive positions increased from zero in 1975—before the election of David Vann, the city's first racially liberal white mayor—to 44 percent of the mayor's top personal executive staff positions (four out of nine positions) and one department head during Vann's administration (Perry 1983, 212). Throughout his mayoral tenure, at least 50 percent of Arrington's top personal executive staff has been black.

In New Orleans, the percentage of black department heads increased from zero in 1969—before the election of Moon Landrieu, the city's first racially liberal white mayor—to 42 percent (five out of 12) during Landrieu's mayoralty. Landrieu appointed the city's first black chief administrative officer, Terrence Duvernay, in addition to "a significant number of blacks to important administrative positions just below the department head level" (Perry and Stokes 1987, 244). During Morial's mayoralty, the number of black department heads increased to seven out of 12, or 58 percent, which included a black chief administrative officer, the city's first black police chief, Warren Woodfork, and a black sanitation department head (Perry and Stokes 1987, 245). Succeeding Morial, Barthelemy appointed a white chief administrative officer and eight out of twelve (67 percent) black department heads. In the administration of the current mayor of New Orleans, Marc Morial, at least half the mayor's executive staff is black.

The appointment of blacks to executive positions in city government is important for several reasons. First, although these positions are few, they provide additional financially rewarding and prestigious employment opportunities for blacks. Second, executive positions are generally policy-making positions; therefore, blacks who hold these positions are able to make or influence policies that advance blacks' interests. Third, because these appointments have historically gone to whites, the appointment of blacks to these positions represents an important symbolic benefit. Finally, service in these key positions provides a small number of blacks with valuable experience, which should make them especially attractive for service in future mayoral administrations or as candidates if they should seek elective office. The experience that black urban government executives are currently gaining in running city government should have positive significance for future urban governance.

TABLE 8.4 Full-time employees of the city of New Orleans by race, 1993

Occupation classification	Black			White			Other			Unknown	
	No.	%	IOR*	No.	%	IOR*	No.	%	IOR*	No.	%
Officials/administrators	167	38.83	0.65	248	57.67	1.43	12	2.79	0.44	3	0.70
Professionals	451	42.31	0.7	561	52.67	1.3	53	4.98	0.79	1	0.09
Technicians	300	42.44	0.71	373	52.76	1.3	31	4.38	0.67	3	0.42
Protective services workers	763	41.81	0.7	1021	55.94	1.38	39	2.14	0.34	2	0.11
Paraprofessionals	281	77.83	1.30	70	19.39	0.48	10	2.77	0.44	0	0.00
Clerical workers	956	84.08	1.4	155	13.64	0.33	22	1.94	0.31	4	0.35
Skilled craft workers	248	68.51	1.14	86	23.75	0.58	25	6.91	1.11	3	0.83
Maintenance workers	736	89.10	1.49	61	07.38	0.18	28	3.39	0.53	1	0.12
Totals	3902	58.12	0.97	2575	38.35	0.95	220	3.28	0.58	17	0.25

*Index of representation.

SOURCE: *Work Force Demographics*, City of New Orleans, Louisiana, 1993. This report was provided by the City of New Orleans, Louisiana.

Minority Business Assistance

Black municipal officials can use the authority of city government's control over contracts for services and products to award city contracts to black businesses and to provide technical assistance to those businesses. This important possibility, until recently, had been ignored in the black politics literature (see Perry and Stokes 1987, 245–246). Because ethnic politics earlier in the twentieth century widely used this practice and because its applicability to blacks has been frequently questioned, this omission is conspicuous.

Increased black political participation in both Birmingham and New Orleans historically has not significantly increased the dollar amount of municipal contracts awarded to black businesses. In Birmingham, the minority business assistance program was begun by a city ordinance in 1977. Arrington acknowledges that his major disappointment has been his failure to advance black businesses in the city. This sentiment is echoed by Arrington's chief of staff: "The city's minority assistance program has not helped black businesses much. Blacks have not moved into the mainstream of the business sector. In every other way, blacks in Birmingham have been successful."[5] Arrington had hoped that his minority business assistance program would create a strong black business sector to complement blacks' outstanding success in the public sector. This had not occurred by 1989.

Mayor Arrington, however, has persisted in his efforts to increase minority participation in the business sector. In 1989, he proposed the "Birmingham Plan" to civic and community leaders. The Birmingham Plan involves partnerships between public and private entities designed to increase the participation of minority and disadvantaged business enterprises in Birmingham's economic development over a sustained period of time (City of Birmingham 1992).

Several societal and legal issues explain why the city's leaders made a concerted effort to ensure minority and disadvantaged citizens' involvement in Birmingham's changing economy by use of the Birmingham Plan. Since 1989, blacks in Birmingham have made up over 60 percent of the city's population. The black majority expected benefits in return for its political support of Arrington and the predominantly black city council. In effect, blacks expected a quid pro quo. In the legal arena, the construction industry opposed the city's minority business assistance programs. In addition, the decisions handed down by the U.S. Supreme Court in *City of Richmond v. J. S. Croson* and *Wilkes v. Birmingham* struck down minority set-aside programs in areas where patterns of discrimination could not be documented.

Three initiatives of the Birmingham Plan are most pertinent to understanding Arrington's efforts to create opportunities for minority businesses: the Birmingham Community Development Corporation, Inc.; the Birmingham Residential Mortgage Program; and the Birmingham Construction Industry Authority (BCIA).

The Birmingham Community Development Corporation, Inc., was created by nine local financial institutions to provide loans for start-up and equipment costs,

---

[5] Personal interview with Dr. Edward LaMonte, former executive secretary to Dr. Richard Arrington, mayor of Birmingham, Alabama.

and as a credit enhancement for new bank financing. As of 1992, $8 million has been pledged by the financial institutions and the city. The Birmingham Residential Mortgage Program was started in cooperation with the city and the same lending institutions. The program makes available $25 million in FHA and VA residential mortgage loans to low- and moderate-income buyers in the metropolitan Birmingham area. Some closing costs are waived and the city provides up to $1,500 for closing costs and down payment assistance. The Birmingham Construction Industry Authority (BCIA) resulted as a settlement of a twelve-year legal dispute involving the City of Birmingham and the Alabama Chapter of the Associated General Contractors over the city's practice of setting goals for minority participation in public projects. The BCIA set voluntary goals for minority and disadvantaged business enterprise participation in public and private sector projects, certification, marketing assistance, and project reporting and tracking (City of Birmingham 1992).

Implementation of the Birmingham Plan has resulted in a marked increase in minority participation in the public and private sectors. In 1991, according to a report prepared by the mayor's office, the city of Birmingham awarded 31 percent of its contracts to minority and disadvantaged business enterprises. By contrast, the University of Alabama at Birmingham, which is the largest employer in the city, awarded minority and disadvantaged business enterprises 5 percent of its contracts. The Birmingham Construction Industry Authority has provided training and development seminars to minority contractors and sponsors scholarships for minority high school and college students pursuing careers in construction. General contractors in the city reported that the minority and disadvantaged business enterprise participation rate in BCIA-sponsored programs was 13 percent of 136 monitored projects. The Birmingham Residential Mortgage Program, as of December 1991, had approved 83 loans in the amount of $2.5 million. As of March 1992, the Birmingham Community Development Corporation, Inc., had approved 80 loans in the amount of over $2.8 million (Office of Mayor Richard Arrington, Jr. 1992).

The New Orleans business assistance program has not been as successful as the Birmingham program. Morial authorized a minority business assistance program in late 1983 by issuing Executive Order No. 83–02, which required 25 percent minority labor force participation; however, the implementation of the program did not begin until 1985. By the end of Morial's second and final term in 1986, the city's minority business assistance program was widely regarded as a failure (see Perry and Stokes 1987). The failure of black political leadership in New Orleans to increase significantly the number of municipal contracts awarded to black businesses and the slow success of comparable efforts in Birmingham demonstrate a limitation of black political participation as a vehicle for producing private sector benefits for blacks. Finally, in 1989, minority business assistance programs were discontinued in Birmingham and New Orleans because of the landmark decision handed down by the U.S. Supreme Court in *City of Richmond v. J. S. Croson*, which ruled that "'minority set-aside' programs must be based on documented evidence of discrimination." The Court ruled that arbitrary goals were unconstitutional. The *Croson* decision in effect mandated that all political jurisdictions had to conduct disparity studies that found evidence of willful discrimination in order to reinstate minority set-aside programs.

A 1993 disparity study conducted for the city of New Orleans indicated that minority businesses were discriminated against in the allocation of city contracts. The study conducted by the Massachusetts-based National Economic Research Associates (NERA) found that Minority Business Enterprises (MBEs) and Women's Business Enterprises (WBEs) have been discriminated against in the allocation of city contracts. WBEs received 3 percent of all construction contracts whereas MBEs received 2 percent of construction contracts, 10 percent of service contracts, and 3 percent of commodity purchasing contracts.

The city of New Orleans sought to improve its record of allocating contracts to minority and women's businesses by setting utilization goals of 17.23 percent for black businesses and 14.78 percent for women's businesses. The city did not set a higher utilization goal for black businesses because of the disproportionately small number of black businesses and the fact that many of them did not own and could not obtain the equipment required to perform contract jobs.

THE SOCIAL AND ECONOMIC IMPACT OF THE INCREASED ALLOCATION OF GOVERNMENTAL BENEFITS TO BLACKS

The benefits that blacks have received from their increased political power and influence in Birmingham and New Orleans have been both symbolic and substantive. Some observers seem to feel that symbolic benefits are not important. To the contrary, symbolic benefits are very important in American politics (see Edelman 1964, 1971, 1975; Elder and Cobb 1983) and blacks, like all other groups in American society, are affected by symbolic politics. Symbolic benefits that confer an aura of legitimacy, respect, and equal standing to previously disadvantaged, discriminated against, and subordinate groups are very important (see Barker 1987). Increased black political participation and especially increased black officeholding have moved the black populace toward enhanced group social standing, which concomitantly has elevated blacks' self-esteem. A derivative of the symbolic benefits that ensue from blacks' holding important governmental positions is that it becomes easier for other blacks to move into important positions of public responsibility. Mayor Arrington's former chief of staff describes the working of this phenomenon as regards the symbolic importance of Arrington in Birmingham: "Arrington provides a personal example for blacks to move into leadership positions. Arrington serving as the mayor has made it easy for other blacks to move into other visible positions. Having Dick Arrington as mayor made it easier for Walter Harris to be appointed superintendent of public schools."[6]

---

[6] Personal interview with Dr. Edward LaMonte, former executive secretary to Dr. Richard Arrington, mayor of Birmingham, Alabama.

In other words, the election of blacks to high positions of public responsibility not only benefits blacks generally by improving their individual and group self-esteem but also makes it easier for whites to accept blacks in other positions of public responsibility. Thus, the benefits that blacks have achieved in the symbolic realm have substantially improved their social status.

The substantive benefits that blacks in Birmingham and New Orleans have received from their increased participation in the political process have significantly improved their social and economic conditions. Minority business assistance and improving police treatment of citizens have not been as successful as municipal employment and executive appointments as payoffs from black political participation in both cities. Increased executive appointments and municipal employment are examples of the substantive benefits that have occurred to blacks in the two cities. These benefits plus the symbolic benefits have collectively enhanced the social and economic conditions of blacks.

It is more difficult to show that improvements in the economic status of blacks follow directly from the benefits blacks have obtained from city government because so many other factors are involved. In New Orleans, the percentage of black middle-class families increased from 10 percent in 1970 to 31 percent in 1985. It is likely that gains in municipal employment have contributed to improved economic conditions for blacks generally by providing significant, stable employment that would not have existed otherwise for them.

BIRACIAL COALITIONS IN THE 1990s

In both Birmingham and New Orleans, the major politically oriented groups are blacks, liberal whites, the white business community, and the remainder of the white populace. In New Orleans, organized labor is another center of power. In both cities, no one center of power is ascendant over all major policy issues. Even the strong biracial coalition of blacks and upper-income liberal whites, which has controlled elections in Birmingham since 1967 and which controlled elections in New Orleans from 1969 to 1986, has not won all or even most policy issues. The same is true for the white business community, which is generally acknowledged to be the most influential group once elections are decided. These observations are supportive of the central tenets of pluralist theory that the decision-making process in the United States is influenced by many different groups and that no single group can dominate the process across all issue areas.

The least identifiable of the groups—the amorphous remainder of the white populace, which principally consists of low-income, conservative whites—has not fared poorly in either city. Arrington reports that he has given more city services to the conservative white areas of the city than any other mayor in Birmingham's history, despite the fact that whites in these areas do not vote for him. The wisdom of Arrington's actions is supported by political developments in New Orleans.

In the New Orleans mayoral election of 1986 in which the two principal candidates were black, whites divided their vote by voting overwhelmingly for the candidate perceived to be less threatening to their interests. In other words, whites are now in the exact same position as blacks were prior to their becoming the majority population. The election result has the potential to stimulate low-income conservative whites to become more organized for political action. If that happens, it would clearly be a significant development, given that low-income whites generally demonstrate little interest in political organizations.[7]

The election results also mean that the biracial coalition that controlled election outcomes in New Orleans between 1969 and 1986 is in all likelihood moribund. Mayoral elections in New Orleans are likely to continue to be contested by at least two viable black candidates, and as long as that condition holds, the once-powerful coalition will not be able to function. Thus, the character of biracial politics in New Orleans is changing, evolving into two biracial coalitions split along ideological lines—a liberal coalition and a conservative coalition. The liberal biracial coalition is made up of a large black majority and a small white minority. The conservative biracial coalition comprises a white majority and a significant black minority. Two points are relevant here. One, having the population of a city align on the basis of two contending biracial coalitions based on ideology is better than having an alignment based on race alone. This is the case given the divisive impact that race as a social cleavage can have on the fabric of a political community in the United States (see Carmines and Stimson 1989). Compared to race, ideology is a much milder social cleavage in American politics. Two, blacks are strongly incorporated in both coalitions and therefore stand to gain from whichever coalition wins.

The 1990 mayoral election in New Orleans confirmed the observation that biracial politics in New Orleans is evolving into two biracial coalitions. The liberal biracial coalition succeeded in influencing Mayor Barthelemy's victory over his opponent Donald Mintz, a white liberal. Barthelemy had the support of a large black majority and small white minority. (The incumbency-ideological-racial character of this election was comparable to the 1981 contest between then-incumbent Ernest Morial and Ronald Faucheaux, a white liberal candidate.) Barthelemy won reelection, capturing 86 percent of the black vote and 23 percent of the white vote, whereas Mintz received 75 percent of the white vote and 14 percent of the black vote (Perry 1990c, 157). The key to Barthelemy's victory was the support he received from the black voter and the significant crossover support from white voters. Surprisingly, high black voter turnout, a feature usually associated with black mayoral victories, was not a factor in Barthelemy's victory. The low turnout among black voters may suggest their lack of enthusiasm for Barthelemy, a phenomenon that makes the 1990 reelection of Barthelemy significant and unique. Most black candidates require strong black voter support and a strong turnout among blacks to win an election (Perry 1990c, 157).

---

[7] This "group" is the least identifiable of the political groups in both cities because it is not nearly as organized as the other groups discussed. In fact, it is more of a latent group than a group in the traditional sense of interest group pluralism. That low-income whites are not as politically organized as other groups, including low-income blacks, is consistent with prior research findings on black and white participation rates (Verba and Nie 1972; Shingles 1981).

In Birmingham, the influence of the liberal biracial coalition over electoral outcomes does not appear to be threatened. Arrington is so firmly entrenched in his informal role as leader of black politics in the city that it is not likely he will face significant black opposition in future mayoral races. Thus, any significant opposition will come from white candidates, which will ensure continuance of the biracial coalition as the most powerful force in the city's electoral politics. In every election, Arrington combined solid black support with limited white support to win. In the 1991 mayoral election, Arrington received solid support from the city's black voters. As in the past three elections, the mayor did not receive much support in the city's predominantly white areas—particularly in the city's eastern section. Because the mayor had no significant black opposition, the biracial coalition had enough political influence to overcome Arrington's lack of substantial white support.

SUMMARY AND CONCLUSION

Black organizations in both Birmingham and New Orleans had enough political resources to successfully energize blacks to increase their participation in politics despite opposition from some white individuals, groups, and political leaders who possessed greater political resources. The principal resource that black organizations used to increase their voting strength was protest activity. Specifically, the protest activities of the civil rights movement in the South resulted in actions and policies by the national government that fully extended the franchise to southern blacks. After southern blacks obtained the full franchise in the middle 1960s, black organizations and political leaders used increased black voting as the principal resource to extract favorable actions and policies from city governments in Birmingham and New Orleans.

Overall, increased black political participation is positively associated with blacks' receiving an increased proportion of resources allocated by city governments in both Birmingham and New Orleans. Consistent with prior research findings, black political participation in the two cities is strongly associated with their receiving increased municipal employment. Black political participation in the two cities is also strongly associated with increased executive appointments accruing to blacks. The benefits in increased municipal employment and executive appointments that accrued to blacks were significant in both cities.

In contrast, benefits in minority business assistance were not as significant as those in municipal employment and executive appointments in both cities. The category of governmental actions and policies in which increased black political participation has exerted its weakest influence in both Birmingham and New Orleans is minority business assistance. That black political participation has not been able to increase significantly the number of city contracts awarded to black businesses in New Orleans and was slow in doing so in Birmingham indicates a limitation of black political participation in producing private sector benefits for blacks. The findings of the chapter provide a mixed assessment regarding the ability of black political participation to substantially reduce police brutality against blacks in the two cities. In Birmingham, the results were uniformly strong in that direction. In New Orleans, black political participation has not substantially reduced police brutality against blacks.

The benefits that blacks have received from their increased participation in the political process in both cities have contributed significantly to improving the social and economic conditions of blacks. To those who would criticize the impact of increased black political participation because it has not revolutionized the social and economic conditions of blacks, an appropriate response is that such an expectation was unrealistic. Moreover, there is no precedent for political participation producing revolutionary outcomes for any groups in American urban politics or American politics generally. Given the inherent limitations of political participation as a medium for social and economic change, blacks in Birmingham and New Orleans have gained significant benefits from their incorporation in the political process.

REFERENCES

Barker, Lucius J. 1987. Ronald Reagan, Jesse Jackson, and the 1984 Presidential Election: The Continuing American Dilemma of Race. In Michael B. Preston, Lenneal J. Henderson, and Paul Puryear, eds., *The New Black Politics: The Search for Political Power,* 2nd ed. White Plains, N.Y.: Longman.

Bobo, James R. 1975. *The New Orleans Economy: Pro Bono Publico?* New Orleans: College of Business Administration, University of New Orleans.

Browning, Rufus P., Dale Rogers Marshall, and David H. Tabb. 1984. *Protest Is Not Enough: The Struggle of Blacks and Hispanics for Equality in Urban Politics.* Berkeley: University of California Press.

Carmines, Edward G., and James A. Stimson. 1989. *Issue Evolution: Race and the Transformation of American Politics.* Princeton, N.J.: Princeton University Press.

City of Birmingham. 1992. Office of Economic Development. *Birmingham Plan at a Glance.*

Edelman, Murray. 1964. *The Symbolic Uses of Politics.* Urbana: University of Illinois Press.

Edelman, Murray. 1971. *Politics as Symbolic Action.* Chicago: Markham.

Edelman, Murray. 1975. *Political Language.* New York: Academic Press.

Elder, Charles D., and Roger W. Cobb. 1983. *The Political Uses of Symbols.* White Plains, N.Y.: Longman.

Eisinger, Peter K. 1980. *Politics of Displacement: Racial and Ethnic Transition in Three American Cities.* New York: Academic Press.

Eisinger, Peter K. 1982. Black Employment in Municipal Jobs: The Impact of Black Political Power. *American Political Science Review* 76 (June): 380–392.

Franklin, Jimmy Lewis. 1989. *Back to Birmingham: Richard Arrington, Jr., and His Times.* Tuscaloosa: University of Alabama Press.

McClain, Paula D. 1993. The Changing Dynamics of Urban Politics: Black and Hispanic Municipal Employment—Is There Competition? *Journal of Politics* 55 (May): 399–414.

Mlandenka, Kenneth R. 1989a. Blacks and Hispanics in Urban Politics. *American Political Science Review* 83 (March): 165–191.

Mlandenka, Kenneth R. 1989b. The Distribution of an Urban Public Service: The Changing Role of Race and Politics. *Urban Affairs Quarterly* 24 (June): 556–583.

Office of Mayor Richard Arrington, Jr. 1992. 1991 Birmingham Plan Year-End Status Report. Birmingham, Ala., February 15.

Perry, Huey L. 1983. The Impact of Black Political Participation on Public Sector Employment and Representation on Municipal Boards and Commissions. Review of *Black Political Economy* 12 (Winter): 203–217.

Perry, Huey L. 1990a. Black Politics and Mayoral Leadership in Birmingham and New Orleans. *National Political Science Review* 2: 154–160.

Perry, Huey L. 1990b. The Evolution and Impact of Biracial Coalitions and Black Mayors in Birmingham and New Orleans. In Rufus P. Browning, Dale Rogers Marshall, and David H. Tabb, eds., *Racial Politics in American Cities*. White Plains, N.Y.: Longman.

Perry, Huey L. 1990c. The Reelection of Sidney Barthelmy as Mayor of New Orleans. In Huey L. Perry, ed., Recent Advances in Black Electoral Politics (Symposium). *PS: Political Science & Politics* XXIII: 156–157.

Perry, Huey L. 1992. The Political Reincorporation of Southern Blacks: The Case of Birmingham. *National Political Science Review* 3 (1992): 230–237.

Perry, Huey L., and Judith C. Delmas. 1992. A Report on Police Abuse in New Orleans, Louisiana. Prepared for the New Orleans, Louisiana Human Relations Commission.

Perry, Huey L., and Alfred Stokes. 1987. Politics and Power in the Sunbelt: Mayor Morial of New Orleans. In Michael B. Preston, Lenneal J. Henderson, Jr., and Paul Puryear, eds., *The New Black Politics: The Search for Political Power*, 2nd ed. White Plains, N.Y.: Longman.

Perry, Huey L., and Alfred Stokes. 1993. Politics and Power in the Sunbelt: Mayor Morial of New Orleans. Reprinted in Harry A. Bailey, Jr., and Jay M. Shafritz, eds., *State and Local Government and Politics: Essential Reading*. Itasca, Ill.: F. E. Peacock.

Schexnider, Alvin J. 1982. Political Mobilization in the South: The Election of a Black Mayor in New Orleans. In Michael B. Preston, Lenneal J. Henderson, Jr. and Paul Puryear, eds., *The New Black Politics: The Search For Political Power*. White Plains, N.Y.: Longman.

Shingles, Richard D. 1981. Black Consciousness and Political Participation: The Missing Link. *American Political Science Review* 75: 76–90.

Stein, Lana. 1986. Representative Local Government: Minorities in the Municipal Workforce. *Journal of Politics* 48 (August 1986): 694–713.

Stein, Lana, and Stephen E. Condrey. 1987. Integrating Municipal Workforces: A Comparative Study of Six Southern Cities. *Publius: The Journal of Federalism* 17 (Spring): 93–103.

Strong, Donald S. 1972. Alabama: Transition and Alienation. In William C. Harvard, ed., *The Changing Politics of the South*. Baton Rouge: Louisiana State University Press.

U.S. Department of Justice, Civil Rights Division, Criminal Section. 1991. *Police Brutality Study*. Washington D.C.

Verba, Sidney, and Norman H. Nie. 1972. *Participation in America*. Chicago: University of Chicago Press.

chapter **9**

The Struggle for Black Empowerment in Baltimore: Electoral Control and Governing Coalitions

Marion Orr

Editors' Note

During the middle 1970s through the middle 1980s, when other big cities with large black populations elected their first African-American mayors, Baltimore, despite its huge black population, was unable to elect a black chief executive. The powerful and popular Mayor William Donald Schaefer was able to retain the mayor's office for several years after Baltimore reached a black majority. In addition, whites maintained a majority of the city council seats until 1995—more than 15 years after blacks reached a numerical majority of the population.

In many ways, the struggle for black political empowerment confirms many of Browning, Marshall, and Tabb's findings. The election of Mayor Kurt L. Schmoke and increased black representation on the city council brought about significant changes in city government. Yet Baltimore offers some important differences, as this chapter shows. The city's southern tradition of segregation and racial exclusion hampered the development of liberal biracial coalitions.

This chapter also raises the issue of who really benefits from black electoral incorporation. Disadvantaged black residents appear to have benefited little from black control of city hall. The chapter concludes with a discussion of what black urban regimes can do to broaden the advantages of black electral incorporation.

In 1935, long before the national civil rights movement, a little-known but excellent study commissioned by the Baltimore Urban League urged black citizens in Baltimore to make more use of their right to vote. The report referred to the underutilized black vote as a "sleeping giant" (Reid 1935, 43).

If ever the Negro population of Baltimore became aware of its political power, the changes in the governmental, economic and racial set-up of the community would under-go a profound change. . . . Despite the curtailment of the vote through registration laws, there is sufficient strength to bring about many reforms which hitherto have been sought through pleading. We refer, particularly, to such matters of librarians, policemen, firemen, et al. The power of organized political strength has never been effectively tested in Baltimore. (Reid 1935, 46)

Black politics in Baltimore have changed greatly since the Urban League released its report over 60 years ago. Today, blacks in Baltimore have achieved what Rufus Browning, Dale Marshall, and David Tabb (1984, 1990) call "political incorporation." Baltimore has a black mayor—in Baltimore's "strong mayor" form of government, political incorporation culminates in the control of the mayor's office. African Americans hold a majority of the 19 seats on the city council, including the seat of council president who is elected citywide. The position of comptroller, a citywide post, is held by a black woman. The administrative leadership of the city is also predominantly black. In short, black Baltimoreans have achieved a high level of incorporation and access to city government.

This chapter examines the struggle of African Americans in Baltimore for political access and responsive policies at the local level. It provides an account of the political challenges black Baltimoreans overcame to gain incorporation in Baltimore city government. It also shows how Browning, Marshall, and Tabb's "political incorporation" theory applies to African-American politics in Baltimore.

The first section provides some important background information on Baltimore's economic, social, and political history. I examine the impact of Baltimore's tradition of machines and patronage on black political empowerment, assess the level of black incorporation in the Baltimore city council, and analyze blacks' effort to gain control of the mayor's office and the election of Mayor Kurt Schmoke. In the second section, I examine the impact of black incorporation on the allocation of policies and benefits to African Americans. Browning, Marshall, and Tabb's incorporation model predicts that black representation and influence in city government can be translated into a change in governmental policies. I test this prediction with data from Baltimore and discuss the limitations of incorporation. In a concluding section, I reflect on the issue of black electoral control and what black-led regimes might do to more fully spread the benefits of black political incorporation.

BACKGROUND AND HISTORY

With its economy built on heavy industry, Baltimore has many of the features of an old frostbelt city (Browne 1980, 177–195). For most of its history, the city had a diversified industrial base with clothing factories, chemical plants, steel mills, and auto assembly plants dotting its boundaries. Such employment opportunities attracted people to Baltimore. During the nineteenth century, European immigrants arrived from Ireland, Germany, and later Italy and Poland, along with smaller numbers from Russia and Lithuania, making Baltimore a city of ethnic neighborhoods (Fee, Shopes, and Zeidman 1991). Blacks and whites from rural Maryland and other southern states also came in search of job opportunities.

Baltimore's location makes it unique among other large industrial cities. Situated just below the Mason-Dixon line, Baltimore has many traditions that are characteristic of the Deep South. Historian Joseph Arnold (1990) described Baltimore as a city with a "southern culture and a northern economy." The majority of whites in the city traced their roots to rural Maryland or other southern states, and they kept black residents firmly in place through a southern system of legal and social segregation. African Americans were never disenfranchised, but they were relegated to second-class citizenship. Racial segregation was enforced by custom and law in the schools, public facilities, neighborhoods, churches, and employment (Reid 1935; Hollander Foundation 1960; Callcott 1988). Baltimore was the first city to enact an ordinance prohibiting blacks and whites from living in the same neighborhood (Power 1983). Supreme Court Justice Thurgood Marshall often described his native city as "up-South Baltimore" (Watson 1990, 81).

In the 1950s and 1960s, the city underwent a profound transformation. First, the suburbanization of the white population triggered the numerical dominance of the city's black residents. By the mid-1970s, black residents became the majority; by 1990, as Table 9.1 shows, blacks made up nearly 60 percent of the total population. This population is composed primarily of whites and blacks. The "new immigrant" groups from Asia and Latin America are less than 3 percent of the residents. Second, the civil rights movement and the rise to power of African-American elected officials changed the social and political life of the city; by the 1980s, in fact, it had shed most of its southern orientation. Third, the economic structure of the city changed profoundly: Baltimore is no longer a manufacturing center (Garland 1980). Since 1950, the number of manufacturing jobs has declined by 65 percent. Growth in the economy has taken place primarily in the service sector, and much of this growth is centered in the Inner Harbor redevelopment area and downtown. Some view the redevelopment of downtown as the most successful redevelopment project in urban America. Yet Baltimore is "a city declining" (Szanton 1986, 45). The suburbanization of middle-class whites (and increasingly middle-class blacks) has left behind

TABLE 9.1 Population of Baltimore 1950–1990 (in thousands)

Year	Total	% Change	White	% Total	Black	% Total
1950	950		724	76	225	24
1960	939	−1	611	65	326	35
1970	906	−4	480	53	420	46
1980	787	−31	347	44	431	55
1990	736	−6	288	39	436	59

SOURCE: U.S. Bureau of the Census (1950, 1960, 1970, 1980, 1990).

many residents who are poor (Rusk 1996). The outmovement of retail and whole-sale trade and manufacturing jobs has contributed to high unemployment and a weakened tax base. Finally, the continued decline of the city's population has di-luted the city's political standing in the state and state government.

Machine Politics and the Black Community

Like many large eastern cities with sizable racial and ethnic communities, Baltimore developed a machine tradition. In most big cities with strong machine traditions, black political leadership and the black vote were often tightly controlled by machine leaders (Banfield and Wilson 1961; Gosnell 1968; Walton 1973, 56–69; Pinderhughes 1987). For example, Banfield and Wilson (1961) observed that blacks in Chicago were organized as a "submachine." Black voters were expected to support the machine's white candidates in return for specific inducement or patronage—city jobs, zoning and housing code decisions, and police matters. In those wards or districts dominated by black voters, the submachine was led by a black "boss." Congressman William Dawson was Chicago's leading black machine-style politician (Grimshaw 1993; Pinderhughes 1987; Walton 1973). In Chicago, machine politics delayed black political empowerment.

Minority mobilization in Baltimore seems to follow the pattern in Chicago and other cities where partisan, ward-based machines were prevalent. From the late nineteenth century until the 1960s, the formal machinery of government in Baltimore was controlled by a multitude of district-level Democratic party organizations or "clubs" (Arnold 1976; Bain 1970; Wong 1990). Between 1930 and the early 1960s, the Fourth District in west Baltimore, where the majority of the black residents lived, was controlled by James "Jack" Pollack, the political boss and leader of the Trenton Democratic Club (Wheeler 1955; Fleming 1964). Although African Americans were a majority of the Fourth District's population, Pollack refused to support black candidates for Fourth District seats on the city council or in the state legislature (Fleming 1964).[1]

In 1954, three black candidates—foremost among them Harry Cole, who later became a justice on Maryland's highest court—defeated Pollack-backed incumbents for seats in the legislature from the Fourth District (Callcott 1988, 151; Fleming 1964; McDougall 1993, 92). One year later, Pollack responded by running Walter Dixon, a black, on his Fourth District city council slate. Dixon won election and became the first black in 25 years to hold a seat on the city council.[2] In 1958, a biracial Pollack

---

[1] Baltimore's six state legislative seats were coterminous to the six council seats. During this time, the Fourth District elected six members to the House of Delegates and one member to the state senate.

[2] In 1890, Republican Harry S. Cummings, an attorney, became the city council's first black member. Six different black Republicans served on the council between 1890 and 1931. The defeat of the last of two of them, Warner T. McGuinn and Walter S. Emerson, meant the exclusion of African Americans from the council until 1955. On Cummings and other black Republican city councilors, see Greene 1979 and Smith 1993, 145–146.

slate recaptured the three legislative seats he had lost four years earlier. Even with partially black tickets, Pollack was not able to control black voters who were moving into his district in the 1950s. Pollack was eventually overthrown by population change.

A smaller but significant number of black residents lived in east Baltimore. The black precincts in east Baltimore were the bailiwick of a black submachine boss, Clarence "Du" Burns (O'Keeffe 1986). Burns was one of only two African Americans working for the Bohemian Club, a party organization led by conservative white ethnics. Burns worked his way up the Bohemian Club "through precinct work" (Russo 1986, 1). Burns carried his precinct for the white bosses and became, in his own words, "one of the boys" (quoted in Russo 1986, 1). Burns acknowledged that he knew he was being used by white bosses, but this did not bother him; he considered it a part of the game of politics. Burns formed his own political club, the East Side Democratic Club, and in 1970 was elected to a seat on the city council.

Machine politics tend to create a considerable amount of distrust and jealousy between black voters and black politicians, and among the political leaders themselves (Nelson and Meranto 1977, 58). Within Baltimore's black leadership, the most important ideological division was between machine-style black politicians and those black leaders whose roots were in the civil rights movement. The influential Mitchell family were leaders in Baltimore's civil rights community (Watson 1990; Callcott 1988; Hollander Foundation 1960). The Mitchells often challenged black machine-style politicians as pawns of white political operatives, criticizing them for forsaking the goals of equality and equal representation for personal and economic gain. Clarence "Du" Burns "received a great deal of criticism . . . because of his willingness to cut deals with white political operatives" (O'Keeffe 1986, 15). Black club leaders and their white patrons were in constant battle with the civil rights leaders for political hegemony in the black community.

Weak Incorporation: 1955–1991

Baltimore's governmental structure is different from that of the ten cities in *Protest Is Not Enough*. Constitutionally, the cities originally examined by Browning, Marshall, and Tabb have council-manager forms of government. Under a council-manager system, all city policy is established by the city council and carried out by the city manager. The Baltimore city charter, however, allows for a strong mayor-weak council form of government (Krefetz 1976). The city council is divided into six districts, each of which elects three councilors. The council is presided over by its president, who is elected at large. Although the council is relatively weak compared to the mayor, several successful politicians have used their tenure on the city council to win election to higher offices.

Weak incorporation best characterizes the position of blacks on Baltimore's city council during much of the postwar era. Figure 9.1 shows the relationship between Baltimore's black population and the number and percentage of black council members for selected years from 1955 through 1995. The data show that African-

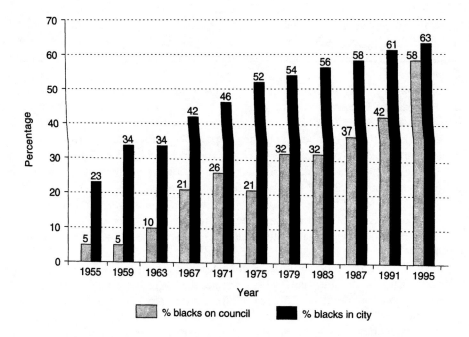

FIGURE 9.1 Black representation on Baltimore City Council, 1955–1995

American representation on the city council did not approach its share of the population until the 1995 elections. For example, in 1955 blacks made up 23 percent of the population but held only one city council seat—just 5 percent of the council seats.[3] Four years later, the African-American population rose to 34 percent but the number of blacks on the council remained at one. In 1987, when 60 percent of the city's population was black, 11 of the 18 council members elected from districts were white, as was the council president. As late as 1991, African Americans made up 61 percent of the city's population, but they held only 42 percent of the city council seats.

What explains black underrepresentation on the Baltimore City Council? After the Supreme Court's decision in *Baker v. Carr*, the city charter was amended to require a redistricting following the results of each census. In 1971, and again in 1980, incumbents in four of Baltimore's six council districts gerrymandered the district lines to dilute the voting power of the city's growing black population (Bachrach and Baratz 1970). With blacks consolidated into a 90 percent black Fourth District, white majorities were preserved in the First, Third, and Sixth Districts. Slim black majorities in the Second and Fifth Districts were overcome by highly organized

---

[3] In 1946, the city charter was amended to allow for a fourth council member in any district with more than 75,000 registered voters. Because two of the six districts satisfied this criterion, the membership of the council stood at 20 from 1955 to 1963. A charter revision adopted in 1966 capped the total number of councilors at 19—three for each of the six districts and a council president.

white political clubs, which often hand-picked a "token" black to integrate an otherwise all-white ticket.

Whites have been reluctant to form biracial coalitions at the district level. To win election to the city council, blacks have had to run in the three majority-black districts. As of 1980, only the Second, Fourth, and Fifth Districts fell into this category. Yet unlike white-majority districts, black-majority districts have shown a willingness to cross racial lines in elections. For instance, although blacks make up more than two-thirds of the Second District's population, they have regularly elected a white to one of its three city council positions. And in the Fifth District, where African Americans account for slightly more than half the population, a white candidate has won one of the three seats (Wickham 1987, 14–15). But in the city's First, Third, and Sixth council districts, where the African-American populations range between 20 percent and 40 percent, white voters continue to reject black candidates at the polls. A commentator for the *Baltimore Evening Sun* observed in 1991, "Black candidates for City Council lose by huge margins in white, working-class precincts controlled by old-line political clubs fielding all-white tickets. No black city council member has been elected from a district with a white majority" (Fletcher 1991, B1).

Black leaders' frustration with their minority status on the city council came to the fore in 1991 during the decennial redistricting. A coalition of councilors, led by the seven blacks and supported both by the white councilors from the majority-black Second and Fifth Districts and by the white council president, pushed through a redistricting plan that established five majority-black districts. Several white council members objected to the plan, describing it as the "rape of our communities" (Thompson 1991). At one dramatic moment, a black councilor took off her shoe and waved it in the faces of her white colleagues, saying, "You've been running things for the last 20 years. Now the shoe is on the other foot. See how you like it" (Olesker 1991, B1). In the ensuing municipal election, a black was elected for the first time to a Sixth District council seat. A black activist, Melvin Stukes, was elected without the endorsement of the district's Stonewall Democratic Club (Banisky 1991). Stukes's election was viewed by many as the beginning of the empowerment of the city's black majority on the city council.

Black incorporation on the council culminated in the 1995 elections. Lawrence Bell became the second black to win election as council president. He was joined by ten other blacks on the council, including the first black to win a Third District seat and the second black representative chosen in Baltimore's Sixth District. Hence, the 1995 council election produced a city council milestone: 105 years after the first black was elected to that legislative body, African Americans for the first time formed the council's majority.

Baltimore's Failure to Elect a Black Mayor

In Baltimore's strong-mayor form of government, gaining control of the mayor's office is the culminating step in the process of electoral incorporation. The mayor appoints all the department heads, has considerable budgetary authority, and controls the important Board of Estimates. Because city council members are for the most part concerned with providing constituent services, the mayor's domination over city affairs is unchallenged.

The groundwork for electing the city's first black mayor was laid in 1967, when Joseph C. Howard won a seat on the Supreme Bench (a city judicial post), becoming the first African American to win a citywide election (Welcome 1991, 193). Three years later, Milton Allen was elected to a prominent citywide post, Baltimore State's Attorney (or district attorney). Also in 1970, Parren Mitchell became the first black from Maryland elected to Congress. These early black citywide victories showed that African Americans could successfully compete in citywide elections.

In early 1971, after Mayor Thomas D'Alesandro, III, announced that he would not run for reelection, there was considerable speculation that Baltimore would follow Gary, Indiana, and Cleveland, Ohio, and elect its first black mayor. With no incumbent, the September 1971 Democratic primary was viewed by observers as a competition to determine which group—the black club leaders or the black civil rights establishment—would dominate as the city became majority African American.[4]

City Solicitor George Russell, a black, was the first to announce for mayor and was a leading candidate. Although Russell had broad support among white and black political leaders (Fleming 1972, 4), he surrounded himself with many whom the civil rights establishment had opposed and was the choice of many of Baltimore's black club leaders, including Clarence "Du" Burns.

The desire of civil rights leaders to direct the political future of Baltimore was a major factor in the decision of State Senator Clarence Mitchell, III, to enter the mayor's race. His candidacy was viewed by many as an effort to siphon black votes away from Russell. Mitchell's candidacy also boosted the candidacy of the principal white aspirant, then–city council president William Donald Schaefer. Schaefer had citywide backing. He developed tremendous popularity with city voters—both black and white (Fleming 1971). In the end Schaefer won the primary with 57 percent of the vote.

Baltimore's failure to elect a black mayor in 1971 was the result of division in the black community. Many blacks who were active in the civil rights movement and who helped elect Judge Howard, Parren Mitchell, and Milton Allen did not work for Russell, did not raise money for him, and refused to endorse any black candidate. Perhaps the best indication of black division is reflected in the statement of Congressman Mitchell who, despite his nephew's defeat, declared the election a victory. "This is a victory night for us," Mitchell said. "We have accomplished what we set out to accomplish" (Fleming 1972, 17).

---

[4] With Democrats outnumbering Republicans in Baltimore by a 9–1 ratio, a win in the Democratic primary is tantamount to victory. The last Republican member of the city council left office in 1942. A Republican has been elected mayor of Baltimore only twice in the last 50 years. Theodore Roosevelt McKeldin was elected in 1943 and again in 1963.

The Schaefer Years: 1971–1987

Many observers agree that William Donald Schaefer became the most powerful mayor in Baltimore history (Levine 1987a, 133; Arnold 1990, 30). He was not seriously challenged in his reelection bids: In 1975, 1979, and 1983 he received 71 percent, 80 percent, and 73 percent of the Democratic primary vote, respectively. After Baltimore became majority black in the mid-1970s, Schaefer was able to hold on to the mayor's office largely because he had developed a close association with black leaders (Arnold 1990, 30; Welcome 1991). When Schaefer became mayor, his black supporters were rewarded and given greater responsibilities in the city government (Wong 1990, 87). For example, he used his formal authority over the city's public school system to maintain black support. The first majority-black school board was named during Schaefer's first term. Many of Schaefer's black supporters were appointed as school administrators and many more received jobs throughout the school district (Wong 1990, 115; Crew et al. 1982).

In general, downtown development became the hallmark of the Schaefer administration. The famous Inner Harbor redevelopment project, the World Trade Center, the National Aquarium, and luxury hotels all were constructed during his fifteen-year tenure (Levine 1987b). Under Schaefer's leadership, Baltimore rose to national prominence as a renaissance city. Black residents, however, were not included in Baltimore's transformation. In 1983, the U.S. Commission on Civil Rights held hearings in Baltimore and found that the city had not done enough to include African Americans in the city's downtown redevelopment projects (U.S. Commission on Civil Rights 1983, 1). Levine (1987b) presents census data showing that during the renaissance era, black neighborhoods continued to experience social and economic decay. To finance downtown redevelopment projects and maintain a good bond rating during Schaefer's years in city hall, city agencies received reduced budgets. Financial support for the city's public schools was reduced (Vobejda and Ifill 1986; Imbroscio et al. 1995). As a result of low spending levels, the city schools operated with a shortage of books and low staffing levels in libraries and counseling offices.

The black community remained patient, waiting for Mayor Schaefer to retire or move on to higher office (O'Keeffe 1986). Their chance finally came in 1987 after Schaefer was elected governor.

The Election of Kurt Schmoke: Strong Incorporation

In the 1987 mayoral election, one thing was certain: Baltimore would elect a black mayor. The Democratic primary was the first all-black mayoral primary in Baltimore history. The two candidates represented radically different generations and backgrounds. Clarence "Du" Burns, 68 years old, largely self-educated and outgoing, worked for 22 years as a janitor at a high school (a patronage appointment), formed his own political club, and was elected to the city council in 1971 (Arnold 1990, 31). In 1983, he ran citywide and became the first black to win election as president of the city council. As council president, Burns automatically became mayor when his friend, Schaefer, resigned to become governor in 1986.

Nearly 30 years younger than Burns, Kurt Schmoke grew up on Baltimore's west side, the son of college-educated parents. Schmoke was a high school and college sports star. A graduate of Yale University and Harvard Law School, he is a Rhodes Scholar. In 1982, in his first bid for elected office, Schmoke was elected state's attorney (Noah 1990). Schmoke was able to unite the black community behind his candidacy. He also received considerable support from liberal whites and many of the city's prominent civic leaders (O'Keeffe 1986, 63–90).

Among the several issues dominating the 1987 mayoral campaign, development and education were perhaps the most important. Schmoke expressed the view that Baltimore's economic development goals had not balanced neighborhood improvement with downtown development. He concluded that Baltimore was prettier but poorer. Schmoke also emphasized his desire to improve the city's public schools (see Orr 1996). He vowed to make Baltimore "the city that reads" (Schmoke 1987, 7).

Burns was less critical of Baltimore's "renaissance." As Mayor Schaefer's floor leader, Burns helped guide many of the city's downtown projects through the city council. He argued that the Inner Harbor and other redevelopment projects were necessary to expand the city's tax base. Burns also indicated that he too was unhappy with the condition of the city's school and would work to improve them.

During the campaign, a grassroots, church-based organization called Baltimoreans United in Leadership Development (BUILD) sought to shape the debate by launching a petition drive to show support for its antipoverty program that included a school compact program, site-based school management, reduction in school class sizes, the creation of more low-income housing, and improvement in municipal services (Orr 1992). BUILD collected more than 70,000 signatures of voters. BUILD is perhaps the most influential community-based organization in the city. As a nonprofit organization, it could not endorse political candidates; instead, BUILD leaders asked each candidate to endorse its antipoverty agenda. While Schmoke did so without reluctance, Burns initially rejected it as "unrealistic." He later changed his mind and confirmed his "commitment and the city's commitment to the BUILD municipal agenda."

Schmoke won the primary election with 51 percent of the total vote. A breakdown of the vote by city council districts shows that Schmoke won all the majority black districts; Mayor Burns won all the majority white districts. In the general election, Schmoke easily defeated his white Republican opponent by securing 90 percent of the black vote and 65 percent of the white vote. Unlike in Chicago, the climax of Baltimore's transition to black leadership occurred without polarization or even any noticeable tension.

Schmoke was reelected in 1991 and 1995. The 1991 Democratic primary was a rematch, with Schmoke challenged by Burns and William Swisher, the conservative, white former state's attorney whom Schmoke defeated in 1982. Schmoke had several advantages in the 1991 race. He was an incumbent and well financed. In addition, his two opponents shared the same base of voter support. Schmoke won reelection handily. In 1995, he was challenged by then–city council president Mary Pat Clarke. Clarke, a white, sharply criticized the mayor's handling of stubborn urban problems and said that it was time for a change in the city's leadership. Schmoke, however, was reelected easily, capturing nearly 60 percent of the Democratic primary vote.

BLACK POLITICAL INCORPORATION IN BALTIMORE: ANALYSIS

In the cities examined by Browning, Marshall, and Tabb, black political incorporation was responsible for important changes in government policies. They conclude that minority regimes were responsive to minority residents in several public policy areas. Following Browning and his associates, I assess the impact of black incorporation in Baltimore on three public sector areas originally examined: executive appointments; municipal employment; and appointment to city boards and commissions.

Executive Appointments

The data on Baltimore confirm earlier studies showing an increase in the number of black government executives—department heads and top personal mayoral staff—with the election of a black mayor (Eisinger 1984; Rich 1989). When Mayor Schaefer left office in 1986, 40 percent of the 15 major departments were headed by African Americans. By 1994, Mayor Schmoke had increased the number of blacks in executive positions to 73 percent. These appointments include a number of departments that were never headed by a black. For example, Schmoke appointed the first black to head the Department of Planning, the agency charged with preparing and updating the city's physical redevelopment plan. In 1992, Schmoke named Herman Williams the city's first black fire chief. As Perry (1990, 145) notes, although the number of executive positions are few, "blacks who hold these positions are able to make or influence policies that advance blacks' interests."

Municipal Employment

The data in Table 9.2 confirm Browning, Marshall, and Tabb's findings that black municipal employment is a function of electoral incorporation and the size of the black population (Browning, Marshall, and Tabb 1984, 171–204; Mladenka 1989). As the black population of Baltimore increased and blacks gained controlled of city hall, black Baltimoreans gained a fairer share of municipal jobs. In 1986, the last year of the Schaefer administration, the black percentage of the municipal workforce had leveled off to 45 percent; by 1994, the proportion of black employees rose to 50 percent. Although the percentage of blacks in the municipal workforce increased across nearly all occupational levels, blacks remain heavily represented in the service maintenance and office categories (74 percent and 65 percent, respectively), jobs characterized by low skill levels and low wages.

Table 9.2 shows that blacks are well represented in the middle-level categories, which generally require more skills and training than the service maintenance and

TABLE 9.2 Black employment: Baltimore city government, 1986 and 1994

1986					
Category	White	Black	Other	Total	% Black
Administrative	266	81	4	351	23
Professional	1,586	785	81	2452	32
Technical	1,447	795	17	2259	35
Protective Services	2,860	1,229	24	4,113	30
Paraprofessional	106	420	1	527	80
Office/Clerical	969	1,214	18	2,201	55
Skill Crafts	206	136	1	343	40
Service Maintenance	1,109	2,368	13	3,491	68
Total	8,549	7,028	159	15,737	45
1994					
Category	White	Black	Other	Total	% Black
Administrative	233	137	11	381	36
Professional	1,231	765	77	2,073	37
Technical	1,359	936	27	2,322	40
Protective Services	2,279	1,290	42	3,611	36
Paraprofessional	99	387	4	490	79
Office/Clerical	665	1,248	11	1,924	65
Skill Crafts	301	246	12	559	44
Service Maintenance	731	2,096	10	2,837	74
Total	6,898	7,105	194	14,197	50

SOURCE: City of Baltimore, Office of Equal Opportunity, State and Local Government Information, EEO-4 Report, 1986 and 1994.

clerical positions. These categories include skill craft workers, paraprofessionals, protective services workers, and technicians. In fact, the largest percentage of blacks are not found at the low skill level; the largest proportion of blacks (nearly 80 percent) are paraprofessionals. The proportion of blacks in protective services rose from 30 percent in 1986 to 36 percent in 1994. These data confirm earlier research that showed black mayors have had a special interest in police and community relations (Saltzstein 1989).

Blacks are also well represented in administrative and professional categories, the two high-skill, high-wage classifications. The percentage of black employees in both categories increased between 1986 and 1994. The largest increase occurred among black administrators—the highest category. In Mayor Schaefer's last year of office, 23 percent of the administrators were black; near the end of Schmoke's second term, 36 percent were black.

Although these data are heartening, they should be viewed in the context of an aging city with an extremely needy population and shrinking revenues. With the erosion of federal aid to cities, Mayor Schmoke is finding it increasingly difficult to align available resources with the demand for services. Because a major portion of Baltimore's operating budget consists of labor- and personnel-related costs, Schmoke has had to downsize city government. In December 1988, the city implemented a general hiring freeze, exempting only teaching positions, critical public safety positions, and positions in the judicial area. There have been long-standing hiring freezes in most city agencies, allowing many jobs to be phased out as workers retire. Between 1990 and 1992, the city eliminated 2,878 jobs, mostly through attrition (Fletcher 1992). The city's 1991 "Strategic Financial Plan" explained that the hiring freeze "has, for all practical purposes, become institutionalized" (City of Baltimore 1991, 15–16). This means that fewer blacks will benefit from black electoral incorporation (Fletcher 1992; Terry 1991).

Appointments to Boards and Commissions

Boards and commissions play a significant role in Baltimore city government. Many boards primarily advise city agencies, the mayor, and/or the city council. Some boards have enforcement powers over local, state, or federal laws; others oversee internal city matters, such as pensions or hiring. Typically, members of boards and commissions are appointed by the mayor with confirmation by the city council.

In 1994, blacks were well represented on many of Baltimore's 47 boards and commissions. Fifty-three percent of the board members and commissioners were black.[5] African Americans chaired 23 of the boards or commissions. In 1994, all members of the Civil Service Commission—which has wide powers over municipal employment practices—were African American. Blacks have held a majority of the nine seats on the board of school commissioners since 1975 and several blacks have served as president.

Black Political Incorporation: Lessons from Baltimore

What lessons do we draw from the Baltimore experience? First, the experience of blacks and machine politics in Baltimore confirms earlier research showing that the tradition of patronage and machines can delay black political empowerment. The Baltimore case shows that machines can hamper the development of strong independent black political leadership and foster internal division within the African-American community. White machine bosses worked to prevent blacks from challenging the dominant power structure and even designated "token" blacks to keep progressive coalitions from challenging the dominant mobilization of bias. Machine-style politics was virtually absent in the ten northern California cities originally examined by Browning, Marshall, and Tabb. The Baltimore experience suggests a need to reformulate the incorporation model to account for existing arrangements and traditions that tend to divide minority communities.

---

[5] Telephone interview with the staff in City Hall, Baltimore, October 1994.

An essential lesson to be drawn from the Baltimore case is that ideology varies from city to city. V. O. Key's (1949) seminal work on southern culture and politics found racial ideology to be a significant contextual variable that determined the political behavior and success of African Americans. Baltimore, a city with a southern culture, has been characterized by an absence of an organized liberal white leadership willing to forge a biracial electoral coalition. For much of the post–World War II era, a majority of the 18 seats on the city council were controlled by whites who represented districts that voted strongly for George Wallace in 1968 and Ronald Reagan in 1980 and 1984.[6] Conservative whites successfully resisted black political incorporation.

A central component of the theory of minority political incorporation is the necessity of blacks to forge electoral coalitions with liberal whites. Strong political incorporation was associated with the presence of liberal whites (Browning et al. 1984, 18–45). Perhaps liberal whites are easier to find in Berkeley, Oakland, and San Francisco than in Baltimore. Before African Americans became a near-majority in the city, there appears to have been an absence of an organized liberal white leadership willing to form biracial electoral alliances. As a result, black incorporation was delayed until Baltimore's black population reached a majority.

In the future, black political incorporation in Baltimore will increase. The percentage of blacks in the city has increased to 63 percent since the last census, as more white residents moved to the suburbs. And the results of the 1995 Democratic primary suggest that white citywide candidates will face an uphill battle in garnering black support. Mayor Schmoke defeated his white challenger in an election characterized by racial bloc voting. The results of this election showed that Baltimore is different from New York, Chicago, and Los Angeles, where white mayoral candidates have emerged to replace black incumbents. Moreover, city comptroller Joan M. Pratt, a black certified public accountant (CPA) and political novice, defeated former state senator Julian Lapides, a white liberal with a long history of voting for civil rights issues. The demographic figures and voting patterns suggest that blacks are likely to hold on to the city's top elected offices. Finally, more blacks are expected to win positions on the city council from the redrawn Third (61 percent black) and Sixth (58 percent black) Districts (Daemmrich 1995). Unlike Chicago, Los Angeles, and other major cities, Baltimore does not have a sizable Latino or Asian-American population. Blacks can lay claim to these positions unchallenged by other minority groups.

Baltimore confirms earlier findings of Browning, Marshall, and Tabb: "the key to control of city government in favor of minority interests" is controlling the city council and the mayor's office (1990, 9). In Baltimore, the election of a black mayor brought about important changes in city government policy. The author of the 1935 Urban League report quoted in the opening of this chapter would be pleased. Sixty years later, blacks are well represented as firefighters and librarians and other mu-

---

[6] The leaders of the political clubs that controlled these districts were typically conservative. Some of them, like Dominic Mimi DiPietro, a councilman from the First District and founding member of the United Democratic Club, occasionally used racial epithets when referring to blacks.

nicipal workers. In fact, the head of the city's public library system is a black woman. The fire department (long a bastion of white ethnics) is headed by a black fire chief. Black electoral incorporation has had a significant influence on the public sector. Today, however, fewer African Americans can look to the city government for employment. Shrinking revenues and budget constraints have led Mayor Schmoke to downsize city government. Between 1984 and 1993, the number of municipal employees dropped by 19 percent. In the early 1980s, at the request of Baltimore officials, the state of Maryland became responsible for the Baltimore jail. With Mayor Schmoke currently appealing to state officials to take over the municipal court system, even more municipal jobs are likely to be lost.

CONCLUSION: GOVERNING COALITIONS AND THE TASK OF GOVERNING

The argument is often made that the benefits of minority electoral incorporation— access to city jobs, contracts, appointments to city boards—go disproportionately to minority middle-class communities (see Barnes 1994; Jones 1978; Reed 1988; Stone 1989). Urban poverty has increased even as the number of black mayors and city council members has risen (Jaynes and Williams 1989; Swain 1993). Figure 9.2 shows that Baltimore is no different. The percentage of all Baltimore families living in poverty households rose from 9.3 percent in 1970 to 10.3 percent in 1980 and 17.8 percent in 1990. The data in Figure 9.2 also show the racial dimensions of poverty in the city. Although only about 8 percent of whites in Baltimore live in poverty, almost a quarter of black households live below the poverty threshold.

Is there anything that black urban regimes might do to expand the opportunities of disadvantaged residents? Is there anything that Baltimore's city government has done or is proposing that shows promise for the needs of the city's growing disadvantaged community? The revitalization of Sandtown—a depressed, low-income area in west Baltimore—is an example of the kind of things that black urban regimes might do to assist in improving the lives of disadvantaged urban dwellers.

In 1990, the Schmoke administration helped launch a program called "Community Building in Partnership" (CBP). The CBP process began when Mayor Schmoke appointed a task force of Sandtown residents, neighborhood leaders, city officials, and the Enterprise Foundation to develop a plan for transforming the neighborhood's future. The plan is a comprehensive initiative designed to make basic systems work in all aspects of neighborhood life, from housing and human services to education and economic development (City of Baltimore 1992). The revitalization project in Sandtown is an attempt to deal with poverty and endow residents with the capacity to sustain their community. More than 50 projects and services have been initiated in Sandtown, including the development of more than 1,000 housing units and a new multipurpose community center; a health outreach program linking pregnant mothers with prenatal and infant care; the planting of more than 30 community gardens; the establishment of a residents' food and clothing cooperative; and the production of a neighborhood newspaper. Resident-led activities, community organizing, and leadership development are central to the CBP effort. Working

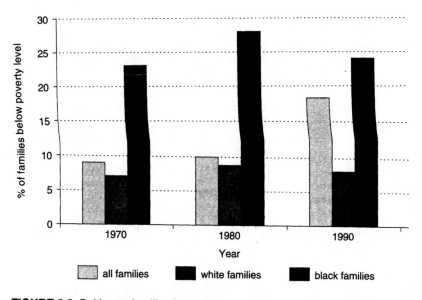

FIGURE 9.2 Baltimore families in poverty
SOURCE: U.S. Bureau of the Census, 1970, 1980, 1990

with BUILD and the Sandtown-Winchester Improvement Association, city officials have supported efforts to strengthen community pride and build neighborhood capacity. The CBP represents the kind of "civic engagement" that Putnam (1993, 1995) advocates as a way to address the ills of urban communities.

The Sandtown project highlights an important point about urban politics and public policy: The power of a governing coalition varies with the nature of the governing task. The governing arrangement depends on what is to be done, who is part of the governing coalition, how the members relate to one another, and what resources the members can bring to the task of governance. If the task is to change governmental practices and institute federally funded social programs, then elected officials are centrally important, as in the issue areas treated by Browning, Marshall, and Tabb. On the other hand, if the task is one of altering opportunities for disadvantaged residents in a changing private economy, the prospects of public-private partnerships play a central role.

Explaining Baltimore's efforts in Sandtown, Mayor Schmoke acknowledged the limited capacity of city government and the need for forging partnerships:

> Declining resources, structural changes in the economy, population shifts, and steady decline in federal support limited the City's capacity to respond to our social problems and needs. Nevertheless, we are working to alleviate the consequences of these changes on Baltimore and its neighborhoods. Our efforts are realistic. We know change requires a full partnership of government, private sector, labor, religious, nonprofit groups, community organizations, and individual citizens. Together, we can "chart a new course of progress." (Schmoke 1994, 1)

In sum, electoral control *alone* does not secure inclusion in the mainstream economy. Something more is needed. Black urban regimes must establish strong links with mass-based political/civic organizations, business leaders, nonprofits, and other nongovernmental institutions.

REFERENCES

Arnold, Joseph. 1976. The Last of the Good Old Days: Politics in Baltimore, 1920–1950. *Maryland Historical Magazine* 7 (Spring): 443–448.

Arnold, Joseph. 1990. Baltimore: Southern Culture and a Northern Economy. In Richard M. Bernard, ed., *Snowbelt Cities: Metropolitan Politics in the Northeast and Midwest since World War II*, 25–39. Bloomington: Indiana University Press.

Bachrach, Peter, and Morton S. Baratz. 1970. *Power and Poverty: Theory and Practice*. New York: Oxford University Press.

Bain, Henry. 1970. Five Kinds of Politics: Politics in Five Maryland Communities. Ph.D. dissertation, Harvard University.

Banfield, Edward, and James Q. Wilson. 1961. *City Politics*. New York: Vintage Press.

Banisky, Sandy. 1991. Increased Black Role Foreseen in Baltimore Politics. *Baltimore Sun* (March 24), B1.

Barnes, Claude W. 1994. Black Mecca Reconsidered: An Analysis of Atlanta's Post–Civil Rights Political Economy. In Marilyn Lashley and Melanie N. Jackson, eds., *African Americans and the New Policy Consensus: Retreat of the Liberal State?*, 179–99. Westport, Conn.: Greenwood Press.

Browne, Gary L. 1980. *Baltimore in the Nation, 1789–1861*. Chapel Hill: University of North Carolina Press.

Browning, Rufus P., Dale Rogers Marshall, and David H. Tabb. 1984. *Protest Is Not Enough*. Berkeley: University of California Press.

Browning, Rufus P., Dale Rogers Marshall, and David H. Tabb, eds. 1990. *Racial Politics in American Cities*. White Plains, N.Y.: Longman.

Callcott, George H. 1988. *Maryland and America, 1940–1980*. Baltimore: Johns Hopkins University Press.

City of Baltimore. January 1991. Preliminary Strategic Financial Plan for the City of Baltimore. Department of Finance.

City of Baltimore. April 1992. Report on the Sandtown-Winchester Community Building in Partnership Initiative.

City of Baltimore. 1993. *City Charter*.

Crew, John et al. 1982. *Effective Public Education: The Baltimore Story*. New York: New Dimensions.

Daemmrich, Joanna. 1995. Council Likely to Reach Race and Gender Balance. *Baltimore Sun*, February 26, C1.

Eisinger, Peter. 1984. Black Mayors and the Politics of Racial Advancement. In H. Hahn and C. Levine, eds., *Readings in Urban Politics*. White Plains, N.Y.: Longman Press.

Fee, Elizabeth, Linda Shopes, and Linda Zeidman, eds. 1991. *The Baltimore Book*. Philadelphia: Temple University Press.

Fleming, G. James. 1964. *An All-Negro Ticket in Baltimore*. New York: McGraw-Hill.

Fleming, G. James. 1972. *Baltimore's Failure to Elect a Black Mayor in 1971*. Washington, D.C.: Joint Center for Political Studies.

Fletcher, Michael. 1991. Blacks May Need More than Numbers to Gain: Political Clubs' Voting Patterns Affect Black Groups. *Baltimore Evening Sun,* March 3, B1.

Fletcher, Michael. 1992. Job Cuts by City Especially Pain Its Black Workers. *Baltimore Sun,* January 26, B1.

Garland, Robert. 1980. Baltimore Is No Longer a Blue-Collar Town. *Baltimore Magazine,* March, 15–21.

Gosnell, Harold. 1968. *Machine Politics: Chicago Model,* 2nd ed. Chicago: University of Chicago Press.

Greene, Suzanne E. 1979. Black Republicans on the Baltimore City Council, 1890–1931. *Maryland Historical Magazine* 74 (September): 203–222.

Grimshaw, William. 1993. *Bitter Fruit: Black Politics in Chicago.* Chicago: University of Chicago Press.

Hollander Foundation. 1960. *Toward Equality: Baltimore's Progress Report.* Baltimore: Sidney Hollander Foundation.

Imbroscio, David, Marion Orr, Timothy Ross, and Clarence Stone. 1995. Baltimore and the Human Investment Challenge. In Fritz W. Wagner, Timothy E. Joder, and Anthony J. Mumphrey, Jr., eds., *Urban Revitalization: Policies and Programs,* 38–68. Thousand Oaks, Calif.: Sage.

Jaynes, Gerald D., and Robin M. Williams, Jr., eds. 1989. *A Common Destiny: Blacks and American Society.* Washington, D.C.: National Academy Press.

Jones, Mack H. 1978. Black Political Empowerment in Atlanta: Myth and Reality. *Annals of the American Academy of Political and Social Science* 439 (September): 90–117.

Key, V. O. 1949. *Southern Politics in State and Nation.* New York: Knopf.

Krefetz, Sharon. 1976. *Welfare Policy Making and City Politics.* New York: Praeger.

Levine, Marc. 1987a. Response to Berkowitz Economic Development in Baltimore: Some Additional Perspectives. *Journal of Urban Affairs* 9 (Spring): 133–138.

Levine, Marc. 1987b. Downtown Redevelopment as an Urban Growth Strategy: A Critical Appraisal of the Baltimore Renaissance. *Journal of Urban Affairs* 9 (Fall): 103–123.

McDougall, Harold. 1993. *Black Baltimore: A Theory of Community.* Philadelphia: Temple University Press.

Mladenka, Kenneth. 1989. Blacks and Hispanics in Urban Politics. *American Political Science Review* 83 (March): 165–191.

Nelson, William, and Philip Meranto. 1977. *Electing Black Mayors.* Columbus: Ohio State University Press.

Noah, Timothy. 1990. The Testing of Kurt Schmoke. *Washington Post Magazine,* May 27, 13–17, 27–31.

O'Keeffe, Kevin. 1986. *Baltimore Politics in 1971–1986: The Schaefer Years and the Struggle for Succession.* Washington, D.C.: Georgetown University Press.

Olesker, Michael. 1991. Recalling the Night that Sheila Dixon Let the Shoe Drop. *Baltimore Sun,* March 21, B1.

Orr, Marion. 1992. Urban Regimes and Human Capital Policies: A Study of Baltimore. *Journal of Urban Affairs* 14 (Summer): 173–187.

Orr, Marion. 1996. Urban Politics and School Reform: The Case of Baltimore. *Urban Affairs Review* 31 (January): 314–345.

Perry, Huey L. 1990. The Evolution and Impact of Biracial Coalitions and Black Mayors in Birmingham and New Orleans. In Rufus P. Browning, Dale Rogers Marshall, and David H. Tabb, eds., *Racial Politics in American Cities,* 140–152. White Plains, N.Y.: Longman.

Pinderhughes, Diane. 1987. *Race and Ethnicity in Chicago Politics.* Urbana: University of Illinois Press.

Power, Garrett. 1983. Apartheid Baltimore Style: The Residential Segregation Ordinances of 1910–1913. *Maryland Law Review* 42 (Fall): 289–328.

Putnam, Robert. 1993. The Prosperous Community: Social Capital and Public Life. *American Prospect* (Spring): 35–42.

Putnam, Robert. 1995. Bowling Alone: America's Declining Social Capital. *Journal of Democracy* 6 (January): 65–78.

Reed, Adolph. 1988. The Black Urban Regime: Structural Origins and Constraints. In Michael Peter Smith, ed., *Power, Community and the City. Comparative Urban and Community Research*, Vol. 1. New Brunswick, N.J.: Transaction Books.

Reid, Ira. 1935. *The Negro Community of Baltimore*. Report of a study conducted for the Baltimore Urban League.

Rich, Wilbur. 1989. *Coleman Young and Detroit Politics*. Detroit: Wayne State University Press.

Rusk, David. 1996. *Baltimore Unbound: A Strategy for Regional Renewal*. Baltimore: Abell Foundation.

Russo, Bud. 1986. The Rise of Clarence "Du" Burns: From Collecting Cardboard to City Council President. *The Baltimore Chronicle*, March 5, A1.

Saltzstein, Grace. 1989. Black Mayors and Police Policies. *Journal of Politics* 51 (3): 525–544.

Schmoke, Kurt L. 1987. Inaugural Address of Mayor Kurt L. Schmoke. Baltimore: Office of the Mayor.

Schmoke, Kurt L. 1994. Baltimore: Building Blocks for a Livable City. Baltimore: Office of the Mayor.

Smith, J. Clay. 1993. *Emancipation: The Making of the Black Lawyer, 1844–1944*. Philadelphia: University of Pennsylvania Press.

Stone, Clarence. 1989. *Regime Politics: Governing Atlanta, 1946–1988*. Lawrence: University Press of Kansas.

Swain, Johnnie D. 1993. Black Mayors: Urban Decline and the Underclass. *Journal of Black Studies* 24 (September): 16–28.

Szanton, Peter. 1986. *Baltimore 2000: A Choice of Futures*. Baltimore: Morris Goldseker Foundation.

Terry, Don. 1991. Cuts in Public Jobs May Hurt Blacks Most. *New York Times*, December 10, A1.

Thompson, Ginger. 1991. City Council OKs Plan for 5 Majority Black Districts. *Baltimore Sun*, March 24, A1.

U.S. Bureau of the Census, 1950, 1960, 1970, 1980, 1990.

U.S. Commission on Civil Rights. 1983. *Greater Baltimore Commitment: A Study of Urban Minority Economic Development*. Washington, D.C.: U.S. Government Printing Office.

Vobejda, B., and Gwen Ifill. 1986. Education Issue May Spell Trouble for Schaefer. *Washington Post*, July 28, C1.

Walton, Hanes. 1973. *Black Politics*. Philadelphia: Lippincott Press.

Watson, Denton L. 1990. *Lion in the Lobby: Clarence Mitchell, Jr.'s Struggle for the Passage of Civil Rights Laws*. New York: William Morrow.

Welcome, Verda, with James Abraham. 1991. *My Life and Times*. Englewood Cliffs, N.J.: Henry House.

Wheeler, Harvey. 1955. Yesterday's Robin Hood: The Rise and Fall of Baltimore's Trenton Democratic Club. *American Quarterly* (Winter): 332–344.

Wickman, Dwayne. 1987. *Destiny 2000: The State of Black Baltimore*. A Report from the Baltimore Urban League.

Wong, Kenneth. 1990. *City Choices*. Albany: State University of New York Press.

part **V**

Latinos

chapter **10**

Hispanic Incorporation and
Structural Reform in Miami

Christopher L. Warren

Editors' Note

Miami is a medium-size city constituting the geographic, political, and economic center of Dade County. Although it remains the hub of urban life in south Florida, it is only one segment of a more complex metropolitan form of government (Metropolitan Miami-Dade County) that encompasses over two dozen separate municipalities as well as a sprawling unincorporated area. Because of the enormous influx of refugees over the last 36 years from Cuba as well as other Latin American and Caribbean countries, Miami has undergone the single most dramatic ethnic transformation of any major American city in this century. Although its multi-ethnic character makes its politics unique, metropolitan Miami may also stand as a portent for other cities with rapidly changing international populations.

Warren shows that in Miami, Hispanics (especially Cuban Americans), unlike blacks and unlike Latinos in many other cities, have achieved rapid economic and political incorporation. They have been successful in Miami's internationalized economy and in a federal court suit brought by Hispanic and black plaintiffs, which overturned the metropolitan government's at-large elections. These achievements, combined with other factors, have made Hispanics the core electoral constituency as well as an integral part of local political-economic elite leadership.

Although Hispanic political incorporation arises in significant ways from growing numerical superiority, economic success, and the structural reform of local government, the dominant coalition that institutionalizes their incorporation is neither likely to include blacks nor be especially liberal. In such a context, the emergence of new minority groups as major players in local politics does not necessarily result in

*shifts in policy or the redistribution of locally controlled resources in ways that en-
hance the political position or policy interests of blacks and low-income Hispanics.*

Miami has always been a place that forces one to reclaim one's past and identity—
or even to discover them for the first time. Playwright William Inge was commenting on this phenomenon when he observed, "It wasn't until I got to New York that
I became Kansan"; so it is for most of Miami's population. In this city of emigres,
migrants, and immigrants, it is attributes such as national and state origin, race, and
ethnicity that usually eclipse other possible bases of identity. Most traditional political participation, therefore, cuts along those same lines. Coalitions between groups,
when they exist at all, are usually strategic and issue- or candidate-specific and are
not broadly conducive to the general shaping or redirection of policy over time.

Of great utility in studying cities like Miami[1] has been the emergence over the
last several years of a number of theoretical frameworks. These have encouraged
research that seeks to characterize local politics broadly in ways that transcend
both the descriptive case study and an exclusive focus on one or a few important variables. Individuals such as Browning, Marshall, and Tabb (1984, 1994),
Mollenkopf (1992), and Stone (1989), whether they speak in terms of *political
incorporation, dominant coalitions,* or *regimes,* have all sought to focus on variables, that while broadly heuristic, nonetheless provide the researcher with common reference points in the study and comparison of otherwise diverse local political environments.

The framework used by Browning, Marshall, and Tabb is particularly apt in the
analysis of this most group conscious of cities, given its more specific focus on minority group mobilization, dominant coalition formation, political incorporation, and
resultant policy responsiveness to minority interests. Insights derived from the study
of Miami might then prove to be a harbinger for other large metropolitan areas affected by the "internationalization" of their populations, economies, and politics.

In the 1990s, the story of Hispanic[2] ascendancy in Miami has evolved into one
in which Dade County's Cuban community is now fully incorporated as the key
player at all levels of Miami's electoral politics as well as in many of its most important economic and civic affairs. A significant capstone for expanded Hispanic electoral clout was the 1992 U.S. District Court decision overturning at-large elections
for the county commission (*Meek v. Metropolitan Dade County,* 1992). As a result of
the decision, Hispanics and blacks were both assured secure seats on Miami's most

---

[1] Even the term *Miami* can be a source of confusion. In common usage, it often refers to the entire metropolitan area, which encompasses all of Dade County and its 26 municipalities. It also refers to the
city of Miami, which is the core municipality in the Miami Standard Metropolitan Statistical Area
(SMSA). In this chapter, Miami will be used to refer to the Miami-Dade County metropolitan area. The
city of Miami will be referred to as such.

[2] Although for many the term *Latino* has become preferred in making references to Spanish-speaking
people from the Americas, in Miami the term is rarely encountered and is infrequently used by Cubans
for self-identification. Therefore, the terms *Hispanic* or *Latin,* which are more common in local usage,
are used throughout the chapter.

important policy-making body. Growing numbers of Hispanics and blacks have also gained entree to the once all-white business and civic associations that have traditionally played a significant leadership role in the community's affairs. Yet, a careful examination of the flow of resources and benefits controlled by local government indicates that much has remained the same. Although minority group representation is now manifest in local government decision making, it does not as yet promise to fundamentally challenge long-standing public policy priorities or the centrality of larger economic interests in shaping the area's primary political-economic agenda. For blacks in particular, ongoing obstacles to effective political incorporation remain evident.

Aspects of Miami's political environment place issues of minority mobilization and incorporation, coalition building, and local government responsiveness to minority policy agendas in a context quite different from those of most other cities analyzed in this book. Four features of the Miami setting are especially noteworthy for the ways they combine to shape the area's minority politics:

1. Miami's distinctive political geography, particularly the ethnic diversity of its population, its neighborhood settlement patterns, and the structure of its metropolitan form of government
2. Heightened group consciousness and conflict resulting from the respective roles played by each of the area's three major ethnic groups in determining election outcomes and influencing local government policy making
3. Growing system complexity, as evidenced by the continued intrusion of international affairs in local politics and the need for the system to manage conflict over policy issues as diverse as the ongoing influx of refugees, neighborhood redevelopment, police violence, white flight, and local anti-communism
4. Ongoing efforts to reform local government structure, including recent federal court suits and rulings as well as the possible incorporation of several new municipalities within Dade County

This chapter analyzes Miami politics in light of these features, with the objective of explaining the following: (1) the basic contours of Hispanic (especially Cuban) and black (especially African-American) political mobilization and incorporation, (2) the area's well-publicized political and social upheaval (for example, massive influxes of political and economic refugees and race riots), and (3) possible scenarios for the future of minority politics in Miami.

THE POLITICAL GEOGRAPHY
OF METROPOLITAN MIAMI

Two aspects of metropolitan Miami's political geography are of particular relevance to minority politics. First, the amazing diversity of the area's international population makes analyses of minority group politics problematic. Second, the area's

unique metropolitan form of government creates patterns that are difficult to analyze. This government system combines mechanisms of a strong county government with those of the area's 26 municipalities. It is superimposed on a paradoxical
neighborhood settlement pattern that variously concentrates and disperses minority
populations, dramatically affecting the relative influence of blacks, Hispanics, and
non-Hispanic whites in the different municipal and county jurisdictions.

Ethnic Diversity and Neighborhood Settlement Patterns

Over the past 35 years, the combined forces of immigration and "white flight" have
brought about in Miami the single most dramatic ethnic transformation of any major
American metropolitan area in this century (Metropolitan Dade County Planning
Department 1986). In an area where close to 50 percent of the population is foreign
born, where the rapidly growing non-Cuban segment of the Hispanic population
comes from well over a dozen countries, and where approximately 25 percent of
the black population is of Caribbean origin, specific mention must often by made of
the particular black or Hispanic national group being referenced (Boswell 1994a).
With the internationalization of Miami's population, non-Hispanic whites (a euphe-
mism used by the local media to replace the term *Anglo,* which some find objec-
tionable) have not only seen their numbers shrink both in relative and real terms
but have also lost external recognition of their own varied ethnic and regional
backgrounds.

As Table 10.1 shows, the rapid demographic change in Dade County is a post-
1960 phenomenon, largely precipitated by the Cuban Revolution and the resultant
influx of refugees. The emergence of a Cuban enclave, combined with the rapid
penetration of international capital into the local economy, had a multiplier effect
on the influx of additional refugees and immigrants from throughout the hemisphere (Portes and Stepick 1993). Today, after post-1990 immigration is taken into
account, the county's Hispanic population unquestionably exceeds 1 million people, likely constituting more than 50 percent of the total. Cubans, the Hispanic
group almost singularly associated with Miami in the popular consciousness, are
now estimated to make up 60 percent of Miami's Latin population—a decline of
more than 10 percent since 1980 (Boswell 1994a, 1994b).

Within Miami's black population, there has always been a significant Caribbean
component. Haitian refugees, especially the "boat people" who came in the late
1970s and early 1980s, have added tremendously to its diversity (Dunn and Stepick
1992; Stepick 1992). However, despite significant increases in the black population
(rising 570 percent during the years 1950 to 1990), as a proportion of the total, the
increase has been slow and gradual, ranging from 13 percent of the total in 1950 to
20 percent in 1990.

Given the difficulty inherent in defining broad categories of minority groups in
Miami, it is still most useful to conduct political analysis within the general context
of the tri-ethnic framework. The hundreds of thousands of immigrants and refugees
from throughout the hemisphere represent a rapidly expanding portion of the over-

TABLE 10.1   Tri-ethnic population of Dade County: 1960–1990

	Non-Hispanic White		Black		Hispanic		Total	
Year	Number	%	Number	%	Number	%	Number	%
1960	748,000	79.8	140,000	14.9	50,000	5.3	938,000	100.0
1970	786,000	61.6	190,000	14.9	299,000	23.5	1,275,000	100.0
1980	776,000	47.3	282,000	17.2	581,000	35.5	1,639,000	100.0
1990	614,000	31.2	398,000	20.3	953,000	48.5	1,965,000	100.0

Note: The non-Hispanic white category includes a small proportion of "other" races. Hispanic is not a race category, and given the presence of small numbers of black Hispanics, there is some slight overlap.

SOURCE: Thomas D. Boswell. 1994. *The Cubanization and Hispanicization of Metropolitan Miami*. Miami: Cuban American Policy Center, Cuban American National Council.

all population and contribute significantly to intragroup diversity, but these other national groups mostly remain politically, economically, and socially insulated and isolated. Questions of immigration status, citizenship, group size, and economic subsistence loom large for many of them, making political mobilization, incorporation, and the shaping of public policy distant considerations.

Another factor shaping minority politics in Miami is the extent to which this diverse population has been superimposed on mostly static political boundaries, resulting in several cities that are predominantly Hispanic (nine cities in all, including the three largest: Miami, Hialeah, and Miami Beach), black (the two small towns of Opa Locka and Florida City), or non-Hispanic white (several of the smallest and medium-size municipalities). At the same time, rapid growth of the unincorporated area population (now far exceeding that of all municipalities combined) has worked to marginalize the influence of the municipal governments on the area at large. City of Miami residents, for example, made up almost 65 percent of the total county population in 1940, but that proportion had dropped to 18 percent by 1990.

Black settlement patterns have had an especially negative effect on efforts at political mobilization. Historically, because of the legacy of southern racism and the conscious placement of some black settlements in unincorporated areas (Mohl 1992, 1987), blacks have played an almost insignificant role in the politics of the municipalities. A majority of the population still resides in unincorporated Dade county, making blacks particularly dependent on the decisions of the county government.

Overall, there are about a dozen indentifiable black neighborhoods spread throughout the metropolitan area. In the northern reaches of the county are found the densely populated public housing developments of Liberty City, which is not a city at all but a mostly unincorporated area bordering the city of Miami in northwest Dade. Other predominantly black neighborhoods lie adjacent to Liberty City, but they are either located in separate municipalities (the city of Miami or Opa Locka) or are more likely to be populated by people from the Caribbean (Little Haiti). Closest to the central business district is Overtown, which historically served as the black downtown section. In the agricultural south end of the county lie several less densely settled black neighborhoods. This settlement pattern, and the extent to which it undermines black influence in both the county and the individual municipalities and complicates grassroots organizing, has been a formidable barrier to political mobilization. Even in the black majority towns of Florida City and Opa Locka, black electoral success has always been tempered by the marginal roles played by these municipalities in the county's affairs. The use of these two cities as a base for the articulation of black political interests is even more profoundly limited by the severe economic problems they face. As of the mid-1980s, both were listed as being among the ten poorest of all suburban incorporated areas in the nation (Johnson 1987).

In contrast to Miami's black population, a majority of Hispanics reside in various municipalities. Also, rather than being dispersed throughout the county, Cubans in particular have settled in a largely uninterrupted corridor of residential areas, extending from the city of Miami's Little Havana section to the western limits of Dade County, and north into Hialeah. This contiguous neighborhood base in Dade's largest municipalities, combined with the growing trend in both state and local government toward district elections, facilitated the emergence of Cuban-Americans as important participants in both municipal and county politics. For many Cubans, political success at the municipal level has been an effective springboard to higher local and state office.

Meanwhile, the declining non-Hispanic white population is now in the minority in most of the largest municipalities. Still, throughout the 1980s, the two major bases of Anglo power remained the metropolitan county commission and the major downtown business, civic, and media institutions that are involved in community affairs. However, as explained in greater detail below, these significant bases of political influence have also experienced dramatic changes in recent years.

In short, in the complex political geography of Miami, the three major ethnic groups are not spread uniformly across the metropolitan area, but instead reside in a mixed pattern of enclaves and neighborhoods, the locations of which determine their respective bases of power and possible arenas for effective political participation.

Metro's Structure and Minority Group Representation

Unlike metropolitan areas such as Boston, Chicago, or Atlanta, where core cities with a clear sense of identity are the dominant governmental structures, Miami's metropolitan government is fragmented, both structurally and in the public consciousness. This configuration blurs jurisdictional lines as well as local governmental responsibility and accountability. In 1957, Miami-Dade County established the first metropolitan form of government in the United States. Metropolitan Dade County government (popularly referred to as "Metro") provided for a two-tiered system that coordinated the workings of the county and municipal governments while granting the county certain powers over the municipalities. The large unincorporated area was to be solely governed by Metro. A metropolitan county commission and a county manager hold policy-making and administrative authority and are the dominant forces in matters of areawide concern (for example, land use and zoning, mass transit and infrastructure, social services, and parks and recreation). The county also sets minimum performance standards for many of those services still provided by the municipalities. For their part, municipalities retain the authority to maintain their own police departments, set municipal taxes, and exceed county standards in zoning and service delivery, among other narrower powers (Sofen 1961, 1966; Lotz 1984).

The Metro commission initially operated under a complex structure that combined district, at-large, and municipal representation. By 1963, reformers won a campaign to reduce the size of the commission to nine members elected at large, on nonpartisan ballots, with provisions for runoffs in the event no candidate for a seat received a majority. A Metro mayor with no executive or administrative authority served as one of the nine commissioners as first among equals. With the more than two dozen other municipalities each having local governments of their own and each with a unique charter and structure, and with metropolitan Miami's population being so transient, it is easy to understand why many residents of Dade County have difficulty distinguishing between county and municipal mayors and commissioners (Mohl 1984).

Metro was created and its structure initially reformed at a time when political power was overwhelmingly in the hands of Miami's non-Hispanic white population. Blacks, who as of the 1960 census were still seriously disenfranchised, made up only 15 percent of the population. Hispanics, mostly noncitizens, constituted a meager 5 percent of the total population, and by one estimate, "probably fewer than 5,000" actually voted (Banfield 1965, 104). Thus, concern for minority representation was not part of the political calculus that created or initially reformed the Metro system, nor was it a significant factor in its subsequent policies (Sofen 1961, 1966).

As of the 1963 charter changes, Metro stood as a model of reformed local government, characterized by a council-manager form of government, nonpartisan/at-large elections, and recognition of an "at-large community interest" in local government policy making. A concomitant deemphasis of party, neighborhood, and minority racial or ethnic interests meant that Metro's structure acted as a buffer against subsequent attempts to use minority and neighborhood-based political power to influence public policy (Stack and Warren 1992).

Over time, at-large elections and the runoff provision proved to be particularly effective deterrents to minority candidates. As of the early 1990s, by which time Hispanics and blacks made up about 70 percent of the population, there still had never been more than one black and one Hispanic commissioner to serve on the nine member Metro Commission at any given time (see Table 10.2). From Metro's inception in 1957 through 1992, a total of five black and two Hispanic officials had served on the commission, and of those, only two blacks and one Hispanic had been elected outright, without first being appointed to fill a vacancy. Ironically, in those instances in which a minority candidate was elected outright, the candidate usually won without carrying the votes of his or her own group. In such cases, the winning candidate proved to be the favorite of non-Hispanic white voters. Indeed, generalized social and political antagonism between blacks and Hispanics, combined with a tendency for bloc voting within all three groups, essentially assured that non-Hispanic white voters would remain the decisive swing vote in most at-large county elections, even as their numbers had declined from over 80 percent of the total population in 1960 to barely more than 30 percent in 1990 (Warren 1991).

The high costs of running countywide campaigns also meant that successful candidates usually received significant financial support from major private sector interests—especially those tied to development and tourism. In races that were competitive, it was common for private interests to contribute to each of the major candidates running for the same seat—a practice known in local campaign parlance as CYA (Cover Your Assets) (Soto 1988). Unless minority candidates were able to attract similar financial backing and combine it with policy stands that could be expected to cultivate non-Hispanic white support, they had little chance of winning office.

Court Intervention

Over the years, one of the few issues that provided common political ground for Miami's black and Hispanic political leadership was reform of multimember and at-large election structures in favor of district representation for both state and local offices. In both the 1982 and 1992 state redistricting efforts, the abolition of multimember districts for state legislative races and the creation of more minority districts dramatically increased Hispanic and black representation from Dade County (Moreno and Warren 1992). Within Metro, however, a steadfast majority of incumbent commissioners resisted all recommendations and attempts to create district elections. As a result, black and Hispanic plaintiffs eventually filed a class action suit against Metro, under Section II of the amended 1965 Voting Rights Act (*Meek v. Metropolitan Dade County,* 1992).

Relying on Congress's amendments to the Voting Rights Act, the federal courts ruled that plaintiffs in voting rights cases no longer had to demonstrate "intent" to discriminate in the creation of at-large electoral systems in order for the at-large sys-

TABLE 10.2   Ethnic representation on the Metro Commission: Pre- and post-court intervention (1992–1993)

	Non-Hispanic White		Black		Hispanic		Total	
	1992	1993	1992	1993	1992	1993	1992	1993
Number of Seats	7	3	1	4	1	6	9	13
Percentage of Seats	78.0	23.0	11.0	31.0	11.0	46.0	100.0	100.0
Percentage of Population	31.0	31.0	20.0	20.0	49.0	49.0	100.0	100.0

tems to be overturned on constitutional grounds. Instead, plaintiffs needed only to demonstrate that under the totality of circumstances, the electoral system had the effect of diminishing minority access to the electoral process and hindered the election of the representatives of their choice (*Thornburg v. Gingles,* 1986). In an elaborate 62-page order, handed down in August of 1992, the judge in the Metro case ruled that Metro's system of elections discriminated against both blacks and Hispanics. Ironically, central to the judge's reasoning was his recognition of "the severe degree of racially polarized voting and the keen hostility that exists between blacks and Hispanics." The judge concluded that such polarization led each group to forge separate strategic voting coalitions with non-Hispanic whites to defeat those candidates most strongly supported by either minority group (*Meek v. Metropolitan Dade County,* 1992). Pursuant to its ruling, the court approved a plan that replaced the nine-member, at-large system with a 13-member commission, all elected from districts—with as many districts as practicable having either Hispanic or black voting majorities. Under the court orders not even the position of mayor was retained. However, separate action taken under the provisions of the county's home-rule charter now call for the creation of a separate mayor's office that will have substantial executive and administrative authority.

With the first election under the new system in April 1993, the county commission went from a nine-member body in which there had never been more than one black and one Hispanic commissioner at any one time, to a 13-member body having six Hispanics, four blacks, and three non-Hispanic whites. Non-Hispanic white representation dropped from 78 percent to 23 percent of the seats (see Table 10.2). After the success of the suit against Metro, many of the same plaintiffs immediately proceeded to bring suit against the Dade County School Board and even against the state, which has at-large elections for county judge seats. A suit against the city of Miami Beach over its own at-large electoral configuration was also filed, and other municipal challenges could follow.

CHANGING POLITICAL FORTUNES

In the face of such changes, Dade County has become a significant testing ground for the extent to which local electoral reform can be a significant force in promoting minority group political power. Certainly, at the level of Hispanic and black representation on locally elected boards and commissions, it is difficult to envision more rapid or fundamental changes than those Miami has been experiencing.

These are not insignificant gains. In the case of black Miamians, to move in 30 years from virtual political exclusion, frequently reinforced by both racist law and practice, to proportional parity on key policy-making bodies, has deep symbolic significance and inherent value in the representation of people and agendas long denied. Cuban Americans have experienced one of the most rapid political incorporations of any immigrant group in American history. Such achievements provide legitimacy, forums for the articulation of policy agendas, the potential to forge new governing coalitions, and an opportunity to steer resources in new directions. However, as Browning, Marshall, and Tabb point out (1994, 18, 12), in the drive by minority groups to attain political power and equality, "it is the nature of issues to change over time from what is urgently demanded to what is taken for granted." There are always the lingering questions of "What difference does it make?" and "What's next?" Thus, the electoral successes of minority group leadership must ultimately be gauged in terms of "the production of policies responsive to the concerns of the group" (1994, 18, 12).

An analysis of policy responsiveness, however, must go beyond the representation of group and constituency interests on policy-making bodies to examine the influence of economic structures and power on local government decision making and the ways in which such influence can either nurture or hinder certain policy outcomes. As Mollenkopf has argued (1992, 38), the two "primary interactions" between the leaders of local government and the numerous other players and forces in urban political systems are, "first, between the leaders of city government and their political/electoral base; and second, between the leaders of city government and their economic environment." It is the broader analysis of these interactions and the extent to which they provide further insight into the political fortunes of Miami's three major ethnic groups to which we now turn.

An End to Non-Hispanic White Dominance in a Pervasive Political-Economic Context

Although non-Hispanic whites have been supplanted in terms of their electoral dominance, they have remained powerful in the major nongovernmental civic, media, and business institutions. These bases of elite power have also been transformed, albeit not as dramatically as elected bodies. Not only have Hispanics and blacks been brought into the leadership ranks of prominent local organizations that historically have been bastions of Anglo power, but parallel business and civic institutions, controlled by Hispanics and blacks, have emerged, such as the Cuban American National Foundation, the Latin Builders Association, and the Black Lawyers Association. In fact, there are three local chambers of commerce—each primarily representing one of the three major ethnic groups (Freedberg and Soto 1989).

Historically, private sector influence in Miami has been especially linked to the establishment and growth of the city's central business district as well as to the development and tourism interests long essential to the health and well-being of the local economy. With rapid growth in the 1940s and 1950s came new demands for physical and social infrastructure and expanded local initiatives to promote and stabilize business activity. Such objectives served to facilitate business leadership in community affairs. As Mohl documented (1987), even early social programs such as slum clearance were shaped by the "hidden agenda of the downtown civic elite," which sought to expand the business section into the black neighborhood of Overtown.

With population growth, the proliferation of dozens of local governments, and resultant fragmentation in local policy making, local elites became active in the effort to establish a metropolitan government. Endorsement of the proposition was also forthcoming from a variety of "good-government" groups, local elite law firms, professional administrators, the *Miami Herald*, and others who saw inherent advantage in being able to work with a more centralized government. This pro-Metro coalition became and has generally remained the dominant force in shaping the community's basic political-economic agenda (Sofen 1966; Mohl 1984). Even in the wake of dramatic demographic changes, Sofen's (1961) early observations regarding Miami's power structure have, to this point, remained essentially valid.

> In the case of Miami, the lack of countervailing organizations in the form of either cohesive labor or minority groups, has meant that the business community had no real competitors in the political arena. Moreover, since the cause of "good government" groups coincided with the desires of the more powerful Miami business organizations, the latter were quite content to allow the newspapers, professional groups, the university professors, and the League of Women Voters to assume the positions of catalytic leadership in civic affairs. (p. 30)

In later years, the role played by the business sector became even more formal and institutionalized through the establishment of organizations such as the ironically self-described "Non-Group" (an association of Miami's top business and civic leaders), the Beacon Council (a publicly and privately funded agency chartered to encourage business development), and various appendages of the traditionally Anglo Greater Miami Chamber of Commerce. Each has served as an important vehicle in the formation and articulation of the policy preferences of major private economic interests—constituting what one former Miami mayor called "the shadow government" (Slevin 1994, 4B).

The major business and civic associations have not entirely denied the existence of minority policy concerns, but they have continued to be central in articulating what the broader "public interest" is in terms of local government policy. In the end, throughout most of its recent history, Miami's business interests and reformist governmental structures and values converged in creating an environment in which issues of primary concern to minority groups and their neighborhoods have been frequently dismissed as not being in the best interest of the community as a whole. The idea that advancement for minorities might require policies inconsistent with the interests of influential economic institutions is generally not countenanced.

Black Incorporation
and the Limits of Structural Reform

As in most areas of the country, the 1950s and 1960s promised a positive political future for Miami's black population. The civil rights movement, federal court decisions, and national legislation encouraged local mobilization efforts. Although lacking the high level of organization and intensity found in some southern cities, blacks in Miami realized substantive gains, through community organizing and protest activity, in the desegregation of public and private facilities and in voter registration.

Once black registration increased, election and appointment to local political office followed. Though never exceeding one seat on either the old nine-member Metro commission or the five-member city of Miami commission, blacks did gain seats on the county school board and eventually won a majority of seats on the Opa Locka and Florida City town councils. In the 1970s and 1980s blacks also gained significantly in the area of appointed office, at various times holding the offices of Miami city manager, superintendent of schools, and numerous other high and mid-level positions.

Advancement for blacks was also apparent in local government employment and contracting with minority firms. Local government jobs have been an essential source of employment for black Miamians, with blacks holding approximately one third of the more than 30,000 county and city of Miami jobs. Although, as some critics point out, many of the jobs are lower level clerical and service positions, over recent years, dissatisfaction over opportunities for blacks in public sector employment has not been a top agenda item. Both Metro and the city of Miami also have ordinances setting goals for the awarding of contracts to minority-owned businesses. Although such programs in other cities have confronted legal challenges in federal court, they continue to be expanded in Dade County.

Yet clearly, apart from overcoming *de jure* segregation, the most significant milestone in black incorporation has been the restructuring of the Metro commission, resulting in the election of four black commissioners. As a result, black officials' share of seats rose from about 11 percent to 30 percent of the total. The most senior of the four commissioners and the only one to have served on the old commission is Arthur Teele, a Republican with a background in banking. Given the absence of a mayor's seat on the new commission, Teele was elected chair by his fellow commissioners and is considered a probable candidate for mayor when that position is established. With appeal that cuts across ethnic lines (he was initially elected in an at-large race in which he did not carry the black vote), a favorable reputation in the business community, and a talent for building ad hoc, issue-specific majorities on policy votes, Teele could be an effective broker in forging a governing coalition that focused more attention on the agenda of the black community. What is lacking, however, is strong leadership from other black officials with strong neighborhood bases to be the primary promoters of the agenda. To date, the remaining three black commissioners have been among the least visible and vocal on the commission.

Although there is no formal policy agenda for black Miamians as such, most of the concerns voiced by black civic leaders fall into one of three major categories. First, concerns that cut across the breadth of law enforcement have been ongoing, including high incidences of crime, generally poor police-community relations, and repeated instances of police violence. Second, housing and neighborhood revitalization have been consistent areas of complaint. Finally, and most significantly, general issues of expanded economic opportunity, especially in the private sector, are not only critically important, but because of the need for sustained responses from the business community, are also particularly resistant to improvement. The perceptions and the realities of limited progress on these issues is indicative of the limitations of political incorporation for black Miamians.

Regarding law enforcement, under the Metro charter incorporated areas maintain their own police departments whereas unincorporated areas, including some of the most densely populated black neighborhoods, are policed by the county force. A long history of friction between blacks and police has been particularly problematic in the unincorporated neighborhoods and in the city of Miami, and it was a catalyst in each of the four riots that took place in the 1980s (Porter and Dunn 1984). At the same time, criminals in these areas, a constant danger to residents, have repeatedly victimized tourists and others who get lost when exiting the expressways that crisscross black neighborhoods. Such incidents not only dominate local news but have received significant national and international press. The obvious need for law enforcement, safety, and stability, combined with a generalized mistrust and resentment toward law enforcement officials, makes the multidimensional problem particularly recalcitrant.

In the 1980s, Liberty City (which experienced one of the most violent riots of this century in May 1980) and Overtown (where there were several nights of disorder in December 1982, in the spring of 1984, and in January 1989) came to replace Watts and Detroit as the contemporary symbols of racial upheaval in America. For some, the pattern of rioting symbolized a host of fundamental problems faced by the black community, leading them to describe the riots as "rebellions" (Marable 1980). Yet in this community, still dependent on tourist dollars and hypersensitive to bad publicity, efforts were often made to downplay recurrent outbreaks of violence. Furthermore, just as the 1980 riots coincided with the influx of upwards to 150,000 Mariel and Haitian refugees, the racial violence of 1989 accompanied the arrival of tens of thousands of Nicaraguan and other Central American refugees. The coincidence of such events seems to reinforce the contention that in Miami, the problems evident in the black community are frequently undercut or upstaged by the pressing needs of the most recently arrived refugees, who are often viewed as receiving more immediate, concentrated, and dedicated assistance from both the local public and private sectors.

In the second policy area of housing and neighborhood revitalization, not only have there been chronic complaints about the administration and maintenance of public housing through the county's "Little HUD" office, but the housing problem is in turn linked to the broader problem that black Miamians frequently lack the power to shape those policies that most directly affect their own neighborhoods. Over the years, a greatly disproportionate number of development projects have negatively affected black neighborhoods. A football stadium to house the Miami Dolphins was built in northwest Dade, disrupting one of the county's few middle-class black neighborhoods. Since the 1930s, Overtown itself has been repeatedly disrupted by redevelopment plans and massive highway construction, virtually none of which have focused directly on improving conditions for residents. The last major effort in the 1980s, called for the area of Overtown bordering the central business district to be the site for the construction of a publicly funded arena to house the Miami Heat basketball franchise and the development of thousands of units of middle-class housing and shops. Only the arena and the first housing units were ever completed, and after six years of operation, the Miami Heat franchise has declared the facility inadequate and now threatens to leave the city if a new arena is not built in a different location at public expense.

In the meantime, mere blocks from the Overtown neighborhood, two major government-subsidized retail projects have been completed on the bayfront, tens of millions of dollars have been spent on a downtown auto race facility used once a year, the main downtown park (which lies mostly unutilized) and the adjoining Biscayne Boulevard have received more than $35 million in improvements in recent years, $120 million has been pledged for construction of an opera and symphony facility, and hundreds of millions more in public funds have been spent within about a three-square-mile area adjoining Overtown. Frequently, even monies initially designated for neighborhood development are subsequently funneled into the business district. One $40 million city of Miami bond issue known as "Parks for People" was approved with support from black voters on promises that most of the funds would be used to create and improve neighborhood parks throughout the city. More than two-thirds of the money was ultimately spent on expanding the downtown Port of Miami and improving the main downtown park (Goldfarb 1992).

Although it is impossible to calculate the direct and indirect returns generated by such projects for local government or business, such anecdotal evidence does at least suggest the general direction of resource allocation. At each juncture, policy-makers have justified such projects in terms of the broader economic interest of the community and the spinoff benefits for blacks and other residents in terms of expanded job opportunities and better overall living conditions. Many blacks have remained skeptical of such justifications insofar as they are either (1) premised on the seemingly contradictory logic that improved circumstances for blacks are often linked to the disruption of their neighborhoods and the dislocation of residents, or (2) linked to expensive projects and programs that provide little or nothing of direct benefit to black residents and neighborhoods, but rather are intended to bring macro-economic benefits. Policies aimed at improving black neighborhoods outright have been few in number, have been of low visibility, and have experienced weak follow-through.

The third category of policy concerns relevant to Miami's black community is directly linked to the need for greater economic opportunity. As a group, blacks confront the worst living conditions, earn the lowest median income, and have the largest percentage of families in poverty, the worst housing conditions, and usually twice the rate of white unemployment. When the city of Miami was designated, based on the 1980 census, as the sixth poorest large city in the United States on the basis of the percentage of the population living below the poverty line, it was largely because the black neighborhoods of Overtown, Little Haiti, the black section of Coconut Grove, and a portion of Liberty City are all contained within the city limits. In sharp contrast to many Hispanics in Miami, blacks are not in a position to use economic clout as a means of enhancing their political status. There are comparatively few black-owned businesses (approximately 6,700 as of 1987), and of those businesses that are owned and operated by blacks, only about 14 percent provide employment for anyone other than the owner (Portes and Stepick 1993, 183).

Even the pledges of public and private support for efforts to promote black economic opportunity that were forthcoming after the 1980 and 1982 riots were short-lived. The Metro-Miami Action Plan (MMAP), which was to be the centerpiece of a coordinated public/private revitalization effort, all but folded after five years of operation. As one Hispanic former MMAP board member stated, "MMAP has been abandoned by almost everyone. There is not a sense of urgency about black problems. . . . A lot of prominent corporate leaders began to disappear after the second year. In Miami, you only get the corporate world to react in times of crisis. There's not a conscience that endures" (Dugger 1987, 1C).

It is too early to determine whether expanded and more secure black representation on the Metro commission or other boards will provide the necessary pressures to assure better follow-through on those programs that are established, much less whether it provides an effective base for actual policy initiation. Protest, though rarely seen in an organized or sustained way, is still viewed as a necessary tool for the black community. One particularly illustrative example was provoked by the snubbing of Nelson Mandela by local government and business leaders when he visited Miami in 1990. Mandela was slated to receive a grand welcome to the city until, soon after his arrival in the United States, he was asked about the support the African National Congress had received in the past from Fidel Castro and Yasir Arafat. By refusing to renounce those who had lent support to him and his organization during the years when most of the West did not, Mandela angered anti-Castro activist groups as well as some of the Jewish community.

In response, local officials (Cuban and Anglo alike) refused to greet Mandela and withdrew the honors that were to be presented. Little organized response was forthcoming from the black community until a prominent local black attorney, H. T. Smith, worked on organizing a convention boycott of Miami. Gradually, the initial call for an apology for the snubbing of Mandela evolved into a more substantive list of demands aimed at expanding opportunities for blacks in the private sector. After three years of the boycott, estimated to have cost Miami tens of millions of dollars in convention business, a 20-point negotiated settlement was announced in May of 1993. At the time of the agreement, Smith reminded community leaders of their poor follow-through in past efforts to focus on issues of greatest concern to the black community. "Failure to keep the promises we have made will have serious consequences, because we believe in the future we will not have the credibility to harness the rage, the frustration, and the indignation of the black community" (Smith 1993, 3). The boycott strategy, effective in this instance, may prove to conceal a tragic flaw over the longer term. By relying heavily on outside players as opposed to local organizing, the boycott may have effectively pressured the private sector, but it also contributed little to longer term mobilization and incorporation efforts that could bring Miami's black citizens and political leaders together in a common cause.

Advances for blacks in voter registration, elections, appointment politics, and public sector employment have provided important opportunities, but to date their incorporation has not helped forge a competitive governing coalition, able to move policy in ways that directly benefit black neighborhoods and their residents or able to capture the attention and commitment of the major business and civic institutions. Group size, holding a minority of seats without consistent allies on fragmented boards and commissions, holding a majority of seats in the two poorest municipalities, and having generally diffused and weak political leadership that has been unable or unwilling to consistently promote an agenda to benefit the black community are all factors limiting the achievements of black political incorporation. Black Miamians may find that even when the electoral structure has "delivered" all that it reasonably can, numerous obstacles to real influence over policy remain.

The Political and Economic Dimensions of Hispanic Incorporation

Standing in a city that has been described as the "capital of Latin America" (Levine 1985), it is difficult to appreciate that 35 years ago Hispanic influence in Miami was practically nonexistent. After the Cuban Revolution of 1959, the first waves of Cuban immigrants did not bring in the dispossessed poor of that country but included numerous accomplished professionals who combined personal initiative with an "open armed" immigration policy and U.S. economic assistance in establishing themselves in Miami. Subsequent waves of immigrants throughout the 1960s brought a large portion of the Cuban middle class as well as an upwardly mobile working class to the area. Although collectively the notions of Cuban wealth are often more valid as allegory than as fact, Cuban immigration has been accompanied by rapid economic incorporation and a number of dramatic success stories. Overall, as of 1986, the median income for Cubans nationally was $26,770 as opposed to $14,584 for Puerto Ricans and $19,326 for Mexicans (Marquis 1989). By 1987, Hispanics in Miami had founded close to 37,000 businesses, including banks, television and radio stations, construction companies, restaurants, and a variety of service and industrial enterprises. Los Angeles is the only city in the United States with more Hispanic-owned businesses, but it has a larger Hispanic population, and the Miami firms tend to encompass more capital and employ more people.

The 1980 Mariel refugees and many of the Cuban entrants since then have included far larger numbers of refugees who were poor, nonwhite, unskilled, and without family ties in the United States. Thus, in more recent years, class and racial differences have sometimes tested the durability of nationalistic ties. However, such divisions have yet to manifest themselves in politically significant ways. Ultimately, it is the numerical, economic, and political force of the middle- and upper-class Cuban community that has the greatest impact on Miami politics.

For many years, the political incorporation of Cuban Americans lagged behind their economic accomplishments. As of the late 1970s, few Miami precincts had majorities of Hispanic registrants, and only a handful of Hispanics held local political office. Fortunes began to change dramatically in the 1980s as Cuban-Americans became more pervasive in municipal and county government as well as in the state legislature and Dade's U.S. House delegation. Bloc voting for Cuban candidates, higher than average voter turnout, and fuller use of the once-weak local Republican party apparatus were all important factors in early Cuban political mobilization.

In the area of appointive politics, Hispanic incorporation has progressed just as rapidly. In what may be the capstone of their ascendancy in this area, Cuban Americans have now long held the positions of county manager, Miami city manager, and superintendent of the county school system. County and municipal employment for Hispanics has progressed apace with these other developments, sometimes leading to charges of political patronage, cronyism, and machine politics. Such charges have been especially common in the Hispanic majority cities of Hialeah and Sweetwater.

The immigrant experience, antipathy toward Fidel Castro, and other more local factors have channeled Miami Cuban politics in particular directions, but it is a mistake to view this group's political activity as monolithic. Some political rivalries were transplanted from Cuba, there are no leaders behind whom Cubans are truly united, and the phenomenon of Cubans running against Cubans is growing in elections at all levels. Thus, the long-term impact of Hispanic incorporation on local policy making is still uncertain, especially in light of the unusual nature of their accompanying policy agenda. In addition to routine issues of service delivery and business development, Miami's Cubans have frequently emphasized issues that in a local context are more symbolic than substantive—especially anticommunism and efforts to oppose various "English only" language initiatives. "On the local level, symbolic politics have . . . frequently been at the core of local political mobilization, candidate selection, and issue articulation. . . . Certain largely symbolic political issues became particularly significant, not only because of the controversy surrounding them but also because of the role they played in galvanizing Cuban ethnic group consciousness and converting it into local political activism" (Stack and Warren 1990, 12).

With political representation now secured at the national level through Cuban representation in the U.S. House and the ongoing lobbying efforts of the Cuban American National Foundation, more of the political energies of the community on foreign policy matters are now directed at Washington. In recent years, some Cuban leaders have been trying to gradually distance themselves from such issues and devote more attention to the substantive concerns of local government. The broadening of Cuban officials' participation in an array of policy areas suggests a new found confidence in the power and influence they have gained, constituting a shift from more militant and internationally oriented exile politics, to a more mainstream, domestic ethnic politics.

Of more critical significance is the extent to which Hispanic economic and political incorporation in Miami has not raised policy issues that challenge the power of the traditionally influential downtown business elites. Although Cuban-American political successes have displaced a number of non-Hispanic white officials, the Latinization of the economy has proven to be functional for the major Anglo business interests, providing international linkages and increased stability. The overlap of Hispanic and Anglo economic interests reduces the non-Hispanic white elite's anxieties over the growing political strength of the Latin population, diminishing any motivation to enlist black support in a non-Hispanic political coalition. This process differs from the political and economic co-optation of minorities described in some cities and represents more of a genuine convergence of economic and class-based interests between Miami's private sector establishment and upper- and middle-class Hispanics.

Overall, Hispanic incorporation in Miami contradicts most generalizations made about other cities with large Hispanic populations in six important ways. First, the makeup of Miami's Hispanic population differs from that of most other cities, being predominantly Cuban and generally more affluent. Second, the level of Hispanic political incorporation has proceeded so rapidly and to such an extent that Hispanics are now the dominant electoral group in local politics, demonstrating significant levels of cohesion and bloc voting. Third, the economic incorporation of middle- and upper-class Hispanics in Miami has facilitated their political incorporation. Fourth, Hispanic incorporation in Miami has preceded rather than followed the incorporation of blacks. Fifth, whereas black and Hispanic mobilization and incorporation may be complementary processes in some cities, in Miami, the political and—just as important—economic incorporation of Hispanics is widely perceived as not benefiting blacks. Finally, Hispanic incorporation in Miami has not been associated with the building of more liberal coalitions but has generally had the effect of complementing rather than challenging the traditional leadership and agenda of downtown business elites.

INCREASING SYSTEM COMPLEXITY

As detailed in all the foregoing analysis, there has been great variation in the respective struggles of blacks and Hispanics in Miami, resulting in neither common patterns of mobilization nor a convergence of political-economic and policy interests. Unlike the gradual, incremental working out of different stands on policy issues discussed by Peter Eisinger (1980), minority politics in Miami has often shown signs of intransigence in an atmosphere of group polarization. Black and Hispanic political mobilizations have often been at cross purposes, as in the New York scenario described by Mollenkopf; but unlike the situation in New York and most other cities, Hispanic incorporation in Miami has outstripped that of blacks in every respect. However, given the coincidence of ethnic and class divisions in Miami, juxtaposing middle- and upper-class Hispanics and non-Hispanic whites with poorer blacks and more recently arrived immigrants and refugees, the substantive policy implications of Hispanic incorporation are very different for non-Hispanic whites and blacks, respectively. In short, while Hispanic incorporation has injected new issues into the community, it has not presented a fundamental challenge to the community's essential conservatism in matters of local government policy.

As the complexities of Miami's politics and the turbulence and unpredictability of its recent history suggest, a thorough assessment of possible scenarios for the future is a risky endeavor. However, based on recent events, it is possible to highlight certain political possibilities relevant to the ongoing efforts by Miami's diverse minority populations to have their disparate interests effectively represented in local policy making.

Political Prospects

Browning, Marshall, and Tabb have discussed the respective roles of both *electoral politics* and *demand-protest* in effective minority group mobilization. They have also underscored the importance of *coalition building* between minorities and supportive whites in challenging more conservative groups in the making of policy. The emphasis placed on these focuses is appropriate in assessing the future of Miami politics. By distinguishing what seems feasible in the context of these factors, as opposed to what might otherwise be viewed by some as ideal, one is able to focus on those political prospects that are most likely to emerge in the near future.

Electoral Politics. The most important determinant in the future of Miami's electoral politics has long been and will continue to be the area's governmental structure. When minority representation rapidly became an increasingly significant factor in local governmental affairs, the Metro system not only did not lend itself to increased levels of minority incorporation; it was also found by the federal court to present an unconstitutional hindrance. For black citizens, the restructuring of Metro has for the first time provided secure representation at a level proportionate to their population on the metropolitan area's most important policy-making body. For Hispanics, long underrepresented as well, the new structure has consolidated their status as the dominant electoral force in the county. In the process, non-Hispanic white representation has declined precipitously.

Because the new system has been in place for only two years at the time of this writing, it is too early to discern the extent to which minority and neighborhood interests and agendas will be represented differently from the way they were under the old system. What is apparent, however, is that representation has been broadened, a few candidates with strong neighborhood bases and without funding from major economic interests have been elected in some districts, and, with a few notable exceptions, commission votes have not cut strictly along ethnic lines. Amid predictions from mostly non-Hispanic white critics of the court ruling that the changes would result in the ushering in of an era of ethnically based "ward politics," and the "Balkanization" of Miami's ethnic groups, in practice, district elections were also likely the best opportunity for non-Hispanic whites to secure their own future representation on elected bodies and to provide at least the potential for the more effective representation of the diversity of group interests.

As the push for district elections continues to affect other county and municipal jurisdictions, change is also evident in various efforts presently underway to incorporate new municipalities. Since the founding of Metro in the late 1950s, only one new municipality of consequence has been created: Key Biscayne in 1991, an affluent island community near downtown Miami. Partly from a sense of accumulated grievance regarding Metro service delivery, partly in response to the successful Key Biscayne effort, and partly as a response to concerns over the new Metro election system, discussions over the possible formation of a number of new municipalities have begun in the past year. Though several more neighborhoods have discussed the possibility, presently four areas have received permission from Metro to proceed with plans to incorporate. Ranging in size from approximately seven to 36 square miles, and in population from 16,000 to 155,000, three of the cities would be predominantly non-Hispanic white and relatively affluent. If these efforts are successful and if future similar incorporations occur, then the feared "Balkanization" of Miami may indeed come—not from district elections but rather from new incorporations that suggest a "circling of the wagons" along socioeconomic as much as or more than along ethnic lines.

Protest. Given the often spontaneous and opportunistic nature of political protest, it is difficult to estimate what its role in Miami politics will be in the future. Of the three major ethnic groups in Miami, blacks have used protest as a tool to pressure local government most frequently, with the recent boycott being one of the most sustained and effective actions ever taken in Miami. In general, however, given that the boycott did not involve local grass-roots citizen mobilization, it remains true that the absence of a sustained and demonstrably effective protest tradition among blacks was probably a contributing factor in the racial violence Miami experienced in the 1980s. Moreover, the lack of substantive results in the wake of numerous promises for post-riot relief has amply demonstrated the limitations of protest as a policy lever. In the end, protest and outbreaks of violence have drawn attention to grievances, but to date, they have been ineffective in assuring a sustained response from either government or the private sector. Even those commitments won through the boycott must be continuously monitored and nurtured.

Protest has been used less frequently to pressure local government by Hispanics and non-Hispanic whites. On occasion, groups of angry residents from a particular neighborhood will turn out at a commission meeting to oppose changes in neighborhood zoning, and there have been numerous instances of demonstrations by Hispanics over immigration policy as well as in displays of anticommunist sentiment, but all such examples fall short of protest that is used as a tool to shape local government policies in any sustained way. Notwithstanding its recurrence in various forms and its being directed at different targets in both the public and private sectors, protest seems unlikely at present to play a substantively different role in the future of Miami politics.

Coalition Building. The entry of new groups and issues into Miami's political process over the past several years and their reinforcement through structural reform might be thought to provide opportunities for the emergence of new political coalitions. However, for years, the city of Miami and Metro systems had made policy according to a fixed, if not always gladly accepted, set of rules. Anglo and private sector elite dominance in the political arena seemed unchallengeable. In the 1960s, efforts at black mobilization and the earlier phases of Latin immigration suggested emergent divisions in the community, transforming Miami's black-white racial setting into a much more complex multi-ethnic political environment. That diversity is now better represented in the electoral and policy-making processes. Yet, while such changes have increased the numbers of groups and actors participating in the community's politics, there has not been a subsequent emergence of new coalitions able to bring about a major shift in the content of local public policies.

The divisions between blacks and Cubans, especially, are so steeped in economic and group differences as well as cultural and ideological sensitivities that finding acceptable compromises between them seems difficult under the best of circumstances. Nor have white liberals played a determinant role in the formation of new coalitions. Liberal political organizations in Miami are few in number, and local government has lacked mechanisms that could bring liberals from various groups together in support of particular candidates or policy initiatives.

Occasional instances of increased voting across ethnic lines does present some opportunity for the creation of new coalitions within the ranks of the electorate. However, the nature of Miami elections, given the absence of a role for political parties, the highly individualistic nature of campaigning, and the ever-changing ad hoc coalitions that are a constant in local policy making, severely limit the opportunity for the building of lasting coalitions between officials on policy-making bodies.

CONCLUSIONS

In the attempts of social scientists to understand black and Hispanic struggles for power and equality in urban politics, the case of Miami is particularly important in suggesting a scenario of increased division between the nation's two largest minority groups. With regard to both substantive and symbolic issues, zero-sum perceptions may widen the gulf between blacks and Hispanics as well as between both groups and non-Hispanic whites.

Those who remain most optimistic about the future of ethnic group relations in Miami have at times been blinded by civic boosterism. On many occasions, Miami has been proclaimed to be addressing, at long last, the resilient problems of its poor and politically disenfranchised who are disproportionately of minority populations. At some junctures, one or more ingredients in fact seem to be in place for just such action. However, bringing the right elements together at the same time, over a sustained period of time, has been a particularly elusive goal. There is now the potential for key policy-making institutions to represent Miami's divergent group interests and provide an arena for the working out of differences between them and political-economic notables on issues of resource allocation. However, although two short years and one election cycle under the new system is too short a period for definitive assessments, to date there is little evidence of significant shifts in agendas or the flow of resources. On occasion, usually in the face of crisis, major private sector players have also been jostled to independent action. However, here again, what has not been observed is the political system's ability to sustain an effort to harness the energies of both sectors in common purpose to deal with long neglected problems.

The political and social problems faced by blacks in Miami require particular attention. Reforms have boosted representation and provided more direct electoral linkages between black office holders and the problems of black neighborhoods. Yet, such changes, without strong leadership promoting a coherent agenda, do little to bring about substantive changes in local policy. This may especially be the case if there is an increased trend for affluent areas to distance themselves from the Metro system through their own incorporation—a move that is usually viewed as a means for neighborhoods to keep more of their resources to themselves. In such an environment, blacks could find themselves becoming more influential over a rapidly shrinking pool of resources.

Miami's experiences may also point to the possibility of Hispanics emerging as a dominant force in the politics of more cities. Although initiatives such as Proposition 187 or pending bills in Congress speak to the possibility of laws that might limit both immigration and the benefits made available to illegal or even legal entrants, the continued growth of Latin populations seems inevitable. With population growth, Hispanics may increasingly achieve political power in some cities on their own, without support from white or black coalitions. Such a pattern may prove especially evident in cities where Hispanic economic and political incorporation are complementary.

Finally, although it is a new twist in the urban politics literature, the alienation and even the underrepresentation of white residents in majority-minority cities and the phenomenon of white flight will likely demand increased attention from policymakers and students of urban politics alike. Although such problems are in many ways different in character and degree from those of groups that historically have been disenfranchised, they nonetheless relate to the continued viability of our cities and the representative nature of their governments. The often-related issues of private economic power, the deference that should or should not be accorded it by local government, and the role of business in shaping important public policies are even more complex when placed against the backdrop of minority group power and agenda articulation. Ultimately, although each urban area faces its own unique circumstances relating to minority political mobilization and incorporation, Miami may represent a microcosm of change, conflict, and adaptation that could alter previous explanations of minority politics in America's cities.

REFERENCES

Banfield, Edward C. 1965. *Big City Politics*. New York: Random House.

Boswell, Thomas D. 1994a. *The Cubanization and Hispanicization of Metropolitan Miami*. Miami: Cuban American Policy Center of the Cuban American National Council.

Boswell, Thomas D. 1994b. *A Demographic Profile of Cuban Americans*. Miami: Cuban American Policy Center of the Cuban American National Council.

Browning, Rufus P., Dale Rogers Marshall, and David H. Tabb. 1984. *Protest Is Not Enough: The Struggle of Blacks and Hispanics for Equality in Urban Politics*. Berkeley: University of California Press.

Browning, Rufus P., Dale Rogers Marshall, and David H. Tabb. 1994. Political Incorporation and Competing Perspectives on Urban Politics. Paper Presented at the annual meeting of the American Political Science Association, September 1–4, New York.

Dugger, Celia W. 1987. MMAP Losing Punch. *Miami Herald,* July 17, 1C.

Dunn, Marvin, and Alex Stepick. 1992. Blacks in Miami. In Guillermo J. Grenier and Alex Stepick, eds., *Miami Now!: Immigration, Ethnicity and Social Change*. Gainesville: University Press of Florida.

Eisinger, Peter K. 1980. *The Politics of Displacement*. New York: Academic Press.

Freedberg, Sydney P., and Luis Feldstein Soto. 1989. Miami Splinters in Three Parts. *Miami Herald*, February 13, 1B.

Goldfarb, Carl. 1992. Time's Right to Help Inner City, Non-Group, Other Leaders Say. *Miami Herald*, May 16, 1B.

Johnson, Dirk. 1987. The View from the Poorest U.S. Suburbs. *New York Times*, April 30, 10.

Levine, Barry B. 1985. The Capital of Latin America. *The Wilson Quarterly* (Winter): 46–69.

Lotz, Aileen. 1984. *Metropolitan Dade County: Two-Tier Government in Action*. Boston: Allyn & Bacon.

Marable, Manning. 1980. The Fire This Time: The Miami Rebellion, May 1980. *The Black Scholar* 11 (July): 2–18.

Marquis, Christopher. 1989. Cubans Still Better Off than Other Latins. *Miami Herald*, February 6, 1B.

Metropolitan Dade County Planning Department: Research Division. 1986. *Hispanic Profile: Dade County's Hispanic Origin Population*. Miami.

Meek v. Metropolitan Dade County. 1992. 805 F. Supp. 967.

Mohl, Raymond A. 1984. Miami's Metropolitan Government: Retrospect and Prospect. *Florida Historical Quarterly* (July): 24–50.

Mohl, Raymond A. 1987. Trouble in Paradise: Race and Housing in Miami during the New Deal Era. *Prologue* 19: 7–21.

Mohl, Raymond A. 1992. Race Relations and the Second Ghetto in Miami: 1940–1960. Paper presented at the annual meeting of the American Historical Association, December 28, Washington, D.C.

Mollenkopf, John H. 1992. *A Phoenix in the Ashes: The Rise and Fall of the Koch Coalition in New York City Politics*. Princeton, N.J.: Princeton University Press.

Moreno, Dario, and Christopher L. Warren. 1992. The Conservative Enclave: Cubans in Florida. In Rodolfo O. de la Garza and Louis DeSipio, eds., *From Rhetoric to Reality: Latino Politics in the 1988 Elections*. Boulder, Colo.: Westview Press.

Porter, Bruce, and Marvin Dunn. 1984. *The Miami Riot of 1980: Crossing the Bounds*. Lexington: Lexington Books.

Portes, Alejandro, and Alex Stepick. 1993. *City on the Edge: The Transformation of Miami*. Berkeley: University of California Press.

Slevin, Peter. 1994. The Non-Group Seeks to Answer, "What Are We?" *Miami Herald*, November 21, 1B.

Smith, H. T. 1993. Speech Announcing the End of the Miami Convention Boycott. May 12. Unpublished photocopy.

Sofen, Edward. 1961. Problems of Metropolitan Leadership: The Miami Experience. *Midwest Journal of Political Science* 5 (1): 18–38.

Sofen, Edward. 1966. *The Metropolitan Experiment*, 2nd ed. New York: Doubleday Anchor.

Soto, Luis Feldstein. 1988. Donors Hedged Their Bets. *Miami Herald*, October 10, 1B.

Stack, John F., Jr., and Christopher L. Warren. 1990. Ethnicity and the Politics of Symbolism in Miami's Cuban Community. *Cuban Studies* 20: 11–28.

Stack, John F., Jr., and Christopher L. Warren. 1992. The Reform Tradition and Ethnic Politics: Metropolitan Miami Confronts the 1990s. In Guillermo J. Grenier and Alex Stepick, eds., *Miami Now!: Immigration, Ethnicity and Social Change*. Gainesville: University Press of Florida.

Stepick, Alex. 1992. The Refugees Nobody Wants: Haitians in Miami. In Guillermo J. Grenier and Alex Stepick, eds. *Miami Now!: Immigration, Ethnicity and Social Change.* Gainesville: University Press of Florida.

Stone, Clarence N. 1989. *Regime Politics: Governing Atlanta, 1946–1988.* Lawrence: University Press of Kansas.

Thornburg v. Gingles. 1986. 106 S.Ct. 2752.

Warren, Christopher L. 1991. Affidavit in Support of Plaintiffs' Motion for Summary Judgement and in Response to the Court's 2/13/91 Order. *Meek vs. Metropolitan Dade County.*

chapter **11**

Latinos and Politics in Denver and Pueblo, Colorado: Differences, Explanations, and the "Steady-State" of the Struggle for Equality

Rodney E. Hero

Editors' Note

Denver presents a case of apparent substantial Latino—and black—political success. Denver elected a Latino mayor, Federico Peña, in 1983 and reelected him in 1987. Also notable, and unique among U.S. cities, that Latino mayor was succeeded by a black mayor, Wellington Webb, elected in 1991 and reelected in 1995. But unlike Miami's, Denver's Latino population is almost entirely of Mexican-American background and it represents but 20 percent of the city's population. And Denver's black population is only 12 percent. In rather stark contrast, Pueblo has a large Latino (Mexican-American) population of almost 40 percent. Yet there is little evidence of Latino political impact.

These two Colorado cities thus present distinct patterns and pose a number of intriguing questions. How, and why, do Latino political "successes" differ so much, even in the context of one state? Do different cities' structure and/or "cultures" make that much of a difference? Are there other important factors to consider? Is the presence of a substantial black population important for Mexican-American political success? What is the relationship between political success (election to office) and other dimensions of group well-being? That is, is formal inclusion in government "enough" for larger political and social progress? If so, what is the likely depth and pace of that change?

Hero suggests that these questions are more complex than they may appear. He also indicates that the "struggle for equality" does not end with substantial formal inclusion; indeed, in many respects, that may be just the beginning.

The struggle of Latinos and blacks to achieve equality in American cities has some common characteristics (Stone 1990; Mollenkopf 1990) but also varies a great deal across regions and across cities in the United States. Even within a single state, political and policy outcomes of minority organizing may differ considerably in different cities (Browning, Marshall, and Tabb 1984; Hero 1992). This chapter examines and compares the political status of Latinos (Mexican Americans) and blacks in two cities in a western (Rocky Mountain) state—Denver and Pueblo, Colorado.

The extent and nature of Latino and black political influence in the two cities—compared with each other as well as with other cities—does not lend itself to easy explanations. Nonetheless, the theoretical model put forth by Browning, Marshall, and Tabb (1984, 1990, 9–18, also see ch. 1 of this volume) provides a useful and systematic approach for assessing minority politics (cf. Hero 1992, ch. 10). The analysis below follows that framework to a large degree. The extent and nature of Latino and black political influence in Denver and Pueblo appear importantly shaped by forces, factors, and processes delineated in the mobilization/representation/incorporation model, including growing minority populations, the potential and reality for coalition partners, and city size. Additionally, governmental structure, individual leadership or political entrepreneurialism, and region within the state (or "political culture") seem significant.

The political gains of Latinos in Denver, by commonly used measures, have been quite impressive and surpassed by Latinos in but a few cities; African-American political influence has similarly been quite high. Yet these successes sometimes seem more apparent than real and are restricted to only some arenas of city governance. In contrast to the ostensible political achievements of minorities in Denver, Latinos in Pueblo are only marginally influential (see Hero 1992). On the whole, the political influence of Latinos (and blacks) in these two Colorado cities, especially Denver, has been as great as or greater than that found in a number of cities, including those in northern California (Browning, Marshall, and Tabb 1984; Hero 1992) and in others such as New York City, Los Angeles, and Chicago (Browning, Marshall, and Tabb 1990; Hero 1992). The grounds for this conclusion, and the conditions that produced these outcomes, are discussed below.

BACKGROUND

Mexican Americans are the largest "minority" group in Denver and Pueblo (and in the state of Colorado, 13 percent in 1990), although their proportion of the population is almost twice as large in Pueblo as in Denver. In 1990, Latinos made up about 21 percent of the population in Denver and almost 40 percent in Pueblo. During the 1980s, a decade when Latinos achieved notable political gains in Denver politics, they represented about 18 percent of the city's population. Mexican Americans accounted for over a third of Pueblo's population during the same period.

The Latino populations in both cities are, in fact, largely "Mexican origin," with only small proportions of Puerto Rican, Cuban, or "other" Latino/Hispanic groups. It is significant that the Latino population in Colorado has relatively few noncitizens; by most estimates, well over 90 percent of Colorado Latinos are U.S. citizens, and the vast majority are native born, with many tracing U.S citizenship back over several generations. These characteristics distinguish Denver and Pueblo Latinos from those in a number of U.S. cities with diverse and/or very large noncitizen or recent immigrant Latino populations (Meier and Stewart 1991). The black or African-American population in Denver is substantial, about 12 percent; in Pueblo, it is only 2 percent.

ANALYSIS

Preconditions to Minority Mobilization

Before we consider minority representation in Denver and Pueblo, we need to examine certain contextual variables or "preconditions" to mobilization. Denver and Pueblo rank somewhat differently on the socioeconomic and sociopolitical variables that affect minority political influence.

In both cities, the minority, especially Latino, populations have grown considerably in the last generation. In 1960, Latinos made up about 17 percent of Pueblo's, and 9 percent of Denver's population. Denver's African-American population has grown modestly from 7 percent in 1960. The Latino population in Pueblo has more socioeconomic resources than do Latinos in Denver. For example, in 1980 Mexican Americans had slightly lower levels of poverty in Pueblo than in Denver (21 percent to 23.9 percent), higher levels of per capita income ($4,677 to $4,510), more education (12 to 11.1 median school years completed), and a larger percentage in managerial/professional occupations (13.5 percent to 11 percent) (Hero 1992).

In both Denver and Pueblo, it is interesting that the black population fares somewhat better than Latinos on several measures of socioeconomic well-being. Black per capita income, median school years completed, and percentages in managerial/professional occupations are above those of Latinos, and their unemployment rate is lower. However, blacks do much less well than do Anglos on these indicators in both cities.

Despite some evidence that would suggest greater Latino political influence in Pueblo than Denver, other factors point in the opposite direction. Denver has a substantial black population whose presence resulted in local organizing during the national (black) civil rights movement. Black efforts served as a model and catalyst for Latino political efforts. Denver was also the home of the "Crusade for Justice," a movement headed by one of the most prominent leaders of the "Chicano Movement" of the 1960s and 1970s, Rodolfo "Corky" Gonzalez. Also, "white liberal" support for minorities has been much greater in Denver than in Pueblo. One example is the electoral support for a Latino mayor; yet Peña's electoral coalition was always somewhat fragile and had its origins in white, middle-class support as much as in the Latino neighborhoods (see Hero 1987; Hero and Beatty 1989). Another instance is the broad-based electoral support for the successful black city auditor and later (successful) mayoral candidate, Wellington Webb (Hero and Beatty 1989).

"Demand-protest" activities have been more extensive in Denver (Hero 1992). The factors of size, socioeconomic inequality, and governmental structure indicate greater mobilization in Denver. Denver is a substantially larger city than Pueblo (468,000 to 99,000 in 1990; 492,000 to 101,000 population in 1980). Although the Latino *percentage* of Denver is lower than that of Pueblo, the actual numbers are over twice as large. There also is somewhat more socioeconomic inequality of Mexican Americans relative to Anglos and/or the general population in Denver than in Pueblo in terms of poverty, per capita income, and education levels (Hero 1992).

Governmental structure is often perceived to be related to more minority political activity and influence (Browning, Marshall, and Tabb 1984, 84–85). "Unreformed" structures provide more outlets for minority political influence. Heavily district based, Denver's governmental structure is relatively unreformed, with a strong mayor-council system and a relatively large council (11 of the 13 council members). Moreover, the Denver mayor is a formally "strong" mayor in having extensive budgetary, appointment and veto powers. In contrast, Pueblo's governmental structure is generally "reformed" with the council-manager system, a numerically smaller council (7), and a smaller percentage of the council members elected from districts (4 of 7, or 57 percent, versus 85 percent in Denver).

New Democratic majorities among voters and on the council is another precondition found to be necessary for minority political mobilization. This phenomenon occurs despite the formally nonpartisan electoral nature of many cities in the western United States, including Denver and Pueblo. Since at least 1963, Denver has had a majority of Democrats on its city council, and since the mid-1970s, that majority has exceeded 60 percent. Democrats appear to have been overrepresented on city council relative to registered Democratic voters. At the same time, however, Republican membership on the council exceeded Republican voter registration for every year until about 1987 (Hero 1992). This overrepresentation of both major parties on the council is partly the result of high levels of "unaffiliated" or "independent" registration in Denver (and, indeed, in Colorado as a whole).

In Pueblo, there has been a long-standing Democratic dominance in terms of council members' partisan affiliation and overrepresentation relative to that of the city's registered voters. But whereas Republican identifiers represented a majority of the Pueblo city council for only the earliest year for which evidence was examined (1964), Republicans have, on average, been more heavily overrepresented relative to registered voters than have Democrats from the 1960s to the present. For example, in 1994, Republicans made up 43 percent of the city council members but only 20 percent of Pueblo's registered voters; Democrats accounted for 57 percent of registered voters in the city and a like percentage of city council members. Also, Democrats in Pueblo city politics are often politically conservative and do not necessarily support the "liberal" or "progressive" policies assumed in much popular and scholarly perception (Browning, Marshall, and Tabb 1984; Hero 1992, ch. 10; Cronin and Loevy 1993, ch. 1).

Minority Representation and Incorporation

Representation. "Descriptive" or "sociological" representation—having city council/mayoral positions held by members of the minority population—is another major dimension of minority politics in cities. Representational *parity* means having representation in approximate proportion to population numbers in the city as a whole.

Denver. From the 1960s to the late 1970s, Latinos in Denver were generally underrepresented (or below parity) on the council relative to their numbers in the general population (Hero 1992). From 1955 to 1975, there were no Latinos on the Denver city council despite the all-district (nine-member) council before 1971 and the expansion of that council (to 13 members with 11 from districts and 2 at large) in a way that was intended to enhance the likelihood of Mexican-American representation (Lovrich and Marenin 1976). (However, there was a single Latino member on the Denver city council, a Republican, who was elected in 1943 and served until the mid-1950s [Leonard and Noel 1990, 393]). In 1975, two Latinos were elected to district-based seats on the Denver city council and held those seats until 1987, when both decided not to seek reelection. Both were succeeded by two Latinas (women) who had been their former aides; both Latinas were reelected to their council seats in 1991 and each has subsequently held the position of president of the council. It thus appears that Latino/a representation on the city council is well established—indeed, even "institutionalized."

In 1983, Federico Peña became Denver's first Mexican-American mayor. He had previously served in the Colorado House of Representatives and had been quite visible and active in several Chicano/Latino policy concerns, but he had no previous city government background. He was reelected in 1987; he did not seek reelection in 1991. Peña's initial election surprised many observers because few minority mayors have been elected in cities with such relatively small minority populations (18 percent Latino and 12 percent black); in fact, the Latinos and blacks represented only about 12 percent and 10 percent of eligible voters, respectively. Peña was able to form a "liberal" electoral coalition by increasing the turnout and gaining the support of minorities, white liberals, labor, and gays (Hero 1992). Peña's campaigns were notable in emphasizing distributive or developmental concerns, and bringing attention to "minority" or "redistributive" concerns only indirectly.

Since the early 1980s, there have been three Latino/as holding city council and/or the mayor's position, producing an essential statistical "parity" between the size of the Latino population and the proportion of mayor/city council members.

The first black was elected to the Denver city council in 1956. From the early 1960s to the present, black representation on the Denver city council has actually been above parity, averaging 2.9 (where 1.0 equals parity); in 1994, two of the 13 city council members were black and the city had a black mayor. Denver elected its first black mayor in 1991; the two candidates in the 1991 runoff election were both blacks.

Pueblo. Latino representational parity on the Pueblo city council has generally been low, lower than in Denver; it has averaged only about half of parity since 1963. It has also been quite erratic. These basic relationships and their erratic quality are due partly to the impact that the presence or absence of one Hispanic council member can have (because of the small total number of councilors, 7). Nonetheless, the drop from three Latinos on city council in 1976 to none between 1983 and 1987 seems substantial. Since 1987, Pueblo has had one or no Latinos on its city council, despite a 38 percent to 40 percent Latino city population.

Latinos in both Denver and Pueblo had substantially higher scores on representational parity—more than double—during the mid-to-late-1970s than was the average for Hispanics in the northern California cities (during the same period) studied by Browning, Marshall, and Tabb. Indeed, the average parity ratio for Denver and Pueblo from the mid-1960s to the mid-1980s, which includes several years in which there was no Latino representation in the two cities, is somewhat greater than the average for the northern California cities in 1975–1978.

Political Incorporation.   Political incorporation refers not only to representation but also to the position of minority representatives vis-à-vis the dominant coalition on the city council. That is, incorporation measures the extent to which minorities are represented in "coalitions that dominate city policy-making on minority-related issues" (Browning, Marshall, and Tabb 1984, 25, 18). My estimates of incorporation, based on interviews and other evidence, suggest that Denver's overall minority incorporation scores in 1984 and 1987 were quite high. They were well above the score of any of the northern California cities, the highest of which was 3 in 1978, and Denver's 1976–1980 score of 2 is well above the average (.5) for the ten northern California cities in 1978. With a black mayor and four minority council members—members who have held important positions within the council and appear to be quite active on issues central to minority communities—the basic patterns found in Denver for the late 1980s continue to hold into the present. This claim is underscored by the programs of Denver's Latino and black mayors from 1983 through 1995 (at least).

Peña's mayoral agenda sought to achieve both economic development, linked to minority opportunities, and governmental "openness." While Peña stressed such issues as building a new convention center and a new airport and bringing a major league baseball team to the city, he linked these projects to minority employment and business opportunities. He also expanded the city's minority contracting program and appointed many minorities to administrative positions and to city boards and commissions. Although the full or "real" benefits for minorities of the Peña administration have been debated (Saiz 1988; Judd and Ready 1986; Hero 1992, ch. 8 and 10), it is clear that Peña's administration was dramatically more "progressive" or liberal than its conservative Democratic predecessors. Many observers view the Peña administration as a watershed in Denver's political history in establishing a more liberal and ethnically/racially aware political regime despite its tenuous electoral base. The election of a black mayor in 1991, who defeated a fellow black and who campaigned to carry on and essentially complete the progressive agenda of his predecessor, suggests more continuity than change. But that continuity was much different from the continuity of the late 1970s.

The early 1990s have thus witnessed a maintenance and consolidation of the black and Latino political incorporation in Denver that emerged in the 1980s. However, that incorporation or presence seems not to be increasing, and there is little evidence that it has had an impact beyond a fairly narrow set of concerns in the governmental arena nor has it altered minority socioeconomic conditions. That is, minority and/or equality concerns do not routinely receive equal footing in general policy processes. And the socioeoconomic status of minorities has declined relative to whites (but large minority [Latino] immigration does not explain this because such immigration has not been a major issue in Denver). Although Denver is willing to extend distributive policies and there has been some redistribution within public sector programs, broader economic imperatives limit much beyond this.

Incorporation in Pueblo, following the pattern of representation, has generally been much lower than in Denver. But its average score in 1976–1980 (1.5) compared favorably with the northern California cities' average (.5) in 1978. However, as there has been little or no Latino presence on the Pueblo city council in recent years, the level of incorporation is almost by definition minimal to nonexistent.

In short, and as anticipated, Latino incorporation is higher in Denver than in Pueblo. Also, these two Colorado cities evidence greater incorporation than do the ten northern California cities.

There are at least two variables that seem significant regarding the higher representation and incorporation in Denver and Pueblo compared to the California cities; these were not considered in the Browning, Marshall, and Tabb study. One is that residential segregation may actually foster the minority representation on the city council (Vedlitz and Johnson 1982) that is a prerequisite for incorporation— and, in turn, policy responsiveness. Denver Latinos have been more residentially segregated than those in Pueblo and the northern California cities studied by Browning, Marshall, and Tabb. Mexican-Anglo segregation in 1970 in Denver was 52.8; it was 41.7 in Pueblo and averaged 37.3 in the five northern California cities for which data were available (see Lopez 1981; Hero 1992). While some changes have occurred over time, the basic patterns of residential distribution remain.

Second, Denver's largely "unreformed" governmental structure seems important. Its strong mayor system, with extensive budgetary and appointment power, permits executive leadership. Its heavily district-based and "professionalized" city council is also distinctive from that of Pueblo (or the cities studied by Browning, Marshall, and Tabb) and research has suggested the importance of such factors. For example, minorities seem more willing to contact city council members about governmental concerns when those members are elected from districts and are themselves minorities (Heilig and Mundt 1984). Legislative professionalism has impacts on policy outputs (Carmines 1974); it may also have a significant role in institutionalizing influence, including minority influence, at the urban level in that it provides resources for councilors to give more time and attention to their legislative and related activities such as "constituency service" or "casework." Denver's city council members are substantially better paid ($18,675 in 1982; $36,000 in 1994) than in Pueblo ($2,400 in 1982) or the

California cities studied (*Municipal Yearbook* 1982). Denver councilors also have a staff person, and the council appears to have a more formalized committee structure than in Pueblo and many other cities. These factors would, in turn, be expected to have implications for questions of policy responsiveness.

Policy Responsiveness

Representation and incorporation are important in themselves but they must also be considered relative to policy responsiveness. The expectation, and finding, of earlier research was that greater incorporation is related to greater policy responsiveness. Several measures of policy responsiveness have typically been used; the major indicators are replicated here for Denver and Pueblo.

1. *City Government Employment.* One measure of policy responsiveness is the proportion of minority employment in city government. When "all occupations" are considered, Denver is, and has been *since at least 1973, above parity* in city government employment for both Latinos and blacks. This employment parity resulted from the demand-protest activities that arose in the mid-1960s in Denver in both the black and Chicano communities. The relatively conservative Democratic mayors during this period addressed the demands in part with limited political appointments and civil service employment. The Peña administration, with the backing of a majority of the council, was very supportive of minority public employment, including employment at the upper levels and viewed this as something to be addressed because it was the right thing to do and not only because of political expediency.

Pueblo has been and remains below parity for Latinos; for example, its parity ratio in the late 1980s was .75 for all occupations. The average Latino employment parity in the California cities in 1978 was .62 (Browning, Marshall, and Tabb 1984, 196, 266). Denver's Latino employment parity was about twice that average (at about the same time—1978) and Pueblo's was very near to that average.

Note, however, that in both Denver and Pueblo, Latinos are heavily concentrated in low-level positions and occupations (Hero 1992). This is also reflected in employment among officials and administrators. In the late 1980s, Denver's parity score for Latino officials and administrators was .62 whereas Pueblo's was .43; the black parity score in Denver for this category of employment was about the same as that for Latinos. The data for the ten northern California cities in 1978 indicates an average of .45; Denver's average at about the same time was somewhat higher (an estimated .57) and Pueblo's was considerably lower (estimate of .26). The parity scores for the higher level (official and administrators) positions have continued to increase for minority groups in both Denver and Pueblo, but Denver's levels have well exceeded those for Pueblo.

2. *Contracting Policies.* A second indicator of responsiveness focuses on minority contracting policies. Several measures were used to evaluate city policies regarding special efforts to allow minority businesses to receive city contracts. First, an assessment was made as to whether the cities had adopted various contracting practices (Browning, Marshall, and Tabb 1984, 161, 284–285) such as "specifically targeting minority contractors even if they are not the lowest bidders." Interview re-

sponses revealed that of the six such practices identified, Denver has adopted essentially *all* of them while Pueblo has adopted none. The actual *implementation* in Denver of those policies was seen as moderately aggressive, according to interviewee responses.

Several points are noteworthy here. First, Denver established its policy under the conservative administration of (Democrat) William McNichols at the behest of minority and liberal white council members. The goals were expanded and pursued more aggressively under the Peña administration. Finally, Denver undertook studies to justify the continuance of such programs in the aftermath of the 1989 U.S. Supreme Court decision in *Richmond v. Croson*, a decision that significantly narrowed the grounds on which such minority set-aside programs could withstand judicial scrutiny. In Pueblo, the question of commitment to assertive implementation has been moot as there is no policy to implement.

Another measure of city minority contracting policies has to do with the Community Development Block Grant (CDBG) Program, a federal program created in the mid-1970s that allocates monies to cities. The legislation called for cities to identify the ethnic/racial background of the owners of firms that receive contracts to carry out work under the program. From 1983 to 1987, estimates indicate that relative to the overall Latino population, Latino businesses in Denver and Pueblo have received respectively 64 percent and 42 percent of the contract dollars they should receive if their share of these dollars reflects their proportion of the city population (based on my calculations and estimates from CDBG data obtained from the Housing and Urban Development (HUD) Regional Office, Denver). The percentage for blacks was somewhat higher, over 80 percent. Although below parity, these percentages appear comparable to the average for the northern California cities at an earlier period: 1978 (see Browning, Marshall, and Tabb 1984, 162).

3. *Membership on City Boards and Commissions.* "Appointments to [city boards and] commissions enable elected officials to reward supporters, to give at least symbolic representation to groups, and to give ambitious activists the opportunity to gain visibility for future political candidacies" (Browning, Marshall, and Tabb 1984, 156–157). Evidence on the extent to which minorities have been represented on boards and commissions in Denver and Pueblo was gathered for recent years. As with the other measures of policy responsiveness, minorities in Denver are considerably better represented than those in Pueblo. By 1987, Latinos in Denver had a parity score approaching 1.0; blacks already were above parity (1.34). As a candidate and as mayor, Peña strongly emphasized the importance of such descriptive representation in his appointments to boards and commissions.

In comparison, Latino membership on city boards and commissions in Pueblo was but half of parity and does not appear to have increased very much recently (based on my calculations from city data sources).

4. *Civilian Police Review Board.* Civilian police review boards have been seen as a way of dealing with concerns surrounding police treatment of minorities (Browning, Marshall, and Tabb 1984). Therefore, the presence (or absence) of such a board was used as a measure of policy responsiveness (Browning, Marshall, and Tabb 1984, 152–155).

Neither Denver nor Pueblo had established a civilian police review board by the late 1980s. Such a board was discussed with some frequency in Denver during the late 1970s and early 1980s. Interestingly, however, the election of Federico Peña as Denver's mayor in 1983 seems to have dampened rather than increased discussions on this matter (Browning, Marshall, and Tabb 1984, 155–156). Peña's election and position as chief executive of the city's bureaucracy with the power to appoint the head of the department of public safety and police chief, seemingly has allayed minority concerns about police treatment (author interviews). However, in 1992, with the leadership of a black city council member and with the opposition of the police department and the black mayor, a civilian review board was established.

CONCLUSION

These findings on Denver and Pueblo suggest that the variables specified by Browning, Marshall, and Tabb are significant in understanding racial politics in U.S. cities. The variables, particularly those concerning city size and governmental structure, seem significant in explaining the different levels of political mobilization of Denver's versus Pueblo's minority communities. They may also explain the considerably higher political mobilization of Denver Latinos versus that in the California cities or elsewhere. At minimum, these findings are important in indicating that the low levels of Latino representation-incorporation and resultantly low policy responsiveness found in most other cities are *not* universal. Denver's minority communities in particular have obtained political influence well beyond that found in virtually all other U.S. cities. And the political achievements of Pueblo's Latinos, while modest relative to Denver's, nonetheless appear greater than those found in other studies (cf. Browning, Marshall, and Tabb 1984).

A complete understanding of why this is the case cannot be provided at this point, but we can speculate. Probably quite important is the impact of governmental structure. The Browning, Marshall, and Tabb study was quite cognizant of the potential impact of governmental structure but was unable to systematically or extensively examine its impact; the ten cities they studied were all basically "reformed"; thus, there simply was not sufficient variation for purposes of analysis. It is therefore notable that in Denver, with its unreformed structure, including a strong mayor system—and minority mayors since 1983—political representation, incorporation, and responsiveness are so much greater than in the northern California cities and in Pueblo. Residential segregation and legislative professionalism may also play a role.

Other differences also seem critical. Denver is the largest and most visible city in the state, the state capital, and the most prominent city in the Rocky Mountain region. These factors, alone and in combination, seem to magnify the importance of such variables as city size, governmental structure, and the like. Moreover, Denver's minority population, while substantial, is not as large or, perhaps, "threatening" as in other cities. And the minority politicians who have emerged have, for the most part, been moderate to liberal but have pursued agendas that are compatible with larger city concerns. In many ways, the successes of Peña and Webb in Denver are similar to those of Tom Bradley in Los Angeles and Norman Rice in Seattle; in some ways, large cities in the West are different.

Pueblo, in contrast, does not have many of the structures or conditions that appear to have been critical to the political impact that Denver Latinos have had. A generally more conservative environment, including an apparent paucity of white liberals, a very small black population, a governmental structure that does not seem to encourage the engagement of minority concerns, and a relative isolation from the state's major social and economic activities have led to little political mobilization, substantial underrepresentation, and little or no incorporation and policy responsiveness.

The struggle of Latinos and blacks for equality in urban politics clearly continues. It also takes different forms but and varies significantly throughout the states and even within states. Emerging trends, both locally and nationally, suggest at most a steady state for minority influence. There may even be a decline as prominent national, state, and local officials are now openly and aggressively challenging policies that contributed to whatever level of minority incorporation and policy responsiveness found in Denver and Pueblo, and elsewhere.

REFERENCES

Browning, Rufus P., Dale Rogers Marshall, and David H. Tabb. 1984. *Protest Is Not Enough: The Struggle of Blacks and Hispanics for Equality in Urban Politics*. Berkeley: University of California Press.

Browning, Rufus P., Dale Rogers Marshall, and David H. Tabb. 1986. Black and Hispanic Power in City Politics: A Forum. *PS* (Summer): 573–575.

Browning, Rufus P., Dale Rogers Marshall, and David H. Tabb. 1990. *Racial Politics in American Cities*. White Plains, N.Y.: Longman.

Carmines, Edward. 1974. The Mediating Influence of State Legislature on the Linkage between Interparty Competition and Welfare Policies. *American Political Science Review* 68 (September): 1118–1124.

Cronin, Thomas E., and Robert D. Loevy. 1993. *Colorado Politics and Government: Governing the Centennial State*. Lincoln: University of Nebraska Press.

Heilig, Peggy, and Robert J. Mundt. 1984. *Your Voice at City Hall*. Albany: State University of New York Press.

Hero, Rodney E. 1987. The Election of Hispanics in City Government: An Analysis of the Election of Federico Peña as Mayor of Denver. *Western Political Quarterly* 40 (March): 93–105.

Hero, Rodney E. 1992. *Latinos and the U.S. Political System: Two-tiered Pluralism*. Philadelphia: Temple University Press.

Hero, Rodney E., and Kathleen M. Beatty. 1989. The Elections of Federico Peña as Mayor of Denver: Analysis and Implications. *Social Science Quarterly* 70, 2 (June): 300–310.

Judd, Dennis, and Randy Ready. 1986. Entrepreneurial Cities and the New Economic Development. In George Peterson and Carol Lewis, eds., *Reagan and the Cities*. Washington, D.C.: Urban Institute Press, 209–247.

Leonard, Stephen J., and Thomas J. Noel. 1990. *Denver: Mining Camp to Metropolis*. Niwot, Colo.: University Press of Colorado.

Lopez, Manuel M. 1981. Pattern of Interethnic Residential Segregation in the Urban Southwest. *Social Science Quarterly* 62, 1 (March): 50–63.

Lovrich, Nicholas, and Otwin Marenin. 1976. A Comparison of Black and Mexican-American Voters in Denver: Assertive versus Acquiescent Political Orientations and Voting Behavior in an Urban Electorate. *Western Political Quarterly* 29 (June): 284–294.

Meier, Kenneth J., and Joseph Stewart. 1991. *The Politics of Hispanic Education*. Albany: State University of New York Press.

Mollenkopf, John H. 1997. New York: The Great Anomaly. In R. Browning, D. R. Marshall, and David H. Tabb, eds., *Racial Politics in American Cities*, 97–115. White Plains, N.Y.: Longman.

Municipal Yearbook. 1982. International City Managers' Association.

Saiz, Martin. 1988. Progressive Politics and Fiscal Austerity: The Experience of the Peña Administration. Paper presented at the Annual Meeting of the Western Political Science Association, San Francisco.

Stone, Clarence N. 1990. Race and Regime in Atlanta. In R. Browning, D. R. Marshall, and David H. Tabb, eds., *Racial Politics in American Cities*, 125–139. White Plains, N.Y.: Longman.

Vedlitz, Arnold, and Charles A. Johnson. 1982. Community Racial Segregation, Electoral Structure, and Minority Representation. *Social Science Quarterly* 63 (December): 729–736.

part **VI**

Strategies and Prospects

chapter 12

The Prospects for Multiracial Coalitions: Lessons from America's Three Largest Cities

Raphael J. Sonenshein

Editors' Note

Politically excluded groups often debate the best strategies to improve their position. Should they go it alone or form coalitions? If they enter into coalitions, will an appeal to shared ideology be sufficient to hold the coalition together or will it be necessary to make major concessions to the material interests of other members? And can the experience gained through the minority incorporation model be helpful in the more diverse and multipolar world of today's big city arena? What does the rise of white-led regimes in most large cities mean for the study of minority incorporation?

In this chapter, Raphael J. Sonenshein explores in the multiracial setting a model of coalition politics he developed in the study of biracial coalitions. His approach begins with a critique of the idea that only self-interest can animate coalitions; ideology is crucial to coalition success. Goodwill alone is not enough, but neither is cold self-interest. But even ideology is not enough without creative and determined leadership to navigate the shoals of interest conflict. He finds that in America's largest cities, the linkages of ideology and interest among potential minority allies have weakened and that progressive leadership for such coalitions is in severe disrepair.

Sonenshein finds that the new white-led regimes have capitalized on interest and ideology conflicts within the minority-progressive alliance and have been able to capture the community's ideological center. Progressive leaders have become bogged down in the politics of diversity rather than developing agendas for solving communitywide problems. To experience a resurgence of minority-progressive influence, leaders of potential coalitions must both relearn the lessons of earlier coalitions and *stake out new and creative territory in issues that concern both minority and non-minority communities.*

The debate over the viability of interracial coalition politics has been an enduring and intensely argued one. Should racial minorities go it alone, join forces with other minorities against the majority, or form alliances with elements of the majority group?

In the previous edition of this book (1990), I presented a theory of interracial coalition within the context of black-white relations. Only a mixture of interest and ideology, shaped by leadership, could overcome the numerous barriers to the success of coalitions crossing racial and ethnic lines. In this chapter, I will apply the same three-part model to the complex task of evaluating the prospects for multiracial coalitions. Are multiracial coalitions viable in political settings of increasing diversity and weakening liberal strength?

A THEORY OF COALITION

Since the mid-1960s, urban politics have been profoundly influenced by race and the ideological divisions that grow out of racial division. Indeed, throughout American politics the racial barrier redefined opinions, attitudes, and alignments. The meanings of conservative and liberal ideologies have been deeply influenced by their relationship to race (Edsall and Edsall 1991; Carmines and Stimson 1989).

As racial matters came to a boil in the mid-1960s, African Americans had to choose among several paths. This practical decision in turn depended on a more theoretical question: What is the most solid basis on which to build coalitions?

Although the debate over interracial coalitions is highly political and pragmatic, it is also an argument over a *theory* of biracial coalitions. The optimists focus on the role of *ideology* and emphasize the enduring and solid character of biracial coalitions based on common beliefs. The pessimists tend to see *interest* as the glue of coalitions and to view biracial coalitions as at best short-lived compromises between self-centered groups.

An active scholarly debate on racial issues divides along roughly the same lines. One school of thought suggests that preexisting racial attitudes deeply influence perception of racial issues; in this sense, racial politics is at its root ideological (Kinder and Sears 1981). Regardless of the political situation, some whites are more racially liberal than others and this attitude shapes their political actions. A contrasting view holds that racial conflict can be understood as a realistic power struggle between groups. As whites identify with other whites in the face of a black challenge, they protect their group interests through racial hostility (Giles and Gatlin 1980; Bobo 1983; Giles and Evans 1986). In this view, political actions are affected by the political situation of individuals and groups.

Thus the study of biracial electoral coalitions can be seen as a test case in a more general debate about the roots of racial conflict and cooperation. What is more important in racial coalitions: goodwill or practical calculation?

In their classic *Black Power* (1967), Carmichael and Hamilton argued that the goodwill that underlay the civil rights movement was no longer adequate for the new era of racial polarization. Rather, they favored self-interest as the glue of coalitions and believed that communities of color and class had the best chance of forming such pragmatic alliances. This view coincided with a widespread move to exclude white liberals from racial politics. As African-American communities began to move toward citywide power in many cities, the evidence both supported and contradicted Carmichael and Hamilton's view.

Minority power arose from a combination of minority unity and mobilization, as suggested by Carmichael and Hamilton, and the support of liberal whites, as suggested by those who favored a role for liberal ideology. Starting in 1967, cities with large African-American populations began to generate black mayoral candidacies. The first black mayors were elected in 1967 in Cleveland and Gary. Newark elected a black mayor in 1970, and Los Angeles and Detroit followed suit in 1973.

Despite enormous differences among cities, the African-American candidates' coalitions, and the alliances that opposed them, bore remarkable similarities. Black mayoral candidates drew overwhelming black support; the youngest, most liberal, and best educated whites, particularly Jews; and mixed support from Latinos. Less educated, less liberal whites provided the hard core of opposition (Pettigrew 1971; Halley, Acock, and Greene 1976; Hahn, Klingman, and Pachon 1976).

Win or lose, African-American candidates could rely on black voters to provide virtually unanimous and enthusiastic support. The margin of victory would come from inroads into white constituencies and increasing support among Latinos. Instead of a class alliance of the economically disadvantaged, the biracial coalitions that carried black candidates into power were a mixture of racial identification among blacks, ideological affinity with some whites, and some racial and class solidarity with Latinos.

Browning, Marshall, and Tabb's study of the political incorporation of minorities in ten northern California cities (1984) found that whether or not African Americans were mayoral candidates, the coalitions for minority "incorporation" involved the same mixture of groups. They found that mobilization and unity among blacks were combined with the support of liberal whites and often Latinos into a winning liberal coalition. Their research strongly supported the roles of race and ideology in the development of minority power. Their work also pointed to the importance of coalitions between African Americans and liberal whites, with additional support coming from Latinos.

My application of the Browning et al. model in Los Angeles found that the same pattern defined Los Angeles politics over the whole modern era from 1964 through the present (Sonenshein 1993). Whether the issues were taxes, board of education races, voting for partisan offices, or ballot measures to ensure police accountability, the pattern was the same: Blacks were the most liberal, joined in coalition to liberal whites and Latinos in opposition to the most conservative whites. Tom Bradley's six mayoral campaigns (all but one successful) between 1969 and 1989 confirmed the pattern, as he carried the African-American community; did extremely well with liberal whites, particularly Jews; and drew increasingly strong support from Latinos (Sonenshein 1993).

The ideological underpinnings of minority political incorporation have been so consistent that ideology must be considered the central factor in the success of such coalitions. Ideological differences among whites, as demonstrated by Browning, Marshall, and Tabb, are indeed crucial to minority political success. But the case of limited and precarious minority incorporation in New York City, where white liberalism has been historically very strong, creates what John Mollenkopf, in this volume, has called "the great anomaly." Los Angeles has been a less liberal city than New York City, but its level of minority incorporation has been far larger and more durable.

Just as Carmichael and Hamilton had predicted, conflict of interest between minorities and white liberals greatly weakened the possibilities for interracial coalitions in New York City. In New York, white liberals were highly represented in the civic institutions, particularly the schools, that came under attack by minority activists in the 1960s. By contrast, the minority surge in Los Angeles was tied to the struggle of white liberals, particularly Jews, for representation in Los Angeles civic life. The alliance of outsiders thus represented a fundamental alliance of interest.

But neither ideology nor interest fully explains coalition outcomes. Group relations are not simply the outcome of objective interests or poll-measured attitudes. Political actions are taken by human beings and therefore are affected by the actions of leaders who themselves seek out trusting relationships with other political actors.

Drawing on Hinckley's critique of coalition theory (1981), I argued that the outcome of interracial coalitions is profoundly shaped and influenced by leadership. Leaders and organizers have an impact on how group interests are perceived. The prospects for biracial coalitions depend heavily on the willingness and ability of leaders to create and sustain such coalitions. In matters of race, leaders may find it easier to overcome interest conflicts among ideological allies than to create an interest alliance among ideological foes.

The presence of outstanding interracial leadership in Los Angeles made a great contribution to the extraordinary success of the black community in winning political incorporation. The trust developed among the long-time Bradley forces made them coherent, cohesive, and united in the face of political challenges. The effective leadership of Harold Washington was critical to the Chicago success story, as demonstrated by the collapse of his coalition after his sudden death in 1987. In New York City, interracial leadership networks were weak, internally divided, and vulnerable to demagoguery from the outside.

Two major changes have now forced a reassessment of the prospects for progressive, interracial coalitions. First, the rise of white Republican mayors in Los Angeles and New York City and moderate white Democratic mayors in Philadelphia and Chicago shows that the electoral base for minority incorporation in big cities has dramatically declined. Second, the shifting demographics of urban America have created a much greater degree of multiethnicity in many cities. With the fall of the biracial regimes and the increased prominence of group relations among minorities, the initial focus on black-white relations has taken a back seat.

What did the rollback of minority political gains mean for the structure of urban politics? Did they suggest the end of a period marked by racial and ideological divisions? Or were they merely a shift of victors in a political structure that had not fundamentally altered? How durable was the realignment of urban politics that began in the mid-1960s, when the racial struggle moved out of the South and into the big cities of the nation? What are the prospects for rainbow coalitions as a replacement for the liberal biracial coalitions of the recent past?

The historical approach to coalition presented by Hinckley (1981) suggests that we should be cautious in declaring the old world dead. Coalition patterns evolve slowly; old patterns die hard and can even be regenerated. The challenge is to separate the consistent from the new in the move from a biracial to a multiracial analysis. Two of these new paths are the conservative and the rainbow.

In the conservative view, the earlier pattern of racial and ethnic division has become obsolete. In this view, African-American mayors were increasingly keeping alive a set of racial divisions against the wishes of the voters. Jim Sleeper, a perceptive New York City journalist, referred to "the rainbow ideology's tendency to deepen racial and other differences in the name of respecting them; in the zero-sum game of urban governance, politics implodes" (Sleeper 1993, 20). Sleeper attributed the victories of new mayors, most of them white, to new coalitions:

> It's a familiar pattern. Beyond New York, the Rainbow habit of crying racism has found itself discounted by voters of all colors who want better governance and less rhetoric. Politically centrist mayoral candidates, many of them, ironically, white men, have drawn substantial numbers of nonwhite voters into new coalitions—call them Rainbow II—by touting a can-do pragmatism and a common civic identity that is more than the sum of skin tones, genders, sexual orientations, and resentments. (Sleeper 1993, 20)

The implication of Sleeper's argument is that there has been some change in the structure of city politics, one that black leaders and their supporters have failed to grasp, in which race and ideology play less central roles than before.

On the other hand, a renewed emphasis on rainbow politics challenges the neoconservative view. In this outlook, the old biracialism erred by overemphasizing the role of whites. In an increasingly diverse society, black-white politics are seen as obsolete precisely because they do not emphasize color enough.

As the Los Angeles civil unrest showed, interminority relations were forcing their way into the public agenda. With increasing immigration to American cities, interminority relations were potential flashpoints. In most major American cities, the dialogue about minority incorporation has been expanded to deal with the wide range of diverse groups entering the political marketplace.

Thus the conservative and rainbow approaches to the postincorporation era offer diametrically opposed critiques of biracial liberal coalitions. Conservatives say that color has been overemphasized, while rainbow progressives seek to expand the definition and political meaning of color.

To assess these approaches to the future of minority politics, we turn to the experience of the nation's three largest cities, in which the defeat of minority-led coalitions and the rise of diverse populations have challenged the nature of coalition politics.

NEW YORK CITY, LOS ANGELES, AND CHICAGO

In my earlier chapter (1990), I proposed to explain why coalition politics had developed so differently in the nation's three largest cities. Why had Los Angeles, the city with the smallest black population, managed to develop by far the strongest biracial coalition? Why had New York City, with its long tradition of liberalism, been most notable for the failure of its interracial politics?

In the 1990s, the cities continue to differ among themselves, but there is also a striking commonality in several areas. All three cities were marked by the succession of white mayors not supported by the vast majority of African Americans to posts previously held by black mayors. Severe problems have arisen in all three cities in the area of interracial politics, and progressive forces have been stymied in mounting a challenge to the new white-led regimes. Therefore, although this chapter still explores some of the key differences in coalition politics across the three cities, its main burden must be to explain the apparent synchronicity of the shifts in coalition strength.

Why did minority liberalism fall in America's three largest cities? What does that failure mean for the future of minority politics? Of the three cities, Los Angeles had by far the longest run of biracial coalition rule: 20 years. In Chicago, Harold Washington's death in 1987 was followed almost immediately by the defeat of the liberal coalition that he had built to win the mayor's office in 1983 and 1987. In New York City, David Dinkins's mayoralty lasted only one term, with his defeat in 1993. By contrast, Tom Bradley held office for 20 years, finally stepping down in 1993. His predicted successor, Michael Woo, was solidly defeated by white Republican Richard Riordan.

The three largest American cities represent alternative urban models. New York City and Chicago are both older cities with traditional party structures deriving from their industrialization period in the nineteenth century. In that sense, they share many qualities with a large number of eastern and midwestern cities. Liberalism and the norms of the welfare state have dominated New York City, while pragmatic governance by a political machine has been the leading force in Chicago.

Los Angeles is a model of the newer western cities developed in the later nineteenth and early twentieth centuries, shaped by midwestern Protestant migrants who hoped to devise an urban alternative to the "old, corrupt" cities of the East and Midwest (Fogelson 1967; Singleton 1979). The antiparty norms of the Progressive movement found their greatest expression in the West (Shefter 1983), and were central to the development of the Los Angeles political community. Party organization has been virtually nonexistent in Los Angeles (Adrian 1959; Carney 1964), representing the polar opposite of Chicago.

TABLE 12.1   Population by group, 1990

	New York City	Chicago	Los Angeles
Whites	43.4	38.2	37.5
Latinos	23.7	19.2	39.3
Asians	7.0	3.7	9.8
Blacks	28.8	39.0	13.9
Total	7,322,564	2,783,726	3,485,398

SOURCE: U.S. Bureau of the Census, 1990.

In demographic terms, the cities represent different points on a spectrum (see Table 12.1). Chicago has the largest black population, nearly 40 percent; Los Angeles the smallest at 14 percent; with New York City in the middle at 25 percent. Whereas both New York City and Chicago have large populations of Eastern European Catholic immigrant groups, New York City is by far the larger center of Jewish population. Together, metropolitan New York and Los Angeles hold 60 percent of · America's Jews (Fisher 1979).

Los Angeles has the largest Latino population (nearly 40 percent) of the three cities, but it lacks the working-class white Catholic group so prominent in New York City and Chicago. Its black population is the smallest of the three cities. Of the three, New York City has the largest Jewish population and Chicago the smallest (3 percent). Los Angeles has the second largest Jewish community in the nation (6–7 percent).

In all three cities, changing demographics have challenged the perception of a black-white politics. But in each city, these demographics have failed to fully dislodge the dominance of politics in black and white.

IDEOLOGY

A central pillar of biracial coalition politics has been ideological affinity between minority groups and whites. Racial liberalism among whites was the principal predictor of white support for minority political interests (Browning, Marshall, and Tabb 1984). A second pillar has been the ideological affinity among minority groups, specifically African Americans and Latinos. Where that affinity has not appeared—for example, in Miami—blacks have experienced severe political isolation.

What does the rollback of minority gains in big cities have to do with ideology? And how should we measure *racial* liberalism? I propose that the African-American community remains the principal base of support for racial equality. If our concern in this volume is the movement toward racial equality, the best way to measure ideology is by comparison to the position of the African-American community. (There are notable exceptions, such as the mixed positions of blacks on immigration, as seen in California's Proposition 187, but no measure is perfect.)

In both the interracial and interethnic dimensions, there is evidence of a significant decline in both white and Latino support for the expressed position of the African-American community. In Los Angeles, New York City, and Chicago, white liberal voters were less likely than in the past to support the mayoral candidate backed by the African-American community. And white conservative voters mobilized at a higher level than minority voters.

In New York City, Mollenkopf (1997) found that Rudolph Giuliani's 1993 mayoral victory was due to several factors. "More than half the margin of change since 1989 came from middle class white Catholic and Jewish election districts. . . . In addition, however, black voters turned out in lower numbers; Latinos both turned out in lower numbers and defected from Dinkins, and white liberals defected" (this volume, 109–110).

In Chicago's 1989 mayoral election, Richard M. Daley reversed Harold Washington's success by taking key shares of the white and Latino vote. He was remarkably effective at winning a huge majority of Latino voters and made strong inroads in the small but key areas of white liberal reform strength on the Lakefront.

In Los Angeles, Richard Riordan did much better among Jews and Latinos than any conservative opponent had ever done against Tom Bradley. Shockingly, he even won the most powerful white liberal council district in the city, the Fifth, with 57 percent of the vote. In modern times, the Fifth District had never supported a conservative candidate over a liberal candidate for any citywide office (Sonenshein, this volume). Riordan broke even among Jews, winning more than 40 percent of their vote. (Bradley had regularly received two-thirds or more of the Jewish vote). Among Latinos, Riordan also exceeded 40 percent, a significantly higher level than previous conservative candidates. And, as in the other cities, turnout was higher in areas of Riordan's strength than in areas of Woo's strength.

Nonetheless, the white liberal constituency remains distinctive from the white conservatives. In each city, white liberals were pulled to the right, but other whites were farther down that road. Exit polls in both New York City and Los Angeles revealed the persistence of this ideological split among whites. At the same time, the shift of other groups rightward left the black community more isolated than it has been in decades. More distant from white liberals and Latinos than it had been, the black community found itself alone on the left.

Thus, in all three cities, mayoral elections revealed a shift in the support and enthusiasm of key groups. Those on the minority-progressive side were less enthusiastic and less supportive of their candidate. Those on the white conservative side were more enthusiastic about their candidate and made significant inroads into the liberal constituency. The citywide momentum of racial politics shifted rightward.

The ideological prospects for multiracial coalitions from the progressive side are therefore mixed. Ideological differences among whites remain potent, but whites as a whole seem to be moving farther away from minority concerns. Among minorities, blacks must compete against conservative and moderate appeals to class and ethnic interests. This could be seen in the support given to white mayoral candidates in all three cities by leading Latino politicians. The main pillar that remains intact is Democratic identification and voting among white liberals, blacks, and Latinos.

Broad support for racial liberalism remains among most blacks, many whites, and many Latinos. There has not yet been a fundamental and irreversible restructuring of political support against black interests and in favor of racial conservatism. Something else is obviously taking place in these cities that holds great implications for the future prospects of minority incorporation.

INTEREST

Carmichael and Hamilton suggested that the ideological support given to blacks by white liberals is contingent on self-interest:

> We do not seek to condemn these groups for being what they are so much as we seek to emphasize a fact of life: they are unreliable allies when a conflict of interest arises. Morality and sentiment cannot weather such conflicts, and black people must realize this. (1967, 76)

Interests helped mightily to explain why biracial coalition politics succeeded in Los Angeles to a far greater degree than in the more liberal New York City. There was a fundamental conflict of interest between blacks and many white liberals in New York City, due in part to the very liberalism of New York. That city developed a huge public sector in which thousands of white liberals held a central stake at the very moment that minority assertion collided with city government in the 1960s.

By contrast, in Los Angeles, blacks and Jews (and other white liberals) were both largely excluded from the city's civic culture. The public sector was poorly developed in Los Angeles, setting up far fewer stakes for intergroup conflict. And as the two groups began to cohere, they were able to simultaneously erase their outsider status by taking over city hall together.

In Chicago, the interests of blacks were in sync with those of the small white liberal reform community that had been excluded by the powerful Democratic machine, and with elements of the Latino community similarly excluded. Thus, there were greater prospects in Chicago for a biracial alliance, oddly, than in the more liberal New York City.

But in the contemporary era of each city, the balance of interests has shifted in a way that is less amenable to liberal coalitions. The new white-led coalitions have managed to appear as guarantors of the interests of many whites and Latinos who would otherwise be open to supporting a citywide minority movement. Unlike the earlier white-led coalitions of raging populists with a strong racist flavor like Frank Rizzo in Philadelphia and Sam Yorty in Los Angeles, the new mayors are pragmatists who are just as open to the ideas of white reformers as black mayors had been. And they are more likely than minority opponents to speak directly to the interests of these communities.

Thus, when Daley campaigned on the Chicago Lakefront, he presented himself much as a black mayoral candidate might: as a pragmatic centrist who would protect the interests of the people in the area and provide good government. One politician noted, "What Richard Daley offered to the lakefront was a combination of what the lakefront, in my opinion, always wanted. It was an efficient, honest operation that works well and is reasonably progressive on social issues" (quoted in Hinz 1991, 77).

Riordan campaigned on the liberal westside of Los Angeles as a centrist, nonideological opponent of crime who understood that even liberal communities are deeply afraid of crime. His slogan, "Tough enough to turn L.A. around," implied a measured strength—no more toughness than absolutely necessary—rather than the alienating bombast of a Sam Yorty.

By appealing directly to the interests of key centrist constituencies, the new white-led coalitions were able to overcome the ideological leaning toward racial equality. Unlike Bradley and Washington, liberal candidates leaned heavily on ideological arguments to win these communities over. For those cross-pressured voters in white and Latino communities, there was a sense of moral obligation to vote for the liberal side but a powerful self-preservation urge to vote for the conservative. In Los Angeles, many people were "mild about Mike," while in New York City, some observers found that many whites voted for Dinkins out of a sense of guilt.

Pivotal to the decline of white and Latino support for black political interests is the changing perception these groups hold about the city and their place within it. White liberals, like many whites, increasingly blame the despairs of city life on the varied faces within the community. In Los Angeles, for example, white liberal voting for Richard Riordan was related to voters' attitudes about immigration (Kauffman 1994). The principal issue that whites mention is crime and the government's response to it. The growing divide between economic classes further separates white and minority interests.

For other minorities, tensions with blacks are built around day-to-day economic and political competition. The rainbow assumption that color will play a special role is under severe challenge between black and Korean-Americans in Los Angeles and New York City. Color is not necessarily an interest. Economic interests are probably far more important than broad appeals to color as a unifying force.

The dilemma for multiracial coalitions is that they have not made a successful argument that they can protect the interests of the key groups they hope to represent. Conservative and moderate coalitions have more successfully addressed this interest question.

The framework of the ideological debate over racial equality in America's three largest cities has shifted so that goodwill is the main pillar of the liberal argument. And goodwill alone is not enough, especially when the conservative side effectively avoids the more blatant opposite of goodwill—racial polarization—in its message. The liberal side says the city will work better if we all get along. The conservative side says we will all get along better if the city works better. The second argument is both more realistic and more appealing to an electoral majority.

LEADERSHIP

In the face of urban stresses and fading ideological affinities, the burden on multiracial leadership has become heavy. In each of these three cities, one fact stands out: On the leadership front, conservatives and moderates have come to overshadow liberals. Just as the black mayors of the 1960s, 1970s, and 1980s contrasted themselves with the often corrupt and even racist mayors they fought, the new white mayors have been able to positively contrast themselves to the leaders generated by the left in urban politics.

A few examples should illustrate the problem. In 1993, Los Angeles voters were asked in a private poll to evaluate the two candidates for mayor on the dimension of leadership. Even though voters only narrowly preferred Riordan in the horse race, they overwhelmingly rated him ahead of the liberal Woo on the dimension of leadership (Sonenshein, this volume). In a comparable manner, New York City voters in the same year—even though closely divided in the horse race—clearly saw Giuliani as a stronger leader than Dinkins. Mollenkopf's analysis (1994) reveals that even among Dinkins's strongest supporters, there were questions about his leadership ability:

> Registered voters were evenly divided on the . . . question of whether Dinkins was a strong leader. Three-quarters of blacks felt so, but all other groups had a much more negative evaluation of Dinkins's leadership. By contrast, a clear majority of the voters thought Giuliani was a strong leader, including 44 percent of the black voters. (214)

The death of Harold Washington in 1987 showed in the most dramatic possible terms that the dynamics of coalition building are not abstract or mathematical but painfully human. Between his first election in 1983 and his reelection in 1987, Washington revealed excellent skills of political leadership in the face of highly entrenched opposition. He held and expanded his political base and became the dominant figure in the city's politics. When Washington suddenly died, the entire framework of minority incorporation literally collapsed.

In both Chicago and New York City, recent black mayors acted in key instances to jeopardize their credibility in protecting the interests of nonblacks. During the Chicago mayoralty of Eugene Sawyer, a top mayoral deputy, Steve Cokely, was quoted as charging Jewish doctors with inventing the AIDS virus in order to kill blacks. This calumny set off a storm in the city, with special intensity among Jews and other whites. Mayor Sawyer delayed firing Cokely until the political pressures became too intense to resist. The firing came far too late to dispel the impression that the mayor could not bring himself to totally disown Cokely without being forced to do so.

Even more damaging were two events during Mayor Dinkins's tenure. A black-led boycott of a Korean-owned grocery store in Brooklyn strained tempers in the city to the boiling point. Dinkins maintained an extremely low profile, only later taking the symbolic action of visiting the store. This delay allowed the perception to grow that he would not oppose black interests in conflict with those of another minority group. Then, when several days of rioting by blacks in the Crown Heights section of Brooklyn terrorized the orthodox Jewish community, Dinkins again seemed to delay the deployment of sufficient police forces to stem the violence. The Crown Heights events left an indelible impression that Jews could not count on Dinkins to protect their most basic interests in life and property.

Interests are not simply objective. People come to understand their interests at least in part by the actions of leaders to either protect or jeopardize them. With interests seen as unprotected, the white vote for Dinkins depended far too heavily on ideologically based goodwill.

The apparent ability of white-led coalitions to consolidate their support indicates something else about the leadership competition: the edge favoring these coalitions depends partly on their greater responsiveness to the concrete problems of their cities. These are not new Sam Yortys; these are generally pragmatists with serious policies. Much like the African-American mayors of an earlier time, they are charting a path down the city's center and holding the high ground on the core issues of public safety and economics. It is very difficult to mount a challenge to these new mayors from the left, as long as the left struggles for a counter-governing philosophy.

Part of the problem is that leadership from the left in urban politics has become trapped between two basic models of progressive politics: the biracial and the rainbow. Basically, progressives need both to reach significant numbers of whites and to unify and mobilize minorities. This task is substantially more formidable than the road taken by black mayors.

Under a biracial approach, pioneered by black mayoral candidates, minority leaders make genuine and extensive efforts to recruit whites to their cause and to make clear that their leadership will cause the city to be safer and better run. Under the rainbow approach, the bond of color and nonwhite status is the vehicle for inclusion. But the two strategies conflict with each other. Leaders have been forced to split the difference, which makes no one happy. A revealing example was Woo's admission in 1993 that he referred to the violence of 1992 as a rebellion in the black community and as a riot among whites. Dinkins, trying to bridge a harsh black-Korean battle in Brooklyn in 1991, ended up seeming rudderless and ineffective.

In the search for rainbow coalitions, the appealing concept of *diversity* has fragmented progressive politics. As a symbol of harmony, diversity is a useful and relatively benign concept. As a political coalition strategy, it is problematic. Diversity appears to be a "soft" way to avoid the hard edges of coalition politics—namely, which groups are potential allies with a serious stake in the system—and also the hard edge of racial polarization.

"Diversity" evades the tough decisions among deserving interests that are the essence of urban leadership. Unlike the successful biracial coalitions of the 1970s and 1980s, the diversity coalition begins with appeals to member groups rather than the crafting of an overall rationale for leadership that will appeal to a number of groups.

In effect, many of the new progressives have confused the inner leadership role (building networks of key leaders) and the outer leadership role (crafting and presenting a rationale for governing). They have misunderstood the experience of biracial coalitions and have *begun* with the coalition question, rather than subordinating coalition to the development of broad political messages and evidence of governing credibility. The diversity discourse about rainbow coalitions has transformed coalitions from a means into an end, and in so doing has forfeited the high ground essential to citywide political victory.

The easy answer becomes to talk less about race (as just another type of diversity) and not to make hard choices among the few truly available partners. And diversity is hardly benign to many voters in American cities, for whom it symbolizes not the "gorgeous mosaic" of David Dinkins or the cosmopolitan walkways of Mike Woo but the very breakdown of the social order.

PROSPECTS: TIME TO GIVE UP?

Looking at the present era in historical perspective, we can see that we are entering uncharted waters. We have reached the end of a great wave of American minority politics, the experiment in minority incorporation. Like all waves, it will continue to flow unevenly, and perhaps permanently, as did the civil rights movement before it. But we should ask, as Martin Luther King, Jr., did in 1967: Where do we go from here? It is by answering that question that the meaning and potential of multiracial coalitions will emerge. After all, creating electoral coalitions for minority incorporation is not an end in itself but, like the civil rights movement, an inspiring tool toward the more profound prize: equality.

If the civil rights movement was about applying moral force against unjust laws and the movement for minority incorporation was about the development of political power to change unjust practices, what is next? The most fundamental battleground in American society is about neither rights nor political power but about gaining majority consent through the art of political communication. Both the civil rights movement and the movement for minority incorporation represented expressions of that broader strategic necessity.

The literature on minority incorporation tends to assume the importance of electoral coalitions and voting alliances as central features of minority success. And indeed participation in a winning coalition did make a significant difference in policy outcomes. But in the postincorporation world of American cities, there are good reasons to go beyond the electoral in searching for vehicles for equality.

In the preincorporation era, minority groups and their liberal allies could see the value of gaining electoral power. But there is also the downside: Power can be lost. A minority strategy that depends only on winning successful incorporation will be subject to the partisan and ideological winds. If incorporation increases positive change, how can unincorporation be hedged against?

The battle over public opinion and governmental power cannot solely depend on turning demographics into political power. Far more than even a decade ago, American political life is now dominated by competing agendas advanced in highly sophisticated ways through the mass media. These agendas are advanced by interest groups, political parties, candidates, bureaucracies, and even foreign nations. In the place of an Establishment that could be appealed to, we have instead a political marketplace. *The movement for minority equality runs the serious risk of not contending on that awesome battleground of public opinion.* The shaping of public opinion rules budgets and determines national, state, and local priorities. It is the ability to compete and succeed in that competitive arena that will underlie the success of multiracial coalitions.

CONCLUSIONS

The prospects for building multiracial coalitions are bleak unless progressives fully understand the wrong turns that can derail the minority search for equality. Coalition politics are means to an end. It is the ability to link ideologies of fairness and equity and to respond to the legitimate interests of groups and masses and the intangible quality of leadership that give them life.

Regardless of the appeal of strategies of color in the search for racial equality, cross-racial appeals are still of fundamental importance. As Mollenkopf noted on New York City: "Proponents of such a [multiracial liberal coalition] must also address the issues that deeply concern all voters, but especially middle-class white voters. Foremost among them is the perception that crime is rampant, the streets unsafe, intergroup relations uncivil, and the quality of life decaying" (1994, 226). Although it is tempting to turn sympathetic whites into "flak-catchers" for the long-unexpressed anger of minority activists, they are actually potential members of a progressive coalition whose interests must be respected and whose values should be appealed to.

A progressive movement cannot, in its desire to move "beyond black and white," make two fundamental errors. One is to treat multiracial coalition politics as simply a numerical extension of the same black-white dynamics that underlie biracial coalitions. Latinos and Asian Americans have their own ideologies and interests, their own internal divisions, and in responding to appeals from conservative forces, may not have the same goals and objectives as blacks and whites.

The other error is to underestimate the continuing power of race in American politics. As Sears and his colleagues have demonstrated (Sears, Citrin, and van Laar 1995), race continues to shape a wide range of issues, including American attitudes toward the very diversity that leads many of us to downplay the significance of black-white divisions.

As an organizing principle for new progressive multiracial coalitions, color is an unreliable glue. Using ethnicity as a bond for coalitions—rather than addressing the serious economic and social issues of community life—will have the paradoxical effect of exacerbating coalition tensions. The evidence from before is that there must be goals beyond race relations to make coalitions succeed. Coalitions must be able to make a difference, to cut deeper, to provide leadership.

We continue to learn that goodwill is not enough, but neither is cold self-interest. While the idea of color-blindness distorts the reality of American life, color alone is an insufficient basis for enduring coalitions for equality. The struggle for equality still requires leaders who can create and sustain enduring systems of belief, manage conflicts of interest, promote interest alliances, and cross society's racial and ethnic barriers in the interest of a humane vision for the whole society.

REFERENCES

Adrian, Charles R. 1959. A Typology for Nonpartisan Elections. *Western Political Quarterly* 12: 449–458.

Bobo, Lawrence. 1983. Whites' Opposition to School Busing: Symbolic Racism or Realistic Group Conflict? *Journal of Personality and Social Psychology* 45: 1196–1210.

Browning, Rufus P., Dale Rogers Marshall, and David H. Tabb. 1984. *Protest Is Not Enough: The Struggle of Blacks and Hispanics for Equality in Urban Politics.* Berkeley: University of California Press.

Carmichael, Stokely, and Charles V. Hamilton. 1967. *Black Power: The Politics of Liberation in America.* New York: Random House.

Carmines, E. G., and J. A. Stimson. 1982. Racial Issues and the Structure of Mass Belief Systems. *Journal of Politics* 44: 2–20.

Carmines, E. G., and J. A. Stimson. 1989. *Issue Evolution: Race and the Transformation of American Politics.* Princeton, N.J.: Princeton University Press.

Carney, Francis. 1964. The Decentralized Politics of Los Angeles. *Annals of the American Academy of Political and Social Sciences* 353 (May): 107–121.

Edsall, Thomas B., and Mary D. Edsall. 1991. *Chain Reaction: The Impact of Race, Rights and Taxes on American Politics.* New York: Norton.

Fisher, A. M. 1979. Realignment of the Jewish Vote? *Political Science Quarterly* 94: 97–116.

Fogelson, Robert. 1967. *The Fragmented Metropolis: Los Angeles, 1850–1930.* Cambridge, Mass.: Harvard University Press.

Giles, Micheal W., and Arthur Evans. 1986. The Power Approach to Intergroup Hostility. *Journal of Conflict Resolution* 30: 469–486.

Giles, Micheal W., and Douglas S. Gatlin. 1980. Mass-level Compliance with Public Policy: The Case of School Desegregation. *Journal of Politics* 42: 722–746.

Hahn, Harlan, David Klingman, and Harry Pachon. 1976. Cleavages, Coalitions, and the Black Candidate: The Los Angeles Mayoralty Elections of 1969 and 1973. *Western Political Quarterly* 29 (December): 521–530.

Halley, Robert M., Alan C. Acock, and Thomas H. Greene. 1976. Ethnicity and Social Class: Voting in the 1973 Los Angeles Municipal Elections. *Western Political Quarterly* 29 (December): 521–530.

Hinckley, Barbara. 1981. *Coalitions and Politics.* New York: Harcourt Brace Jovanovich.

Hinz, Greg. 1991. Lakefronters. In Paul M. Green and Melvin G. Holli, eds., *Restoration 1989: Chicago Elects a New Daley,* 74–90. Chicago, Ill.: Lyceum Books.

Kauffman, Karen. 1994. Us versus Them: A Group Conflict Analysis of the 1993 Los Angeles Mayoral Election. Paper presented at the annual meeting of the Western Political Science Association.

Kinder, Donald R., and D. O. Sears. 1981. Prejudice and Politics: Symbolic Racism versus Racial Threats to the Good Life. *Journal of Personality and Social Psychology* 40: 414–431.

Mollenkopf, John. 1994. Afterword. *A Phoenix in the Ashes: The Rise and Fall of the Koch Coalition in New York City Politics.* Princeton, N.J.: Princeton University Press (paperback edition).

Pettigrew, Thomas. 1971. When a Black Candidate Runs for Mayor: Race and Voting Behavior. In Harlan Hahn, ed., *People and Politics in Urban Society,* 99–105. Beverly Hills, Calif.: Sage.

Sears, David O., Jack Citrin, and Colette van Laar. 1995. Black Exceptionalism in a Multicultural Society. Paper presented at the annual meeting of the American Political Science Association.

Shefter, Martin. 1983. Regional Receptivity to Reform. *Political Science Quarterly* 98 (Fall): 459–484.

Singleton, Gregory H. 1979. *Religion in the City of the Angels: American Protestant Culture and Urbanization, Los Angeles, 1850–1930.* Ann Arbor, Mich.: UMI Research Press.

Sleeper, Jim. 1993. The End of the Rainbow? America's Changing Urban Politics. *The New Republic,* November, 20–25.

Sonenshein, Raphael J. 1993. *Politics in Black and White: Race and Power in Los Angeles.* Princeton, N.J.: Princeton University Press.

chapter **13**

Has Political Incorporation Been Achieved? Is It Enough?

Rufus P. Browning, Dale Rogers Marshall, and David H. Tabb

In the 21 cities examined in this book, have blacks and Latinos achieved strong political incorporation? Sometimes.

Have they held the power they built? Not always. They and their liberal allies have suffered significant defeats in several cities, and the fear arises that these reversals might result in renewed exclusion and subordinate status.

Where they did achieve incorporation, have minority-oriented city governments produced gains for minority people? Yes, in significant, but limited, areas.

Have these governments achieved the broader goals of the movement that produced them? No.

We first summarize the findings of the preceding chapters on minority mobilization and incorporation. Then we take up questions of the record of minority-oriented city governments, their adequacy, what we have learned about the coalitions that sustain them, the recent reversals they have met in several cities, and their possible futures.

MOBILIZATION AND INCORPORATION: FUNDAMENTALS

Withholding for the moment judgment about the value of minority incorporation in city governments, we bring together here findings and interpretations about resources for mobilization and incorporation, and barriers to it.

Weak and Strong Forms of Minority Incorporation

Representation alone gained little influence for minorities; minority participation in liberal dominant coalitions led to much stronger minority influence in city governments and greater policy responsiveness; coalitions led by black mayors typically incorporated still stronger commitments to minority objectives.[1] As Stokely Carmichael and Charles Hamilton put it in 1967:

> When black people lack a majority, Black Power means proper representation and sharing of control. It means the creation of power bases, of strength, from which black people can press to change local or nationwide patterns of oppression—instead of from weakness.
>
> It does not mean merely putting black faces into office. Black visibility is not Black Power. (1967, 46)

In our terms, Carmichael and Hamilton's "proper representation" was potentially achievable through participation in liberal dominant coalitions; "sharing of control" was the fundamental premise of the most successful of those coalitions.

Interest Group and Electoral Strategies

Mobilization that produced sustained incorporation built on interest-group organization, demand, and protest as well as on electoral effort, including the formation of party or partylike coalitions. Electoral mobilization and coalition were the essential foundation of enduring incorporation. Group organization, demand, and protest were the foundation for successful electoral effort, in spite of instances where too intense protest hindered and delayed the formation of coalitions.

Cities in which blacks or Latinos achieved the most powerful participation in electoral coalitions, and subsequently in city governments, were those in which the development of autonomous, solidarity minority leadership and organization preceded it, confirming Carmichael and Hamilton's argument:

> The concept of Black Power rests on a fundamental premise: Before a group can enter the open society, it must first close ranks. By this we mean that group solidarity is necessary before a group can operate effectively from a bargaining position of strength in a pluralistic society. (1967, 44)

The linkage between the achievement of solidarity within the minority group and the achievement of strong incorporation was very close in the cities studied. The early strong incorporation of blacks in Berkeley depended on the unusually

---

[1] Mollenkopf suggests in ch. 4 that New York may be an anomaly in this regard—that a regime in which blacks are weakly incorporated nevertheless produces substantial benefits for them. We deal with that possibility later in this chapter.

strong organization of black leadership in the Berkeley Black Caucus. Conversely, the long delay in the election of a black mayor in Oakland was the result in part of the split between the Black Panther Party and middle-class black leadership (see ch. 1). Failure to achieve solidarity both within and between minority populations in New York explains in part the failure of blacks and Latinos to obtain incorporation corresponding to their numbers in that city (see ch. 4). Breaking away from the Democratic machine and organizing a grass-roots process to pull black community organizations together, and the inclusion of Latinos in a coalition, were prerequisites for Harold Washington's victory in Chicago (see ch. 5).

The Importance of Coalitions

Regardless of election system (partisan or nonpartisan), the political incorporation of minorities—the extent of their role in dominant coalitions that controlled city government—depended on their ability to form and maintain cohesive electoral coalitions. In particular, where blacks and Latinos constituted a minority of the effective electorate, their incorporation depended on the formation of bi- or multiracial coalitions that selected candidates, controlled the number of minority candidacies so as to prevent splitting the vote for minority candidates, organized slates, coordinated campaigns, and controlled city councils and departments.

Fundamental resources of group size formed the basis of these coalitions. Depending on historical patterns of competition and conflict, on leadership, and on the sizes of black, Latino, and supportive white groups, coalitions were variously composed of blacks and whites, Latinos and whites, or all three groups.

The Importance of Leadership

Because competition and conflict between groups are typical historically, the structure, size, and timing of new coalitions depended on the ability of leaders to overcome divisions and to shape issues so as to minimize antagonism and sustain joint effort. The flow of issues, partly under the control of coalition leaders, and the willingness and ability of the available leadership to reach out across racial boundaries—a difficult task—shaped the structure of the coalitions that actually formed, won control of city government, and maintained their commitment and position (see ch. 12). The structure of local leadership, as well as the dynamic of group conflict, is shaped by historical experience—for example, the innovative cooperation that took hold and became accepted practice in Philadelphia (see ch. 3).

GROUP SIZE AND PATTERNS OF MOBILIZATION

We set forth in chapter 1 expectations about mobilization based on sizes of racial/ethnic groups in the California cities—namely, that a successful multiracial coalition will form and take control of city government where the minority population plus support from liberal whites approaches 50 percent of the electorate. Patterns of

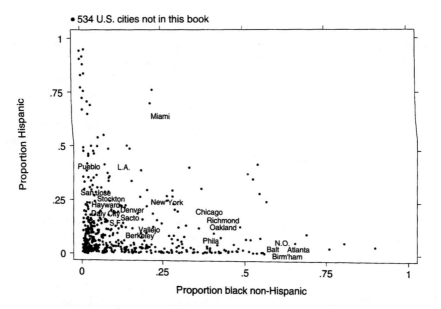

FIGURE 13.1 Proportion Hispanic by proportion black non-Hispanic, 555 U.S. cities with populations 50,000 and over in 1990

Key to abbreviated city names: Balt = Baltimore, Birm'ham = Birmingham, L.A. = Los Angeles, N.O. = New Orleans, Phila = Philadelphia, Sacto = Sacramento, CA. Richmond is Richmond, CA.

mobilization that emerged in the other cities analyzed in this book correspond in part to those expectations. Figure 13.1 places our 21 cities in the context of all U.S. cities with populations of 50,000 and over with respect to the sizes of their Hispanic and black populations. Atlanta, Baltimore, Birmingham, New Orleans, Oakland, and Richmond (California) are arrayed along the horizontal axis (proportion black) of Figure 13.1, with majority or near-majority black populations already in 1980. In all these cities, black mayors who led bi- or multiracial coalitions were elected, though in cities where blacks constituted a majority of the electorate on their own, they were no longer dependent on support from other groups. In Birmingham and New Orleans, as Huey Perry carefully delineates in chapter 8, biracial coalitions had formed earlier and had first elected racially liberal white mayors, then black mayors. Similarly, in Miami and Pueblo (upper left of Figure 13.1), Latinos constituted majorities or near-majorities already in 1980 and elected Latino mayors.[2]

In a second group of cities, neither blacks nor Latinos constituted majorities in 1980, neither group had an overwhelming share of the city's population of people of color, but the two groups together made up at least 40 percent of city popula-

---

[2] The proportion black and especially the proportion Hispanic measures in Figure 13.1 exaggerate the political strength of these groups in city electorates. Group proportions of city *electorates* are smaller than these proportions of city populations and many, sometimes most, Latinos in these cities are not eligible to vote because they are not citizens.

tion: Los Angeles, Philadelphia, Chicago, and New York.[3] In all these cities, a bi- or multiracial electoral alliance with a strong commitment to minority (primarily black) interests had taken control of the mayor's office by 1987. In New York, this was a biracial coalition under Mayor John Lindsay, elected in 1967 and 1971. Thus, the experience in these cities was at first glance consistent with the simple model, derived from the California experience, that predicts coalition formation and takeover of city government.

However, New York has oscillated back and forth between explicitly multiracial coalitions—Mayor Lindsay's and an uneasy coalition that elected David Dinkins mayor in 1990—and considerably less liberal coalitions led by mayors Edward Koch and Rudolph Giuliani. The inability of multiracial coalitions to sustain themselves in New York are anomalous in terms of the simple model, as Mollenkopf argues in chapter 4. In Chicago, a successful black-Latino-liberal coalition led by Harold Washington also could not maintain itself after his death.

New York since 1975 and Chicago before and after Harold Washington all exemplify co-optation, in which segments of black and Latino leadership and electoral support are brought into a dominant coalition in which whites play primary roles and which does not make so strong a commitment to minority interests. We discuss these cities and cities with similar group-size and political characteristics below in the section, "Barriers to Incorporation."

Denver constitutes a modest anomaly on the other side, with a combined black and Latino population of only 30.8 percent in 1980 but a Latino mayor by mid-decade. But as Hero explains in chapter 11, Federico Peña's campaign for mayor of Denver fell a good deal short of the model of a multiracial electoral alliance with a strong commitment to minority interests. A Latino mayor was elected, but minority interests were not strongly incorporated.

BARRIERS TO INCORPORATION

The passage of time since the first edition of this book has seen the defeat of biracial and multiracial coalitions in several cities. This recent history enlarges our view of the barriers to incorporation. Now we see not only the problems that prevented or restricted incorporation in the first place but also the decline of once-successful minority-oriented coalitions and the threat of countermobilization and the resurgence and success of conservative coalitions. Maintaining a coalition that supports minority interests during a period of governance is different from mobilizing to

---

[3] The 40 percent minority figure is a rule of thumb—an approximation for circumstances that vary from city to city. An illustration will show its plausibility. Suppose the black plus Latino population is 40 percent and the white non-Latino population is 60 percent. Evidence from many cities suggests that typically 10 percent to 20 percent of the white population will support a biracial coalition (see Preston, Henderson, and Puryear 1987). This amounts to 6 percent to 12 percent of the total population. Combined with a 40 percent minority population, we have a potential coalition of 46 percent to 52 percent of the population, within striking distance of an electoral majority if the coalition's supporters can be mobilized.

elect it in the first place. And restructuring a coalition after defeat is likely to be different still, requiring altered expectations, new visions, and different skills. We review first the barriers to incorporation that are apparent in the history of minority incorporation in cities since the 1950s, then we turn to the threat of reversal and the fear of renewed exclusion that defeat brings to the fore.

Urban Machines

New York since 1975 and Chicago before and after Harold Washington present characteristics that were not found in the California cities and that constitute additional barriers to minority mobilization and incorporation. In these cities, we find party organizations that have co-opted minorities into their organizations—bringing in carefully selected minority activists and officeholders who are expected to remain loyal to the party and its leadership rather than to an autonomous leadership that arises from the minority community itself.

The machines are well-institutionalized coalitions that predate the widespread minority mobilization of the 1960s. Not oriented toward reform and determined to protect the power of the organization and the economic interests of its ultimately white leadership and business support, the machine attempts to prevent the formation of multiracial challenging coalitions through co-optation, building on and generating divisions among minority leaders and groups, and establishing minority officeholders against whom other minority people find it difficult to run. The machine creates some minority incorporation and produces some minority-oriented policies but helps to prevent the mobilization of a more liberal, unified minority-based coalition.

Thus the machine stands as a barrier to the formation and success of reform-oriented coalitions, in which more autonomous minority leadership could play central and dominant roles. Some benefits flow to minority populations from such machines, as they do from co-optive regimes generally—such benefits as city government employment and contracts from the city—but the machines will not undertake efforts to reorient city government across a broad range of policy areas.

In Chicago, unlike New York, a weakened machine was defeated by a multiracial coalition led by black insurgents. Harold Washington's election as mayor and then his success in gaining a council majority show that even a long-entrenched machine and its structure of co-optation can be overthrown, given appropriate leadership, fundamental resources of minority population, and some support outside the minority community.

But the Chicago case also demonstrates the difficulty of accomplishing an overthrow. As Pinderhughes shows in Chapter 5, Washington's coalition and leadership were unusual (see also ch. 4 and 12). The coalition conducted an extraordinary grass-roots mobilization and involvement in the decision to select Washington as the coalition's candidate for mayor in the first place. Washington himself was capable of reaching out across racial lines to Chicago's Latino population, including them as respected partners in his ultimately victorious coalition. Not every leader with the ability to win majority support in his own group also has the will, the credibility, and the skill to create a liberal biracial or multiracial coalition. (See ch. 12 for a discussion of the importance of leadership.)

The fragile dependence of such coalitions on leadership was sadly illustrated when Washington died in office and black candidates competing to succeed him split his coalition, leading to the election of the white machine candidate, Mayor Richard M. Daley, in 1989.

Fragmentation of Minority Groups

In addition to the party machine as a barrier to minority mobilization, New York illustrates also the possibility and consequences of extreme fragmentation of minority groups. The 1980 census counted more than 45 percent of New York's population as black or "of Hispanic origin," and these groups probably made up more than half of New York's population by the late 1980s. By the standards of the other cities studied in this book, resources of such size should have been more than ample to found a liberal multiracial coalition that could control city government over a long period of time. A major reason this has not happened, as seen in chapter 4, is the extent to which both blacks and Latinos in New York have been divided.

In contrast to the California cities, where most blacks and Latinos have arrived since World War II, New York's black and Latino populations have had a long history of competition, conflict, established leadership, and political division. This is not new clay that a skillful leader can readily mold into a unified force, but a congeries of minority populations between which divisions are deep and solid. Blacks and Latinos in New York are further split within each group by ancestry and nativity—blacks of West Indian birth or origin as well as blacks of southern origin; Latinos of Puerto Rican birth or ancestry but also Dominicans and other Latino immigrant groups—and by place of residence in the boroughs of the city.

Fragmentation of minority populations in New York is not only a result of differences in ancestry and nationality; it stems also from a long history of conflict and competition and the habituation of organizations and leaders to that history, as Mollenkopf notes (ch. 4). This is utterly unlike the experience of black communities in the California cities. Blacks arrived in large numbers in California mainly during and after World War II. Coming predominantly from the American South, they were not divided by different ancestry. Organizational structure and leadership still emerging, they were mobilized by the civil rights and Black Power movements and were presented with an opportunity to overthrow conservative regimes, if they could coalesce among themselves and with others. For California blacks, the civil rights movement was the formative influence for political mobilization. In contrast, the political fragmentation of New York's black population was well established long before the civil rights movement. This population's ability to overcome fragmentation was tested again in the 1989 New York mayoral election that pitted Mayor Koch against David N. Dinkins, the black Manhattan borough president, who formed a biracial coalition. Dinkins won, but his coalition subsequently lost support and was defeated in his bid for reelection in 1993.

Intense fragmentation between and within minority groups impedes the formation of multiracial coalitions. Anthony Downs draws the lesson:

> In many big cities minorities need to overcome their own fragmentation into groups and their deliberate co-optation by the white politicians who long dominated local politics before they can fully control their local government. (1985, 291–292)

New York, Chicago, and San Francisco all illustrate the difficulty of combining the potential electoral strength of two or more racial/ethnic groups. We should expect it to be more difficult to form the multiethnic coalitions that will be necessary to take control of city government in such settings than it is to form biracial, black-white or Latino-white coalitions in cities where one "minority" group dominates. It is not impossible—witness Sacramento and the sometimes-successful efforts of multiethnic coalitions in all these cities—but it is more difficult and therefore more dependent on circumstances and on special qualities of leadership.

Fragmentation of racial/ethnic groups can obstruct stable coalition building in cities where no political machine is established—witness San Francisco. But fragmentation makes co-optation a convenient tool for a well-organized machine—witness New York.

Issues, Interests, and the Loss of White Support

The formation and survival of bi- and multiracial coalitions depend in part on the ideological commitment of liberal whites to the minority cause. Mollenkopf's analysis of New York (ch. 4) and Sonenshein's comparative study of New York, Chicago, and Los Angeles (ch. 12) delineate the limits of that commitment; the New York case especially illustrates the potential for drastic loss of earlier support and the long-term eclipse of progressive multiracial coalitions.

In some cities, certainly in New York and Los Angeles, Jews have accounted for a large share of white support for blacks, reflecting the experience of Jews with discrimination and their special moral determination to oppose it. Unfortunately for the cause of coalition, blacks and whites generally but Jews in particular have a special potential for conflict of interests around anti-Semitism, city government fiscal problems, residential and labor market succession, and control over city government functions and employment.

Anti-Semitism.   A few black leaders express openly anti-Semitic attitudes; the expression of anti-Semitism and the failure of some black leaders to denounce them reduces support for biracial coalitions among Jews. In New York, as a result, two-thirds of the Jewish voters defected from the Democratic Party in 1989 and 1993 to support a Republican for mayor.

Fiscal Problems.   In New York again, fiscal crisis has dominated the agenda of city government for years and turned white supporters away from the problems of minority groups. The Koch administration "undid the spending patterns of the Lindsay years," and the Giuliani administration has also "dramatically reduced funding for programs designed to incorporate minority interests" (ch. 4).

Residential and Labor Market Succession. In New York in particular, many Jews have been affected in recent years by the transition of Jewish lower-middle- and working-class neighborhoods to black or Latino neighborhoods. Such transitions are likely to kindle racial, class, and cultural antagonisms and thus reduce support for coalitions.

Control over City Government Functions and Employment. In the 1968 school strikes in New York, black activists were

> pitted . . . as "outs" against a school bureaucracy led and staffed dispro-portionately by liberal and moderate whites (including many Jews). Liberals were cast as "ins" in traditionally liberal New York City; it was a strike against [White] institutional liberalism. The high degree of black-Jewish conflict produced by the strikes shifted much of the city's liberal base into a moderate/conservative alliance with white Catholics; this link became the base for the Koch regime. The result left blacks without political incorporation. (Sonenshein 1993, ch. 11)

It is apparent that conflicts arising from these and other issues can destroy or prevent the formation of bi- and multiracial coalitions. Liberal coalitions have split and lost power in many cities:

- In Los Angeles as Latinos and Jews moved to a conservative coalition
- In Philadelphia as a nonreform coalition of Democrats replaced a reform-oriented Democratic coalition
- In New York as conservatives exploited conflict within the liberal multiracial coalition
- In Chicago as blacks split among themselves and were unable to retain the allegiance of Latinos
- In San Francisco as progressive whites and blacks split over social and environmental issues
- In New Orleans as both conservatives and liberals formed biracial coalitions

Although the issues described above involved conflict between whites and blacks, it is easy to think of tensions and issues that divide blacks and Latinos, whites and Latinos, blacks and Asians, and so on. Thus, the general problem is the management of issues so as to form and maintain an effective coalition, even in the presence of actual or potential conflict with respect to interests.

LATINO MOBILIZATION AND INCORPORATION

Latinos are different. They are, first of all, not black except in relatively small numbers; thus they do not suffer the stigma of blackness in American society, and many consider themselves to be whites of Hispanic origin. Second, they are much more diverse than blacks, and the diversities count: Cuban Americans are not Puerto Ricans, who are not Dominicans, and Mexican Americans are not Central Americans, either culturally or in socioeconomic status.[4] Third, they are more likely to be Roman Catholic. Fourth, they are less likely than blacks to see political action as a preferred means of improvement. Finally, although poverty continues to be a major problem in many Latino communities, Latinos on average appear to assimilate economically more rapidly than blacks and are less concentrated geographically than blacks.

They are different in other political respects as well. Warren reports that of the Latinos in Dade County, Florida, who are registered to vote, about 75 percent are Republicans (ch. 10). Opposition to the Castro regime in Cuba is a central tenet of their political program, even at the local level, and they are strongly growth oriented and increasingly successful in business.

Federico Peña, mayor of Denver, with a strong-mayor form of city government, was not the product of minority electoral mobilization or demand-protest and was not endorsed by established Mexican-American politicians. In a city with only 18 percent Latino population (31 percent black or Latino in 1980, but a smaller percentage of the electorate), he did not emphasize his Mexican-American identity in his campaign, but he had a "proven track record" for Mexican Americans and with liberal whites as a state legislator, and he was strongly supported by Mexican-American voters and the liberal wing of the statewide Democratic party.

With Denver experiencing a severe recession, Peña lost the support of important Democratic party leaders, barely won reelection, and never had control of a majority of the city council. This is clearly not a case of strong minority incorporation, in spite of the election of a Latino to the mayor's office.

Denver city government has been opened to minority participation—not a small achievement. Given the relatively small size and weak mobilization of Denver's minority population, perhaps it is surprising that a Latino mayor was elected at all. A somewhat larger Latino population in San Jose has not elected a mayor; but San Jose's black population, which would support a liberal coalition, is very small, unlike Denver's.

Latinos can be mobilized to vote for multiracial coalitions led by whites (Sacramento) or blacks (Chicago), but they are not very likely to generate strongly minority-oriented programs and coalitions themselves. This is not to say that they have not done this to some degree in some cities, such as Miami. In the first edition, we said that if Latino economic assimilation were to proceed with reasonable speed, it was unlikely that Latinos as a group would mobilize strongly around demands of the sort articulated by the black power movement.[5] In the 1990s, continued immi-

---

[4] With respect to socioeconomic differences among Latinos in the eastern United States, see Fitzpatrick and Parker (1981).

[5] William Julius Wilson (1985, 148) raises the possibility that rapidly growing urban Latino populations, with both continued immigration and high birth rates, might experience a worsening of their social and economic conditions, including an increase in joblessness, crime, teenage pregnancy, female-headed families, welfare dependency, and ethnic antagonism directed toward them.

gration and high birth rates have produced dramatic increases in the absolute and relative size of the Latino population in many cities and corresponding increases in Latino mobilization, as the chapters in this edition show.

In the meantime, Latino incorporation, as we see it in the cities studied in this book, is different. It draws more narrowly from the comprehensive socioeconomic goals of the black power movement and has a more limited view of the proper role of government. Latino political leadership has responded to an electoral base that has been more diverse and, typically, more conservative.

The conservatism of Latino mobilization and incorporation has of course implications for the responsiveness of city governments in which Latinos are incorporated—responsiveness to what? To whose demands and interests? To what ultimate goals? We should expect Latino-run city governments to end discrimination in hiring, certainly, in the routine administration of city affairs, and in the award of government contracts to minority-owned businesses. Should we expect such governments to equalize the delivery of city services and improvements generally? Perhaps somewhat, alleviating the most glaring inequities, but not much, if it means significantly reallocating municipal resources toward low-income neighborhoods, their residents, and their businesses, and raising taxes to pay for new programs.

As we have noted, studies in this book confirm the difficulty of forming multiracial coalitions including blacks and Latinos. The tensions between these groups are often high as they compete both in labor markets and for political position and governmental benefits. The obstacles seem greatest in New York and Miami, where the two groups are in direct conflict; but political relationships are problematic in Los Angeles as well. The most successful black-Latino coalition seems to have been Harold Washington's in Chicago. The process of coalition formation in that city should be a model for similar efforts elsewhere. However, the collapse of that coalition when Washington died underscores again the special problem of maintaining multiracial coalitions and the special importance of leadership in such settings.

BLACK POLITICAL INCORPORATION: IS IT IN DECLINE?

The cities examined in this book reveal many patterns of change in black political incorporation. In some cities, strong black political incorporation was achieved and sustained over time. In others, coalitions that strongly incorporated black leadership have been defeated. In still others, strong black incorporation has not been achieved.

In 1988, with the important exceptions of New York and Miami, where black incorporation was weaker than we might expect on grounds of black population alone, blacks were well placed in dominant coalitions in all nine cities (of the 21 studied in this book) in which they constituted at least 20 percent of city population in 1980: Berkeley, Atlanta, Los Angeles, New Orleans, Oakland, Birmingham, Chicago, Philadelphia, and Baltimore. Where blacks were smaller proportions of the populations, they have fared less well. Nevertheless, there is no denying the enormous gain from the virtual exclusion of blacks in 1950 to their achievement of governmental positions and leadership in 1988.

In 1996, the picture is more complex. Liberal coalitions in four cities have experienced defeat since 1990: New York, Los Angeles, Chicago, and San Francisco. In these cities, previously dominant liberal coalitions have been turned out of office, the alliances that sustained them were significantly weakened, and their futures are highly uncertain. San Francisco already represents a reversal of a reversal, however: Willie Brown, the African-American former speaker of the California Assembly, won election to the mayor's office in December 1995—a gift of term limits to splintered liberal, progressive, and multiracial groups in San Francisco.

In 13 other cities, bi- and multiracial coalitions have not experienced defeat: Atlanta, Birmingham, New Orleans, Philadelphia, Baltimore, Miami, Denver, Pueblo, and Berkeley, Oakland, Richmond, Sacramento, and San Jose, California.

The levels of incorporation that groups achieve are changeable. The aging of coalitions in office, demographic change that presents new interests and challenges, the investment of coalition leadership in the successful commitments and statuses of the past, and the likelihood that their mistakes and their programs will eventually stimulate opposition—these are all at work to undermine established coalitions in which African Americans are strongly incorporated.

The growth of Latino and Asian populations is rapid and important in many cities. The growth of these groups shifts the ground beneath biracial coalitions based on the premise that the fundamental alliance is a compact between blacks and whites.

The chapters of this book provide many examples of the ways competing coalitions exploit differences within liberal biracial coalitions, the potential for fragmentation of groups once they have achieved some success or lose a unifying leader (Chicago), and the difficulty of translating successful electoral coalitions into successful governing coalitions (Chicago, New York, Philadelphia).

DEFEAT

Several of the authors of chapters in this book write of *rollbacks* in black or Latino political incorporation. The term seems to signify a return to an earlier stage of minority political incorporation. The possibilities are really more diverse than rollback implies, and it is important to be clear about the possibilities.

What happens when a governing coalition is defeated in an election and loses its control over the legislative and executive functions of city government? Defeat certainly does not mean a return to the 1950s. Minority communities typically have far greater resources at their disposal now than they did then—resources of money, leadership, experience, education, political awareness, organization, position, and relationships in private, public, and nonprofit organizations. Defeat is not the end of the road for the interests in a losing coalition because these resources do not go away with defeat. Instead, they are likely to be organized so that organizations and leaders conduct vigorous advocacy on behalf of their communities. Later, they are likely to turn to building and rebuilding alliances.

Even in defeat, a coalition is not without resources. Perhaps the most important resource of a defeated coalition is its potential for regrouping and competing again.

A coalition that maintains its structure even though it has lost an election, especially a close one, is likely to instill caution in the victorious coalition. The cautionary impact of a still-viable coalition is a form of influence over policy and programs. Although not as good as control, it is much better than nothing.

Defeat may be more serious than that, however. It may signify the disintegration of a coalition—its perhaps irretrievable demise. The end of the Bradley era in Los Angeles may be such an instance. But even the complete disintegration of the Bradley coalition obviously does not mean the end of the political road for people of color in Los Angeles. By opening up political space, the end of a coalition creates opportunities for new leaders and new alliances at the same time the old patterns fall apart. New alliances of people of color are likely to form eventually to take advantage of their potentially mobilizable numerical advantage.

Three scenarios are less optimistic. One is a scenario of *multiracial competition*. In this scenario, most cities will evolve toward multiracial populations. People of color in these cities will typically find it difficult to form coalitions because of their cultural differences and different positions in a racially obsessed society, and therefore different interests. Unless leaders can develop agendas that are more successful in bringing groups together, this scenario has division, not coalition, as its typical state, and political weakness as its typical result.

Another possible scenario, the scenario of *political isolation,* reflects a fear of some African-American observers now. In this scenario, cities become increasingly multiracial, but Latino and Asian-American populations grow more rapidly than black populations. The first two groups are increasingly assimilated—at least their relatively light-skinned and educated members—and co-opted into white-dominated coalitions from which African Americans are largely excluded. The latter find themselves increasingly unwanted partners in urban political alliances. This scenario is given impetus both by legitimate apprehension about the pervasiveness and persistence of racism and by knowledge of the real differences in political orientations and social values and identities between these groups. Richard DeLeon's data on the political isolation of African Americans in San Francisco lends support to this possibility (ch. 6).

A third scenario is the Atlanta model as described by Stone and Pierannunzi (ch. 7): *politico-economic co-optation*. In this scenario, black politicians control city government, but they have been co-opted by a white economic elite. An African-American economic and professional elite emerges that enriches itself but abandons low-income blacks, who are politically isolated and powerless. In this scenario, the great escape from black political exclusion engineered in the sixties and seventies ends in the assertion of class interests and power and the perpetuation of poverty and hopelessness determined by both class and race.

IS INCORPORATION ENOUGH?

No one who favors political equality objects in principle to the formation of multiracial coalitions or to minority officeholding. The question is, what do minority officeholders and coalitions do with their positions? Do they make city government responsive to the interests and needs of minority communities? Especially, do they use the powers of city governments to pursue the broader aims of the black power movement, including expansion of assistance and provision of employment to economically marginal populations, and redistribution of the resources of city governments?

There is "an inherent value in officeholding. . . . A race of people who are excluded from public office will always be second class citizens" (McCain 1981). Officeholding *does* confer legitimacy on a hitherto excluded group, as Perry argues (ch. 8). These are symbolic but nonetheless terribly important considerations.

Still, some of the authors of this book set forth criticisms of some largely black regimes and some black leaders, criticisms that lean toward a conclusion that these leaders are not as active as they should be in redistributive efforts; that they are less powerful than their political positions imply, because of the pervasive systemic power of white business interests and a progrowth ideology that may simply ignore the needs of ordinary citizens; and that they are too narrowly self-interested, too focused on their own interests, the interests of the black (and white) middle and upper class.

Stone and Pierannunzi, writing on Atlanta in chapter 7, conclude that the city's black middle-class political leadership is in a "tight alliance with the white business elite"; he reports the remark of one activist that a meeting of black and white leaders in Atlanta "is nothing but a roomful of people trying to cut a deal." The city's biracial coalition leaves out a range of lower-class interests, including neighborhood organizations and affordable-housing groups. The dominance of the governing biracial coalition replicates the extreme inequalities in the socioeconomic sphere—Atlanta is second only to Newark in poverty rate among U.S. cities, and the mass of black constituents remains effectively excluded.

In such a situation, we might hope eagerly for black political incorporation, but when it arrives, find that it is an obstacle to achievement of a broader set of goals. Even if we do not conclude that incorporation is *only* a sham, only the illusion of empowerment, we might still be profoundly ambivalent toward it.

The authors of this book do not conclude that black incorporation is only a sham. Biracial regimes have accomplished substantial good overall. What has been accomplished varies from city to city, however, and it is clearly not *enough*—not enough to prevent the perpetuation of racial discrimination, disadvantage, poverty, and social decay.

HAVE MINORITY REGIMES BEEN RESPONSIVE?

By *minority regimes,* we mean city governments dominated by bi- or multiracial coalitions in which blacks or Latinos play significant roles. Primarily these are biracial regimes in which blacks play leading roles.

City Government Employment

All the minority regimes studied in this book have effectively reduced discrimination in city government employment. Often they have created strongly affirmative recruitment and hiring practices that have resulted in minority workforces close to or above parity with the size of minority populations. Even governments like New York's, with limited minority incorporation, have pushed ahead rapidly with minority hiring (ch. 4). All the minority regimes have greatly increased minority representation in professional, managerial, and executive positions, including department heads.

Some commentators deride city government employment as the weakest of weak rewards, "a few government jobs" with which elites buy off minority protest. We do not agree. One analysis concludes:

> About 55 percent of the increase in black professional, managerial, and technical employment between 1960 and 1976 occurred in the public sector, and employment in social welfare programs accounted for approximately half of that increase. (Murray 1984, citing Brown and Erie 1981, 308)

This suggests that gains in city government employment contributed significantly to middle-class black employment gains generally during this period. Our own analysis of city workforces in the ten California cities showed that minority employees of city governments ranged from 2 percent to 6 percent of total minority residents in the workforce, more in the older, larger cities with the highest proportions of black residents, again not an insignificant contribution to total minority (especially black) employment.

The argument is also sometimes made that the advantages of city government accrue almost entirely to middle-class blacks and Latinos; but the pattern varies a great deal from city to city. Older cities with broader governmental functions also hire large numbers of blue-collar workers. Bolstering the employment opportunities of middle-class or potentially middle-class minority persons is obviously not the same from an antipoverty perspective as enhancing employment opportunities for low-income persons; on the other hand, support for a nascent minority middle class is not to be scoffed at, either.

Police-Community Relations

Establishment of civilian police review boards was one of the points at which minority incorporation in the ten California cities did make a difference, and some of the authors in this volume report progress along these lines. Police review boards are, of course, only one of several strategies for reducing the use of lethal force against minority people. Minority hiring onto police forces and changing top leadership are common and probably more effective steps taken by minority regimes. Reviewing the literature on black regimes, Adolph Reed concludes:

> Black regimes generally have been successful in curbing police brutality, which often has been prominent among black constituents' concerns. . . .
> Black regimes have made substantial gains in black police employment, which contributes to the reduction in police brutality. (Reed 1988, 156)

Development of Minority Businesses

Development of minority business is typically supposed to be accomplished by set-asides or other special efforts to channel city spending for supplies and services to minority-owned businesses, thus encouraging the growth of the minority-owned and operated private sector. The record of minority regimes in this area is murky. Perry reports little or no progress in New Orleans and Birmingham (ch. 8), and the record in other cities is mixed. Minority contracting is sometimes distorted by favoritism for a few firms with special ties to the regime (Stone and Pierannunzi, ch. 7), as governmental contracting frequently is. In some cities, some minority contractors have been found to be paper corporations, fronts for white-owned businesses. There are success stories of city government support for minority businesses, but recent Supreme Court decisions make set-asides more difficult to implement, even when city governments are willing to develop strong programs.

Appointments to Boards and Commissions

All the minority regimes studied in this volume have made substantial numbers and proportions of minority appointments to city boards and commissions. No doubt the significance of these appointments varies enormously. In some cities, they may be entirely symbolic; in others, they are key steps in the extension of control over city government and associated agencies. In Oakland, for example, minority control of commissions with real governmental authority was essential to the establishment of control over city departments and over public authorities associated with the city, such as the Port Authority. This in turn allowed the dominant coalition to change the policies of those agencies to emphasize direct minority hiring, employment-related development, increased provision of facilities and services to minority residents and neighborhoods, and coordination with other minority-oriented programs of city government.

In these respects, the minority regimes studied here have typically been responsive. We simply do not have sufficient evidence in this volume about other areas of need in which minorities may or may not have made substantial progress. Adolph Reed, reviewing the available evidence, concludes that "the presence of a black mayor or regime has some, but less than dramatic, racially redistributive effect on allocation of public resources" (1988, 139). It may be too much to expect more than "some" racially redistributive effect. Yet worsening poverty and other signs of social breakdown in inner-city populations would seem to be critical conditions that a city government must deal with, certainly a government that purports to be responsive to its minority population, as minority regimes do. Several authors of this volume note that the regimes they studied had done little to meet the needs or even heed the objections of lower-income minority populations.

Unfortunately, it is extremely difficult for city governments to have much impact on poverty. The federal government can no longer be depended on to lead the effort to reduce poverty, and city governments lack both the fiscal resources and the structural capability to do so, even if they were willing to take up where the federal government left off.

THE STRUCTURAL LIMITS OF MINORITY REGIMES

The painful truth is that many of the forces shaping the conditions under which the mass of low-income minority people live are not under the control of city governments, even governments run by minority regimes (Peterson 1981). Big cities with large minority populations are undergoing two radical transformations that have been under way for several decades and are continuing (Kasarda 1985; Wilson 1985; Downs 1985). One of these transformations is economic: the shift from manufacturing and distribution activities to administration, information, and other services, many highly technical in nature. The number of low-skill jobs in such cities is dropping.

Big-city populations are being transformed as well: as blacks and Latinos, mainly poor and unskilled, increase in number, whites are leaving, partly for racial reasons:

> This transformation is occurring in part because of the white majority's deliberate policy of segregating itself from both poor and nonpoor minority group members. Such segregation . . . operates by excluding nearly all poor households and most minority households from new suburban areas. Segregation is less evident in workplaces, although residential segregation also produces massive racial separation of jobs.
>
> As a result, many minority group members live in areas that provide a much lower quality of life in every respect than that enjoyed by most whites. Confronted by a triple handicap of shrinking job opportunities, poor education, and low-quality neighborhoods [and increasing competition for low-skill jobs from new immigration and from high birth rates in the inner city], these minority citizens are caught in a situation from which there appears to be no escape. (Downs 1985, 285)

Not only the white population but also its taxable wealth and the investments of corporations are being suburbanized. At the same time the minority populations of big cities are facing increasingly severe and intractable problems, their cities are losing resources to cope with them.

The roots of this knot of problems and constraints are many; again, they are essentially outside the control of city governments. Since the 1970s, increased competition from foreign manufacturers and national policies that fought inflation by keeping interest rates high—thus increasing demand for the dollar, raising the exchange value of the dollar, and raising the prices of U.S. goods—led to the closure of many older manufacturing plants, typically in big cities where African Americans are concentrated.

Long-standing policies that had nothing to do with race in their origins now yield racially distributed outcomes. Construction of freeways beginning in the 1950s helped to accelerate suburban development relative to the central city. The income tax deduction for mortgage loan interest increased the demand for new homes, which were built and continue to be built in the suburbs.

Trends and pressures and the shifting strength of coalitions at state and national levels are also at work. Republicans made major gains in state legislatures in 1994 as well as taking control of both houses of Congress. Even though public support is weak for Republican initiatives to overturn 40 years of social policy, it is possible that Republicans will control all three branches of the federal government after the 1996 elections. Further cutbacks in federal aid to cities, together with state-imposed spending and taxing limits, will make it that much more difficult for liberal-to-progressive coalitions to find the resources to achieve their goals. The aid that is available is more likely to be funneled to suburbs and more likely to find its way to cities with Republican than with Democratic mayors.

Thus the tendency of whites to segregate themselves from people of color is compounded by global economic trends, by long-standing national policies, by the American tradition of local government that permits the wealth and incomes of suburban populations to be separated from the problems of the central city, and by recent Republican gains. The forces operating against big cities and their minority populations are so powerful and manifold that it is difficult to see any immediate or direct way out of their dilemmas.

WHAT SHOULD BE DONE?

It is in the nature of partly successful movements that their accomplishments, once taken as great victories, are more or less quickly taken for granted. Leadership, a vision, and an agenda emerged from the early civil rights movement and mobilized millions of people against great odds. The movement's great accomplishments—including the establishment of voting rights and the election of many thousands of African Americans to public office—were not enough to end discrimination or to lead or assist sufficient numbers of other African Americans out of poverty. In the shadow of these persistent and painful problems, we should not be surprised if the widespread achievement of an end to discrimination in city government employment does not shine as brightly as it did and cannot be accepted as enough.

The civil rights movement drew power from the great ideas of freedom, equality, justice, and brotherhood, and from "the American dream that one day this nation will rise up and live out the true meaning of its creed—we hold these truths to be self-evident, that all men are created equal" (King 1992 [1963], 104). In the 1990s, when African Americans are found in considerable numbers at high levels of achievement in the professions, in government, in universities and schools, and in business, can a renewed movement draw with energizing fervor on those ideas and the hope they offer? Can such a movement draw in others as well—Latino, Asian, Native American, European American?

If a renewed movement could emerge, what would it want? What concrete steps would it demand? It is one thing to demand an end to legal segregation of public accommodations and of public universities and schools, and to get affirmative action in city government hiring. It is quite another to get equal financing for inner-city schools and suburban schools, or to get equal employment rates for people of color and for whites. If whites move to suburbs in part to avoid racial integration, the achievement of integrated housing such that people of color would have the same rate of access to suburban schools as whites lies at still another level of impossibility.

The U.S. Supreme Court's decision in *Brown v. Board of Education* (1954) was an attack on separate but unequal education, yet de facto segregation and grossly unequal education are still largely what we have. Perhaps a renewed movement would mount a renewed attack on de facto segregation, perhaps not.[6] Even if integration is a dream still to be deferred, much better education must be high on the rational priorities of inner-city families of all races. More jobs and better neighborhood conditions are also common goals of people of color in many settings—not only African Americans but Latinos, Asians, and Native Americans as well.

Jobs, education, better neighborhoods, available and affordable health care, drug prevention and treatment programs, affordable day care—a plausible set of concrete goals is not much of a puzzle. The mobilization that would be necessary to achieve them *is* a puzzle, though local efforts pursue them now in countless different settings, with limited success overall.

WHAT CAN BE DONE?

City governments and the coalitions that control them are not, however, entirely without resources. As Downs points out, "Minority control over big-city government"—we would say, control by minority-oriented coalitions—"greatly increases the bargaining power of minorities in relation to major property owners who pay taxes, and increases their political power in Congress and the state legislatures" (1985, 291). Although this is true, it is also true that the suburbs are gaining population and political power more rapidly than the big cities.

Minorities need allies, not only to win elections but to mobilize to the fullest extent possible the resources of the community to improve education and job training. Whereas in earlier decades supporters of minority demands for improved education and job training were powerful at the federal level, that is no longer true. Now, as Downs put it in 1985,

> The best natural allies are those who stand to lose most if the minority community cannot produce competent workers. That means businesses locked into the city itself, such as downtown property owners, nonbranching banks, or newspapers. They might support more ghetto enrichment as a quid pro quo for further integrated core development benefiting them. (Downs 1985, 292)

---

[6] Anthony Downs's analysis written more than a decade ago (1985, 290) is probably still accurate: There is no point in advocating racial integration as the central social strategy for coping with big-city problems. . . . The political leaders of all large metropolitan areas do not have the slightest interest in pursuing this strategy in any meaningful way. . . . So devoting scarce political energy and resources to integration must be considered a marginal activity.

Of course, "ghetto enrichment" such as greatly increased financing for schools is likely to involve raising property taxes, where a pro-minority coalition will face an electorate as well as business interests.

The governments of large cities that are economic and administrative centers with stable or growing economies are in a better position to bargain with business interests and to extract some concessions about the form, location, and mix of development, and about use of minority-owned firms and employment of minority workers. The record of minority-oriented regimes in actually extracting such concessions is mixed and not a solution to all the problems of education, jobs, and poverty, but such regimes clearly do more in this regard that non-minority regimes.

As Adolph Reed explains, this strategy means "neither a reflexive opposition to economic growth nor an adversarial relationship with concrete business interests." Rather, the goal is to use "public authority to articulate policy agendas that accommodate economic growth as much as possible to the needs of the municipality and its citizenry rather than vice versa" (Reed 1988, 167). Downs and Reed both emphasize the leadership role of the minority community and minority mayors in particular. Reed suggests that regimes use the "cultural authority of office to draw attention to unpalatable conditions that affect constituents but are beyond the scope of municipal control." They can also engage in forms of official protest, such as

> passing unconstitutional tax ordinances, to dramatize existing inequities, thereby opening them to public awareness and debate and providing opportunities for political mobilization. Along each of these dimensions of advocacy for justice and equity, the record of black regimes is poor. (Reed 1988, 168) [We would say the record of minority-oriented regimes is poor.]

Downs too stresses possibilities for effective advocacy that go beyond the current political efforts of minority-oriented regimes. One tactic that might be effective "is constantly emphasizing that spending more on educating minority group children is investing in the city's future, not just aiding the poor." Another tactic "would be launching a series of nonviolent demonstrations in white areas and schools about the poor quality of minority schools," resembling civil rights protests of the 1960s (1985, 292). Such advocacy might lead eventually to metropolitan tax sharing or other measures to channel state or local funds to inner-city schools, investment, and employment programs. Minority-oriented regimes could do more to organize and publicize demands on suburban governments in metropolitan regions and on state and national governments for resources and programs to alleviate their problems.

Although these are tactics that could be undertaken, there are strong reasons that big city mayors and other elected officials are not likely to pursue them with great vigor. These officeholders have typically won office without such tactics in the first instance; if they harbor ambitions for higher office, they will typically have to appeal to a less minority-oriented constituency than the one that elected them. This creates a disincentive to use dramatic or radical tactics.

Self-help in minority communities can be important to the communities' development and success. Although not political in the narrow sense, self-help has important social and political implications. Even if the path of political mobilization is unpromising, self-help efforts can make an enormous difference in the lives of individuals and groups. Some Asian communities, for example, have successfully operated loan pools so that immigrants can acquire small businesses. Self-help efforts and the discipline they demonstrate also probably help minority communities appeal successfully to middle-class and business interests (Downs 1985, 292). African-American, Latino, and Native American communities have also initiated forms of self-help that we simply do not know enough about.

Minority-oriented regimes can play an important leadership role in the development of self-help, and with relatively modest governmental resources or private support, can help communities organize self-help activities that involve recyclable financial resources. Leadership in self-help efforts would be an effective tactic politically as well as for the direct help it generates, because it would assure nonminority people that minority communities are doing what they can to help themselves while it gave minority communities increased hope and confidence in the relevance of local government.

The fundamental point is that many minority-oriented regimes, even with the constraints they operate under, could undertake significant new efforts. For this to happen, however, may require new coalitions faced with "greatly increased and informed pressure from the black electoral constituency" (Reed 1988, 196) and from liberal whites, which in turn implies broad public debate on the issues—a debate that is not now heard.

Clarence Stone has written elsewhere of the possibility of an "opportunity-expansion" regime—a coalition of public and private interests in cities that would pursue "enriched education and job training, improved transportation access, and enlarged opportunities for business and home ownership" for the lower-class residents of big cities (1993, 20). Although no city is wholly of this kind, several large cities (San Francisco, Cleveland, Boston) have undertaken "significant moves to open benefits to the lower class. . . . Each of these cities has edged toward a more class-inclusionary regime" (Stone, Orr, and Imbroscio 1991, 236). The achievement of such a regime would require at least some mobilization of a lower-class constituency, "overcoming a cycle of disappointment and cynicism" (Stone 1993, 21).

By this vision, coalitions should form around the goals of much better education, more jobs, better neighborhoods, and enlarged opportunities for ownership. These are key goals for many members of diverse groups, including liberal and progressive whites, and might be cast convincingly as goals for some business interests as well. With vigorous and persistent effort and skillful leadership, such coalitions might be able to mobilize and unite a broad range of groups and interests around issues of fairness, equal opportunity, and reduction of social conflict and crime through better education and access to employment.

Multiracial coalitions are difficult to form and sustain. Nevertheless, because American cities are becoming increasingly multiracial, we see no alternative but to continue to explore the possibilities of multigroup coalitions and to learn what works to bring groups together. Clearly what does not work, in a multiethnic setting, is a single-minded focus on one's own race or ethnicity. Leaders and activists who hope to put together multiracial coalitions will have to formulate issues and ways of dealing with each other that both focus on common interests and respect the status and histories of each group and the differences between them. These are not new skills in the history of coalition formation but they will be new to many established leaders whose careers are based on cultivation of their group alone, or on cultivation of biracial relationships.

Political incorporation must be the start but cannot be the limit of minority governmental effectiveness. Minority-oriented regimes—and prospective challengers that adopt a broader opportunity-expansion program—possess unique resources with which to pursue renewed mobilization and advocacy, so that issues of poverty, employment, housing, isolation, and terribly inadequate education, for disadvantaged whites as well as for people of color, find their way onto local, state, and national agendas. Understanding the histories of leadership, mobilization, coalition formation, and incorporation described in this volume will, we hope, help people fashion the vision and the coalitions that will carry to a new plane the historical struggle to build democracy and a greater equality out of the centuries-long practice of racial domination.

REFERENCES

Brown v. Board of Education, 347 U.S. 483, 494 (1954).

Brown, Michael K., and Stephen P. Erie. 1981. Blacks and the Legacy of the Great Society: The Economic and Political Impact of Federal Social Policy. *Public Policy* 12 (Summer): 299–330.

Carmichael, Stokely, and Charles V. Hamilton. 1967. *Black Power.* New York: Random House.

Downs, Anthony. 1985. The Future of Industrial Cities. In Paul E. Peterson, ed., *The New Urban Reality.* Washington, D.C.: The Brookings Institution.

Fitzpatrick, Joseph P., and Lourdes Traviesco Parker. 1981. Hispanic Americans in the Eastern United States. *Annals of the American Academy of Political and Social Science* 454: 98–124.

Kasarda, John D. 1985. Urban Change and Minority Opportunities. In Paul E. Peterson, ed., *The New Urban Reality.* Washington, D.C.: The Brookings Institution.

King, Martin Luther, Jr. 1963. I Have a Dream. Speech to the March on Washington, August 28. In James M. Washington, ed., *I Have a Dream: Writings and Speeches That Changed the World.* Glenview, Ill.: Scott, Foresman, 1992.

McCain, Tom. 1981. Quoted in *American Civil Liberties Union News.*

Murray, Charles. 1984. *Losing Ground: American Social Policy 1950–1980.* New York: Basic Books.

Peterson, Paul E. 1981. *City Limits.* Chicago: University of Chicago Press.

Preston, Michael B., Lenneal J. Henderson, and Paul Puryear, eds. 1987. *The New Black Politics,* 2nd ed. White Plains, N.Y.: Longman.

Reed, Adolph. 1988. The Black Urban Regime: Structural Origins and Constraints. In Michael Peter Smith, ed., *Power, Community and the City.* Comparative Urban and Community Research, Vol. 1. New Brunswick, N.J.: Transaction Books.

Sonenshein, Raphael J. 1993. *Politics in Black and White: Race and Power in Los Angeles.* Princeton, N.J.: Princeton University Press.

Stone, Clarence N. (1993). Urban Regimes and the Capacity to Govern: A Political Economy Approach. *Journal of Urban Affairs* 15 (1): 1–28.

Stone, Clarence N., Marion E. Orr, and David Imbroscio. 1991. The Reshaping of Urban Leadership in U.S. Cities: A Regime Analysis. In M. Gottdiener and Chris G. Pickvance, eds., *Urban Life in Transition*, Vol. 39, *Urban Affairs Annual Reviews.* Newbury Park, Calif.: Sage.

Wilson, William Julius. 1985. The Urban Underclass in Advanced Industrial Society. In Paul E. Peterson, ed., *The New Urban Reality.* Washington, D.C.: Brookings Institution.

Index

About the Authors

Rufus P. Browning is professor of political science and director of the Public Research Institute at San Francisco State University. An earlier book that he wrote with Dale Rogers Marshall and David H. Tabb, *Protest Is Not Enough: The Struggle of Blacks and Hispanics in Urban Politics*, received two awards from the American Political Science Association.

Richard E. DeLeon is professor and chair of the Department of Political Science at San Francisco State University, where he has taught since 1970. He is author of *Left Coast City: Progressive Politics in San Francisco, 1975–1991.*

Rodney E. Hero is professor of political science at the University of Colorado at Boulder. He is the author of *Latinos and the U.S. Political System: Two-Tiered Pluralism,* and recipient of the 1993 Ralph J. Bunche Award from the American Political Science Association. He also has written a number of articles addressing Latinos and urban politics in the United States.

Richard A. Keiser is assistant professor of political science at Carleton College where he teaches a course on urban politics and minority political empowerment. He is the author of the forthcoming book *Subordination or Empowerment? African American Leadership and the Struggle for Urban Political Power.* He is currently working on a book on the transformation from exclusionary to inclusionary urban regimes.

Dale Rogers Marshall is president and professor of political science at Wheaton College in Massachusetts. Previously she was academic dean at Wellesley College and before that was professor of political science and associate dean of the College of Letters and Sciences at the University of California at Davis. She has published widely in urban politics and has been active in both the Western Political Science Association and the American Political Science Association.

John Mollenkopf is professor of political science and sociology and director of the Center for Urban Research at the at the City University of New York Graduate Center. Author or editor of six books on urban policy and politics, he was educated at Carleton College and Harvard University. He was program director for urban initiatives at the Social Science Research Council from 1991 to 1993 and director of the economic development division of the New York City Department of City Planning in 1980 to 1981. He has served on many editorial and research advisory boards, including the National Puerto Rican Coalition, and was consultant to the New York City Districting Commission and the Charter Revision Committee.

Marion Orr is an assistant professor of political science at Duke University. He earned his Ph.D. from the University of Maryland, College Park. His research interests are the areas of race and politics, urban politics, and urban public policy. His articles have appeared in several journals. He is completing a book on race and politics in Baltimore and Detroit.

Dianne Pinderhughes is professor of political science and Afro-American studies and director of the Afro-American Studies and Research Program at the University of Illinois Urbana-Champaign. She is the author of *Race and Ethnicity in Chicago Politics: A Reexamination of Pluralist Theory* and numerous other publications on race, public policy, and electoral politics. Active in many professional associations, she was vice-president of the American Political Science Association in 1995–1996 and president of the National Conference of Black Political Scientists from 1988–1989.

Huey L. Perry is professor of political science and coordinator of the Office of Research and Services at Southern University, Baton Rouge. Perry's principal area of research focuses on the impact of the increased black political participation that has occurred in the South since the national civil rights legislation of the middle 1960s. His research examines the political, social, and economic impact of black political participation in the South. His publications include two edited books, *Blacks and the American Political System* (co-edited with Wayne Parent) and *Race, Politics, and Governance in the United States.* The first book was published by the University Press of Florida in 1995. The second book will be published by the University Press of Florida in 1996. Perry's publications include several articles in refereed journals and several book chapters.

Raphael J. Sonenshein, professor of political science at California State University, Fullerton, received his Ph.D. in political science from Yale University. He is the author of *Politics in Black and White: Race and Power in Los Angeles,* winner of the 1994 Ralph J. Bunche Award from the American Political Science Association as the best book in political science on the subject of racial and ethnic pluralism. He is currently studying the politics of diversity in contemporary Los Angeles.

Clarence N. Stone is professor of government and politics at the University of Maryland. His most recent book is *Regime Politics: Governing Atlanta, 1946–1988*, winner of the American Political Science Association's Ralph Bunche Award in 1990. Currently he is directing an 11-city study, "Civic Capacity and Urban Education," funded by the Education and Human Resources Directorate of the National Science Foundation.

David H. Tabb, professor of political science at San Francisco State University, has written or co-authored over 20 articles and three books on the politics of race and political incorporation. His current research involves assessing the variation in political capacity of local governments to deliver federal programs to disadvantaged minorities.

Christopher L. Warren is associate professor and chair of the Department of Political Science at Florida International University where he teaches urban and American politics. His research and publications have focused on the politics of ethnicity and class, Miami politics, and the reform of local governmental structures. He is presently co-authoring a book on Cuban-American politics.